The
Political Economy
of
Social Policy

A. J. CULYER
University of York

D1448634

Martin Robertson · Oxford

First published in 1980 by Martin Robertson, Oxford.
Reprinted with corrections 1983

British Library Cataloguing in Publication Data

Culyer, Anthony John
   The political economy of social policy.—
   Revised ed.
   1. Social service—Finance
   2. Social policy
   I. Title   II. Economics of social policy
   338.4'7'361   HV70

   ISBN 0-85520-369-2 (Hb)
   ISBN 0-85520-370-6 (Pb)

Typeset by Santype International Ltd., Salisbury, Wilts
Printed and bound at T J Press Ltd, Padstow.

for Tom and Alex

The complicated analyses which economists endeavour to carry through are not merely gymnastic. They are instruments for the bettering of human life. The misery and squalor that surround us, the injurious luxury of some wealthy families, the terrible uncertainty over-shadowing many families of the poor—these are evils too plain to be ignored. By the knowledge that our science seeks it is possible that they may be restrained! Out of the darkness light!

A. C. Pigou

Enthusiasm for the ideal in faith, in hope, and in charity is the best of human possessions; and the world owes very much to those who have been thrown off their balance by it. But, on the other hand, a responsible student of social problems must accept mankind as he finds them; and must base his estimates on that which is practicable. He must nourish the ideal in his heart; but his actions, his conversation, and even his thought must be occupied mainly with the actual; he must resist every temptation to make a short cut to the ideal. For indeed a traveller in a difficult country, who makes for his ultimate goal by a straight course, is likely to waste his time and strength and perhaps to meet disaster.

Alfred Marshall

Contents

Preface

This book is much more than merely a new edition of my *The Economics of Social Policy*. Any author would naturally hope to have met all the objections raised against a first edition and to have neatly excised all blemishes. But in a field as intellectually unstructured as social policy and in a field, moreover, that is inherently controversial, such hopes must be vain. In response to the mostly friendly criticism I have had, as well as my own experience of using the earlier book, I have nonetheless made some major changes. Partly these are matters of reorganisation. Partly they are also matters of elimination—I have omitted, for example, the discussions of drug dependence and the economics of crime and the law from the present book for reasons of space; the cost is that it now contains less material to stimulate 'lateral' thinking. On balance I judge this cost to be worth incurring.

The major changes consist in entirely new material. On the theoretical side this includes an introduction to the theory of production, human capital, uncertainty and the measurement of dispersion or inequality. On the applied side these changes have their chief impact in Parts II and III, which now correspond to the 'cash' and 'kind' aspects of the Welfare State. The discussion of income redistribution in Part II now includes more on statistical measures and a much more extensive treatment of poverty. Part III has four chapters: on the social services in general and on health, education and housing in particular. I have not included a chapter on what are often called the 'personal' social services on the grounds that a consideration of the myriad economic problems therein arising would pose no new conceptual or empirical difficulties not discussed elsewhere and hence—supposing me to be right in this judgement—serve no pedagogic purpose. I have also added a section on the political economy of pensions (in chapter 6) though I have not thought the issues there worth a whole chapter.

Part IV contains applications of analysis in social policy that are not associated with the *special* character of health, education, housing, etc. A much expanded set of illustrative studies is now included.

I have tried to draw illustrative examples from a variety of countries, since the earlier book found some favour abroad. Inevitably, however, with a British author most are British in origin. But since illustrations have an *analytical* rather than a *descriptive* purpose, and have been chosen for this reason, I hope that the preponderance of British applications will not limit the general usefulness of the book.

As before, the audience aimed at consists of students who have had no more than an introductory course in economics. All material not normally taught in such courses—as well as some that is—is fully explained in the text. The emphasis, as before, remains on the *use* of theory rather than the description of institutions and policy. The continuing interplay of values in the analysis of solutions to social problems that may be considered in terms both of justice and efficiency is emphasised, as is the importance of the Paretian approach in minimising the personalisation of social values by those wishing to be social analysts rather than social propagandists: a distinction I not only continue to believe is possible but that I also hold dear.

Twenty questions are appended to each chapter (save the first). These are designed to afford an opportunity to check understanding of the chapter contents and to delve deeper into some of the issues raised. Where possible, answers written for submission to teachers and tutors should contain clear technical expositions of the basic analysis as well as criticisms and developments of it.

The result of all this will be, I hope, a helpful book for students of social policy, capable of use in a wide variety of different kinds of course catering for a varied clientele.

A.J.C.

Acknowledgements

Colleagues with whom I teach have some responsibility for the shape and content of the following pages. In particular, Keith Hartley, Alan Maynard, Alan Williams and Jack Wiseman are more implicated than any of them would probably prefer. In addition, for reading the typescript in part or whole, and for making helpful suggestions (some of which I have actually used!) my thanks to Les Castle in Auckland, Mike Jones-Lee in Newcastle, Alan Maynard and John Posnett in York, and Martin Ricketts in Buckingham. I have benefited greatly from the comments made by Mike Cooper in Dunedin on the earlier book, which helped me not only in my resolve to write the new book but also in its actual writing. Mike Cooper deserves special thanks since it was during three months as his guest at the University of Otago that the bulk of the final writing was done. It was a memorable visit. Finally, to Gail Shepherd, who inherited a rotten task of typing and collation and did it all in next to no time, my heartfelt appreciation. She knows me too well for me to think it worth promising her not to let it happen again!

PART I

Prelude

CHAPTER 1

Introduction

Those of you who study this book will normally have had an introductory course in economics. Those who have not may find chapter 2 rather elliptical and the remaining chapters rather tough. For such readers, a brief—but intensive—period of study of the microeconomic sections of any major introductory text in current university use would be of great benefit. For those who have had such an introduction, however, whether they be mainstream economists, social or public administrators, or social scientists of other breeds, this book should present no great technical difficulty. The full interpretation of some of the econometric results of later chapters (especially chapter 11) requires more knowledge than commonly had by the people I have in mind, and this is why these results are presented, so far as possible, without much statistical analysis. The hope is, of course, that these examples will whet appetites to develop such statistical skills. But the rest of the analysis, especially if the review to be found in chapter 2 is conscientiously worked through, should impose no great burden on today's students of social policy.

Interplay of Positive and Normative Questions

As we shall repeatedly see, the analysis of social policy using techniques of economics cannot be free of ethical content. It follows that there must be more than economic science in the economics of social policy. It is therefore useful and important to identify those elements of analysis that may be termed 'positive' and those that may be termed 'normative', for while the criteria one will use to evaluate normative questions may *include* those used to evaluate the positive questions, the criteria used to evaluate positive questions *exclude* some of those used to evaluate normative ones.

Consider a proposition widely used in the analysis to follow: a subsidy on the price of a service will lead to an increase in the amount of that service demanded. This is essentially a *positive* (non-normative) statement about human behaviour that can be tested and, in principle, falsified by reference to what people actually do when subsidised services are introduced. Lying behind this positive statement, which is, as chapter 2 shows, itself derived from more fundamental (positive) propositions about human behaviour, is of course a set of normative considerations. After all, why is anyone interested in the behavioural effects of a subsidy? The answer invariably turns out to be that they have an ethical, or moral, or political, or religious, reason for caring about the consequences. For example they may believe that, in the absence of a subsidy on (say) health care consumption, individuals who are ill may take too little health care or they may believe that, with a subsidy, they take too much. In either case a value judgement is involved. If one takes the position that health care ought to be provided free of charge, one is typically making both a *value* judgement (for example, that people ought to consume more care than they would if it carried a charge) and a *positive* judgement that reducing the price to zero would increase consumption. But the fact that a positive analysis may have a normative *motive* does not of itself make that analysis normative. Nor does the fact that normative analysis includes positive analysis make positive analysis normative.

We shall spend a good deal of time exploring both positive judgements and value judgements in this book. Note that both involve *judgement*: one can never be perfectly *sure* either that a behavioural prediction will actually be borne out (our theories are too imperfect for that) or that others will interpret the evidence in the same way as oneself (the evidence is rarely unambiguous enough for that), nor can one be perfectly *sure* either that one's values are shared by others or that one's own values are perfectly consistent with one another. There is, however, an important difference of principle between the two kinds of judgement, for in the case of positive judgements concerning 'what will happen if . . .' it is possible to reduce arguments, where people differ in their judgements, to questions concerning the relevant and valid use of logic and the relevant and valid interpretation of the facts. In the case of value judgements, argument ultimately boils down also to questions of logic and fact but also—and herein lies a major difference—to differences in views about equity, social justice, political values, and so on: in short to differences in what may turn out to be fundamental views of what constitutes the good society.

This poses a great problem for textbook writers for, if a useful analysis of social policy cannot escape making value judgements, is it then not impossible to write a text that is inherently not *political*? And if it *is* inherently political, then is it not inevitable more controversial than a purely scientific (or positive) book? Is it not inevitably a *tract*?

My own conclusion is that the answer to each of these questions has to be in the affirmative. But this is not to say that the value content of a text book such as this has to be *particular*. It is not to say that the value content must exclusively be, say, socialist, egalitarian, liberal, or Christian. Indeed, since I believe it to be the case that the division of opinion in society is substantially greater in matters concerning the appropriateness of different criteria of value than it is in matters concerning criteria of scientific results, and since it is not my intention to write merely for the subscribers to one particular set of values, it is important to explore a variety of *different* values. Thus, while my commitment to a single set of principles of positive analysis (mainly logical validity and empirical validity) implies that those (few) who do not subscribe to these will find very little of value in the following pages, my refusal to be committed to any single set of value judgements implies, I hope, that those subscribing to any particular set will nonetheless (and providing, of course, that they accept our basic scientific procedure) find much that is of value.

The Pareto Principle

The procedure as regards values is basically two-fold. In the first place extensive use will be made of what is termed the *Pareto principle*, which states that any change to which no one objects and that at least one person approves is good. Conversely, any change that no one approves and to which at least one person objects is bad. This principle is adopted for the obvious reason that such changes are, as is obvious, uncontroversial. This is, of course, a very weak value judgement to make, and it will not take us very far in the analysis of social policy, for it needs only one person to object to a change for us, on the Pareto principle, to reject it as good. It is an inherently conservative judgement to make. It does not (and this should be emphasised) imply that one supports the *status quo*, it implies only that using the Pareto principle alone may not warrant our changing it. (We may have other good reasons for changing it.) For obvious reasons, the Pareto principle is sometimes called the consensus principle. Where there is no consensus, the Pareto principle simply cannot reach a verdict.

Consider a single employer, A, and a single worker, B. If B works for A, A gains the value of B's labour. B will usually lose since he or she probably has better uses for their own time than promoting A's wealth. The Pareto principle cannot, therefore, pronounce that B working for A is good (but neither can it pronounce it bad!). Now suppose that A may offer B a wage. After some bargaining about this wage, conditions of work and so on, A and B reach a mutually advantageous contract, and B agrees voluntarily to work for A on the agreed terms. In this case since both parties agree to the proposal, it is judged good by reference to the Pareto principle. Or is it? Strictly, it can only be judged good if no one else objects. Suppose B, in working for A, creates noise and nuisance for C (without compensating him for it) or suppose that C believes that wage relations between employers and employees degrade, alienate or exploit persons such as B. In either case, the consensus is destroyed and the Pareto principle cannot sanction the contract.

One of the prime functions of markets is to provide a complex inter-locking system of compensation such that losers from any proposed change are persuaded voluntarily to accept it. In so far as the markets are complete and work well, the scope for interpreting the consequences using the Pareto principle is widened. In so far as they are not, or do not work well, its scope is restricted.

Although the Pareto principle is not a scientific principle, it has one important thing in common with scientific principles—it is relatively un-controversial (indeed, it is arguably *less* controversial than scientific prin-ciples since any objector can prevent its reaching a verdict).[1] But because its uncontroversial nature derives from its weakness as an ethical principle it is by no means enough—and it may not be enough even in those cases where it is able to give us a verdict. The second procedure as regards values will therefore involve *supplementing* the Pareto principle in various ways and at various times.

In general the nature of the supplementary principles will be determined by *my* perception of what it is that people commonly think it important to consider in any given context. For example, questions of income and wealth differences crop up continuously in social policy. In such contexts (particularly in Part II) I shall discuss various supplementary principles such as the idea that people have different deserts, or the idea of equality, or the idea of need, or the idea of maximin. In other cases we shall often find (especially in Part III) that rival supplementary value judgements may relate to specific social services where concern is with minimum standards, or equality of consumption, or equality of opportunity.

The purely positive economics of social policy will thus be supplemented in this—admittedly *ad hoc*—fashion both to explore the consequences of different value assumptions and to minimise the risk of tract-writing. Doubtless many readers will think they can infer my own values from all this. I cannot pretend, of course, to have suppressed them completely. I am reasonably confident, however, that it is not easy to spot them, for those who have thought that they have identified them in the past, and have told me as much, have usually been wrong. They have usually been wrong for making the naive mistake of supposing that those value judgements I assert to be commonly held are also those that I myself hold.

This is the only occasion on which the first person singular will appear in this book. I have used it in order to 'come clean' and to try to clarify a matter over which much confusion reigns in the analysis of social policy. Clearly one value I hold is that my own values (other than this one!) should be of no great interest to the reader. An economist's skills, such as they are, lie in economic analysis and its application, not in the advocacy of particular value systems. I hope my readers, when acting in their role as economists, will be as conscientious as I have tried to be. In the age of the dominant expert, it is no business of ours to attribute to experts more than their expertise warrants. Experts on economics, sociology, social or public administration, etc., are *not* more 'expert' than others at making (as distinct from *identifying*) value judgements, particularly on behalf of other people, and the sad fact that many experts feel no inhibitions in allowing their true expertise to lend a spurious authority to their personal value judgements is a matter to be most profoundly deplored. It is not merely arrogant; it brings social science into disrepute among those who are sophisticated enough to see through such pretentions.

The Organisation of This Book

The general principles followed in the arrangement of material are three-fold: (1) that analysis should precede application only where there are clear advantages in so doing, (2) that mere description or advocacy should be completely eschewed, (3) that applications should be chosen principally for the opportunity they provide of illustrating the principles at work and secondarily to demonstrate the wide applicability of the principles.

Part I contains mostly analysis. In general, it is a good rule not to teach theory divorced from application (hence principle (1) above). The reason for doing so here is that the analysis in chapters 2 and 3 is so frequently used in subsequent chapters that there seemed a clear advantage of economy in getting it out of the way early.

The middle parts of the book deal first with questions of distribution and redistribution (Part II). Parts III and IV are so divided that Part III (The Welfare State) discusses economic analysis of the principal social services where those social services have *special characteristics* differentiating themselves from other services in the nature of the problems posed, while Part IV (Methods of Economic Appraisal) examines common methods of analysis that are applicable in the social service area generally. In this part, the applications are drawn from a wide sphere of activity.

The chapters are best read in order, since there is some degree of reference back in each of them. Readers who have had an introduction to welfare economics, externalities and public goods, time preference, and uncertainty, should—despite their expertise—refresh memories by reading chapter 2.

NOTE

1. One may raise the question here as to whether *any* objector can legitimately veto a proposed change: for example busybodies, prudes, the insane, children. This is an important question. Clearly, the more categories of person with a legitimate

(but compensatable) veto over any option the less likely the Pareto principle is to be a useful guide, for the more difficult full compensation for all adversely affected parties will become. Having noted this 'constitutional' difficulty we shall merely pass on without giving it the full consideration it deserves. It will emerge in later chapters that implicitly we deny the veto to fools, knaves and (over some issues) children, but allow it to all those *physically* affected by a choice and all those motivated by noble sentiments. This is admittedly rough justice.

FURTHER READING

Three classics worth reading are:

Pareto, V. (1935) *The Mind and Society* (ed. by A. Livingston and trans. by A. Bongiorno and A. Livingston). New York: Harcourt and Brace (especially chapter 12).
Pareto, V. (1971) *Manual of Political Economy* (trans, by A. S. Schweir, ed. by A. S. Schweir and A. N. Page). New York: Kelley. The 'Pareto criterion' is explicitly stated at chapter 6, para. 33 and in the Appendix at para. 89.
Weber, M. (1949) *The Methodology of the Social Sciences* (trans. and ed. by E. Shils and H. Finch). Glencoe: The Free Press.

and an excellent assessment of Pareto is:

Tarascio, V. J. (1968) *Pareto's Methodological Approach to Economics*. Chapel Hill: University of North Carolina Press.

For some modern writings in the 'Paretian' tradition:

Arrow, K. J. (1963) *Social Choice and Individual Values* (2nd edition). New York: Wiley.
Bowen, H. R. (1948) *Toward Social Economy*. New York: Rinehart.
Buchanan, J. M. (1959) Positive economics, welfare economics and political economy. *Journal of Law and Economics*, 2, pp. 124–38.
Dahl, R. A. and Lindblom, C. E. (1963) *Politics, Economics and Welfare*. New York: Harper.

For scientific method in general, consult:

Kuhn, T. S. (1962) *The Structure of Scientific Revolutions*. Chicago: University of Chicago Press.
Popper, K. R. (1945) *The Open Society and Its Enemies*. London: Routledge and Kegan Paul.
Popper, K. R. (1963) *Conjectures and Refutations*. London: Routledge and Kegan Paul.

and for positive economics:

Friedman, M. (1953) The methodology of positive economics. In *Essays in Positive Economics*. Chicago: University of Chicago Press.
Hahn, F. and Hollis, M. (eds) (1979) *Philosophy and Economic Theory*. Oxford: Oxford University Press.

Melitz, J. (1965) Friedman and Machlup on the significance of testing economic assumptions. *Journal of Political Economy*, *73*, pp. 37–60.

Robbins, L. (1932) *An Essay on the Nature and Significance of Economic Science.* London: Macmillan.

CHAPTER 2

The Fundamental Economics
of Social Policy

In this chapter the basic economic analysis required for subsequent examination of social policy is presented. Like bikinis, this chapter covers only the bare essentials but these form the basis for the whole of the rest of the book. Some additional complications and limitations are discussed later in the contexts in which the theory will be applied. The Further Reading contains some references for those wishing for greater sophistication. This chapter *is* on the long side and it would be best read in the three principal sections into which it has been divided. It is well worth spending time making sure you have grasped the essence of this chapter before moving on, for later parts will take an understanding of this for granted.

The economic approach is about choices. The majority of choices that are made, by individuals, managers, administrators, are in practice *marginal* choices. That is, they are choices between a little more or less of this or a little less or more of that rather than all or none of this or that. For example should another 50p be added to the retirement pension? Should 5p be added to the marginal rate of income tax? Should another ward be added to the local Area Health Authority's bed complement? Should the output of primary school teachers be reduced or increased by 5 or 6 per cent a year? Should the probability of death by road accident be reduced by 5 or 10 per cent? Should police constables' salaries be increased by £100? Should the noise level in York's Coney Street be reduced from 75 perceived decibels to 70? Should the level of air pollution in asbestos textile factories be reduced from 12 fibres per cubic centimetre to 10? Should Joe Smith take a higher wage, higher risk or a lower wage, lower risk job? Most, though not all, of our analysis will concern marginal choices. As will be seen, marginal analysis also provides a good starting point for analysing even non-marginal choices.

A. Optimality and Externality

In setting out the basic economics of choice a highly simplified paradigm will be used initially. Subsequently, some of the simplifications will be

10

dropped, especially those that prevent its effective application to social policy, but not all. The task of incorporating social policy into a really complex microeconomic model of general equilibrium will not be undertaken in this book. Fortunately, however, a great many problems can be handled quite satisfactorily without such complexities.

The fundamental assertion that is made and upheld without exception in this book is the following law:

The more any individual has in a given time period of any entity that he or she regards as desirable, other things remaining the same, the lower its marginal value to him or her.

To illustrate this, consider an individual confronting a choice between two desired entities, X and Y, in a given period of time. X and Y are measured on the axes of Figure 2.1. Suppose that the individual has x_0 of X and y_0 of Y denoted by point a. If we were now to ask the minimum increase in Y he or she would require in compensation for a loss of $x_0 x_1$ we would establish the value to the individual of that amount of X in terms of Y *when he or she has x_0 of X*. In Figure 2.1 we suppose this amount to be $y_0 y_1$, so that the individual would be neither better nor worse off at point b than at a—as the individual saw it. If we now consider some other point c where the individual has more X $(0x_2)$ and the same amount of Y $(0y_0)$ then the law stated above asserts that a *lesser* increase in Y will now be regarded as the minimal acceptable compensation for the same reduction in X. In the figure this is marked as $y_0 y_3 < y_0 y_1$. The individual regards combinations d and c as equally desired, but the slope of the line dc

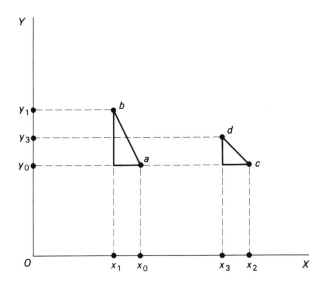

FIG. 2.1 Diminishing marginal value of one thing in terms of another.

must, according to the law of diminishing marginal value, be flatter than that of the line *ba*.

In short, the marginal value (or the value of a little more or less) of *X* falls in terms of *Y* the more *X* an individual has. The same, of course, is asserted about the marginal value of *Y* (holding *X* constant).

It will be clear, of course, that this concept of marginal value is *relative*; in particular, the marginal value of *X* will depend not only on the amount of *X* but also on the amount of *Y*. It is also subjective. Although an individual may reveal in his actions what value he places on goods or services at the margin, what he reveals is a subjective value. In this sense we are adopting an *individualist* foundation for propositions about value attached to goods and services.

It is often useful to represent this idea of value in an alternative way. Suppose we let *Y* stand for income. Then the values placed upon increments or decrements of *X* in Figure 2.1 would be expressed in *money* terms. Again they would be relative values—the value put on *X* relative to the other things income could be used for—and again they would depend upon the size of a person's income (as well as their preferences). But in this interpretation it is particularly convenient to plot the marginal value (MV) of any *X* per time period on a diagram in which *X* is on the horizontal axis and its MV in money on the vertical axis. The law of diminishing marginal value implies, of course, that the relationship between MV and the amount of *X* be negative as in Figure 2.2.

Suppose the individual has x_0 of *X* in Figure 2.2 and that its marginal

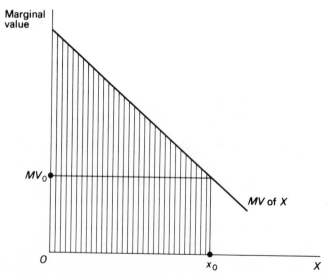

FIG. 2.2   Diminishing marginal value in terms of money.

value is MV_0. This is not, however, its *total* value to the individual. The total value is the vertically hatched area in Figure 2.2, as the MV of one unit of X only per time period is given by the height of the MV curve slightly right of the origin, the MV of two units of X per time period is given by the height of the MV curve a little more to the right, and so on. The total value to the individual is obviously the sum of all these small increments, and is therefore the hatched area in the figure. In this way marginal analysis can be applied to non-marginal choices about X relative to Y.

Provided that the marginal value placed on income remains constant for changes in X consumption, which will be the case if either the elasticity of demand for X and related goods and services is unity or if the amount of income spent on X is an insignificant part of total income, the MV curve in Figure 2.2 can be taken as a close approximation to the demand curve for X. The individual will adjust the consumption of X, or any other good or service, until the MV of X (MV_x) is equal to the price that must be paid, i.e. $MV_x = P_x$.

An alternative way of seeing this is in terms of utility theory. This approach rests on the presumption that individuals will maximise the subjective value, or utility, to them of their consumption. Since the payment of a price detracts from utility while the acquisition of a good adds to it, the individual who maximises in this way, and who consumes at least *some X*, will extend his rate of consumption of each good or service such as X until

$$MU_x = P_x \cdot MU_m$$

where MU_x is the marginal utility of X, P_x is its price and MU_m is the marginal utility of money. Since MU_x falls the more is consumed, while P_x and MU_m do not change with an individual's X consumption, the individual will consume at all rates for which $MU_x > P_x \cdot MU_m$, clearly gaining therefrom, but will not consume at rates for which $MU_x < P_x \cdot MU_m$. To preserve the equilibrium condition above, rises in P_x must be accommodated (MU_m constant) by rises in MU_x, which require reductions in the rate of X consumption, and *vice versa*. In Figure 2.3 a case is illustrated where a rise in P_x from P_x to P'_x is accompanied by a fall in X consumption from x_0 to x_1.

It is usually convenient to suppress the MU_m term by taking it to be equal to unity, so that the marginal values may be directly measured on a money scale. But it should be clear from the foregoing that when we speak of $MV_x = P_x$, an alternative, utilitarian, way of saying much the same thing is that $MU_x/MU_m = P_x$. MV_x is the behavioural indicator, measured in money units, of the subjective ratio MU_x/MU_m. Later in the text we shall use the utilitarian analysis explicitly, especially in the analysis of uncertainty and where income differences between individuals assume importance.

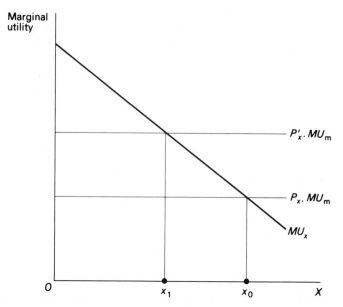

FIG. 2.3   Utility-maximising consumption rates for an individual.

The reference to elasticity of demand in the foregoing relates to the responsiveness of changes in demand to changes in price. It is formally defined as

$$\eta = -\frac{dX}{dP_x} \cdot \frac{P_x}{X},$$

where dX/dP_x is the ratio of the change in quantity demanded of X to the price change. When the elasticity is unity, the *proportional* change in X is the same as the *proportional* change in price. Consequently there is no change in expenditure on X, hence money income for spending elsewhere remains the same, hence its marginal value remains the same.

There are, of course, many refinements of this theory, of which some will be met later in the book. For the moment, the main purpose is to demonstrate how a purely abstract logical theory of choice has been turned into a *refutable* theory. The implication that MV equals price implies the so-called 'law of demand':

> *The higher the personal cost of obtaining any entity, the less will be acquired in any period of time.*

It also implies that the prices voluntarily paid by individuals to gain an increment of a good, or receivable to compensate for the loss of a good, provide an observable measure of MV. This result is of profound importance in social policy. It forms the basis, for example, of much cost–benefit analysis.

Production

Social policy is frequently concerned with *produced* goods and services (for example, housing, hospitals, milk and medicine are produced goods; teaching and medical care are produced services) or with *produced* changes in the characteristics of people (for example, better nutrition, higher educational attainment, improved health). The process of production invariably involves the transformation of *inputs* into *outputs*. Often in the sphere of the social services this is complicated by the fact that a service is being performed *on* a client. The homes of the disabled are modified and aids given them so as to make them more mobile, patients go to hospital or are treated in the community, young people (and some older ones) go formally to places of training and education. Sometimes it is very hard to identify what the output actually is. Where people are involved, it is easy to think of 'bodies dealt with' as output—but this is false, for they are either a kind of input or else are *throughput*. Output is the object of production; throughput and input are not the object or end of production, they are *means* to an end or ends such as a 'healthier' patient or 'better educated' student.

Some problems in the measurement of output will crop up several times later in this book. At this stage we emphasise the mechanics of production and the concept of efficiency in production.

Production is the process by which one set of resources (inputs) is 'transformed' into another (outputs). A *production function* is a specification of the maximum rates of output that can be had from a variety of combinations of inputs and it is therefore a technical relationship determined by the prevailing knowledge about transforming inputs into outputs and the existing techniques available to make the transformation.

A typical production function will relate several inputs to several outputs and the relation between them is likely to be complex. In the social services these complexities are made still more complex by the fact that usually there exist differences in expert opinion as to the nature of the production functions (this is, as we shall see, particularly true in the fields of education and health) and that—as already hinted—the very notion of an output is often hazy and incomplete. While these complexities are (or ought to be) the stuff of scientific (social scientific as well as other) research, and are touched upon later in this book, at this stage we shall focus on three things: some general features that are commonly believed to characterise most production functions; the idea of productive efficiency; and the relationship between production functions and costs.

Two features of production functions that it is useful to understand relate to *returns to scale* and *returns to an input*. Returns to scale describe what happens to output when each input is increased by the same proportion. If output increases by a larger percentage than the increase in (all) the inputs, then the production function is said to exhibit *increasing returns to scale*; if it increases by a smaller proportion than (all) the inputs, then the function is said to exhibit *diminishing returns to scale*; if output increases by the same proportion as (all) the inputs, then the function is said to exhibit *constant returns to scale*. Returns to an input describe what happens to output as one increases only one input, holding the remainder at the same level as before. Again, these returns may increase, be constant or decrease. We shall shortly see why.

Table 2.1 shows a production function for an imaginary process using only two inputs, which we shall use to illustrate the concepts introduced above. The inputs are labelled *A* and *B* for generality, though you may imagine them to be, say, bed-days and nurse-days per year (with 'output' defined as inpatient cases per year) or books and teachers (with 'output' defined, say, as 'A' level scores from a constant pupil population per year).

TABLE 2.1   *Cobb-Douglas Production Function* $(X = 4A^{0.4}B^{0.6})$

Amount of	10	10.0	15.2	19.4	23.1	26.4	29.4	32.3	35.0	37.5	40.0
input *A*	9	9.6	14.6	18.6	22.1	25.3	28.2	30.9	33.5	36.0	38.3
per time	8	9.2	13.9	17.8	21.1	24.1	26.9	29.5	32.0	34.3	36.6
period	7	8.7	12.9	16.5	19.6	22.4	24.9	28.0	29.6	31.8	34.7
	6	8.2	12.4	15.8	18.8	21.5	24.0	26.3	28.5	30.6	32.6
	5	7.6	11.5	14.7	17.5	20.0	22.3	24.4	26.5	28.4	30.3
	4	7.0	10.6	13.4	16.0	18.3	20.4	22.4	24.2	26.0	27.7
	3	6.2	9.4	12.0	14.2	16.3	18.2	19.9	21.6	22.9	24.7
	2	5.3	8.0	10.2	12.2	13.8	15.5	17.0	18.4	19.7	21.0
	1	4.0	6.1	7.7	9.2	10.5	11.7	12.8	13.9	14.9	15.9
	0	1	2	3	4	5	6	7	8	9	10

Amount of input *B* per time period

The outputs (X) in the table have in fact been generated by the production function

$$X = aA^{\alpha}B^{\beta}$$

where $\alpha + \beta = 1$ and a is any positive constant. This is a famous form of the production function known as the Cobb–Douglas function and is often used to estimate real-world production functions. The parameters used to calculate the values in the table, however, were $a = 4$, $\alpha = 0.4$, $\beta = 0.6$, which were simply taken out of your author's head!

It is important to realise that the outputs in the table represent the *maximum* rate of output obtainable from the given inputs (given conventions about working hours and so on). In other words, a production function assumes that the production process is *technically efficient*. This is an overstatement, however, for while in empirical work concerned with estimating functions like this in the real world it is *usually* assumed that technical efficiency obtains, this is not invariably the case. Particularly in the empirical analysis of hospital production functions many economists have felt that the assumption of technical efficiency is hard to justify (some would maintain that the assumption is hard to justify even in the case of ostensibly profit-maximising firms). In such cases the interpretation is that one is estimating a *behavioural* production function that may not be technically efficient but is nevertheless, for the purposes in hand, taken as given. An example of such an empirical study is given later in chapter 11.

The Cobb–Douglas function with $(\alpha + \beta) = 1$ always exhibits constant returns to scale: doubling or halving all the inputs doubles or halves the output. You can check this for yourself in Table 2.1 (any discrepancy is due to rounding). Other formulations would produce increasing or decreasing returns to scale. In fact, keeping the same general form of the function but letting $(\alpha + \beta) > 1$ turns it into an increasing returns function, and $(\alpha + \beta) < 1$ turns it into a decreasing returns to scale function. The selection of the appropriate form is not a *theoretical* issue but an *empirical* one: given any process to study, the task is to find the functional form that most accurately summarises what seems to be happening in the real world.

The Cobb–Douglas also exhibits decreasing returns to each input. For example with A constant at (say) 6, you can see that output increases as we add more Bs, but at a decreasing rate: the *marginal product* of B falls as we add more. The marginal product of B is 8.2 when there is one B (rather than none), 4.2 (12.4 − 8.2) when there are two rather than one, 3.4 when there are three, 3.0 when there are four, and successively 2.7, 2.5, 2.3, 2.2, 2.1 and 2.0. Similarly, the marginal product of A falls as more is used for any *given* amount of B. You can also see that the marginal product of one input is not at all independent of the amount of the others. As we shall see later, this is important in evaluating the argument one sometimes hears that inputs (especially human ones) *deserve* the value of their marginal products as reflected by wages, for even if wages do reflect the value of the marginal product, it is somewhat strange to say that one 'deserves' something that is determined not only by his own efforts.

A feature of the Cobb–Douglas production function, and indeed all 'neoclassical' production functions in economics, is that they assume that there is the possibility of continuous substitution between the various inputs keeping output approximately constant. This feature has been much discussed, and it is clearly possible to envisage situations where further substitution (of, say, hospital porters for hospital doctors) cannot be made without diminishing output (or its quality) quite substantially. In the generality of cases, and particularly when one is considering only relatively small variations in the inputs (say of an order not exceeding 10–20 per cent), there are good reasons for supposing that substitution in production is not only possible but much more possible than is commonly believed. Skilled and professional human resources have not only a vested interest in asserting their own indispensability (as has everyone) but also, by virtue of the extensive control they typically have over production methods, they have power to implement it. For this reason alone there is *propaganda* value in assuming substitutability rather than its converse. An example of how substitutability turned out to be greater than is usually propagated by the professionals is given later in chapter 11.

The coefficients of the Cobb–Douglas production function (α, β etc.) can usefully be interpreted as measuring the responsiveness of output to changes in the amount of each input (the others remaining the same). Thus, $\alpha = 0.2$ implies that output would increase by 0.2 of 1 per cent if input A increased by 1 per cent. Another term for this is *elasticity* of output with respect to input:

$$\frac{dX}{dA} \cdot \frac{A}{X} = \alpha.$$

So much, then, for the main technical features of production functions. We turn now to considerations of cost. Clearly, the choice of which output to produce cannot—or at least should not—be made without regard on the one hand to the value placed on the output by the decision maker and, on the other, to the cost. There is, prior to this decision about output, a decision required related to the method of producing any given rate of output. For example, suppose it has been decided to produced about 20 units of output per time period. From Table 2.1 you can see that there is more than one input combination that will produce this result (this follows from the fact of substitutability in the Cobb–Douglas function). Thus, $10A$ and $3B$, $7A$ and $4B$, $5A$ and $5B$, $4A$ and $6B$, $3A$ and $7B$, or $2A$ and $9B$ all produce between 19.4 and 20.4 units. The *cost-effective* combination is the one that costs the decision maker least. Clearly, the cost-effective combination will depend upon the prices of the inputs or (as we shall see later), if their prices do not reflect the true costs, some imputed prices.

The general relation between output and cost assumes therefore that the activity in question is carried on not only in the technically most efficient way but also in the most cost-effective way. Thus a curve (or curves) showing the relationship between average (or marginal) cost and output, as in Figure 2.4, implicitly embodies within it the two assumptions that *at each* rate of output the operation is being carried out with technical efficiency and with cost-effectiveness.

The most common finding about cost curves is that they generally take the form of an L or shallow U: the greater the time allowed for adjustment in the combination of inputs the shallower the U tends to be. For analytic purposes it is often convenient to assume that the curve is simply a horizontal straight line, invariate with respect to output. In this case average and marginal cost are the same (as you can check for yourself) and the diagrams are consequently less cluttered with lines.

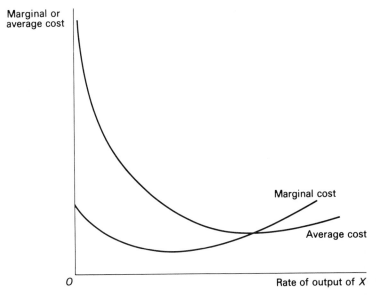

FIG. 2.4   Characteristic shapes of marginal and average cost curves.

Before moving on to bring the production/cost side and demand side together we shall look briefly at a technique of analysing production relations that has been applied with increasing frequency in the social services areas, particularly in health services. This technique is known as *linear programming.*

Suppose a management is responsible for the production of two outputs $(X_1$ and $X_2)$ with three inputs $(Y_1, Y_2$ and $Y_3)$. It is known that the amount of inputs available (at least in the short term) is $Y_1 = 3,200$, $Y_2 = 4,800$ and $Y_3 = 10,000$ and that with current technology the *minimal* amount of input required per unit of each output (whatever the output) is: for X_1, $8Y_1$, $4Y_2$ and $20Y_3$, and for X_2, $2Y_1$, $6Y_2$ and $10Y_3$. This information, summarised in Table 2.2 (the technology matrix), establishes the by now familiar *technically* efficient method of production for the management, given the constraints implied by resource availability.

Figure 2.5 shows the technically attainable levels of output for each

TABLE 2.2   *Technology Matrix*

Input \ Output	X_1	X_2	Total available inputs
Y_1	8.0	2.0	3,200
Y_2	4.0	6.0	4,800
Y_3	20.0	10.0	10,000

input and the heavily drawn line ABCD indicates the maximum feasible production possibilities, given the amount available of all three inputs. Thus for an output mix of X_1 and X_2 along AB, only the Y_2 constraint is binding. Between B and C, neither Y_1 nor Y_2 is binding. Between C and D only the Y_1 constraint is binding. Given an objective (such as maximise the output of X_1 and X_2), known as the 'objective function', the cost-effective point on ABCD can be found—it can readily be seen, in this example, to be at B where the line EE with a slope of minus one is farthest from the origin (hence maximising output, given the inputs available) without going beyond the production frontier ABCD.

Formally, it is sought to maximise the objective function

$$Q = X_1 + X_2$$

subject to the following constraints

$$(Y_1) \qquad 2X_1 + 8X_2 \leq 3200$$

$$(Y_2) \qquad 6X_1 + 4X_2 \leq 4800$$

$$(Y_3) \qquad 10X_1 + 20X_2 \leq 10000$$

$$X_1, X_2 \geq 0$$

At B we see that the Y_1 constraint is not binding so the inequality holds (there will be some spare capacity) while the other two inequalities will, in fact, be equalities. Solving these two simultaneous equations (Y_2 and Y_3) we derive $X_1 = 700$, $X_2 = 150$ and $Q = 850$.

This result is not independent, however, of the *weights* used in the objective function. In the example just presented the weights are unitary and the slope of EE line (the geometric version of the objective function) is minus one: the ratio of the weights. One way of interpreting these weights is to call them marginal values. For example, if X_2 were regarded as three times as important as X_1, it could receive a weight ($= MV$) of 3 with the weight of X_1 remaining unity. This means that instead of one X_1 being regarded as equivalent to one X_2, *three* X_1's are now needed to be equivalent to one X_2. The objective function correspondingly has a slope of minus three as in line E'E', and the new most efficient point C is located.

It can readily be seen that if the decision makers produce in a technically efficient way (i.e. locate somewhere on ABCD) then it is possible to discover the slope of the objective function or, what is the same thing, the ratio of implicit MVs. This method, known as inverse programming (the 'inversion of acriteria planning models'), is used in chapter 11 to make explicit the implicit values of decision makers who can then be confronted with them and asked if they really mean these. Likewise others—such as clients or experts—can see more clearly if current practice accords with the relative priorities they think ought to exist. Thus, if the decision makers

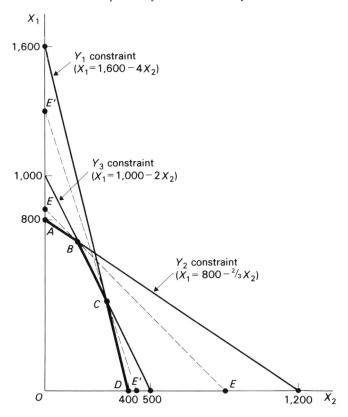

FIG. 2.5   Production frontier with linear constraints.

have located at B, then the implicit ratio of MVs is between $3:2$ and $1:2$ (the limiting slopes set by the slopes of AB and BC). If they have located at C, the ratio must lie between $1:2$ and $1:4$. If they have located between B and C, the ratio is unambiguously $1:2$, and one may reasonably ask 'Is it really right that we regard 1 of X_2 as equivalent to 2 of X_1?' The answer, of course, is up to the policy makers who, in a complex world, often without prices and other aids in establishing priorities, very, *very* frequently have only the haziest notions of what is actually going on and whether it is consistent with their preferred policies.

Likewise, it is not surprising that, in the real world where many managers and decision makers have to grapple with very many outputs and inputs, businessmen have found linear programming a useful technique for choosing profit-maximising output rates. In this case the weights in the objective function are objectively revealed, or subjectively anticipated, prices.

Pareto Optimality

The word 'efficient', as it is popularly used, frequently means that a given activity is being performed at a given rate *at the least cost*. This is what we have called cost-effectiveness. The economic concept of efficiency is, however, wider than this and runs as follows:

> *A society has allocated its resources efficiently when no input and no output can be transferred to some alternative use without making at least one person worse off, even if the welfare of others is improved.*

Clearly this definition, whose close relation with the Pareto principle will be obvious, includes the least cost notion of efficiency, for if a given output of anything could be obtained at less cost, then someone can gain without anyone losing. For example, less inputs could be used in that activity and devoted to increasing output elsewhere. But it also says more than this, for it specifies that even if every good is obtained at least cost, these goods must be so distributed among the members of the society that no redistribution may take place among them that benefits some without harming others. Suppose, out of a stock of an available good, one person places a higher marginal valuation upon his share than another places upon his. Economic efficiency exists only when the marginal values are equal, for otherwise there will be some sum of money that the person with the high MV will give the person with the low MV, and which lies in between the two MVs, that will persuade the latter to surrender some of the good to the former so that both may gain with no one losing. The person surrendering some of the good must be compensated by a price at least equal to his MV if he is voluntarily to exchange with the other. The person acquiring more of the good will value the addition not less than the price he must pay. Only when MVs are equal is there no further scope for *mutually* beneficial redistribution—one person may gain but only at the expense of another. Clearly, when MVs are different as between individuals they will normally, in their own interests, seek to exchange with one another.

A situation in which there is no further scope for mutually beneficial exchange of goods, in which everything that is produced is produced at its lowest marginal cost and in which marginal cost is equal to marginal valuation is a *Pareto optimum*: an economically (or socially) efficient allocation of resources in which no one's welfare can be improved without harming someone else. Related to this, and of great practical importance, is the notion of a *Pareto improvement*, when at least one person's welfare is *raised* without harming anyone else, although the notional optimum may not be attained.

Clearly, there are many cases in the world with which we are familiar when some people benefit at the expense of others. Are such cases efficient? The answer, according to the Pareto criterion, is that *they may be but we cannot tell*. The Pareto criterion does not tell us that such allocations are *bad*, only that we cannot tell if they are good. The reason for this is important and should be well understood. It is as follows. If one individual takes some good from another individual, assuming the good to be efficiently produced and allocated, then the former gains and the latter loses. We could say that social welfare may have also improved if we could specify *how much* benefit the one had gained and *how much* the other had lost. Unfortunately, unless the loser voluntarily *gives* something to the gainer or the gainer voluntarily compensates the loser enough for the loser voluntarily to surrender the good, we cannot make this comparison, for welfare is a subjective experience. Only when individuals voluntarily agree to perform certain actions can we be sure that their welfare is increasing—but even then we cannot tell how much one gains relative to another. Nevertheless, if no one loses and someone gains we can safely say that social welfare has increased. Conversely, if no one gains and someone loses we can safely say that social welfare has fallen. When some gain and others lose without compensation for their loss we cannot, unless we are prepared to place *our own valuation* upon the gains and losses of others, or make the comparison between the two sets of people in some other way, say anything at all about changes in social welfare.

The objection to a policy analyst, such as a student of social policy, placing his or her own valuation on the gains and losses of others is, as we have seen, that his or her expertise lies elsewhere. If observer A and observer B place *different* values on the gains and losses, we have no means of selecting the correct one. All that we have is a subjective evaluation of someone else's subjective experience! As we shall see, this impropriety of making interpersonal 'utility' comparisons has proved an obstacle in social policy evaluation, especially where redistribution of income is important; a number of attempts have been made to overcome it, which will be investigated later. For the moment we do not attempt to go beyond the restrictions imposed upon us by the Pareto criterion: that is, beyond efficiency analysis.

Although it is restricted, the Pareto criterion is far from useless. For one thing, it is good for enthusiastic students of social policy to discover the limits to which they may (as social scientists) go. Academic commentators on social policy are notorious for the assertion of their own values about social policy, which can be a pity since at least some good *scientific* ideas have fallen into disrepute by being associated with particular political positions. For another, the concept of economic efficiency is famous for the production of some famous *qualitative* results. A major result of this kind is that a competitive market will, like an 'invisible hand', guide resource allocation (given an initial income distribution) to a Pareto optimum. Under competition with costless markets where all goods are priced, and where certain other conditions are satisfied, the price system is such that the forces of supply and demand create a unique price in every market where the quantities demanded and supplied are equalised. At this price the market is cleared—everyone has as much as he wants of each thing at the current price. The price is the amount he must pay to someone else in compensation for parting with some good so that one is, on balance, worse off as a result of any exchange. This system gets everything produced efficiently, produced in the right quantities and distributed to those who derive most benefit from it (given an initial distribution of income). ... Or does it?

If the world were really as we have so far assumed, we would, as logicians, have to agree that it did, though we need not agree that it was a just as well as an efficient system. But the world is not, of course, quite like this. In practice lots of things happen to make the ideal described above absolutely unattainable. In the real world the future—and much of the present—is uncertain. Substantial costs have to be incurred to acquire and evaluate information, to arrange and enforce agreements, and so on. All these have been left out of the competitive paradigm. In practice one must allocate the resources used in these processes in an efficient way. In the real world the social framework in which we live is beset by monopolies, falling rather than rising marginal costs, and countless other phenomena that vitiate any simple conclusion about the market. Sometimes society tries to correct some of the more obvious imperfections but even then one cannot be certain that the cure is better than the disease. Sometimes society, recognising that the market is rather inept at revealing the social interest, substitutes government allocation for market allocation. Unfortunately, the political process is also rather inept at revealing the social interest (for example, with simple majority decision rules, 51 per cent of the people can overrule the preferences of 49 per cent). Nevertheless, some people would maintain that it is easier to attain a Pareto optimum or make Pareto improvements with socialist planning than with markets and argue their case for socialism on these grounds more than on any other. Others argue similarly for capitalism! In this book we shall be concerned a great deal with making comparisons between these two methods of allocation, one centralised, one decentralised. One may rest assured, however, that they are each imperfect. The student of social policy has to find the least imperfect method of approaching a relatively efficient allocation of resources. The task of devising modifications to existing social institutions so as to improve social welfare, or to invent entirely new ones, is fortunately exciting and difficult; we may thereby perhaps be compensated for the knowledge that the ideal is beyond our reach!

In this book, four respects in which the simple competitive supply/demand approach is inadequate will consistently crop up. This quartet of complications contains the following: external effects of individual or collective actions; public goods and bads; time; and the problem of uncertainty and ignorance.

Externalities

Let us assume for the moment that no complications exist. We would then say that if A's marginal valuation of, say, bread were equal to the marginal cost of providing it then the result would be efficient. Remember that A's marginal valuation (call it MV_A^A) is his or her valuation of his or her own consumption—it is an *internal* valuation. If we drew a diagram such as Figure 2.6 we would say that social welfare was at a maximum (if nothing else changes) if he or she obtained OQ^* bread per year. Note that we are here assuming for convenience that the marginal cost is constant.

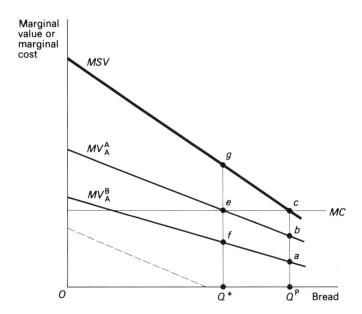

FIG. 2.6   Individual and social marginal valuations.

Now let us introduce the first kind of complication. Suppose that there exists someone else (B) who, in addition to caring how much bread he himself gets, also cares how much A gets. There is a sense, of course, in which *everyone* cares how much everyone else gets, for the more everyone else gets the less there is for oneself. This effect is, however, transmitted readily through the price mechanism and has helped to determine the competitive price. The kind of concern that our B has is different from this: we suppose that, in his opinion, A does not get enough to eat—B has a preference about A's bread consumption. Bread consumed by A benefits, in other words, not only A but *also* B. Let us suppose that the marginal value placed by B on A's bread consumption (call it MV_A^B) falls in the usual way. It may look something like the MV_A^B curve in Figure 2.6. Thus, when A is consuming OQ^* bread A obtains a marginal (internal) benefit of Q^*e *and B obtains a marginal (external) benefit of Q^*f.*

If A were to consume another loaf (per year) his additional benefit would be just slightly less than Q^*e and B's would be just slightly less than Q^*f, but together their additional benefit would be greater than the marginal cost of producing the additional loaf. Clearly then, social welfare would, according to the Pareto criterion, be increased if A ate more bread. In fact, with this externality, the Pareto optimal, or efficient, allocation of bread to A is OQ^P rather than OQ^*, for at OQ^P the additional benefit to both A *and* B (marginal *social* valuation, or MSV) is just equal to the marginal cost of obtaining the additional benefit. With external benefits, therefore, our original rule for allocational efficiency must be modified. Instead of having

$$MV^A = MV^B = MC$$

we must now write:

$$MSV = MV_A^A + MV_A^B = MV_B^B = MC.$$

Marginal *social* valuation of A's consumption should be equal to that of B's consumption (which is MV_B^B, with no marginal externality) and equal to marginal cost, where MSV is the sum of A's MV of his own consumption (MV_A^A) and B's MV of A's consumption (MV_A^B).

This concept of external benefit is of crucial importance in social policy. As we shall see, it provides one of the major reasons why, for example, education and health are subsidised by the state for, with external benefits, too little may be consumed. For the moment, however, let us pause to note three things about the (qualitative) result we have obtained.

First, the mere fact that B receives an external benefit from A's actions is not sufficient in deciding whether social welfare might be increased by arranging some means (a subsidy, perhaps) by which A can be persuaded to engage in more of the externality generating activity. The external benefit must be a *marginal* external benefit at A's current rate of activity. If, for example, MV_A^B were the dashed line in Figure 2.6, though B would benefit from A's consumption, A is still consuming the right amount. Note, furthermore, that even at the efficient rate of consumption, B derives a positive marginal external benefit (Q^Pa) but this does *not* imply that A ought to get more. *A Pareto-relevant marginal external benefit exists only where the sum of internal and external marginal values exceeds marginal cost.* Today, when 'externalities' have begun to become an incantation in popular journals and newspapers and where a divergence between social and internal benefits is held to warrant a whole range of government—or private—compensating actions, it is as well to emphasise that the relevant divergence is between social benefits *at the margin* (i.e. the sum of internal and external marginal benefits *at the margin*) and marginal costs.

Second, note that the Pareto criterion will evaluate a move from Q^* to

Q^P as a good one only if the externally affected parties (in this case there is only one: B) subsidise the additional consumption. In our example, the minimum B will have to pay is *ecb*, the sum of the differences between A's *MV* of additional units and the price he will have to pay over the range $Q*Q^P$, which B would be prepared to pay since he derives an additional external benefit of $Q*faQ^P$. If a third individual, C, does not care about A's bread consumption, it is no use A and B getting together to force C to pay for the subsidy (even though if there were only three people they would have a majority) for C would lose some benefit without being compensated and we have no means of telling whether the extra benefit accruing to A and B exceeds the loss they impose on C.

Third, we may ask, if B stands to benefit from helping A to eat more bread, why the 'invisible hand' has not already forced him to do so—if A and B can mutually benefit by a move from $Q*$ to Q^P, why on earth might it be necessary to get, say, the government to subsidise bread production? Why have A and B not already taken advantage of these potential gains? The answer is that sometimes they do. A great deal of charity has always existed without government intervention. But there are also good reasons why individuals may not have an incentive to reap the potential gains and these arise especially when there is a large number of externally affected parties. We shall return to these reasons below when we discuss public goods.

We have discussed divergences between social and internal benefits. It is a relatively easy matter to do the basic analysis of the case where there is a divergence between social and internal cost. Let us suppose that no one cares how much bread other people eat. We return to a situation in which the optimum is where the *horizontal* sum of internal marginal valuations, rather than the vertical sum, equals marginal cost. We are thus at $OQ*$ bread consumption in Figure 2.7.

Now let us suppose that, although he pays for all his normal inputs in bread production in an entirely proper way, a baker emits a quantity of smoke from his ovens. The more he bakes the more they smoke. The more they smoke the more frequently neighbours must wash, etc. Spring-cleaning, with $OQ*$ bread production, takes place in Summer, Autumn, Winter, as well as Spring (we shall be dealing with far less trivial cases later in the book). The baker, of course, does not incur these costs, he merely imposes them on others. Let MC^P represent the producer's internal marginal cost, as before. Let MC^R represent the (external) marginal cost imposed on the rest of society. Thus, at $OQ*$ bread production, marginal value is $Q*e$, but marginal costs are $Q*e$ incurred internally by the baker *plus eg* incurred externally by his neighbours—a total *marginal social cost* of $Q*g$.

If the baker reduced his output by a loaf a year, the sum of these marginal costs (marginal social cost) would fall while marginal value

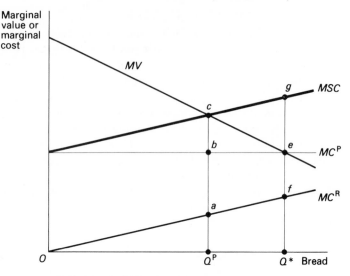

FIG. 2.7   Individual and social marginal costs.

would rise—a net social gain would take place. The astute reader will immediately recognise that the optimum will be at OQ^P, with less bread being baked, where the marginal benefit to all bread consumers is just equal to the sum of internal and external marginal costs, i.e. marginal social costs. Thus, instead of having

$$MV^A = MV^B = MC,$$

we must now write:

$$MV^A = MV^B = MC^P + MC^R[= MSC].$$

Once again, all the warnings concerning the interpretations of external benefits apply to external costs. Moreover, do not fall into the common trap of identifying external costs with social costs. Social costs (unless we exclude the baker from society, which he will justly resent) are the *sum* of internal and external costs. To identify social with external costs is to ignore internal costs, which is as silly as ignoring external costs.

Before turning to the interesting problems of public goods, which have been promised an investigation, two final warnings are in order in relation to the policy inferences to be drawn from the existence of externalities of either kind—benefits or costs. Where Pareto-relevant marginal externalities exist there will either be too little of an activity (in the case of benefits) or too much of it (in the case of costs). First, this does not imply that in the case of an external benefit the goods or service should necessarily be given away free. Nor, in the case of an external cost does it necessarily imply that the activity ought to be banned altogether. Second, externality relationships are (like all relationships) reciprocal. Consider, for example, the imposition of an external cost by some productive activity that creates pollution. We may presume that the polluter has (by default possibly) the right to pollute and he therefore imposes external costs on others. Suppose, however, that we changed the system of rights so that neighbours have the right to a pollution-free life. Then *they* impose an external cost on our original polluter. From the *allocation* point of view it frequently does not matter who has the right. The important thing is that the right be exchangeable so that, if the factory owner has the right, neighbours can compensate him for reducing pollution and increasing thereby his internal opportunity costs. Conversely, if neighbours have the right, the factory can compensate them for accepting some level of pollution. In general, with private property rights that can be exchanged, externalities tend to be internalised (i.e. compensated so as to produce some efficient rate of the activity) or else it is inefficient to internalise them—the social costs of arranging property rights may be too great. Most of the problems we shall meet in the externality field derive from the absence of exchangeable private property rights— frequently they are not feasible. It is ironical that much criticism has been made of private property and capitalism for creating massive externalities whereas most externalities can easily be seen to be created in situations where property and capitalism either do not or cannot be expected to obtain. However, as we shall see later when we investigate the role of government, it may often be more efficient to internalise externalities through formal planning procedures.

The essential economic problem of the government's role is to establish its and the market's appropriate range of activities, as determined by the contribution made to social welfare. We shall not prejudge this issue by, for example, false assumptions about the efficacy of universal private property on the one hand or the efficiency of the 'socialist conscience' on the other.

Public Goods and Bads

Let us begin by reviewing the kinds of goods discussed so far. We began with private goods whose characteristics are two-fold: (a) the benefit a person derives from them depends upon how much *he or she* has, and (b) the more he or she has of any good the less someone else must have. We then investigated *externalities* whose characteristics are also two-fold: (a) the benefit a person derives depends upon how much *someone else* has, and (b) the more of a good he or she has the less someone else must have. *Public goods* form a third category with the following characteristics: (a) the benefit a person derives depends upon how much of the good *exists in society*, and (b) the more a good is produced for him or her the *more* there is for everyone else. In this section we explore the consequences of this type of good (or bad). Some examples of public goods (though they are not all 'pure' public goods) include: defence, national parks, immunisation against communicable disease, fire engines and good ideas. Some examples of public bads are: smog, poverty, criminals, asbestos dust and bad ideas.

Most goods and bads are mixtures of public and private. For example, if an additional fire engine is added to the stock, every property owner in the area will gain as the probability of fire spreading to his home falls and as the probability of serious damage also falls—but if another person builds a house and moves into the area that will diminish, even if only by a little, the protection available to everyone else by raising the probability of an outbreak of fire and hence the probability that the fleet will be attending to that person just when someone else may need it.

With public goods, everyone need not have the same *quantity* as everyone else. To use the fire engine example, households nearest the fire station get more protection than those living some distance off. Moreover, even if they did receive the same quantity, they would not normally place the same value upon it because individuals' tastes differ. The case where everyone has an identically equal amount of a public good is usually termed a 'pure' public good case. But even in this case, whatever the quantity of a public good produced, individuals' marginal valuations will, as a rule, be different. One characteristic of publicness is thus that *marginal valuations cannot be brought into equality*. This in turn implies that we are not concerned with the efficient allocation of public goods between individuals once the goods are produced (the analogue to this problem becomes, where relevant, the problem of where to site the fire station). Instead we are faced with the problem of how much of them to create. If A valued an additional unit of some public good at £5, B valued it at £10 and C at £15, then the total increase in benefit from providing the extra unit (in a three person world) would be £30. Clearly, if it cost less than £30 to create the extra unit, it ought to be provided according to the Pareto criterion. This gives us the general rule for the efficient production of a public good: it is where the sum of all internal marginal values (marginal social value) is equal to marginal cost:

$$MSV = MV^A + MV^B + MV^C = MC.$$

Using our by now familiar diagrammatic technique, efficient production is OQ^P in Figure 2.8 where the sum of the marginal values is Q^Pe and is equal to marginal cost but, in this case, no single person's marginal valuation is ever alone sufficient to warrant any production at all because, for everyone, internal valuations are always less than cost at the margin. This situation is very commonly the case with public goods and bads: few people, if any, have sufficient wealth, and value defence enough, for it to be worth their while providing it for themselves individually and, even if they did, they would not provide as much as *should* be provided to maximise

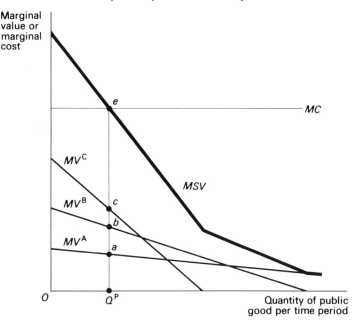

FIG. 2.8   Efficient output of a public good.

social welfare. Few people, again, have sufficient wealth or interest to make, by themselves, any significant dent in the poverty problem. With public goods, individual action is seldom either desirable or desired by individuals themselves. Instead, they clearly have an incentive to act *collectively* to create public goods and destroy public bads.

Collective Action, Democracy and the Free Rider Problem

In the practical world the existence of public goods and externalities affecting many people creates two enormous problems that are closely related to one another. The first is deciding how much to provide, e.g. how much pollution to abate, how much to rectify income deficiencies, how much public health service to provide. The second is how to pay for it. The problems can be well enough illustrated by a simple example. A small township of 500 persons contains an orphanage for forty children. There is a general feeling in the village that it would be nice to provide the children with a touring holiday. Each day of the tour will cost £25 plus a progressive allowance for every extra day the driver and supervisors spend away from home being driven potty by the children. Thus a one-day holiday costs £25, a two-day holiday £55, a three-day holiday £90, a four-day holiday £130, etc. The problems for the community are (a) how long a holiday to give the children and (b) how to pay for it. Let us suppose the 500 members of our community to be divided into two types of person: 200 of them are very kindly people valuing each additional day touring at a (constant) 15p (for simplicity, and only on this occasion, we assume away *diminishing* marginal values); the remaining 300, while kindly, are less kindly and/or poorer—they value each additional day at 10p. Finally, let us assume that there is a general presumption that the total costs of the tour will, in the end, be divided equally among the inhabitants. We note in passing that if the children are to get any holiday at all it *has to be* by the *collective* action of the villagers. Individual initiative is not enough even to provide a single afternoon's coach trip.

A village meeting is called and as is the wont in such community-spirited places, everyone turns up. The meeting has the job of deciding—democratically of course—what to do. The chairman of the meeting, being used to giving a lead, suggests that the children be given a day out in the coach at a cost of £25. That implies a per capita charge of 5p per villager and receives everyone's unanimous support (the more generous people each valuing it at 15p and the less generous at 10p). Obviously someone will suggest that the chairman's proposal is a bit on the mean side. Why not two days? Cost per person is 11p (marginal cost, 6p); again everyone supports the idea. Similarly, everyone will support a three-day holiday, which will cost each person 18p, and consensus is obtained up to a six-day holiday costing 45p each. One of the more generous villagers now proposes a seven-day holiday, costing each member of the meeting an additional 11p, or 56p in all. Suddenly the happy unanimity with which everyone agreed that previous proposals were miserly disappears. This time the matter is actually put to a vote and 200 people approve the motion; 300 vote against. The meeting has decided that a six-day holiday is what the children shall have.

Let us now assume that the village, as a whole, is more kindly than had been supposed before. Suppose now that 300 instead of 200 value additional days at 15p and that 200 instead of 300 value them at 10p. It can readily be foreseen that the meeting would, under these circumstances, vote for an eleven-day holiday, for the 300 will outvote the 200 when a seven-day holiday is proposed, but no one will vote for a holiday in excess of eleven days.

We may compare these results with what our theory tells us ought to be the length of the children's holiday. This is, one may recall, the holiday such that the sum of all 500 marginal valuations is equal to the marginal cost of an additional day touring. A little heavy arithmetic soon tells us that the ideal length of the children's holiday, according to the views of the whole village, is eight days when the sum of the marginal valuations (£60) is equal to the additional cost of the eighth day. (Alternatively it is nine days if 300 rather than 200 are relatively generous.) Can it be that collective action in general, and democracy in particular, has failed so disastrously to attain the ideal?

It has to be admitted that even in our rather perfect democracy described here (where everyone voted and there was no deliberate misleading of anyone by anyone else) the result has turned out to be unsatisfactory. It is also salutary to learn, however, that collective, or political, mechanisms for decision taking can be imperfect in much the same way as individualistic, or market, mechanisms (though it is, perhaps, less surprising when one realises that few institutions are so perfect that they enable individuals fully to reveal their preferences, good or bad, and that increasing the perfection of any institution is itself costly). Note that, in the case of the village we have described, the argument that at least collective action produces *some* holiday for the children is not necessarily a good one, for it need not be the case that the net community benefit from the holiday that is too long exceeds that of no holiday at all. Note also that our democratic procedure does not make any allowance for the benefit received by the children. All that counts is *their welfare as perceived by the villagers*. The villagers could, if they wished, give the children full voting rights in the village meeting (it would make no difference in the case we have discussed, but imagine the consequences of majority voting if the children outnumbered adult villagers or even exceeded the numerical difference between the two groups of villagers!). Alternatively we could, if we wished, include children in our definition of the 'society' whose welfare is to be maximised and thus include their marginal valuations in the efficiency criterion. In fact, however, we do not normally do this in human societies. The only welfare that counts as far as children are concerned is their welfare as perceived by others (parents, teachers, social workers, the population at large, etc.) which is how we have treated them in our example.

A general conclusion we reach is that majority decision rules tend, if people with strong feelings have a majority, to devote too many resources to producing public goods and if they have a minority to devote too few resources to such activities. There is a conceivable way out of this difficulty. Suppose a six-day holiday had been decided. The less generous majority will not vote for any longer holiday unless the additional costs are borne entirely by the more generous minority or, alternatively, that the minority compensate the majority for the higher costs they will incur. It is quite conceivable that a scheme could be devised whereby each individual would agree to an eight-day holiday, *provided that the marginal cost to him never exceeded his marginal benefit*. In this way, a political consensus similar to the consensus of the 'perfect' market would dictate an eight-day holiday. But it clearly requires a 'perfect' political mechanism—which is, unfortunately, just about as rare as the 'perfect' market—so that the relatively generous (or rich) compensate the relatively mean (or poor) for extending the holiday beyond the point the latter prefer.

The principal reason for this imperfection of the collective decision process, apart from the great costs sometimes incurred just in reaching *any* decision, is known as the *free rider problem*. Markets frequently fail to function efficiently because of this problem, and so do collective decision-making organisations. The problem is this: although everyone stands to gain by getting together and acting collectively, each individual will gain *even more*, as he sees it, if he misleads everyone else about his true preferences. Thus, if one villager pretended not to care at all about the provision of a public good such as the children's trip, with a little luck the rest of the village may organise it and he would—inescapably—benefit from it without having to contribute a penny. In short, as well as the children, he gets a 'free ride' at the expense of everyone else. Obviously, if everyone tries to act as a free rider, nothing will get done at all. This is one reason why the contribution scales are often agreed in advance, so no one can be a free rider. The trouble is that this prevents the adjustments to the cost-sharing agreement that are necessary for the ideal to be attained.

There are quite a large number of other methods devised to overcome the free rider problem. One is to 'fence off' the public good so that non-contributors can be excluded from enjoying it. This is possible with some public goods (such as light waves from cinema screens, theatres and television sets) but not others (such as lighthouses, or the benefits of defence and poverty eradication). Another is to tie in some private good benefit with subscription to public goods production. This is, in fact, a very common technique and can be seen in operation when people who support good (public) causes can be observed sporting badges letting the world know about their good deeds, or when subscribers to the National Trust (which lobbies on our collective behalf) get free admission to National Parks. Finally, and most important, members of the community may make a prior agreement that all will contribute to produce public goods. Acceptance of compulsory taxation is implicitly such an arrangement—a sort of social contract. Of course, none of these methods *guarantees* the efficient production of public goods. What we emphasise, however, is the great difficulty of ensuring an efficient rate of their production under *any* kind of institutional framework. We shall be returning to these problems many times in the course of this book and later some methods will be suggested by which the government may improve decisions about public goods production.

B. Human Capital

Although we have complicated the initial model quite substantially, we have continued to assume a timeless and certain world. This section provides an introduction to the role of time and the idea of investment in human beings. In the next section we consider some consequences of uncertainty. The role of time is of importance in social policy for many reasons. Some of these are: that there is no identity between individuals' income flows in any time period and their preferred consumption—they may therefore choose to save or dissave, arrange for retirement, etc; that making investments in, say, hospitals involves the incurring of costs and the receipt of benefits in varying ratios over a long time period; that, by sacrificing current work opportunities to acquire more training or education, future earnings may be increased.

Time Preference

Costs and benefits accruing later are weighted less than those accruing earlier because early resources are preferred to later ones. A pound next year must be less valued by any member of society than a pound (of equal purchasing power) this year, for one has a whole year between now and then to use the present pound. This latter set of options is not available if the pound is coming only next year. Therefore, on the fundamental principle that *more is preferred*, a future pound is always valued less than a present pound. Since this principle clearly does not apply to services, which cannot be stored, some economists prefer simply to assert that consumption in one time period is just *different* from consumption in another in such a way that earlier consumption is preferred. Whichever view one takes, we can say in symbols:

$$P = F \times D, \qquad 0 < D < 1$$

where F is a future pound (next year), D is the fraction or discount factor by which it is discounted to get P—the present value of a future pound. Thus, if 100p next year ($F = 100$) are worth 75p today ($P = 75$), $D = 75/100 = 3/4$. The relative values of P and F are $F/P = 100/75$ so the future value of the future pound is $33\frac{1}{3}$ per cent higher than its present value, i.e. $F/P = (P + 0.33P)/P$ or $P(1 + 0.33)$. $33\frac{1}{3}$ per cent is the *marginal rate of time preference* of the individual and it measures the rate at which an individual will accept a small (marginal) reduction in present consumption in exchange for an increase in consumption at some future date. For convenience, the periods in which consumption takes place are usually taken at yearly intervals.

To illustrate this kind of preference, consider an individual who, by sacrificing £10 this year can enjoy £12 next year. Whether he would make such an investment will depend upon his marginal rate of time preference. If the rate is, say, 10 per cent, then he would need £10 $(1 + 0.1)$ to induce him to make the investment. In this example, since £10 $(1 + 0.1) <$ £12, the condition is more than just met. Let us term the marginal rate of time preference r, then

$$D = \frac{1}{1 + r}$$

which, since $0 < D < 1$, implies $r > 0$.

Substituting this equation into the previous one we get

$$P = F[1/(1 + r)]$$

so the present value of a future pound can be found if the marginal rate of time preference is known.

If the pound is deferred for two years instead of only one, the formula can easily be calculated. The present value of F a year hence (F_1) is $F_1[1/(1 + r)]$. Similarly its present value two years hence (F_2) is $F_2[1/(1 + r)][1/(1 + r)] = F_2[1/(1 + r)^2]$. Deferred three years

$$P = F_3[1/(1 + r)^3]$$

and deferred n years

$$P = F_n[1/(1 + r)^n].$$

If one receives a set of benefits through time, the present values of each are simply added up:

$$P = \frac{F_1}{1 + r} + \frac{F_2}{(1 + r)^2} + \frac{F_3}{(1 + r)^3} + \cdots + \frac{F_n}{(1 + r)^n}.$$

If some benefit occurs at once (at time 0) we amend this equation to:

$$P_0 = F_0 + \frac{F_1}{1 + r} + \frac{F_2}{(1 + r)^2} + \cdots + \frac{F_n}{(1 + r)^n}.$$

What we are dealing with here are the values that individuals place upon present and future costs and benefits to them. These values depend upon their preferences—hence the term *time preference*.

Time preference is taken as a universal phenomenon but *interest rates*, which are commonly supposed to be the same thing, are the product of markets. Just as marginal value can exist without a market, so can marginal time preference. The relationship between time preference and observable interest rates is similar to that between marginal value generally and prices. Interest rates are the product of individuals making exchanges with one another in dated commodities (e.g. I will supply you with so much of X next year if you give so much Y now, or the year after, etc.) and, of course, of actually investing in productive resources. Just as there can be an equilibrium in a timeless market model, so an intertemporal equilibrium may exist that occurs when each has his marginal rate of time preference brought into equality with the other, which is, in turn, equal to the rate at which current resources can actually be converted into future ones. This revealed trading ratio is the rate of interest. Typically, since there is a host of complicating factors, there are many such rates.

If we assume that benefits and costs may not accrue simultaneously (the costs, as is often the case, are largely incurred prior to the benefits), then it is useful to separate them out. We assume (for the moment) that such costs and benefits are expressed in money terms. The equation now becomes:

$$P_0 = \sum_{t=0}^{n} \left[\frac{B_t - C_t}{(1+r)^t} \right]$$

where the Bs and Cs are benefits and costs and the ts refer to the time periods. If

$$P_0 > 0$$

the investment is worth undertaking in the sense that the present value of an individual's income is raised.

If $(B - C)$ is constant through time, the previous equation simplifies to

$$P_0 = (B - C)[1 + 1/(1+r) + 1/(1+r)^2 + 1/(1+r)^3 + \cdots + 1/(1+r)^n]$$

from which we derive[1]

$$P_0 = (B - C) \left[\frac{(1+r)^{n+1} - 1}{r(1+r)^n} \right],$$

and if n is a very long time away, since $1/r(1+r)^n$ becomes negligible we get

$$P_0 = (B - C)/r.$$

Human Investment

Consider the application of this analysis in a problem of *human capital formation*. An individual is considering, we suppose, a choice between two programmes: the first involving no additional acquisition of skill and the second involving a programme of training. Let us assume for simplicity that the non-pecuniary aspects of the alternatives are the same. This enables us to take as a maximand the present value of the differential income stream net of the cost to the individual of the training programme, since the only things that differentiate the two options are monetary factors. Denote the present value of the choice involving no skill change by U

and the other by S, then $S \gtreqless U$ according as

$$(E_0^s - E_0^u - C_0) +$$

$$\frac{E_1^s - E_1^u - C_1}{1 + r} + \frac{E_2^s - E_2^u - C_2}{(1 + r)^2} + \cdots + \frac{E_n^s - E_n^u - C_n}{(1 + r)^n} \gtreqless 0$$

(where the Es are skilled (E^s) or unskilled (E^u) earnings at time t, and the Cs are tuition costs). Further supposing that $E_0^s = 0$ and $C_1, \ldots C_n = 0$, then the comparison is between costs incurred in the present time period $(E_0^u$ and C_0, which are, respectively, forgone earnings plus direct tuition costs) and future earnings differentials. Denote full costs $(E_0^u + C_0)$ by K. Suppose also that the earnings differential in each year is a constant $\Delta E = E_1^s - E_1^u = \cdots = E_n^s - E_n^u$, then the condition becomes, using a result we already have:

$$-K + \Delta E \left[\frac{(1 + r)^{n+1} - 1}{r(1 + r)^n} \right] \gtreqless 0$$

or, where n is a very long way off:

$$-K + \frac{\Delta E}{r} \gtreqless 0.$$

The earnings differential that would *exactly* compensate for the cost is derived from

$$\frac{\Delta E}{r} = K,$$

viz.

$$\Delta E = rK,$$

so if ΔE is larger than rK, then the investment in skills would have been worthwhile. It should be clear that if one can suppose that an individual's marginal rate of time preference is equal to an interest rate at which he actually borrows or lends, then this analysis can be applied to assess—or predict—what decisions are likely to be taken by individuals as regards their training or education.

But do not jump to the conclusion that, if this last equation is not *at least* satisfied, the investment will not (or should not) be undertaken. Recall that we omitted non-pecuniary factors from the analysis by assuming them to be the same for each option. We can easily show that equations like these can mislead, by supposing that there *are* non-pecuniary differentials between the options. The point can be made most simply by assuming that non-pecuniary net benefits, ΔN, attach to the skilled option and that they are constant through time. With N, the choice depends on:

$$-K + \Delta(E + N) \left[\frac{(1 + r)^{n+1} - 1}{r(1 + r)^n} \right] \gtreqless 0$$

or

$$-K + \frac{\Delta(E + N)}{r} \gtreqless 0$$

when n is a long way off. In this case, supposing a subjective shadow price to be attached to the N, the training programme is *just* worth doing if

$$\Delta(E + N) = rK,$$

which implies, of course, that

$$\Delta E < rK,$$

which makes our point: an earnings differential *less* than the annuitised costs does not mean that the investment in human capital either would not or should not have been made. Conversely, however, $\Delta E > rK$ would imply an *a fortiori* argument that the investment was worthwhile.

The basic apparatus of human capital theory underlies much of the economics of social policy, especially in areas concerned with the family, population size and growth, labour force participation, the demand for training and education, the demand for health, and determinants of the distribution of income. We shall, accordingly, be meeting it several times in this book.

C. UNCERTAINTY

The final complexity that we shall need to tack on to the basic analysis concerns the evident existence of uncertainty and ignorance. A great deal of social policy is, of course, justified by, and devoted to, ameliorating the effects of uncertainty and ignorance. Lack of perfect knowledge about both the present and the future arises for the simple reason that all information is costly to acquire. Indeed, much information, even of a probabilistic kind, may be impossible to acquire.

In general, any individual, when confronted with a situation or choice the outcome of which is inherently uncertain, may do two things about it. First he may seek to acquire more information and thus reduce his uncertainty. For example, a person seeking a job would normally be well-advised to discover—if he can—how likely it is that he will be laid off or made redundant. Secondly, he may seek to avoid some of the consequences of the risks he faces by insuring against them. For example, in addition to taking measures to reduce the probability that he might need a surgical operation in hospital, a person may insure against that contingency so that some of its consequences (e.g. the costs of treatment) are borne by someone else.

Both these alternatives have in common the fact that they are costly—information is costly to acquire, and one cannot pass on the risk of loss to someone else without compensating him for it. Our preceding analysis would suggest the nature of an efficient treatment of uncertainty if we assume that, as uncertainty is reduced or its consequences shifted to others, additional reductions or shifts have a declining marginal value. These efficiency conditions are, first, that the marginal value of extra information be equal to its marginal cost and, second, that the marginal value of risk-shifting be equal to its marginal cost. The latter principle implies in particular that the marginal value of risk-shifting ought to be proportional to the risk—the cost of insuring against the consequences of a disaster with a 50 per cent probability should be greater than those of insuring against that disaster if it has only a 25 per cent probability, for those who accept the risk are accepting a higher expected loss of their own wealth or welfare—a higher additional cost.

The treatment of uncertainty (which we assume to be a 'bad') is thus on all fours with the treatment of other allocation problems. Two things in particular, however, are of great importance. The first of these is that information is a public good—if someone discovers that every worker in an asbestos mine has a 10 per cent chance of dying of asbestosis before the age of sixty, the fact that one worker has this information does not reduce the amount of information available to everyone else. Moreover, it is frequently the case that there are economies of scale in information collection—the unit costs, for example, of large agencies collecting a wide variety of data relating to employment are likely to be lower than those of numerous small agencies each doing little bits. An obvious consequence of these two factors is that it is frequently desirable for individuals to act collectively in the provision of information, usually via the government.

Risk Aversion and Insurance

The second implication that is of importance relates to insurance. While there are many events that may occur in the future that cannot be wholly prevented or whose consequences cannot be mitigated by insurance, events that result in the loss of assets with a market value or of income and wealth often can be insured against. As an example of something whose consequences are best avoided in some other way, consider the misery of being ill. This may readily have its probability of occurrence reduced by personal changes in life-style by, for example, not smoking, or eating less, avoiding contaminated water and other sick people, and so on. But it is also usually possible to insure in western societies against the *financial* hardship of sickness, or the financial consequences of not being able to work, as it is to insure against the *financial* consequences of one's house burning down.

It is a fairly simple matter to show why any individual, for whom the marginal value of income falls the more he has, will often choose to insure against uncertain future loss of income or wealth. The basic reason for this is that if the marginal value of income falls, then an individual will be averse to taking risks. Suppose you have £100. I offer you a 50/50 chance of gaining £25 or losing £25. Will you accept? Not if you have a diminishing marginal utility of income, because the marginal value of the £25 you may gain must be less than the marginal value of the £25 you may lose: the value of the risky option is less than the value of keeping your £100. Suppose I offered you a 50/50 chance of gaining £25 or losing £20. The expected size of the change in you income if you accept my offer is 0.5 times £25 less 0.5 times £20. This amounts to +£2.50. Will you accept my offer? Quite possibly not: it all depends on whether the value of the £25 you may gain is larger than the value of the £20 you may lose. Economics does *not* assume that individuals, in an uncertain world, maximise expected income just as it does not assume them to maximise income under assumed conditions of certainty. What we do assume is that individuals maximise expected utility (or subjective value) under uncertainty. Thus, so long as the marginal value or utility of income falls, individuals will be averse to risk.

The point can be illustrated more generally by using Figure 2.9, which

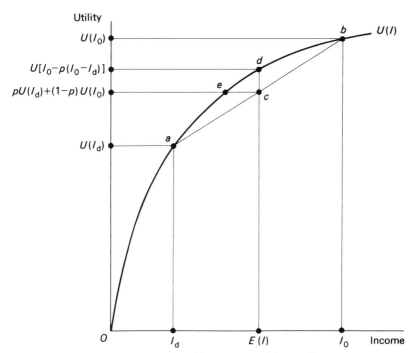

FIG. 2.9   Utility of income and risk aversion.

plots utility (which we have to assume in this case is measured on a ratio scale, like money, weight or height) against income with the $U(I)$ curve showing how utility increases at a decreasing rate with respect to income. Let I_0 on the horizontal axis represent the individual's current income, which we assume he expects to have in some future time period. But he cannot be certain about this and, indeed, there is some chance that his income will be only I_d, representing what it would be if a 'disaster' struck such as his house burning down, or his having to pay heavy medical bills, or his becoming disabled and not finding employment at the same wage. Let us also suppose that the probability of such events occurring for an individual such as ours is known—usually by extrapolating past experience of the frequency of such disasters into the future. If this probability be denoted p, then his expected income next year is $I_0 - p(I_0 - I_d)$: his income now less the probable loss of income, or writing it a different way,

$$E(I) = (1 - p)I_0 + p(I_d)$$

where $E(I)$ is expected income. If we knew what p is, we could readily calculate expected income, given I_0 and I_d. A point corresponding to $E(I)$ for $p = 0.5$ is marked on the horizontal axis of the figure. Now turn to the vertical axis. The utility of I_0 is then marked as $U(I_0)$ and the utility of I_d is marked $U(I_d)$. What is the expected utility of the uncertain combination of I_0 and I_d? Clearly the expected utility is the probability of getting the utility of the one added to the probability of getting the utility of the other, or

$$EU(I) = pU(I_d) + (1 - p)U(I_0),$$

which is marked on the vertical axis and can be located by measuring (for $p = 0.5$) half the distance along ab, or half the distance between $U(I_0)$ and $U(I_d)$.

'Fair' and 'Unfair' Premiums

Now suppose that the individual may purchase actuarially fair insurance, that is, he can completely insure against the financial consequences of the disaster by paying an insurance premium equal to the cost of the disaster times its probability of occurrence. What, in terms of our notation, is this premium? Since the financial cost of the disaster is $I_0 - I_d$, the fair insurance premium is plainly $p(I_0 - I_d)$. Will the individual choose to insure? The answer, under diminishing marginal value of income must be that he will. This can be shown by noting that the utility of income *net* of paying the premium is $U[I_0 - p(I_0 - I_d)]$ and, as can be seen on the vertical axis of Figure 2.9, this is a *higher* utility than that of the uncertain prospect.

Note that

$$I_0 - p(I_0 - I_d) = (1 - p)I_0 + p(I_d)$$

and both of these correspond to $E(I)$ on the horizontal axis. What is *not* the same is the utility of each, for we have just shown that the utility of income net of a certain loss in the form of a premium is higher than the expected utility of either I_0 or I_d occurring.

This is the essence of the economics of insurance against uncertainty. We might briefly note the consequences of supposing that actuarially fair premiums are not available. After all, insurance agencies incur costs of administration, and may charge monopoly rates. Do actuarially *unfair* premiums destroy the utility of insurance to individuals? We can use the analysis just learned to show the circumstances under which they would. Suppose that loading (as mark-ups on the 'fair' premium are known) is a proportion l of the premium. The premium therefore becomes $p(I_0 - I_d) + lp(I_0 - I_d) = (1 + l)p(I_0 - I_d)$. The question is therefore: is

$$U[I_0 - (1 + l)p(I_0 - I_d)] > pU(I_d) + (1 - p)U(I_0)?$$

Clearly l can become so large that individuals will prefer not to insure. In fact, if l is so large that utility from income net of the premium falls from d to below e on $U(I)$, then non-insurance will be preferred.

Issues concerning the size of l become important when one is discussing the question of whether public insurance or compulsory insurance against hazards such as ill-health are to be preferred to private voluntary arrangements. Evidently, there is the possibility that scale economies exist, causing l to be smaller with larger organisations. These and other issues will be taken up later in the book at appropriate points, as will be the important distinction between insurance as we have used the term and *social* insurance as it has evolved.

We have looked at some of the implications that the existence of uncertainty has for our basic analysis. Let us finish by stating some of the things that it does not imply. It does not imply that individuals are stupid or cannot make sensible choices. It does not imply that uncertainty in itself prevents the attainment of an optimum. It does not imply that risk and uncertainty can be abolished. It does not imply that it is socially non-optimal for some individuals who dislike risk still to bear some. It does not imply that somebody who knows the probabilities best ought to make decisions for those who know them less well.

With the basic equipment of this chapter we are now in a position to tackle a large variety of the problems of social policy. In later chapters we shall relate this analysis to the use of cost–benefit analysis in social policy, to social indicators, to the running of individual social services, to their financing, to the role of the public and private sectors, and to other types of problems in social policy.

The analysis of this chapter will be used many times over in what is to follow, so if you are not confident that you have grasped it at the first go, have a second try and remember that what may look rather complicated always begins from a simple beginning and proceeds step by step in complexity. Since the starting points are simple, and each step is easy, you should, provided you are careful, find no difficulty in understanding (and being able to reproduce by working from first principles) the more complicated material.

NOTE

1. To see this, multiply the equation by $(1 + r)$ and subtract the original equation, thus:

$$P_0(1 + r) = (B - C)\left[(1 + r) + 1 + \frac{1}{1 + r} + \frac{1}{(1 + r)^2} + \cdots + \frac{1}{(1 + r)^{n-1}}\right]$$

$$-P_0 = (B - C)\left[1 + \frac{1}{1 + r} + \frac{1}{(1 + r)^2} + \cdots + \frac{1}{(1 + r)^{n-1}} + \frac{1}{(1 + r)^n}\right]$$

$$P_0 r = (B - C)\left[(1 + r) - \frac{1}{(1 + r)^n}\right]$$

$$= (B - C)\left[(1 + r)\frac{(1 + r)^n}{(1 + r)^n} - \frac{1}{(1 + r)^n}\right]$$

$$= (B - C)\left[\frac{(1 + r)^{n+1} - 1}{(1 + r)^n}\right]$$

and

$$P_0 = (B - C)\left[\frac{(1 + r)^{n+1} - 1}{r(1 + r)^n}\right].$$

QUESTIONS ON CHAPTER 2

1. Why do marginal valuation curves have a negative slope?
2. What is the difference between an individual's demand curve and an individual's marginal valuation curve?
3. Why are individual marginal valuation curves sometimes added vertically, sometimes horizontally and sometimes both vertically and horizontally?
4. Distinguish between returns to scale and returns to an input.
5. Why does the average cost curve in Figure 2.4 not touch the vertical axis?
6. What assumptions are made with linear programming that are not made with the Cobb–Douglas production function?

7. Define a Pareto optimum. Does it require productive efficiency and cost-effectiveness?
8. When would the existence of external effects on either the demand side or the supply side *NOT* imply inefficiency in a private equilibrium?
9. Distinguish between external cost and social cost.
10. In what respect does a public good differ from an external benefit? Give examples.
11. Under what conditions will voting produce an optimal output of a public good?
12. Distinguish between time preference and the rate of interest.
13. Distinguish between human and physical capital.
14. Derive $P_0 = (B - C)/r$ from $P_0 = B - C + \dfrac{B - C}{1 + r} + \dfrac{B - C}{(1 + r)^2} + \cdots$
15. What is risk aversion?
16. Is insurance desirable?
17. Distinguish between 'fair' and 'unfair' insurance premiums. In what sense are they 'fair' or 'unfair'?
18. What major imperfections in the market inhibit the attainment of efficiency?
19. What major imperfections in political decision making inhibit the attainment of efficiency?
20. Whose welfare is being maximised in welfare economics?

FURTHER READING

The basic material in this chapter can be found in most introductory general economics texts. Their coverage of some aspects is, however, typically rather sketchy and for these topics the following are recommended:

On welfare economics:

Arrow, K. J. and Scitovsky, T. (eds) (1969) *Readings in Welfare Economics*. Harmondsworth: Penguin.
Buchanan, J. M. (1968) *The Demand and Supply of Public Goods*. Chicago: Rand McNally.
Winch, D. M. (1971) *Analytical Welfare Economics*. Harmondsworth: Penguin.

On collective action:

Buchanan, J. M. and Tullock, G. (1962) *The Calculus of Consent*. Ann Arbor: University of Michigan Press.
Olson, M. (1965) *The Logic of Collective Action*. Cambridge, Mass: Harvard University Press.

On time:

Sugden, R. and Williams, Alan (1978) *The Principles of Practical Cost–Benefit Analysis*. Oxford: Oxford University Press, chapter 2.

On uncertainty:

Friedman, M. and Savage, L. J. (1948) The utility analysis of choices involving risk. *Journal of Political Economy*, 56, pp. 279–304.

For the same basic themes in a socialist planning context:

Dobb, M. (1969) *Welfare Economics and the Economics of Socialism.* Cambridge: Cambridge University Press.
Lerner, A. P. (1944) *The Economics of Control.* London: Macmillan.

On human capital:

Becker, G. S. (1975) *Human Capital* (2nd edition). New York: Columbia University Press.

CHAPTER 3

Collectivism, Caring and Need

A. PUBLIC GOODS AND PUBLIC PRODUCTION

In this chapter we come closest to treading on the preserve of political science. We shall also be trying to search for answers that many students of social policy, drawing immediately upon their personal predilections, will—in their various ways—take for granted. Thus we ask, following the arguments of the last chapter, whether the social services are 'different' in such a way as to warrant, on grounds drawn from social science, government provision. We ask whether government provision is to be preferred to government financing. We investigate the fundamental reasons why government activity *in general* is warranted and, related to this, why it is and how it is that the behaviour of government and the behaviour of those who operate government institutions is different from the behaviour of individuals in general and of those who operate private institutions. We shall then proceed to an economic analysis of the phenomenon of caring and relate this to ideas of justice, efficiency, need, and the Welfare State. By relating the analysis of these matters to the objectives of social policy we shall in later chapters be able to make a consistent analytical critique of some of the controversies concerning current institutional arrangements and indicate a basis upon which students of social policy can seek answers to these weighty questions.

The traditional view has it that public goods will be produced at inefficient levels in the private sector; therefore they should be produced— or at least financed—by government. There are three elements in the argument: first, that private markets have an inherent inability to produce public goods efficiently; second, that government has characteristics that enable it to produce efficiently; third, that some meaningful distinction can be drawn between 'private' and 'public' sectors on *a priori* grounds (i.e. in terms of what they ought respectively to be doing rather than counting up what each actually does). We begin by showing that the usual form of the traditional argument has some severe shortcomings and then seek to establish rationales for government intervention.

Free Riders

The standard argument why the market 'fails' is that the nature of public
good production is that it provides each potential consumer or client with
an incentive (a) not to pay for the service and (b) to understate his own
demand leaving it to others to provide it. In each case the individual would
get a 'free ride' and, since everyone faces the same opportunity of 'getting
something for nothing', too little of the good will be produced—indeed
none will be produced at all! Recalling the example of the village coach
trip from chapter 2, the first incentive amounts to the villagers colluding to
arrange the trip and then failing to pay the tour operator and the second
amounts to each individual pretending he does not value the trip at all,
leaving it to the rest of the village to provide it.

The incentive not to pay for the trip, however, is unrelated to the
question of *public* goods; it concerns the general enforceability of any
contract between the providers of a service and demanders where delivery
of the service and payment do not take place at *precisely* the same moment
in time. If the market fails here it is because the law, custom, etiquette or
moral sanctions do not enforce contracts. The problem exists whether the
contract is between private individuals, between individuals and government or between governments. The answer lies plainly in the rule of law,
the development of interpersonal agreements such as downpayments,
which make contract breaking unprofitable, and in the development of a
moral climate in which obligations are recognised and honoured.

The second incentive is more subtle. The optimal length of a coach trip
is determined by its marginal cost and by the sum of marginal valuations
across the whole community. If one, some, or all members of the community
hide their true MVs, clearly a suboptimal length of trip will result. But why
should individuals 'free ride' when its inevitable consequence is that they
will lose from such activity? Even if, in the village community, there existed
one or two persons who valued the tour so much that they were prepared
to pay for *some* trip regardless of what others did, free riders would still
lose by virtue of the fact that, if the planned trip were too short according
to the Pareto criterion, their own marginal valuations would exceed some
potentially agreeable share of the marginal cost of extending the trip. There
would be *some* distribution of marginal cost among 'free riders' such that
each would benefit from a longer trip. Clearly, each person has an incentive
to come to some agreement with his fellow villagers whereby these gains
can be realised. In coming to this agreement, each may try to hide his own
MV in order to increase his bargaining power and incur a smaller financing cost, but sooner or later the trip has to take place. If by that time
agreement has not been reached such that the optimal trip is being
provided then the 'free riders' will be 'punished' (along with everyone else)
by the provision of a suboptimal trip, or no trip at all.

The true incentives in each case therefore work in favour of, not against, the provision of an optimal trip. In the first case it is in everyone's long term interest to have the rule of law or to invent ways of overcoming the possibility of contract abrogation. In the second case, while individuals may haggle over terms, *in the end* it pays them to reach an optimal agreement. As we shall see later, if individuals care for one another, this increases the probability that a satisfactory outcome will result.

But, it may be objected, is not all this bargaining wasteful? Would it not be more efficient for the government, the local authority, etc., to impose the ideal solution thereby saving all this trouble—perhaps the resources saved from bargaining could be devoted to a longer outing for the children? If bargainers expected to gain from the imposition of ideal terms by a third party we should expect them to seek their services. People would voluntarily seek out the agency of such a third party. But where would the outside agent get the knowledge required to impose the ideal solution? In the real world, only individuals know their true MVs. If they agree to reduce bargaining costs by inviting an 'imposed' choice from outside they will do so only if, in their experience, the third party can be trusted to act *on their behalf* and they will normally seek powers of control over him. In reality, the preferred solution will not be an *imposed* one at all but a *delegated* one. *Accountable* collective choice is thus implied by the existence of public goods.

Government and Social Contract

The real world is full of such mechanisms for delegated decisions. The profusion of clubs, charities and other private collective organisations bears witness to the variety of ways in which individuals, *in the private sector*, voluntarily seek to produce efficient outcomes in the production of public goods. Government, interpreted generally as the ultimate coercive force in a society, is neither necessary nor is it implied by any of the foregoing considerations. *Democratic government*, as a kind of club, however, *is* so implied. The delegation of collective decisions to a government over which citizens have some control is an extension of the general interest each has in getting public goods efficiently produced, and is, indeed, the appropriate agent where the affected community is the whole community under the jurisdiction of a government. There is a general presumption that collective interests of a village—such as the children's tour—are most efficiently run by a local collectivity (e.g. the local church, the parish council, the British Legion).[1] Collective interests of a whole country—such as law and order, the health and education of the nation— are plausibly most efficiently implemented by a national collectivity (i.e. the central government). Clearly, depending on the nature and scope of the public good in question, there is a large variety of collective institutions that will be appropriate for different decisions. In every case, the delegation of decision making can be seen as a rational response of private individuals to the high costs of reaching agreements on every single issue involving public goods. In short, they are 'market type' reactions.

The usual dichotomy between 'the market' and 'the state' is misleading, implying either a dominant state that imposes its will regardless of the wishes of the community (which cannot be evaluated by our normative theoretical apparatus and is certainly not justified by it) or else some omniscient organisation, composed of superhumans, capable somehow of identifying community interests independently of their expression by the community (which is a myth). A preferable distinction is between individual and collective decision making—the latter being appropriate where it is in individuals' interests to delegate decisions. But to the extent that government power is wielded arbitrarily, or in the interests of a cabalistic few (whether they be saints or sinners), then the intervention of government in the decision-making process can have no basis in economics.

It is curious that, despite the fact that much of economic theory has been founded on a narrow conception of self-interest (narrower than that adopted in this book), many students of the economics of social or public policy have failed to note that if the market 'fails' then it must contain within itself its own self-correcting procedures. To jump from the observation of market failure to the assertion that the government can 'do things better' is, however, a hopeless *non sequitur*. Sometimes it may, and sometimes it may not, for, as we saw in chapter 2, collective allocation can also 'fail'. Nevertheless, government intervention can be in the social interest. We must now examine more closely the differences that exist between decision makers acting on their own behalf and those acting on the behalf of others. The nature of these differences provides the fundamental rationale for some of the economic analysis of social policy to follow. Moreover, since the foregoing arguments imply only that collective *financing* may be one of an efficient set of ways of making decisions we also seek to establish whether there may be additional roles for government to play—for example, not on financing but *producing* services. (In our example the village *hired* the bus. It did not set up its own bus company.)

Governmental Behaviour and Its Control

It is sometimes naively supposed that the individuals with executive and administrative functions in government are 'different' from such individuals as, say, consumers or businessmen, and for some this is a sufficient reason for transferring decision making from one sector to another. This view cannot, however, be realistically sustained. Their behaviour may certainly be different, depending upon the function they perform, but economics asserts that their behaviour is different not because they are different *kinds* of people but because the *nature of the constraints* upon their behaviour is different. In particular, the costs of different choices will vary according to the constraints that govern those choices. The behaviour of persons working in a profit-seeking business, a non-profit charity, a public utility, a government department or a local authority will differ not because they are essentially different kinds of people but because the constraints on their behaviour differ.

What are these constraints? At the broadest level they consist of the range of rights owned by an individual in resources. They include not only the monetary wealth at his disposal (whether his or someone else's) and his time, but all other rights he possesses—rights to use, in specified ways, resources such as the air, rivers, office space, manpower, public parks, *etc.* Fortunately, it is not necessary to identify and measure the total constraint on behaviour for our purposes. It is sufficient to assume that there exists *some limit* to a person's rights (a realistic enough assumption); we then can investigate the consequence of changing the constraints—the rights structure—by using the fundamental implication of economic theory outlined in chapter 2: the higher the personal cost of obtaining any entity or engaging in any activity, the less will be acquired or engaged in during any period of time. The behaviour of a businessman who has effluent to dispose of will be different if the river by his factory is owned by someone else than if it is publicly owned or owned by no one (How?). The behaviour of a businessman working on his own account will differ from that of a similar businessman responsible to shareholders (How?). The behaviour of a businessman who can pay whatever wages he likes will be different from that of the businessman who must pay a minimum wage (How?). For our present purposes, however, the important distinction is between individuals who make decisions in the public or government sector, whatever activities may be included in it, and those who make similar decisions in the private sector.

Profit and Non-Profit Motivation

An evidently frequent difference between organisations in the public and private sectors is that usually (though not invariably) the former are non-profit and the latter (again not invariably) are for-profit. This distinction is of great importance in social policy. The question therefore is: why is it that public ownership suppresses the profit motive so effectively? The answer lies in two key constraining elements to the rights of the owners: non-transferability of ownership and non-convertability of revenues.

Transferability of ownership means that the *consequences* of one's ownership can be concentrated upon individuals. In a community of 1,000 with 10 separate organisations that are publicly owned but are nevertheless supposed to make profits (we assume), each individual has a 1/1,000th share in each organisation. The consequences of his actions to improve the profitability of any organisation will be that he 'gets' 1/1,000th part of the additional profit with the other 999/1,000ths going to the other 999 members of the community. Only if the others behave as he does in each organisation will he receive the full benefit of his product. By contrast, if ownership could be transferred, each person might have a 1/100th share of *one* organisation (still with 'equal' distribution of rights) and the benefits of an individual's actions would depend more upon *his own* activity and less upon the activity of others. Divide each organisation into 100 smaller organisations so that each can have sole ownership and the cost–benefit consequences of each individual's activity will be entirely concentrated upon that individual. If the objective was, as we assumed, to make profits, it is perfectly obvious that the ability to transfer and concentrate ownership will be more conducive to profit making—it only needs one person in the community who wants more wealth (and will work for it) for it to be worth his while to buy other people's ownership shares and more effectively concentrate the rewards of his own activity upon himself (also the consequences of his own mistakes) thereby relying less upon the wealth-seeking motivation of others to get his rewards and being less dependent upon their foolish choices. Moreover, since profit maximising implies technical efficiency and cost-effectiveness in production, such firms are also likely to be efficient on the production side. In a more realistic world where individuals have different managerial capabilities, different technical knowledge, different attitudes to risk and so on, the transferability of ownership will tend to be even more productive of profits. Conversely, non-transferability, or public ownership, will be relatively more effective in emasculating the profit motive. This first argument thus shows why, even if publicly owned organisations are supposed to be every bit as profitable as privately owned organisations, they will tend in practice not to be so profitable, because the costs of not making profits are lower for each individual while the benefits of making more profits are less.

Even, however, if profits are not the objective, the cost–benefit consequences of decisions are less fully thrust upon owners, which means that they will have less incentive to control closely the behaviour of the management of publicly owned organisations. The absence of this incentive, or its weakening, means that other incentives are needed to replace those that are absent. In social policy, it is frequently the case that profit seeking leads to a neglect of some important social costs and benefits of the activities of an organisation. Public ownership is one important method of emasculating the incentive to make profits but, at the same time, if the incentive to operate in the social interest, more widely construed, is not also to be emasculated, and if technical efficiency and cost-effectiveness are to be maintained, additional constraints on the behaviour of management are required. The techniques of subsequent chapters in Part III, such as output budgeting and cost–benefit analysis, are intended to provide precisely such decision-making aids and such a decision-making environment.

Non-transferability of ownership, while not unique to public ownership, is for our purposes its most important characteristic. Having thus weakened the profit motive it is a short step to prohibiting it *effectively* in social policy organisations. This done, the second element constraining the rights of public decision makers comes to the fore: non-convertibility.

Non-convertibility means that whatever revenues are brought into the organisation through its activity cannot be converted by the owners into personal wealth and is a constraint on owners of all non-profit organisations, whether publicly or privately owned. The inability of owners to take wealth out of the non-profit organisation means that other owners, customers, patrons and suppliers of funds (whether subscribers or taxpayers) are protected against the—possibly self-seeking—behaviour of any individual owner. But this constraint on owners implies that they will tend to seek other ways of increasing their wealth at the expense of the organisation. If they cannot do it by paying themselves agreed dividends or by selling their ownership, there exist other, less open methods. An owner who happened to be a manager, for example, could pay himself (and his fellow managers) relatively high salaries; they could use luxury office accommodation; they could employ larger staffs than are strictly necessary. There are constraints on the extent to which these sources of wealth can be tapped, of course. For example, salaries cannot be 'unreasonably' high (i.e. so high as to be noticeably high) or the executive will be fired. But not all such activities can be easily monitored. For example, instead of paying themselves higher salaries, inadvertent profits could be invested in safe securities thus ensuring the management a more secure and long-lived salary—which is equivalent to a higher salary. Such effects are often termed '*x*-inefficiency'.

Why should the not-for-profit form of organisation be chosen in view of these potential dangers? The reason is that whatever profits the organisation earns should be devoted *not* to the wealth of owners but to the well-being of those for whose benefit the non-profit organisation has been formed. It is a guarantee to clients and, more important, to the suppliers of funds, that the objectives of the organisation will not be changed at an individual owner's discretion. Hospitals, for example, are almost universally non-profit organisations and in Britain they are mostly publicly owned as well. This guarantees that the costs and benefits of hospitals can be allocated in ways that are different from profit organisations. To be sure, the owners of a profit organisation could devote their profits to charitable purposes *at their discretion*, but if the discretion of a few individuals is thought to be unreliable, the non-profit form of organisation guarantees that the costs to manager–owners of taking out profits are raised. Moreover, if the institutions in question are publicly owned by the whole community, the policies of these institutions can be designed to serve the wishes of agents interpreting the welfare of the whole community—for example to internalise community externalities.

Privately owned non-profit institutions tend to be formed to internalise externalities felt by the owners. Thus, free schools for certain types of children are or have been observed (e.g. for sons, sons of clergymen, daughters, Roman Catholic children, the very poor). Similarly, charitable hospitals have been operated, serving particular areas, illnesses or classes of patient. More generally felt externalities, however, are more effectively internalised by *publicly owned* non-profit institutions that discriminate among their clients on a less narrow and specific basis. Nevertheless, they will still have to discriminate (hospitals and universities, for example, have substantial excess demands for their services from clients legally eligible to receive them). The cost–benefit consequences of ownership rights on management are not such as to guarantee that they will operate *automatically* in accordance with the objectives of the organisation. Again, additional constraints will have to be supplied if they are to fulfil their functions properly (which patients should be assigned to hospital waiting lists and how long, on average, should they have to wait? Which of the many qualified students should be admitted to university? Would you trust doctors and university teachers to exercise their own discretion?).

Equality and the Ownership of Rights

Throughout this discussion we have not mentioned what, for many, is the major reason for state intervention through public ownership: to reduce inequalities in the ownership of wealth (and, thence, political power and influence). The reason for this is twofold. In the first place we have already seen that non-voluntary wealth redistribution (if that is how public ownership is to come into being) cannot be evaluated in the economic scheme we have set ourselves—it necessarily involves one set of members of the community imposing their values upon another. If erstwhile private owners are fully compensated, however, no effective redistribution takes place. Secondly, we have already seen that although public ownership does imply the 'equal' ownership of property by citizens, the rights in that property are not the same as the rights they have in private property—for example, the right to transfer ownership. Equality in ownership rights does not necessarily require public ownership, moreover, as we have seen in the illustrative example above, for rights to various types of private property may be distributed in a variety of ways. The view that 'property is theft' derives not from the nature of private property itself but from some historical point in time at which private rights were reassigned—perhaps some people had their property rights expropriated in what they thought was an unjust way (the enclosure movement is one example and the history of the British Empire provides endless examples of expropriated rights). There may well indeed be theft in a literal sense, but this refers to the *allocation* of private rights, not to their *existence*.

What a system of transferable private property rights *does* imply, however, is that the rights will tend to become distributed towards those who value them most or can increase their exchange value most. For example, the most able managers will tend to acquire more rights over wealth than the less able; people who enjoy taking risks will, if they take risks successfully, collect more wealth than people who dislike taking risks. Exchangeable private property enables individuals to specialise in the kind of wealth management in which they have a comparative advantage. Thus, private property systems require a more or less continuous redistribution of rights or wealth if egalitarian objectives are to be pursued, especially if the starting point is one in which there is already an unequal distribution of ownership rights. The need for this is absent with public ownership. Instead, one needs stringent controls over the stewards of publicly owned wealth and guidelines to indicate how best they might deploy publicly owned wealth in the social interest.

Whether, on balance, the constraints on the behaviour of private decision makers are more effective in promoting socially desired behaviour than the constraints on the behaviour of public decision makers is a moot point. Most readers will have a prejudice about it (and for many if will tie up closely with the view they take about 'freedom' and 'equality'). As professionals, however, the best view we can take is probably that in some circumstances the one method is preferred and in others the other. In addition one should be seeking continuously to find new ways of so altering the environment that constrains behaviour that decisions actually reached accord more fully with the social interest. In the public sector, with which most of this book is concerned, some of these new ways include cost–benefit analysis and output budgeting. In the private sector, methods include the imposition of taxes and subsidies or reassigning—or assigning—private property rights. The political analogues to taxes and subsidies and reallocation of rights concern reforms of the democratic political system, for example to help voters more efficiently to express their wishes, to make politicians respond more efficiently to their wishes or to reduce the extent of 'majority tyranny'. Reluctantly, we shall have to draw back from an investigation of the economics of politics in this sense though, for the serious student of social policy, the insights to be gained from such a study are a rich diet—one not to be left unsampled.

Much 'market failure' results in the creation of harmful external effects simply because ownership rights have not been established in physical things. Remember, no one owns 'things'; they own rights—if they have any at all—in ways to use things. One does not, for example, usually own the right to use one's property to destroy other people's property physically. In America, forests were often destroyed because no one had rights in living trees—only in lumber. To establish these rights, forests were frequently destroyed and the cause of conservation may irrevocably have been harmed. No one bewails the disappearance of domestic cattle—they are not disappearing because they are owned—but the North American bison did not have the fortune to be owned by anyone. Nor did the dodo!

It is not coincidence that many of the most serious threats to our environment, a major problem for social policy, take place in 'property' that no one owns or that is common property (i.e. owned and used in common). One is assailed by noise because property rights in the use of the air for transmitting sound waves are not usually established. One is assailed by smells and ugly sights (or the removal of beautiful sights) for much the same reason. Garbage and poisonous filth are poured out into commonly owned property, or non-owned property, at such a rate today that it is recognised that a social 'problem' now exists.

One method of solving the problem would be for the government to take over specific ownership of such property and to use cost–benefit type analysis to establish what the optimal rate of destruction of the environment should be by weighing the benefits of reduced environmental hazard against the costs in, say, lost production and lower money wealth. Many of the key variables required to make such an analysis more than merely an enumeration of points to consider—for example, the social value placed upon reduced noise from jet aircraft—are enormously hard, if not impossible, to calculate, and the establishment of property rights where they do not exist and where external effects are the likely consequence[2] is a method that can sometimes obviate the need for immensely complex, costly and possibly inconclusive cost–benefit calculations.

To summarise the principle conclusions so far: neither the existence of externalities nor public goods justifies government production or financing of social services, though if the nature of the externality is such that it is both experienced by the whole community and generated by non-specific sectors of the community then both government collective provision and a fairly universal provision is the likely outcome—a *prima facie* desirable outcome—of individual wants. The corollary is that there is no automaticity in getting social wants translated into social action unless the behavioural environment in which the administrators and operators of social services work is specifically designed to promote socially desired behaviour. The economic techniques applicable to publicly owned non-profit organisations are the same, in principle, as those applicable to the private non-profit organisations though in what is to come in Parts III and IV, given the ubiquitous heavy public commitment in social policy we shall concentrate exclusively upon the public sector. Choice between institutions—whether private or public—thus depends upon the nature of the externality, not the nature of the social service produced, and upon the effectiveness with which social control can be exercised over those who formulate and carry out policy.[3]

Most readers will be under no illusions about the efficiency of democratic institutions in improving social welfare. It may be the best form of government most can imagine but there is some hope that, as more thought goes into devising better voting systems and as technology improves,[4] democratic government will undergo considerable evolution and, in the process, become both more democratic and participatory. We have, however, already revealed part of the hand that is to be played in Part IV where methods of controlling collective decision makers by output budgeting, cost–benefit analysis and related techniques are to be discussed in the context of social policy.

Cost–benefit, cost-effectiveness, and output budgeting are essentially ways of presenting information. They do not, as such, impel governments or government departments to act in the social interest. The greater the degree of publicity associated with the techniques, however, the more embarrassing it is for governments, officials and politicians not to act in the potentially better ways suggested by the information. It is not, therefore, surprising that governments are reluctant to reveal all the information used as the basis of a decision or plan. But even if they did, the basis itself provides only a minor incentive for efficiency. Its proper use is far too heavily dependent at the moment upon the public-spiritedness of officials and politicians and upon the extent to which they believe that they can make a career, or prolong their political power, by advocating efficiency. Democracy is not so perfect that it forces them to be socially efficient or socially just. While the economic techniques are a step in the right direction one must not be over sanguine about the extent to which it is in the private interest of public decision takers to use them. Much further work remains to be done in developing methods of ensuring a closer relationship between official responses to their personal interests and appropriate public policies.

CARING

The nature of the externality that would appear to underlie the Welfare State is not of the sort that suggests that a *private* property right/market exchange solution is likely to be satisfactory. The reason for this is that an important foundation for analysis of social policy lies in the proposition that individuals *care about one another*.

Historically speaking, economists have not been much enamoured of the view that man may be seen usefully for social science purposes as, at least in part, unselfish. D. H. Robertson, in 1954, asked what it was that economists economised? ''Tis love, 'tis love', said the Duchess, 'that makes the world go round'. 'Somebody said', whispered Alice, 'that it's done by everyone minding their own business'. 'Ah well', replied the Duchess, 'it means much the same thing'. So economists economised, in the spirit of individualistic libertarianism, on love. Robertson's predecessor at Cambridge, A. C. Pigou, dominated a generation or two's economic vision with his definition of economic welfare: that portion of human welfare capable of being brought into relation with the measuring rod of money. Alfred Marshall, who was in turn Pigou's predecessor, in a saying often quoted by Robertson averred 'progress chiefly depends on the extent to which the *strongest* and not merely the *highest* forces of human nature can be utilized for the increase of social good'.

But the tradition is not only a Cambridgean one. W. S. Jevons, regarded by many as the father of modern (neoclassical) economics, sought to define the scope of economics by 'assigning a proper place for the pleasures and pains with which the Economist deals. It is the *lowest* rank of feelings which we here treat'.

Nor is the tradition post-utilitarian. Perhaps the best-known quotation from Adam Smith's *Wealth of Nations* is 'It is not from the benevolence of the butcher, the brewer, or the baker, that we expect our dinner, but from their regard to their own interest'. Perhaps most cynical of all early precursors was Bernard Mandeville, whose most famous aphorism is 'Pride and Vanity have built more Hospitals than all the Virtues together'.

There have, perhaps, been but two great economists who have taken the idea of 'caring' more than a little seriously in their contributions. One was F. Y. Edgeworth, a marginalist if ever there was one:

> . . . between the two extremes, between the frozen pole of egoism and the tropical expanse of utilitarianism, there has been granted to imperfectly-evolved mortals an intermediate temperate region; the position of one for whom in a calm moment his neighbour's happiness as compared with his own neither counts for nothing, nor yet 'counts for one', but counts for a fraction. We must modify the utilitarian integral . . . by multiplying each pleasure, except the pleasures of the agent himself, by a fraction—a factor doubtless diminishing with what may be called the social distance between the individual agent and those of whose pleasures he takes account. [1881, pp. 102–3]

Aside from the utilitarian assumptions embodied in this, the only real trouble with it is that Edgeworth did not see fit to investigate the *sources* of one's neighbour's happiness (or misery) and focussed rather determinedly on the total independently of its multivarious sources.

Not so with Karl Marx. His discussion of the character of the communist society, immediately upon its emergence from capitalism and in a mature phase, is worth quoting at some length:

> What we have to deal with here is a communist society, not as it has *developed* on its own foundations, but, on the contrary, just as it *emerges* from capitalist society; which is thus in every respect, economically, morally and intellectually, still swamped with the birthmarks of the old society from whose womb it emerges. Accordingly, the individual producer receives back from society— after the deductions have been made—exactly what he gives to it . . . . He receives a certificate from society that he has furnished such and such an amount of labour (after deducting his labour from the common funds), and with this certificate he draws from the social stock of means of consumption as much as costs the same amount of labour . . . .
>
> In spite of this advance, this *equal right* is still constantly stigmatized by a bourgeois limitation. The right of the producers is *proportional* to the labour they supply; the equality consists in the fact that measurement is made with an *equal standard*, labour.
>
> But one man is superior to another physically or mentally and so supplies more labour in the same time, or can labour for a longer time; and labour, to serve as a measure, must be defined by its duration or intensity, otherwise it ceases to be a standard of measurement. This *equal* right is an unequal right for unequal labour. It recognizes no class differences, because everyone is only a worker like everyone else; but it tacitly recognizes unequal individual endowment and thus productive capacity as natural privileges. *It is, therefore, a right of inequality, in its content, like every right.* Right by its very nature can consist only in the application of an equal standard; but unequal individuals (and they would not be different individuals if they were not unequal) are measurable only by an equal standard in so far as they are brought under an equal point of view, are taken from one *definite* side only, for instance, in the present case, are regarded *only* as *workers*, and nothing more is seen in them, everything else being ignored . . . .
>
> But these defects are inevitable in the first phase of communist society as it is when it has just emerged after prolonged birth pangs from capitalist society . . . .
>
> In a higher phase of communist society, after the enslaving subordination of the individual to the division of labour, and therewith also the antithesis between mental and physical labour, has vanished; after labour has become not only a means of life but life's prime want; after the productive forces have also increased with the all-round development of the individual, and all the springs of cooperative wealth flow more abundantly—only then can the narrow horizon of bourgeois right be crossed in its entirety and society inscribe in its banners: From each according to his ability, to each according to his needs! [1875, pp. 248-9]

From our point of view, the chief thing that is wrong with this is its ordering of events required to transcend bourgeois values. The final paragraph comes desperately close, indeed, to utopianism since it appears to envisage the elimination of scarcity (of goods not only to satisfy selfish, but also to satisfy unselfish, desires). But, even if this were not the case, Marx insists on the transitional phase of receipt according to contribution (of

labour) as prior to that of allocation according to need. Chinese commun-
ism of course, has attempted to reverse this ordering, by having allocation
by need in the agricultural communes.

But what is more relevant for our purposes is that bourgeois society has
also evolved a set of institutions, for convenience labelled the 'Welfare
State', that allocate services or cash benefits to individuals on criteria of
'need' rather than ability and willingness to pay. There are three main
issues requiring discussion here. One set relates to the distinction between
justice and efficiency, another relates to the distinction between caring in
general and caring in particular, the third relates to the distinction between
demand and need. We shall consider each in turn.

Justice and Efficiency

One of the many ways in which economists have traditionally divided their
analysis is into a box concerned with equity and social justice and another
concerned with efficiency. There is a great deal more, one may note, in the
efficiency box than the other. Historically, there has also been a strong
political call not to confound the two. An eloquent advocate was Henry
Simons:

> 'It is urgently necessary for us to quit confusing measures for regulating rela-
> tive prices and wages with devices for diminishing inequality. One difference
> between competent economists and charlatans is that, at this point, the former
> sometimes discipline their sentimentality with a little reflection on the
> mechanics of an exchange economy'. [1948, pp. 83]

This influential dogma has seriously confused a couple of generations of
economists and has held back a truly *interesting* economic discussion of
equity, for it suggests that relative prices and consumption of goods and
services are a matter of efficiency rather than equity. It identifies the difference between equity and efficiency in terms of the objects of social concern
rather than, as would seem more correct, in terms of the *source* of the
concern. The source of value for the making of judgements about efficiency
is ultimately the preferences of individuals; whereas the source of value for
making judgements about equity lies outside, or is extrinsic to, preferences.[5]
One reason for this characteristic of equity is clear in the quotation from
Marx cited above: 'right by its very nature can consist only in the application of an equal standard'. The whole point of making a judgement about
justice is so to frame it that it is (and can be seen to be) a judgement made
independently of the interests of the individual making it. The poor man
arguing for redistribution of income from rich to poor may be arguing that
he wants more for himself or for those like him (both of which are
questions of preference), or he may be arguing that there is a principle to

which he is appealing and that transcends—it may even militate against—
his preferences, and this principle implies that such a transfer ought to take
place. A source for such a principle may be held to be a divine command-
ment, or it may derive from a conceptual experiment capable of being
made by anybody so long as he will draw the same conclusions from the
experiment. Or it may lie elsewhere. The nature of the rationale for
efficiency and equity is thus quite distinct and the possibility clearly exists
that the two types of consideration may conflict: one may feel that one
ought not to do what one prefers, or one ought to do what one does not
prefer—there are sins of commission and sins of omission.

It is important to keep this distinction clear because there are several
ways in which these two kinds of consideration can become awkwardly
entangled. For example, classical utilitarianism regards the maximisation
of total utility as the criterion of *both* equity and efficiency and, on this
view, there is little point in making a distinction between them. This is a
way of thinking that has proved to be particularly attractive to economists,
some of whom seem unaware that utilitarianism is not the only ethical
system of thought held by man. Others might concede the value of distinguishing between the categories 'equity' and 'efficiency', which gives rise to
the possibility of describing various states of society as having varying
degrees of efficiency *and* varying degrees of justice, but insist that since
in the end one has to choose the kind of society one prefers, then one must
trade off justice and efficiency. This trade-off will be a matter of preference
and so the 'top-level' choice is ultimately one of efficiency. Such economists
might typically enquire: what is the optimal amount of justice? We shall
not go so far in this book, and the reason is a simple one—that nothing
much will be illuminated by so doing. It is of great interest in social policy
to ask what is just, and why. And it is also interesting to ask what is
efficient, and why. It is, moreover, interesting to identify policies by their
just and efficient characteristics. But neither philosophers nor economists
have any guidance to offer decision makers as to how (or even whether)
one set of characteristics ought to be traded off against the other—even
though someone, somehow, may have to balance the two.

Confusion between the categories 'equity' and 'efficient' has yet a further
source, which is particularly potent in the economics of social policy and
which derives its roots from externality theory. Let us suppose, as we did in
chapter 2, that individual B cares about the amount of bread that A consumes. Referring back to Figure 2.6 we may infer that for A to consume
OQ^* would be *inefficient*. For him to consume OQ^P would, on our assumption, be *efficient*. The argument here is rooted entirely in the preferences of
A and B. The argument has *not* been that it is just, or fair, or equitable that
A should eat more bread; only that B prefers—and is prepared to sacrifice
resources so that—A should eat more bread. In short, B *cares* about A.

Characteristically, appropriate consumption of goods and services, and appropriate redistributions of income, are discussed using the vocabularly of social justice. This is not the same as the language of compassion or, as we have termed it, the language of caring. Social justice is not a matter of preference; compassion and caring are: they are descriptive of the kind of preferences most people regard as being the most admirable.[5]

Although the overwhelming bulk of this book is concerned with questions of efficiency, it would be wrong not to mention some of the principal ideas of social or distributive justice. We shall not discuss utilitarianism, since that will come up in the next chapter as an efficiency case. Three other commonly discussed concepts of distributive justice are, however: distribution according to desert; distribution according to Rawlsian maximin; and distribution according to need.

Desert as a principle of distributive justice has had at least three important historical roles in the justification of particular social policies. First there is the idea that individuals deserve their *earnings* because, at least under certain conditions, this measures the value of their contribution to output. This argument has been chiefly popularised by J. B. Clark. In broad terms it is clearly justificatory of capitalist institutions (and it is usually so intended). Related to it in its desert-status, but otherwise quite different, is the second historical argument, the Marxian view that labour— both direct labour as well as that embodied in machines—deserves the whole of net output since, along with nature, labour is the ultimate source of all value. Neither of these arguments can serve as an argument for distributive justice as between individuals, however, for the reason that if a specified individual is to be held deserving of a reward, his desert must be independent of the acts of other people. But, as we saw in our discussion of the marginal product in chapter 2, the output of any worker is dependent upon the contributions of other workers and other inputs: the number and type of machines available, and so on. No one can therefore claim sensibly to deserve an income based on 'their' contribution, since 'their' contribution is in fact determined in part by others. In a Marxian sense, *everyone* may deserve the net output, but *no one* deserves his share of it!

The other classic way in which desert has been used in social policy is in the distinction between the deserving and the undeserving poor. For many years it was argued (and the argument may still be occasionally heard today) that social security benefits should go only to the 'deserving' poor. First, note that this argument implicitly accepts that the category 'poor' may involve just entitlement to a benefit. The point is that some poor may be justly excluded from benefit. The general idea behind this argument seems to be that there is little point in awarding rights to benefit when there is reason to suppose that the benefit will be used in ways not approved by those making them available (e.g. by being spent on gin rather than milk). The deserving poor thus become those poor people who, the evidence suggests, will use benefits efficiently in the ways approved by benefactors. Viewed like this (and alternative views are hard to sustain) this notion of desert dissolves into a description of a patronising *preference* pattern held by the relatively rich. Desert, in this context, really has nothing to do with justice at all.

Rawlsian maximin, as the name implies, is a principle of distributive justice developed by John Rawls, whereby the just rule for income distribution is to maximise the welfare of the least well-off person (Rawls, 1972a, b). Rawls suggested a variant of the Pareto criterion to be used in a kind of 'social contract'. The question asked is: what general principles would be unanimously agreed by the members of a community in appraising the justice of the institutions and rules that regulate their conduct *independently* of whatever present position they may occupy in society? To get independence from current privileges, values, and so on, Rawls suggests that each individual, when considering whether an arrangement be just or not, imagine himself behind a 'veil of ignorance' so that he is to decide some general rules for distribution without knowing whether, for example, he himself will be rich or poor, bright or dull, assiduous or lazy, black or white, mean or generous. Rawls suggests that a consensus would be reached on three basic principles that together constitute the criteria for a 'fair' or 'just' framework, that is, each individual when conducting such an experiment will come to the same conclusions as regards the principles. The three principles are:

(i) Each person engaged in an activity or affected by it has an equal right to the most extensive liberty compatible with a like liberty for all.

(ii) No inequality is just unless it is *to the advantage of* the most unfortunate individual. Thus, if the removal of some inequalities would, in the process, harm the interest of the less well placed individuals, it would not be a just removal, i.e. inequalities must work to everyone's advantage.

(iii) Inequalities deriving from positions or offices held in society should be equally available to all to compete for on the basis of their ability.

The strength of the Rawlsian approach is in its attempt to derive general principles of just distribution from independent rational individuals, each of whom pursues self-interest (if so desired) behind the veil of ignorance. There are obvious attractions in this rival to the main alternative, which consists of appealing to basic tenets in the hope they may be shared by others (tenets such as it is (the only) good to maximise the sum of utility in society; or each should get his deserts), for if by introspection of the sort Rawls proposes men *would* agree on the principles, then the intuitive appeal of the approach clearly becomes very strong indeed.

Need cannot really serve as the basis of an argument for a just distribution of income or goods. The reason for this is that need is invariably *instrumental*: it serves a more ultimate purpose. When we say someone needs a council house, we are really saying that if he is to arrive in some desired state (that is, being adequately sheltered) he should have a council house. Endless confusion can be caused by failing to note this. Two types of confusion in particular often arise. First, although the end-state may be uniquely just, *there may be more than one means of achieving the end-state*, since need is instrumental. Indeed, since there is almost always a variety of ways of doing anything, delivering *any* service, arranging payment of benefit, etc., only after these alternative means have been investigated may it be possible to say that any individual needs *a service* or *a specific means*. The choice of means is usually a technical matter: the choice of which surgical operation has the higher probability of healing your duodenal ulcer is a technical matter even if we grant that you need your ulcer healed. The second kind of confusion is between rationales justifying the end-state. One may 'need' resources to implement an *efficiency* policy for internalising externalities, or one may 'need' those resources for effecting a more equal distribution on grounds of *justice*.

The language of need can indeed be misleading. On the whole it is best to enquire as to the ultimate aim being sought when 'needs' are asserted to exist; to consider whether they concern justice, or efficiency, or neither; and to consider the variety of means available to accomplish the end.

Specific versus General Caring

It has been observed (e.g. by James Tobin) that even those who are strong in their defence of inequalities of income and wealth are often also strong on *specific egalitarianism*. This is the view that certain specific scarce goods and services ought to be distributed less unequally than the ability to pay for them. Such a view implies that concern over distribution, whether rooted in an external notion of justice or in an individual's preferences, cannot be restricted only to concern over the income distribution and is in direct conflict with the kind of view illustrated by the quotation from Henry Simons on p. 60. The point has been put clearly enough (indeed somewhat overdrawn) by James Buchanan:

> The mere fact that some members of the community are poor does not, in and of itself, normally impose an external diseconomy on many of the remaining members. What does impose such an external diseconomy is the *way* that certain persons behave when they are poor. It is not the low income [alone] of the family down the street that bothers most of us; it is [also] that the family lives in a dilapidated house and dresses its children in rags that imposes on our sensibilities. [1968, p. 189; the two words in brackets have been added by me to make Buchanan's assertion less extreme.]

This view has strong intuitive appeal and its obvious policy implication, that there be subsidies attached to *specific* forms of consumption (e.g.

health services, education, housing), seems commonsensical. It may therefore be a surprise to find that the tradition of economics has nevertheless
denied the efficiency of specific subsidies. The argument runs thus: the
welfare of the recipient will be higher with cash grants than the provision
of a (non-tradeable) good or service since he will have a greater choice of
what to purchase with the cash and may choose to spend at least *some* of
the cash on goods *he* prefers. What this argument fails to note is that if the
income supplement failed to induce the desired increase in specific consumption (perhaps because the demand for the service was not of the sort
that rises as income rises) then there is really little point in those who
finance the transfer making it in the first place. More generally, why rely on
income effects alone anyway: by changing the relative *price* confronting the
consumer (perhaps reducing it even to zero) it may be cheaper to those
who finance it to effect a given desired change in consumption.

Thus, if concern for the consumption levels of others is specific, it is
unlikely that *general* redistribution in terms of income or wealth will internalise the relevant externalities efficiently, and possibly not internalise them
at all. After all, it is not only the relatively poor who may be judged to be in
need of social services.

Were caring not in large part specific, we would be hard put to explain
the existence of the Welfare State, and familiar arguments for subsidies, free
services, vouchers, etc., would have no economic rationale. The evidence,
however, seems to suggest that social concern, despite the traditional assertions of economists, is not only of the general type and perhaps not even
mainly of this type. It is, instead, specific.

The Appendix to this chapter analyses in great detail the basic economics of income transfers, subsidies, free provision and vouchers in the
context of a specific concern, using indifference curve analysis. For readers
with a background sufficient to cope with indifference curves, now is the
time to turn to this Appendix. (Others may proceed without it.)

Is Caring a Realistic Assumption?

The very *existence* of the Welfare State is evidence *for* the proposition that
specific caring exists, for if individuals did not care for one another then no
externality would exist and there would be little reason for collectivist
action. Moreover, the evidence strongly suggests that, to the extent that
caring *does* exist, it is not a *general* concern but, as has been suggested
above, is associated with specific aspects of consumption. The analysis thus
suggests that attempts in the past to provide a *conceptual* definition of the
Welfare State will be doomed to failure; public expenditure on what is
called the Welfare State will be determined, as regards its pattern and
amount, ultimately by people's *preferences*, not by characteristics *intrinsic*

Collectivism, Caring and Need

to social welfare. The items of spending will be those where a caring externality exists. This is less a matter for specific prediction than for observation. What we observe about the size and structure of spending on areas where 'caring' seems *a priori* plausible can be seen approximately presented in Table 3.1.

TABLE 3.1 *Public Expenditure on the Welfare State in Britain 1956, 1966 and 1976 (current prices)*

		1956		1966		1976	
		£m	% total	£m	% total	£m	% total
1	Employment services	26	0.9	71	1.0	689	2.1
2	Housing	496	16.7	979	14.1	5190	16.1
3	Education	636	21.5	1700	24.4	7340	22.8
4	NHS					6182	19.2
		654	22.1	1486	21.4		
5	Personal social services*					1128	3.5
6	School meals, etc.	89	3.0	141	2.0	454	1.4
7	Social Security benefits	1062	35.8	2577	37.1	11233	34.9
	TOTAL	2963	100.0	6954	100.0	32216	100.0
	Total as % of all public expenditure		44.9		48.1		55.1
	Total as % of personal income before tax		17.7		21.6		28.7

* In 1969 some local authority services were transferred from the National Health Service to Social Services.

Sources: Central Statistical Office, *National Income and Expenditure* 1966–76, HMSO, 1977 (for 1966 and 1976); *National Income and Expenditure* 1967, HMSO, 1967 (for 1956).

The items of expenditure included are those labelled 'social services' in the National Income Blue Book, with the addition of employment services, which includes the services administered by the Department of Employment, services to the disabled, sheltered employment and redundancy payments. It excludes several possible categories such as public health services (local authority maintenance of public conveniences, inspection of food and drugs, etc.) on the grounds that these services are more likely to be collectivised due to 'physical' externalities rather than the caring type we have discussed in this chapter.

The high share taken by social welfare expenditure out of both personal income (before tax) and public expenditure is quite consistent over the period 1956–76 (see Table 3.1). It is not particularly influenced by social security payments for, although unemployment in (say) 1976 averaged 5.8 per cent compared with 1.4 per cent in 1966, and although social security expenditure rose more than four times in nominal terms, its share of social welfare expenditure by no means changed proportionately. Social spending has increased steadily over the last twenty years both as a proportion of public expenditure and, since public expenditure has also been rising as a proportion of personal income before tax, even more markedly as a share of personal income.

In broad terms, and with only minor exceptions, items 1–6 inclusive in Table 3.1 are grants provided *in kind*, that is, the financial magnitudes measure the cost of the resources used up in supplying services directly to the public. Item 7, by contrast, is grants provided in cash. Cash grants have consistently taken rather more than one third of social welfare spending. One can therefore plainly see that the bulk of this expenditure seems to be in response to a concern about *specific* distributive efficiency. The *prima facie* evidence is against those who argue the reverse.

Of course it is open to anyone to deny the relevance of this evidence. One could assert, as might Henry Simons (had the public sector been of the size in his day that it is in our own), that its size and composition are not the response of rational individuals to a commonly experienced externality of the sort we have postulated but are the product of years of deceit by power-seeking politicians who have convinced their electors that they really can 'have something for nothing'. Or one may suppose instead that the electors have foolishly not understood the lessons of economics and the results are all a dreadful mistake. However, both the assumption that individuals are *persistently* conspired against without discovery and the assumption that they *persistently* fail to convey their (perfectly rational) wishes to government are assumptions that are not normally invoked in economics—nor indeed in any social science—and seem, on the face of it, more implausible than the alternative.

However, although the evidence is consistent with the postulate that both specific and general caring exist, it should also be noted that the Welfare State provides services to satisfy purely selfish desires as well as (and often simultaneously with) unselfish ones. For example, a free hospital bed that is available is available both for me and for those I may care about—family, friends, colleagues, even strangers. One should not, therefore, jump to the conclusion that the acceptance of unselfishness implies that individuals are only unselfish. This would be as unrealistic (possibly more unrealistic) than assuming them *only* to be selfish.

In addition to assuming that individuals are neither wholly selfish nor wholly unselfish, it seems also realistic to assume that they are not 'too' altruistic. What 'too' altruistic means can be illustrated from an imaginary case of two individuals who each have a general care for the income of the other, as in Figure 3.1. Suppose the points E^A and E^B represent A's and B's preferred distribution of wealth between the two of them. As can be seen, both are altruists since A does not prefer point *A* (where he had all the

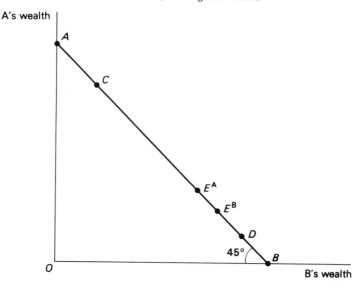

FIG. 3.1   Excessive altruism.

wealth in society) and B does not prefer *B* (where he rather than A has all the wealth). Neither, however, are they *wholly* unselfish since A does not prefer point *B*, nor does B prefer point *A*. If *C* is the initial distribution between them, then A will voluntarily transfer some of his wealth to B until E^A is reached. If B's preferred point is E^B, then the usual theory (i.e. indifference curve analysis) implies that he too will prefer E^A to *C*. Or suppose the initial distribution were at *D*. Then B will transfer to A until E^B is attained. A, too, will prefer E^B to *D*. Both E^A and E^B are Pareto optima (a move from one point to the other will benefit one person but 'harm' the other).

The problem of excessive unselfishness arises when E^A lies south east of E^B (or conversely, E^B north west of E^A). In such a case, their preferred distributions are initially inconsistent and we have the problem that A wants to give more to B than B is willing to receive because of his concern for A, and vice versa. It is only the relative positions of E^A and E^B that count, not the absolute degree of altruism each may have. As can be seen in the figure, A is exceedingly caring for B since his preferred distribution is E^A which, if the starting point is *C*, involves him in giving B more than half his wealth. We accordingly have a possible society of altruists where each individual's altruism is not 'too much' relative to the others. To assume more would be 'unrealistic' in the sense that it would lead to unstable and irreconcilable preferences.

The postulate that individuals care about one another has important implications for how one interprets the idea of 'need' in social policy. We have already seen that 'need' is an *instrumental* concept. Unless we are prepared to go so far as to assert that the purposes for which a set of resources are held to be needed are moral absolutes that must be accomplished regardless of cost, it seems sensible to interpret at least a part of these purposes as determined by the preferences of those who care—or the preferences of those who act on behalf of those who care. We take this up in the next section, where the idea of 'need' is related to the more familiar idea of 'demand'.

Demand versus Need

As we saw above, need involves the idea of instrumentality: if a particular service is a *necessary* condition for the accomplishment of a desired end-state, then that service is *needed*. Or if some unspecified service is necessary for an end-state to come about, some unspecified service is, in the same sense, needed. In this book the need for resources is interpreted as relating only to the means of achieving end-states. This requires us to focus attention on the nature of the claims made about the end-state and also upon the effectiveness of the proposed means that may be needed to attain it.

As we have seen, the source of concern about end-states may lie either in a caring externality (one feels compassion for someone or some group) or in a notion of equity (one appeals to some general principle of justice). Most discussions of need do not make this distinction very clear. But in either case it is the *condition* of the individual or individuals in question that is of concern: whether they are integrated in society, whether they are sick, ill-housed, ill-fed, over-burdened with worry, illiterate, etc. This suggests, in turn, that an important focus of social policy analysis ought to be on such attributes of individuals, and that the success or otherwise of social policy should be judged with respect to such attributes or characteristics. In later chapters, the analysis of *outcome* will occupy us a great deal, where outcome is measured—at least in principle—in terms of changes in individuals' attributes.

Much discussion of need has failed also to emphasise its instrumentality. This failure has led to too great neglect of the 'production functions' in social services: the relationship between the inputs (which are what—if anything—are needed) and the outcomes. Again, attention to these matters will occupy much of the remaining text.

Whether needs are interpreted as absolute or relative will depend very much on the source of concern. If it is an externality deriving from the preferences of third parties, then it is most likely to be *relative*: an individual's need will be seen as depending in part upon the cost of meeting that need. If, on the other hand, the source of concern lies in a notion of social justice, then need may be absolute: it may be, for example, that people feel that all ought to be entitled *as of right* to a specified minimum of (say) food, regardless of the cost to the rest of society. The Welfare State probably reflects both sources of concern: social justice requires the existence of minima; caring preferences determine any excess provision over the minima—a realm in which costs and benefits are balanced at the margin and in which the level of provision is in overall terms determined by the wealth of the community.

Whichever view one takes of need, one should note that they *each* involve a judgement being made independently of the receiving individual's preferences. It is this that makes a need based on caring preferences different from demand, for a demand is a want for some good or service backed by a willingness to sacrifice resources for it. Where demand and need come together is when one individual wants something for someone else and is prepared to sacrifice resources for it. Need is thus an *external* demand. It represents one party's view of what another should have.

Another view of need has been given by Bradshaw (1972). He identified four types:

(a) *normative* need (that which the expert or professional, administrator or social scientist, defines as need in any situation. A 'desirable' standard is laid down and is compared with the standard that actually exists);

(b) *felt* need (here need is equated with want. When assessing need for a service, the population is asked whether they feel they need it);

(c) *expressed* need (felt need turned into action: expressed need is illustrated by waiting-lists for hospital care as an—imperfect—indicator of current need);

(d) *comparative* need (if there are people with similar relevant characteristics to those in receipt of a service but not themselves in receipt, then they are in need).

Each of these meanings is doubtless in use, but none really begins to resemble the usage adopted here. Bradshaw's 'normative' need consists in technical judgements made by professionals that doubtless relate service inputs to end-state outcomes but it is not clear whence comes the moral imperative of the outcome or why it should be the professionals who should evaluate this. (The question of who *should* be arbiter about the ends is a fundamental political question.) His 'felt' need is clearly not a need at all in our sense. It is not even a demand. His 'expressed' need is a demand for service for oneself (possibly at zero money price). His 'comparative' need presupposes that a need exists (which *may* be a need in our sense) and that it is simply a question of identifying those in need but not in receipt. (A matter 'simple' in principle though not, one may add, nearly so 'simple' in practice.)

There is, then, a role for the idea of need in the economics of social policy—though many economists have frowned upon it. One set of reasons for this frowning is expressed in the following:

> the word need ought to be banished from discussion of public policy, partly because of its ambiguity but also because . . . the word is frequently used in . . . 'arbitrary' senses. Indeed . . . in many public discussions it is difficult to tell, when someone says that 'society needs . . .' whether he means that *he* needs it, whether he means society ought to get it in *his* opinion, whether a *majority* of the members of society want it, or *all* of them want it. Nor is it clear whether it is 'needed' *regardless* of the cost to society. [Culyer *et al*, 1972, p. 114]

It seems, however, impossible to banish 'need' from public and academic discussion, and so its meaning requires greater elucidation. At least the meaning used in this book will, it is hoped, be clear, as well as the reasons for adopting this, rather than some other, meaning.

APPENDIX: INDIFFERENCE CURVE ANALYSIS OF
REDISTRIBUTION IN CASH AND IN KIND

Consider the individual whose indifference map, showing preferences between I (income) and X (an unspecified good or service) in the vertical and horizontal axes respectively, is represented in Figure 3.2. Imagine an initial situation with the individual taking x_0 of X, spending Ii_0 (the distance between I and i_0) leaving him with Oi_0 income to spend on things other than x. He will be at E_0 on indifference curve U_0. Now suppose that others care about him, specifically that the rest of society takes the view that x_0 is too low a level of X consumption by this individual; for example, it represents 'inadequate' housing or 'too little' health care as judged by them. Let us suppose that the level of consumption preferred by the rest of society for this individual is x_1—actually more in this case than the individual could consume even if he spent his *entire* income (OI) upon X. What policies might the rest of the community (let us henceforth call it the government) adopt, without coercing the individual in question, to ensure consumption of x_1? We explore four possibilities:

(i) a cash grant or income supplement;
(ii) a subsidy on the price of X;
(iii) provision of X directly at no cost to the individual;
(iv) a 'voucher' or conditional cash grant (conditional in that it may be spent only on X).

The cash grant required if the individual is to consume x_1 rather than x_0 is measured by the distance between I and I_1—for short, II_1—which would give him the new budget line I_1X_1 and a chosen consumption bundle E_1. In this particular case we see that not only is the socially desired level of consumption attained, but also the individual has more income left after

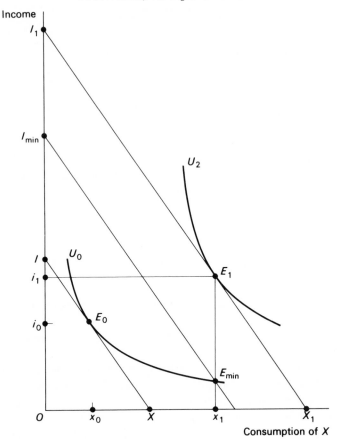

FIG. 3.2 Efficient cash grant.

his expenditure on X than he previously had (Oi_1). He is also, of course, on a higher indifference curve (U_2) than before when he was on U_0.

The subsidy on the price of X required to induce the individual to consume x_1 is indicated by the budget line IX_2, shown in Figure 3.3, under which circumstances the individual will choose the bundle E_2 on indifference curve U_1. This is equivalent in money terms to a cash grant of II_2 which is plainly less than II_1. The value of the subsidy can be seen to be measured by II_2 by the following reasoning: in Figure 3.3, Ox_1 of X is measured by the length of the line i_2E_2. The cost of this at the market price is given by the slope of IX or the slope of I_2E_2 and, using the latter, is evidently I_2i_2—the amount of income that must be sacrificed to get Ox_1 of X at the market price. At the *subsidised* price (slope of IE_2) the recipient of X pays Ii_2, leaving II_2 to be met by the rest of society. For the rest of society, therefore, the price subsidy represents a less costly way of obtain-

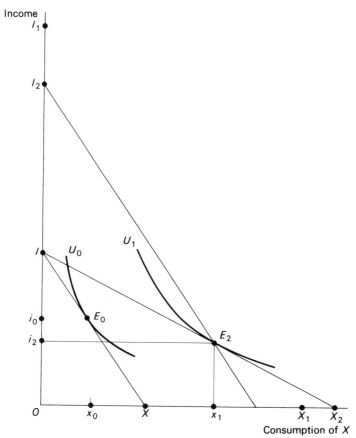

FIG. 3.3 Efficient price subsidy.

ing a given level of X consumption (x_1 in this case). The reason for this is that a substitution effect is strengthening an income effect.

Provision of X in kind directly to the individual will not require the full amount of x_1 to be provided so long as the individual is permitted to supplement the grant in kind with further purchases of his own. The amount of X in kind is, in fact x_2 (less than x_1) in Figure 3.4, which effectively produces the budget line II_3x_1 having the kink at I_3. The individual supplements his 'free' supply of X (in the amount Ox_2 or II_3) by purchasing x_2x_1 additional units himself at the market price. Ox_2 is the *minimum* necessary provision in kind, where voluntary extra purchases are permitted, since the idea is to shift the budget line out to the right so that, when supplementary purchases have been made, the individual will have voluntarily chosen Ox_1. He will thus select point E_1 if X is a normal good, whose demand increases with income. Gifts of X less than Ox_2 will not

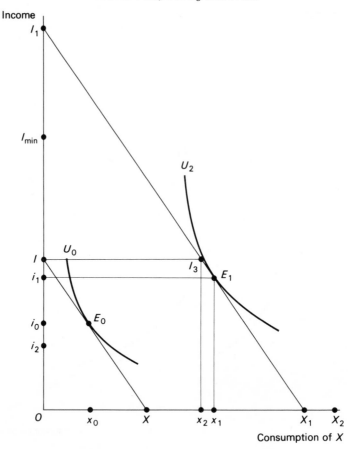

FIG. 3.4   Efficient provision in kind.

shift the budget line far enough to the right to enable the tangency to occur above x_1. Gifts of X more than Ox_2 would enable the recipient to attain a higher indifference curve than U_2 and a higher X consumption than Ox_1.

The cost of this policy to the rest of society is II_1, precisely the same as with the income supplement. If the individual were *not* permitted to purchase additional units of X (as is the case under the National Health Service if we consider X as health care) then the rest of society must provide the whole of x_1 at a cost of $i_1 I_1$, which is larger than under either the income supplement or the provision in kind with supplementation allowed. Note also that, in this case, if the individual is not satiated with the good at E_1, that is, if his indifference curves have not become flat at this point, he will demand more of the free care than is actually supplied (x_1). Consequently, some other form of rationing X will have to be used in order to prevent excessive (from the viewpoint of the rest of society) utilisation of X.

The conditional grant (*or voucher*) is directly similar in effect to the in-kind grant. If the voucher has the value II_1, and supplementation is permitted, E_1 is attained at a cost to the rest of society of II_1. If supplementation is not permitted, the voucher's value must be i_1I_1.

These results are based upon the assumption (among others) that X has a positive income elasticity (which seems plausible since most of the subsidies and grants in the real world had their origin, and frequently have their continued justification, in the assistance they offer to the relatively poor members of the community).

Conflict of interest as regards 'recipients' and 'donors' is clearly apparent from this analysis. In particular, it is clear that consumers of X will prefer (that is, reach higher indifference curves with) those methods of ensuring a given consumption that are most costly to donors while donors, for the obvious reason, will prefer the least cost methods, which tend toward the specific subsidy end of the spectrum.

In a system where transfers in cash or in kind are entirely voluntarily made, one may expect the preferences of donors to dominate those of recipients since, so long as recipients gain (in utility) from the subsidy, donors will prefer to attain their objective at least cost. But one may equally plausibly look at it the other way round: since donors gain from recipients' increased consumption (they too must reach higher levels of utility, otherwise they would not subsidise it), recipients would prefer the subsidy system that most increased their welfare subject to donors making some minimal gain. In practice, since the interests of 'donors' and 'recipients' are interpreted by politicians rather than the two groups directly 'trading' with one another, the mixture will be determined by political forces: the greater the political power of the relatively well-to-do, the more one would expect to see specific subsidies on the price of commodities, since these encourage consumption not only by generating income effects but also create substitution effects in favour of consumption of the service in question. For recipients, however, receipt of (tradeable) transfers in kind, income supplements, or vouchers will be seen (transaction costs aside) as broadly equivalent. In principle, the least cost way to induce an increase in X consumption is to eliminate income effects altogether (more precisely, *very nearly* altogether) and rely entirely upon substitution effects. By offering X on terms that bring recipients to a point such as E_{min} (Figure 3.2) on the original indifference curve (or, more correctly, an indifference curve very slightly above the original one), the recipient has had a minimal increase in his welfare and donors pay only II_{min}. In practice this is likely to be somewhat hard to achieve perfectly, though who can doubt that many transfers, whether made by private charities or by the state, while increasing consumption in specifically desired dimensions, have not permitted much utility gain for the recipients over and above their original starting point? Indeed, sometimes it seems to have been the case that an object of policy, in addition to increasing X consumption (whatever X may have been), has been to do so in a way that was not only cheap but had the characteristic that the recipient should not increase his overall welfare (whether or not this made the policy cheap). It is only relatively recently that 'stigma' has become an *undesired* characteristic of social transfers to those in 'need'.

NOTES

1. It is most unlikely that the citizens of Bradford would be prepared to pay for an outing for the children of Barmby Moor—though (perhaps because!) they are both in what some still regard as Yorkshire. Unfortunately, in a collectivity that included Bradford and Barmby Moor, Bradford would outvote Barmby many times over.
2. An externality is *invariably* the result of absence of defined property rights but undefined property rights do *not* invariably result in externalities.
3. Note that the profit-maximising environment supplied by a competitive capital market (where ownership can be transferred cheaply) is one form of social control of managers and is appropriate where profit maximising leads to socially desirable results—as it frequently does (especially where property rights are fully defined and are exchangeable).
4. The use of computers and mechanised voting procedures is in its infancy at present. In the not too distant future people may vote more frequently, on more specific issues, from their own homes!
5. The distinction here is similar to that made in Sen (1977) between 'sympathy' and 'commitment' and in Harsanyi (1955) between 'subjective preference' and 'ethical preference'. See also Nagel (1970).

QUESTIONS ON CHAPTER 3

1. What is the free rider problem and how may it be overcome?
2. Why may it be to the advantage of individuals to delegate decisions to government? What sort of decisions, if any?
3. Why does public ownership effectively inhibit the profit motive?
4. What characteristics of private property are needed if the market is to operate efficiently?
5. Is private property inconsistent with equality? What kinds of equality?
6. The Welfare State may be seen as a response of rational individuals to:
   (a) the furtherance of their own interests,
   (b) the internalisation of caring externalities,
   (c) the pursuit of social justice,
   (d) some combination of the foregoing.
   How would you assess the relative importance of each of these factors?

7. Can a person ever be held to deserve his or her wage?
8. What is Rawlsian maximin?
9. Distinguish between specific and general caring.
10. What is 'need'? Distinguish 'need' from 'demand'.
11. Can people be too altruistic?
12. Why subsidise specific goods and services rather than give cash grants?
13. Why is health care usually subsidised but not food?
14. Who decides what is needed? Who should decide?
15. Look at note 2 to this chapter. Justify that assertion.
16. Can private charity be an adequate substitute for the Welfare State?
17. If one decides to subsidise a specific good or service, what in general is the least cost way of doing so?
18. External effects and public goods may warrant public subsidy but do they also warrant public production?
19. How would you evaluate two alternatives, one of which was characterised by greater efficiency but less justice than the other?
20. Is 'economic' man recognisably human?

FURTHER READING

On the structure of decision making with public goods or externalities:

Baumol, W. (1952) *Welfare Economics and the Theory of the State.* Cambridge, Mass.: Harvard University Press.

Buchanan, J. M. (1962) Politics, policy and Pigovian margins. *Economica* no. 29, pp. 17–28.

Coase, R. H. (1960) The problem of social cost. *Journal of Law and Economics 3*, pp. 1–44.

Demsetz, H. (1969) Information and efficiency: another viewpoint. *Journal of Law and Economics, 12*, pp. 1–22.

Demsetz, H. (1970) The private production of public goods. *Journal of Law and Economics, 13*, pp. 293–306.

On property rights and delegated decision making:

Alchian, A. A. (1965) Some economics of property rights. *Il Politico*, December, pp. 816–29. Reprinted in A. A. Alchian *Economic Forces at Work.* Indianapolis: Liberty Press, 1978.

Alchian, A. A. and Kessel, R. A. (1962) Competition, monopoly and the pursuit of money. In *Aspects of Labor Economics.* Princeton: National Bureau of Economic Research.

Cheung, S. N. (1969) Transaction costs, risk aversion and the choice of contractual arrangements. *Journal of Law and Economics, 12*, pp. 23–42.

Clarkson, K. W. (1972) Some implications of property rights in hospital management. *Journal of Law and Economics, 15*, pp. 363–84.

Crocker, T. D. (1971) Externalities, property rights and transactions costs: an empirical study. *Journal of Law and Economics, 14*, pp. 451–64.

Culyer, A. J. (1970) A utility-maximising view of universities. *Scottish Journal of Political Economy, 17*, pp. 349–68.

Culyer, A. J. (1972) On the relative efficiency of the National Health Service. *Kyklos*, 25, pp. 266–87.
Jacobs, P. (1974) A survey of economic models of hospitals. *Inquiry*, 11, pp. 83–97.
McKean, R. N. (1972) Property rights within government, and devices to increase governmental efficiency. *Southern Economic Journal*, 39, pp. 177–86.
Newhouse, J. P. (1970) Towards a theory of non-profit institutions: an economic model of a hospital. *American Economic Review*, 60, pp. 64–74.
Niskanen, W. A. (1971) *Bureaucracy and Representative Government*. Chicago: University of Chicago Press.
Schweitzer, S. O. and Rafferty, J. (1976) Variations in hospital product: a comparative analysis of proprietory and voluntary hospitals. *Inquiry*, 13, pp. 158–66.
Williamson, O. E. (1964) *The Economics of Discretionary Behaviour*. Englewood Cliffs, N.J.: Prentice-Hall.

On caring:

Boulding, K. (1962) Notes on a theory of philanthropy. In F. G. Dickinson (ed.) *Philanthropy and Public Policy*. New York and London: National Bureau of Economic Research.
Buchanan, J. M. (1968) What kind of redistribution do we want? *Economica*, 35, pp. 185–90.
Collard, D. (1975) Edgeworth's propositions on altruism. *Economic Journal*, 85, no. 338, pp. 355–60.
Collard, D. (1978) *Altruism and Economy: A Study in Non-Selfish Economics*. London: Martin Robertson.
Culyer, A. J. (1973) Quids without quos—a praxeological approach. In A. A. Alchian *et al. The Economics of Charity*. London: Institute of Economic Affairs.
Edgeworth, F. Y. (1881) *Mathematical Psychics*. London: C. Kegan Paul.
Harsanyi, J. (1955) Cardinal welfare, individualistic ethics and interpersonal comparisons of utility. *Journal of Political Economy*, 63, pp. 309–21.
Marx, K. (1875) *Critique of the Gotha Programme*. In D. Caute (ed.) *Essential writings of Karl Marx*. London: Panther, 1967.
Nagel, T. (1970) *The Possibility of Altruism*. Oxford: Oxford University Press.
Sen, A. K. (1977) Rational fools. *Philosophy and Public Affairs*, 6, pp. 317–44.
Titmuss, R. M. (1970) *The Gift Relationship*. London: Allen and Unwin.

On justice:

Barry, B. M. (1965) *Political Argument*. London: Routledge and Kegan Paul.
Clark, J. B. (1902) *Distribution of Wealth*. New York: Macmillan.
Judge, K. (1978) *Rationing Social Services*. London: Heinemann.
Nozick, R. (1974) *Anarchy, State and Utopia*. Oxford: Basil Blackwell.
Perelman, C. (1963) *The Idea of Justice and the Problem of Argument*. London: Routledge and Kegan Paul.
Rawls, J. (1972a) Justice as fairness. In P. Laslett and W. G. Runciman (eds) *Philosophy, Politics and Society*. Oxford: Basil Blackwell.
Rawls, J. (1972b) *A Theory of Justice*. Oxford: Clarendon Press.
Rescher, N. (1966) *Distributive Justice*. New York: Irvington.
Runciman, W. G. (1966) *Relative Deprivation and Social Justice*. London: Routledge and Kegan Paul.
Sen, A. K. (1975) Rawls versus Bentham: an axiomatic examination of the pure distribution problem. In N. Daniels (ed.) *Reading Rawls*. Oxford: Basil Blackwell.
Simons, H. (1948) *Economic Policy for a Free Society*. Chicago: University of Chicago Press.

Tobin, J. (1970) On limiting the domain of inequality. *Journal of Law and Economics*, *13*, pp. 263–78. Reprinted in E. S. Phelps (ed.) *Economic Justice*. Harmondsworth: Penguin, 1973.
Weale, A. (1978) *Equality and Social Policy*. London: Routledge and Kegan Paul.

On need:

Barry, B. M. (1965) *Political Argument*. London: Routledge and Kegan Paul.
Bradshaw, J. (1972) A taxonomy of social need. In G. McLachlan (ed.) *Problems and Progress in Medical Care*, 7th Series. London: Oxford University Press.
Culyer, A. J., Lavers, R. J. and Williams, Alan (1972) Health indicators. In A. Shonfield and S. Shaw (eds) *Social Indicators and Social Policy*. London: Heinemann.
Marshall, T. H. (1973) The philosophy and history of need. In R. W. Canvin and N. G. Pearson (eds) *Needs of the Elderly*. University of Exeter.
Williams, Alan (1978) Need—an economic exegesis. In A. J. Culyer and K. Wright (eds) *Economic Aspects of Health Services*. London: Martin Robertson.

On the Welfare State:

Bruce, M. (1968) *The Coming of the Welfare State* (4th edition). London: Batsford.
Davies, B. and Reddin, M. (1978) *Universality, Selectivity and Effectiveness in Social Policy*. London: Heinemann.
Glennerster, H. (1975) *Social Service Budgets and Social Policy*. London: Allen and Unwin.
Pinker, R. (1979) *The Idea of Welfare*. London: Heinemann.
Rein, M. (1970) *Social Policy: Issues of Choice and Change*. New York: Random House.
Sandford, C. (1977) *Social Economics*. London: Heinemann.
Sleeman, J. F. (1979) *Resources for the Welfare State: An Economic Introduction*. London: Longman.
Watkin, B. (1975) *Documents on Health and Social Services*. London: Methuen.
Williams, A. and Anderson, R. (1975) *Efficiency in the Social Services*. Oxford: Basil Blackwell.

PART II

Redistribution

CHAPTER 4

Normative and Positive Theories of Efficient Redistribution

In this Part of the book we shall not be concerned to examine in any detail the various theories that have been put forward to account for the *distribution* of incomes or how social policy can affect the underlying income distribution (for example, with regard to encouraging and controlling the activities of trade unions and employers' associations). Instead, our main focus will be on *re*distributing incomes already received by individuals and upon the problem of poverty, or income deficiency, in particular. In this chapter the methods in which redistribution and poverty have been incorporated into economic analysis will be explored. In the next chapter problems of measurement are discussed. In the third chapter of this Part (chapter 6) the policy problems concerned with methods of redistribution and methods of abolishing poverty will be investigated. Note the focus on incomes, or *general* redistribution. As we saw in chapter 3, *specific* redistribution is also very important. This, however, we leave mainly to the discussion of the Welfare State in Part IV.

As with all social phenomena, one may adopt two stances: one normative, the other positive. The normative approach to income redistribution asks what distribution we should aim for and how it should be achieved. The positive approach seeks to explain why the redistribution that occurs takes place and how it would alter if certain changes were to be made. The approaches to be considered here will be positive or normative in these senses. A thread of continuity will be that the basic unit for analysis in each case will be the individual. Thus, in the normative analysis, the touchstone of what is good will be taken to be the individual preferences of the members of society, not some (mythical) omniscient outside observer or some group of benevolent (or otherwise) dictators. In the positive analysis, it will be taken for granted that the behaviour of individuals acting alone or in concert determines the social policies that are actually adopted. Such, at least, would seem a reasonable presumption in societies describing themselves in broad terms as 'democracies'.[1]

As we have seen in the previous chapter, a great deal of the redistribution that takes place in modern societies such as Britain or the USA is not merely a redistribution of money income, nor is it necessarily a *vertical* redistribution from the rich to the poor but rather *horizontal* within income groups. To begin with, however, we shall suppose that the purpose of redistribution is to transfer money from the rich to the poor. Subsequently we shall investigate some theories attempting to explain why the direction of flow need not be from the rich to the poor.

A. NORMATIVE ANALYSIS OF REDISTRIBUTION

Equality and Utilitarianism

One normative approach to the problem of deciding an appropriate inter-personal (interfamilial) distribution of money income is primarily of histor-ical interest only, but since it can still be found, often only implicitly, in some modern writing we shall give it some attention.

For utilitarians such as Bentham and Sidgwick, the objective of society was the maximisation of the sum total of individuals' utilities. To maximise utility was both efficient *and* just (no effective distinction really being made). With an appreciation of the 'law of diminishing marginal utility' (which stated that each addition to a person's money income per year yielded less utility than the previous addition, though the total continued to rise) coupled with an assumption that all individuals are fundamentally alike in their preference and their capacity for enjoying the good things of life, a normative argument for egalitarianism can be made to follow on quite naturally from the utilitarian approach (though it will not follow automatically by market processes).

The egalitarian argument can be shown quite easily in a simple diagram such as Figure 4.1. On the vertical axis is measured the marginal utility of money income. On the horizontal axis we have the size of money income. The curve *Macb* shows how for two individuals, A and B, the marginal utility of money income falls as income increases. Now suppose that A has *OA* income and B has *OB*, i.e. B is the richer of the two. A's marginal utility is *Aa*, which is higher than B's *Bb*. The sum total of utility in our society of two individuals is *OMaA* plus *OMbB*. The utilitarian argument for an equal distribution would run thus: that by removing *BC* income from B and giving it to A, B will lose less than A will gain, since B's marginal utility is lower than A's throughout this income range. With equal incomes of *OC*, each has the same marginal utility of money income and the sum total of utility in society is maximised, being equal to twice *OMcC*, which must be larger than *OMaA* plus *OMbB*.

In its strict form, the argument for absolute equality depends crucially

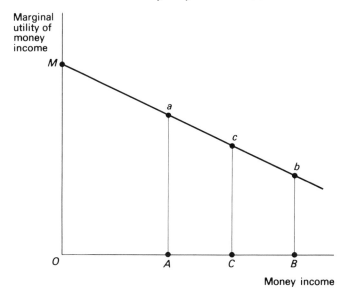

FIG. 4.1   Utilitarian redistribution with identical preferences.

upon an identity of tastes for money income among the population. (Alternatively, one could argue that they *ought to be treated* as identical.) But a weaker form will still hold even when tastes differ. In Figure 4.2 for example, B, the rich person, has a marginal utility curve that is everywhere higher than A's. A possible reason for this is that his great wealth has enabled him to appreciate delights such as Cordon Bleu cooking and opera, tastes that A has not had the opportunity to acquire.

According to this less radical utilitarianism, with different tastes, equality is not required in order to maximise the sum total of individual utilities. One still requires that the marginal utilities of each individual's income be the same but this is now achieved with a transfer of $BB'(= AA')$ from B to A—inequalities are reduced but not eliminated.

At this point the reader will doubtless be aware of a possible perversity in the argument: what if the marginal utility of income for the rich man (B) is *higher* rather than *lower* than that of the poor man? This seems to be a perfectly possible contingency. If the rich man were to say that he got more utility from the ability to buy an additional egg than the poor man, who could gainsay it? But if this were the case, then income should be transferred from the poor man to the rich man! The egalitarian argument of this school of thought thus depended upon the assumption of similar preferences. You may find it odd to conceive that the rich man could derive *more* utility from an additional unit than the poor man. One reason for this may be that you are not really considering the subjective utilities of the two but are really bringing in *your own* values. One way of doing this is to ask

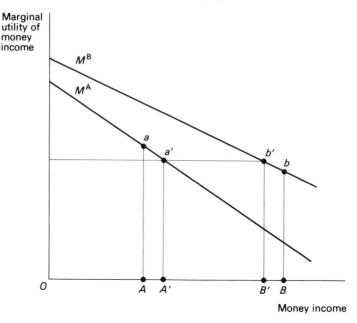

FIG. 4.2   Utilitarian redistribution with differing preferences.

'would I rather be the poor man with an additional unit or the rich man?'
If you answer 'the rich man' then *your* utility would be higher and, on the
usual assumptions, your *marginal* utility would be lower. But though this is
an interesting way of making interpersonal comparisons (and it is one we
shall look at later in the chapter) it is not the same as comparing the
utilities of the rich and poor. It is left to you to draw various M^A and M^B
curves (try some that intersect) to discover which of them implies greater
equality (given a starting point) and which greater inequality, and to recognise the importance of the relative *marginal* utilities at any division of the
total income. The principal lesson from all this is that utilitarianism without identical preferences is by no means necessarily also egalitarian.

   The utilitarian view of distribution survived in essentially the form presented here, together with the assumption of near identical preferences,
until after the First World War. For example, Pigou, in his classic *The
Economics of Welfare*, which first appeared in 1920, wrote:

> It is evident that any transference of income from a relatively rich man to a
> relatively poor man of similar temperament, since it enables more intense
> wants to be satisfied at the expense of less intense wants, must increase the
> aggregate sum of satisfaction. [1932, p. 89]

Similarly Dalton, in *Some Aspects of the Inequality of Incomes in Modern
Communities* also appearing in 1920, wrote:

Put broadly, and in the language of common sense, the case against large inequalities of income is that the less urgent needs of the rich are satisfied, while the more urgent needs of the poor are left unsatisfied ... this is merely an application of the economists' law of diminishing marginal utility ... [1920, p. 10][2]

(Clearly, as put, Dalton's sentence is an application of *more than* merely the law in question.)

There are, of course, many objections to utilitarianism, both scientific and ethical. For our purposes, however, the chief of these relates to the possibility of making comparisons of the quantity of utility that different individuals receive at the margin. One difficulty lies in the use of the word 'utility' among earlier economists. It was, for example, frequently identified with 'satisfaction'. But this raises problems of meaning, for while it may make sense to talk about zero utility, as an abstract idea, it clearly does not make a great deal of sense to talk about zero satisfaction. More fundamentally, however, what kind of sense does it make to say that one person has more utility (or satisfaction) than another? Clearly *some* meaning can be conveyed by such statements. It is not ridiculous to say that 'John is happier today than he was yesterday' or that 'John is happier than Fred', but it is very difficult to say *how much more* happy he is. It is also very difficult to be quite sure that in making such judgements one has not interpreted John's or Fred's behaviour quite mistakenly, and the relative happiness of two persons with different incomes is usually harder to observe than their relative happiness with their Christmas presents.

Since people's tastes do undoubtedly differ and therefore their marginal utilities of money income will differ (even if they have the same income) the absolute equality of incomes cannot be defended on these utilitarian grounds. Similarly since utility is not an observable quantity and the relationship between it (or satisfaction) and a man's income is not at all clear, all we can say is that *we think* that John is more satisfied than Fred—and John need not be the richer man. It also seems impossible to make the interpersonal comparisons of utility with anything like the degree of accuracy we would need to evolve a redistribution policy. Nor have we any reason to suppose that satisfaction varies systematically for all people in society in the way such a basis for policy would require. Even if we allowed that one poor man received less satisfaction than one rich man, it would be unsurprising to find another poor man who was more satisfied than either of them.

As a result of these, and other, considerations it is hardly surprising that the classical utilitarian case for redistribution of incomes from the rich to the poor has been cast into limbo. Which is where we shall leave it.

The Uncertainty Arguments for Equality

In his classic book, *The Economics of Control* (1944), Abba Lerner attempted to overcome the objections raised above by putting forward the following theorem: if it is impossible, on any division of income, to discover which of two individuals has a higher marginal utility of income, the utility of income will *probably* be maximised by dividing income equally.

Lerner's argument, like the previous one, can easily be illustrated in a simple diagram. In Figure 4.3, M is one individual's marginal utility of

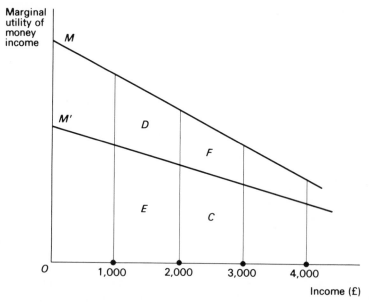

FIG. 4.3   Utilitarian redistribution with uncertain preferences.

income curve and M' is the other's. The two individuals have, we suppose, differing tastes and therefore different marginal utility of income curves. Empirically, however, we do not know where they lie relative to one another and, in particular, we do not know whether M belongs to A and M' to B, or vice versa. What we do know is that marginal utility falls and that their incomes can be measured (at least, approximately).

Suppose that between them A and B have £4,000 distributed such that A has £1,000 and B £3,000. Then by redistributing £1,000 from B to A, each has a post redistribution income of £2,000 (we assume zero incentive or disincentive effects and zero transaction costs). If A's curve is M and B's is M', then B will have lost area C of utility but A will have gained areas D + E. It follows from the diminishing marginal utility of income that

$E > C$; therefore $(D + E) > C$ and A's gain exceeds B's loss. But, of course, A's curve may have been M' and B's may have been M. In this case, the redistribution will have cost B the areas $(C + F)$ and A will gain only E. We know that $E > C$ and that $(D + E) > (F + C)$ but this is not enough to tell us whether $E > (F + C)$. How then do we get out of the apparent impasse?

Lerner suggested that we are as likely to be incorrect in assigning M curves to individuals as we are to be correct. We therefore have a 50 per cent chance of gaining $D + E$ but losing C and a 50 per cent chance of gaining E and losing $C + F$. From redistributing incomes equally we therefore have an *expected gain in total utility* of:

$$0.5[(D + E) - C + E - (C + F)].$$

What can we say about the sign of this term? If it is positive, of course, then we will have shown that equality leads to an increase in the probable sum total of utility. Comparing the terms in the round brackets, one can immediately see that $(D + E) > (C + F)$, which follows simply from the negative slope of M in Figure 4.3. Therefore the latter subtracted from the former will leave a positive sum. It is also clear that $C < E$, which follows from the negative slope of M'. Therefore the former subtracted from the latter will leave a positive sum. Since the sum of two positives is positive, and half of a positive sum is also positive, if follows inexorably that the whole term is positive. Therefore, *to maximise the probable sum total of utilities requires that income be equally distributed.*

Note that the Lerner theorem does not tell us whether, once the redistribution has taken place, there has been any *actual* utility gain to society as a whole, for we are still ignorant about the shapes and relative heights of marginal utility functions. All one can say is that *if* net gains were made they are larger than *if* net losses had been made. Thus there can be no absolute certainty of gain but, as Lerner himself has said, 'if I were offered 11 cents for every "head" in return for 10 cents for every "tail" on 100 million tosses of an unbiased coin, I would consider the probability of gain certain enough' (1970, p. 443). Since all social policy decisions are taken under conditions of uncertainty the argument seems fairly powerful.

Although the Lerner argument has many attractions, it is also not without disadvantages. It continues to assume, like utilitarianism, that utilities can simply be added up (even though it does not require us to observe them). Secondly, although it grants that the utility people receive is not statistically dependent upon their relative incomes, it still requires that the utilities of different people be commensurable. Third, it assumes that one is *equally* uncertain about a loss as one is about a gain. Each of these assumptions is somewhat metaphysical: we can test none of them—not even indirectly by their implications. Of the first it may be said to be highly improbable, for even if the utility received from X be known as well as that from *Y*, common experience suggests that the utility of *X and Y* together may be greater or smaller than the sums of their independent utilities. This is as true of an individual's personal view of different income distributions (for example, A may derive utility from the fact that B has more, or less, income than he has) as it is of shoes and shoe laces.

A common objection to the Lerner argument is indeed that the assumptions and implications upon which it rests are untestable. The assumption of equal ignorance might be acceptable if we could, *ex post facto*, test for the utility consequences of any redistribution. But since even Lerner admits we cannot, we remain ignorant. As Ian Little has said of the Lerner theorem, 'from complete ignorance nothing but complete ignorance can follow' (1950, p. 59). Yet, of course, if we could know something of the relative position and slopes of the *M*-curves, utilitarianism, as Milton Friedman (1947) has pointed out, need not imply egalitarianism at all—as indeed we have earlier seen. Despite the fact that the assumption of equi-probability is untestable (which may not concern you anyway!), the Lerner theorem derives its implication (almost) impeccably from its assumptions. Thus, if you are uncomfortable about the egalitarian result, look to the assumptions.

The really fundamental objection to the Lerner theorem is, however, that it contains a logical slip, which is why there is an 'almost' in the penultimate sentence of the last paragraph. This slip lies in the identification of *ignorance* about which *M*-curve belongs to whom with *equi-probability* of being wrong or right. An ingenious way round this problem has been developed by Amartya Sen (1973). In Sen's argument we suppose that for any marginal utility of income curve it is *possible* that an individual has it. Since nothing at all is now being said about probability, we cannot take the probable sum of utilities as our maximand. Let us therefore take another rule: *to maximise the minimum possible total utility* or *Sen's maximin principle* (to be distinguished from the *Rawlsian maximin* principle discussed in chapter 3). In other words, since we do not know which marginal utility of income curve belongs to whom, let us, for each possible distribution of income, take the lowest possible total utility and, from the resulting lowest possible total utilities, select the highest. We thus select the best of the worst possible outcomes.

Sen's proof that *this rule also implies that it is best to distribute incomes equally* is technical, but a good idea of its gist can be got by considering Figure 4.4. For illustrative purposes we assume there are just two individuals and that each could have one of only two possible *M*-curves, marked, as before, *M* and *M'* in the figure. *OJ* on the bottom axis represents total (fixed) income for distribution between A and B. Now let us enquire what logically possible sum totals of utility are associated with distribution at *E* (equality). Clearly, since there are two individuals and two marginal utility of income curves, there are, at any division along *OJ* four possible total

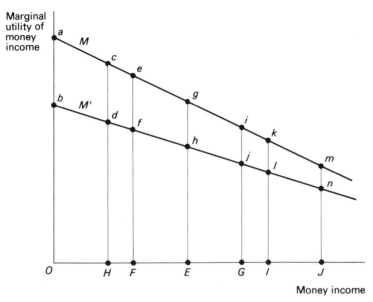

FIG. 4.4 Maximin redistribution with non-intersecting marginal utilities of income.

utility outcomes. At *E*, either A has *M* and B has *M'*, or B has *M* and A has *M'*, or both have *M*, or both have *M'*. The total utility associated with each logically possible outcome can be set out as follows:

At *E*, if

$$
\left. \begin{array}{l} \text{A has } M, \text{ B has } M' \\ \text{A has } M', \text{ B has } M \\ \text{A has } M, \text{ B has } M \\ \text{A has } M', \text{ B has } M' \end{array} \right\} \text{ total utility is } \left\{ \begin{array}{l} OagE + ObhE \\ ObhE + OagE \\ OagE + OagE \\ ObhE + ObhE. \end{array} \right.
$$

These are the logical possibilities. We do not know which is more probable but the least desirable—having the lowest utility—is (by inspection of Figure 4.4) *ObhE + ObhE*.

Now consider some other divisions of the income *OJ* between A and B. *F* and *G* describe such another, where *OF + OG = OJ = 2 × OE*. We shall take it that A is the poorer of the two individuals.

At (*F, G*), if

$$
\left. \begin{array}{l} \text{A has } M, \text{ B has } M' \\ \text{A has } M', \text{ B has } M \\ \text{A has } M, \text{ B has } M \\ \text{A has } M', \text{ B has } M' \end{array} \right\} \text{ total utility is } \left\{ \begin{array}{l} OaeF + ObjG \\ ObfF + OaiG \\ OaeF + OaiG \\ ObfF + ObjG \end{array} \right.
$$

and the least of these is *ObfF + ObjG*.

Consider points such as H and I $(OH + OI = OJ)$:

At (H, I), if

$$
\left.
\begin{array}{l}
\text{A has } M, \text{ B has } M' \\
\text{A has } M', \text{ B has } M \\
\text{A has } M, \text{ B has } M \\
\text{A has } M', \text{ B has } M'
\end{array}
\right\} \text{ total utility is }
\left\{
\begin{array}{l}
OacH + OblI \\
ObdH + OakI \\
OacH + OakI \\
ObdH + OblI
\end{array}
\right.
$$

and the least of these is $ObdH + OblI$.

At $(0, J)$, if

$$
\left.
\begin{array}{l}
\text{A has } M, \text{ B has } M' \\
\text{A has } M', \text{ B has } M \\
\text{A has } M, \text{ B has } M \\
\text{A has } M', \text{ B has } M'
\end{array}
\right\} \text{ total utility is }
\left\{
\begin{array}{l}
0 + ObnJ \\
0 + OamJ \\
0 + OamJ \\
0 + ObnJ
\end{array}
\right.
$$

and the least of these is $0 + ObnJ$.

And so we may go on identifying the lowest total utility possible at each division of total income. When we come to compare these *worst possible outcomes*, we find that

$$(ObhE + ObhE) > (ObjF + ObjG) > (ObdH + OblI) > (Obnj).$$

In this ranking, the first is the equal division, which clearly produces the best utility outcome of all these worst possible outcomes. This is the *maximin* division of income. This result does not depend upon interpersonal comparisons, nor on attaching probabilities to anything, nor on the marginal utility curves not intersecting. All it requires is that the marginal utility of income for each person should fall, which is a proposition that is not in serious dispute.

It may be helpful (lest you suspect some geometrical *leger-de-main*) in seeing the force and generality of Sen's argument briefly to consider a case where the M-curves intersect one another but where, as before, each continuously falls from left to right. In Figure 4.5 M and M' intersect twice, once between O and F and again to the right of G. As before, OJ represents total income and, at the equal division, where each has OE, if

$$
\left.
\begin{array}{l}
\text{A has } M, \text{ B has } M' \\
\text{A has } M', \text{ B has } M \\
\text{A has } M, \text{ B has } M \\
\text{A has } M', \text{ B has } M'
\end{array}
\right\} \text{ total utility is }
\left\{
\begin{array}{l}
OagE + ObhE \\
ObhE + OagE \\
OagE + OagE \\
ObhE + ObhE.
\end{array}
\right.
$$

Now in this case, it is not immediately obvious by inspection whether $OagE \lessgtr ObhE$ and we cannot immediately identify the worst of these possible outcomes. Let us nevertheless press on and consider an alternative division of the income at F and G.

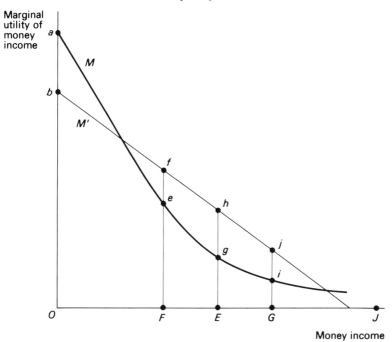

FIG. 4.5   Maximin redistribution with intersecting marginal utilities of income.

At (F, G), if

$$
\left.\begin{array}{l}
\text{A has } M, \text{ B has } M' \\
\text{A has } M', \text{ B has } M \\
\text{A has } M, \text{ B has } M \\
\text{A has } M', \text{ B has } M'
\end{array}\right\} \text{ total utility is } \left\{\begin{array}{l}
OaeF + ObjG \\
ObfF + OaiG \\
OaeF + OaiG \\
ObfF + ObjG.
\end{array}\right.
$$

Once again you may think it not obvious by inspection which of these possibilities is the lowest in terms of total utility. These difficulties can be resolved once we see that it is the income range OF that causes the difficulty for it is not clear whether the total utility of OF income is higher with M or with M' ($OaeF$ compared with $ObfF$). Ranges FE and EG are, however, unambiguous. Let us therefore divide the areas for each possible outcome at E and (F, G) respectively into the sub-areas shown in Figure 4.5. This is done below:

At E:

    (1) $OagE + ObhE = (OaeF + FegE) + (ObfF + Ffhe)$

    (2) $ObhE + OagE = (ObfF + FfhE) + (OaeF + FegE)$

    (3) $OagE + OagE = (OaeF + FegE) + (OaeF + FegE)$

    (4) $ObhE + ObhE = (ObfF + FfhE) + (ObfF + FfhE)$

At (F, G)

(5) $OaeF + ObjG = OaeF + (ObfF + FfhE + EhjG)$

(6) $ObfF + OaiG = ObfF + (OaeF + FegE + EgiG)$

(7) $OaeF + OaiG = OaeF + (OaeF + FegE + EgiG)$

(8) $ObfF + ObjG = ObfF + (ObfF + FfhE + EhjG)$.

It is clear that at E, (1) and (2) are the same. Whether (3) or (4) is smaller depends on the relative size of $OaeF$ and $ObfF$ compared with $FegE$ and $FfhE$. If $(OaeF - ObfF) > (FfhE - FegE)$, then $(4) < (1)$ and (2), and $(4) < (3)$ so that (4) is the worst possible outcome. If, however, $(OaeF - ObfF) < (FfhE - FegE)$, then $(3) < (1)$ and (2), and $(3) < (4)$ so that (3) is the worst possible outcome. Therefore either (3) or (4) is the lowest utility outcome for an equal division of income at E.

At (F, G) it is clear that $(6) < (5)$, since $(FfhE + EhjG) > (FegE + EgiG)$. But are (7) or (8) even smaller? The answer clearly depends on whether $(OaeF - ObfF) \gtrless (FfjG - FeiG)$. If $(OaeF - ObfF) > (FfjG - FeiG)$, then $(8) < (6)$, and $(8) < (7)$ so that (8) is the worst possible outcome. If, however, $(OaeF - ObfF) < (FfjG - FeiG)$, then $(7) < (8) < (6)$ and (7) is the worst possible outcome.

Comparing the two divisions of income at E and (F, G) we may therefore conclude that

—at E the lowest possible utility is either (3) or (4),

—at (F, G) the lowest possible utility is either (7) or (8).

Which, then, is the higher of these pairs of minima? Note that if $(OaeF - ObfF) < (FfhE - FegE)$ then *a fortiori* $(OaeF - ObfF) < (FfjG - FeiG)$. Thus, if (3) is the smaller of (3) and (4), (7) will also be the smaller of (7) and (8). Conversely, if $(OaeF - ObfF) > (FfjG - FeiG)$ then *a fortiori* $(OaeF - ObfF) > (FfhE - FegE)$. Thus, if (4) is the smaller of (3) and (4), (8) will be the smaller of (7) and (8). Consequently we need compare (3) only with (7), and (4) only with (8) to determine the maximin division of income. Clearly, $(3) > (7)$ by virtue of diminishing marginal utility along M, and $(4) > (8)$ by virtue of diminishing marginal utility along M'. Once again, therefore, we find that the maximin solution is the equal distribution of income at which either (3) or (4) describes the lowest possible level of total utility.

If you take the depressing view that the government is most probably going to get its assumptions about relative marginal utilities wrong, then the strategy for a distribution that is *least bad* is equality.

The egalitarian argument has thus proved to be extremely robust in the face of criticism and certainly should not be dismissed too readily. Note that in this discussion we have at no time postulated equality *itself* as an ideal (though clearly some may have a preference of this sort, a possibility discussed on p. 64) but have instead *derived* egalitarian implications from utilitarian ethical assumptions that do not obviously imply it and indeed were not necessarily selected because, as it turns out, they do imply it.

Utilitarianism in the various forms we have considered it is, as has been noted in chapter 3, only one of a variety of ethical principles that can be used to evaluate the income distribution. Others may include equality itself as a principle, need, ability, virtue, merit, effort, achievement, productivity, desert. Some of these have been touched on earlier in chapter 3 and for further analysis the further reading for chapters 3 and 4 is recommended. Note also that we have assumed that the total income to be divided is unchanging: in short, we have assumed the absence of disincentive effects on the production side that generates real income. We shall postpone a discussion of disincentives to chapter 6.

The 'New' Welfare Economics Approach

The 'old' welfare economics, with which this chapter has so far dealt, attempted to give a fully integrated treatment of both allocative and redistributive efficiency. With a common professional consensus among most economists that interpersonal comparisons of utility could never be made in a scientific way, interest in—or at least the ability usefully to discuss as professionals—redistributive questions fell off dramatically, despite the continuing undercurrent of analysis by economists like Sen, and despite the fact that theorems about redistribution do not, as we have seen, *have* to rely on interpersonal comparisons. One consequence of this revolution in the methodology of economics was that matters of allocative efficiency became completely separated from matters of distributive efficiency or justice.

The 'new' welfare economics described the necessary conditions that must be met for an efficient allocation of resources, some of which have already been described above in chapter 2. The efficient allocation of resources, such that no individual can be made better off without at least one other becoming worse off, depends however upon the initial distribution of money income. Consequently, there exists a variety of optima, choice amongst which will depend upon the associated (resultant) income distribution, and each of which is such that no changes could be made without harming somebody. The 'new' welfare economics placed an embargo upon interpersonal comparisons of utility in defining the optima but was compelled to introduce explicit comparisons of this sort when it came to selecting the *optimum optimorum*—the efficient allocation with the best income distribution of all the various optima. But redistribution, of course, would mean some people *are* made worse off in order to make others better off.

So either they could say nothing about it or they invented a mythical 'superman' to make the choice (which is another way of saying nothing!).

The new welfare economics, therefore, was almost entirely empty of relevant analysis of income distribution problems.

Efficient Redistribution

Until very recently, the 'new' welfare economics remained emasculated in this regard. The next significant development derived from a brave facing-up to the fact that individuals in society have *preferences* about income distributions, despite the fact that they may also hold moral views about the justice of various distributions. Consequently, it seemed not unreasonable to include within the choice set of each individual a set of choices to be made about transfers. In short, individuals 'derive utility' from alleviating poverty or in assisting those families who have what they regard as special needs. Thus, both vertical and horizontal equity could be brought under the same methodological umbrella as allocational efficiency. One could describe an 'efficient' redistribution policy. This approach to income distribution is based not on 'what utility does A get from his income and B from his' but on 'what utility does A get from his *and* B's income and what utility does B get from his *and* A's'.

The argument can be illustrated in a diagram similar to the classical utilitarian diagrams, but crucially different in its interpretation. In Figure 4.6, marginal valuations are shown in the vertical axis and the incomes of two individuals along the horizontal axis. MV^A is A's marginal valuation of his own income and MV_B^A is A's marginal valuation of B's income.

Suppose that A has £4,000 income per year and B £1,000. At the pre redistribution level of incomes A's marginal valuation of his own income of £4,000 is ab. The MV placed by A on B's income is $ac > ab$. To increase his own utility he will therefore transfer some of his income to B. In our diagram, his welfare is maximised when he has transferred £1,000. At this point the marginal utility from a pound's worth of income retained for his own use equals the marginal utility (to him) of a one pound increment in B's income. Thus, for social welfare to be maximised, the transfer *ought* to be made. Distributional efficiency obtains where, for A, $MV^A = MV_B^A$. The analysis gives explicit recognition to the fact that many people are (a) concerned about the welfare of others and (b) generous. If MV_B^A (A's marginal utility from B's income) were everywhere zero, he would be indifferent to B's welfare and therefore neither concerned nor generous. If it had positive values but lay below MV^A everywhere to the left of a, A would be concerned but not actually generous—he would not care *sufficiently* to make the transfer. In both these cases a 'corner solution' exists at which $MV^A > MV_B^A$ and it is inefficient to make the transfer.

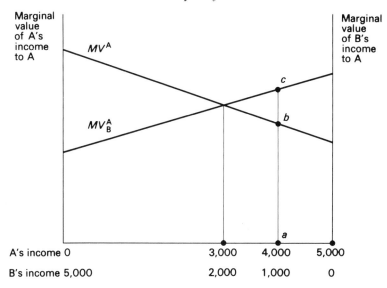

FIG. 4.6 Efficient redistribution when there are preferences about income distributions.

Does the efficiency approach to income distribution imply that society ought to adopt a progressive, proportional or regressive tax structure? The conclusions worked out by Harold Hochman and James Rodgers, who pioneered this approach (1969) and applied it in a large numbers setting rather than the two-person expository model employed here, are that the answer depends upon both the shape of the size distribution of income *and* the responsiveness of each person's 'demand' for transfers (to others) to changes in income differentials. Assuming identical preferences at each level of income with an income distribution that is skewed to the right (a higher proportion of families have incomes below the average income than above it) and with a responsiveness of the demand for transfers such that the size of the preferred transfer increases in proportion with the initial income differentials, the Pareto-optimal pattern of redistribution is effected through *progressive* taxes on income. Even if the demand for transfers is independent of the size of the differentials, the tax structure, while somewhat complex, also ought to have marked progressive characteristics.

Thus, the Pareto criterion can be used to assess the goodness even of income distributions. The test of a socially beneficial redistribution is that it should be voluntarily undertaken, for we take voluntary behaviour to be behaviour that is not against the interest of the person or persons concerned. Usually, however, some judgement (but not a value judgement) will have to be exercised to decide the *fact* of voluntariness and this is sometimes quite difficult with collective actions. Essentially, however, the Pareto criterion can be used to evaluate *efficient* redistributions. There will usually be a set of efficient redistributions and, moreover, the set will vary according to the initial distribution from which one starts.

An efficient redistribution is not, nevertheless, the same as a *just* or a *fair* one. To take an extreme example, the starting point may be one where one person owns *all* society's wealth and is, moreover, totally ungenerous. In this case, the initial distribution would be an efficient one, for no transfer could be made that would not harm this extraordinarily rich man. But it is not likely to be viewed as a *just* distribution—even by the extraordinarily rich man. He may *prefer* to keep his own wealth rather than redistribute it even though he regards his own act in so doing as unjust. As we have emphasised earlier, efficient behaviour may be unjust, and inefficient behaviour may be just, for efficiency depends upon preferences and justice is defined by criteria external to preferences. Each aspect needs to be evaluated separately for an overall judgement to be reached—an overall judgement that it seems sensible to describe as producing neither general efficiency nor justice, but consisting in some balance of both types of consideration: a balancing act we cannot, as social scientists, make ourselves.

Redistribution can thus be justified that may actually harm some members of society, and such redistribution, though not warranted by the efficiency criterion, would be warranted on grounds of justice (which is not, of course, the only remaining relevant criterion. There are other criteria too, such as whether the social structure is liberal, conductive to invention, or productive of variety). Further redistribution may then be justified on the narrower interpretation of economic efficiency. Note, however, that the broader framework of justice, like the narrower one of efficiency, in redistribution, does not imply or prescribe a *uniquely* just and efficient distribution of income. Nor does it imply any particular form of ownership of resources.

B.   POSITIVE ANALYSIS OF REDISTRIBUTION

Positive theories of income redistribution, i.e. those theories that attempt to *explain* why the redistribution that takes place does take place, may be divided into three. The first is a positive version of the Paretian system outlined above based on generosity and is due to Harold Hochman and James Rodgers. The second is based on the selfish proposition that in a democracy the poor use their votes to effect transfers to themselves from the rest of society and is due to Anthony Downs. The third is more eclectic, drawing on elements of the other two theories and is due to Gordon Tullock.

Redistribution through Generosity

The Hochman–Rodgers positive theory of redistribution is based upon the foregoing normative analysis. Individuals in a democracy are assumed to be utility-maximisers, where the sources of utility for any individual are not necessarily selfish. For example, it is the key to their theory that one individual may derive utility from an increase in another person's income. The theory also requires that the democracy in question is a 'perfect' democracy in that no decisions can be made that harm anyone. In short, a *consensus* is required for any action, such as redistribution, to be taken— each citizen has a veto. This is, of course, a rather extreme departure from the majority decision-making rules that characterise the democracies with which we are most familiar, and it is one that is relaxed in the other positive theories we shall discuss. Nevertheless, it is interesting to see how much can be obtained that is consistent with the world we know, even though this assumption (ruling out coercion) is somewhat extreme. In addition, the theory assumes that the larger one's income, the lower the ratio of its marginal utility to the marginal utility one derives from the existence of another person's income. Thus, it is quite clear that the existence of altruism or caring is implied: an individual derives utility not only from his own income but also from others'—the more income they have the more utility the altruist must necessarily gain.

Thus the greater the income possessed by a (generous) person, the greater the differential between his income and that of the lowest income classes and the lower the ratio of his marginal valuation of his own income to his marginal valuation of the lowest income classes' incomes. As a consequence, in a world in which individuals have approximately the same preferences at each level of income, the greater the income differential the greater the amount of the transfer that the relatively rich will want to make to the relatively poor. This in turn implies that the observed calculation of 'fiscal residuals' (the differences in the value of transfers received and taxes paid) will decline as one moves successively up through various income classes. The evidence on actual redistribution is broadly consistent with this implication, though the estimation of the residuals is extremely hazardous. Thus, for the UK in 1977 persons in the highest income decile, with an average income of £11,079, lost from the redistribution that actually took place; persons in the middle income brackets (at around £3,000) seemed, more or less, to break even; those in the lowest brackets received definitely positive net gains in cash and kind from the redistributive process. (see Table 5.5 in chapter 5). As we shall see in chapter 5, Gillespie's results for the USA in 1960 have a similar pattern of redistribution between income classes.

It therefore seems that the Hochman–Rodgers theory, which specifies the pattern of an optimal redistribution, succeeds in explaining *observed* distributions approximately, despite the consensus assumption upon which the model is based. We turn later to an alternative model based upon a majority decision rule rather than consensus. Clearly, in practice, the consensus assumption can only be an approximation to the truth. How good an approximation depends on the facts which, in this case, seem consistent with it.

In modern (large) democracies it is quite obvious that majority-type decisions may imply a substantial divergence from the consensus assumption, according to which any change hurts (in utility terms) nobody. In practice, political decisions do evidently harm some people without any compensating advantages being offered. Nevertheless, it remains the case that the unrealistic consensus assumption may be sufficiently accurate for the results of the theory to be interpreted as a plausible explanation of reality—if, of course, they are not inconsistent with the facts. In particular, we might note that the *smaller* the political unit effecting the redistribution, and the easier it is for individuals to move from one unit to another, the more the consensus assumption holds true. One would accordingly expect the Hochman–Rodgers theory to apply even more effectively in, say, Switzerland, where the cantons are primarily responsible for income taxation and expenditure than in, say, the UK.

Another reason why one would expect an imperfect match between the Hochman–Rodgers theory of *general* income redistribution and actual patterns of fiscal residuals is, as we have seen in chapter 3, that not all concern takes the *general* form invariably associated with vertical redistribution. Horizontal redistribution within income class (or even reverse-vertical redistribution from relatively poor to relatively rich) can arise from a specific concern over the distribution of, say; health or education services. Families with numerous children may not be distributed in the same way as family income, but the need for school places may reasonably be thought to vary directly with the number of children. This again is seen in Table 5.5.

Another important insight offered by the Hochman–Rodgers approach relates to the valuation of public expenditures received by individuals. The convention is to value benefits provided in kind at cost of provision and thence to infer that this is the value (or a minimum value) of the benefit received. The Pareto approach to redistribution invites the question 'value to whom?' It is quite conceivable for the personal valuation placed upon, say, free education by the children of the poor to be less than the cost of provision. The explanation of why the education is provided is that there are externalities that benefit the educated well-to-do when poor children receive schooling, which is why the (caring) relatively rich are prepared to provide it. If, in the spirit of Hochman–Rodgers, we assume that ideal amounts of education are provided, the benefit of the redistribution accrues to two sets of individuals: the poor *and* the rich at one and the same time—both place a value on the redistribution. If the poor would not have consumed education in an ideal amount without free provision, it follows that their marginal valuation of schooling is less than its marginal cost. The remaining differential of cost over benefit accrues to the relatively rich. There are thus two elements that make in-kind provision less progressive than the arithmetic of chapter 5 will indicate. First, the value of benefits in kind *to the poor* may be less than the cost used as a proxy and, second, the rich also benefit. Two implications follow from this:

(1) The voluntary consensus view implies that in terms of *real income* (utility) *all* gain from redistribution, so the net distribution of *real income* may not be different after the redistribution of resources from the distribution previously prevailing. It may even move in favour of the rich! Redistribution of real income to benefit the poor can only be guaranteed if coercion is applied to the rich so that they are forced to do what they would otherwise not do.

(2) In terms of the private valuation of beneficiaries and the private costs of tax payers the redistribution may be overstated because the former will usually be less than the cost data used as a surrogate for benefit received. There is a strong case for ignoring external valuations in *measuring* redistribution (but not in *explaining* it) because our concern is normally with the private value of resources received and lost rather than their social value—the rich, egalitarians, liberals are concerned about the well-being of the poor rather than the well-being that the rich derive when the poor are made better off. But if this is true, then the use of cost data as measures of benefits is of dubious value. Direct enquiry would be one method of eliciting the various values placed upon such benefits, but it too runs into great difficulties, not least of which is the incentive individuals would have to conceal their true valuations if they believed that the results might be used to shape future social policy.

The general predictions of the Hochman–Rodgers model are not wildly inconsistent with the results of chapter 5, as we shall see. Unfortunately the theory does not specify, for example, *how* progressive the net benefit structure will be (beyond the prediction that it will be progressive), for this depends entirely upon knowledge of people's preferences regarding income redistribution and also probably on prevailing notions of fairness, which are not in the Hochman–Rodgers or the caring models.

Redistribution through Selfishness

The economic theory of democracy invented by Antony Downs has implications for income redistribution and approaches the 'positive politics' of the problem from the opposite end to Hochman and Rodgers. Instead of the phenomenon of redistribution being explained primarily by the generous impulses of the relatively rich, Downs' explanation is couched in terms of the relatively poor using their political power to obtain transfers from the rest of society. Coercion is introduced.[3]

Downs' economic theory of democracy assumes that politicians who comprise the leadership of political parties seek office solely to enjoy the income, prestige and power that go with running the government apparatus. The policies of rival political parties are therefore seen strictly as a means of gaining votes in elections—they do not seek to gain office in order to carry out certain preconceived policies or to serve any particular interest groups; rather they formulate policies and serve interest groups in order to gain office.[4] The Downs hypothesis implies that the government always acts so as to maximise the number of votes it will receive at the next election, as will its rival opposition parties (though, of course, one is unlikely to hear politicians admit as much). The citizens in Downs' theory are viewed as utility-maximising individuals who vote for whatever party they believe will provide them with the highest utility from government action. (These sources of utility need not be narrow and selfish: citizens may approve of governmental acts that may penalise them economically in order to help others. For the moment, however, we assume selfish citizens.) The Downs model has many fascinating implications and seems to explain many contemporary phenomena. Our concern, however, is with its implications for income redistribution.

The pre-tax distribution of income in most countries is such that a few persons have large incomes and large numbers have relatively small incomes. One way for a government to gain votes is therefore through redistribution, by depriving a few persons of income (thereby alienating them) and transferring it to many others (thereby gaining their support). A redistribution towards equality is therefore predicted as a consequence of democratic politics.

Three complicating factors in the Downs theory prevent the attainment of perfect equality. The first is that taxes and transfers have side-effects (for example, on willingness to work) that are believed to reduce the total (pecuniary) wealth of the community. Since citizens believe in this effect and are averse to wealth reductions, they tend also to be averse to *complete* equality. As a consequence, vote-maximising governments will not go for complete equality. Secondly, because the future is unknown, low-income persons may hope one day to be rich themselves and this subjective probability (no matter how small the objective probability) will tend to make them prefer *some* degree of inequality. Finally, in an uncertain world, even in a one man, one vote democracy, the relatively rich have more political power, for they can use their wealth to create it, by affording time to organise pressure groups, by buying mass media communication, and so on. All three of these effects act as countervailing forces to the natural tendency of democratic governments to redistribute incomes from the rich to the poor. Indeed, the last effect may be so strong as to overwhelm the natural tendency altogether, though in general this would not appear to be the case, for all the countervailing effects derive from the existence of uncertainty and ignorance (about, for example, the future and the probable consequences of various government programmes). Only when uncertainty and ignorance are higher than is commonly found in literate democracies would one expect the countervailing effects to be overwhelming.

Thus, the fundamental explanation of redistribution in a democracy according to the Downs theory is that it pays governments in terms of votes to transfer from the relatively few rich to the relatively many poor. Insofar as the relatively few rich are also persons of charitable instincts, the theory will tend to apply with even greater force.

According to Gillespie (1965) (see next chapter), the bulk of redistribution in the USA is from the richest 14 per cent of families to the poorest 23 per cent. These relative proportions are consistent with Downsian theory, though the fact (if it is a fact) that a majority of families loses from redistribution would appear to be inconsistent with it. But in the American data it is rather inconvenient for the Downs theory (at least in its simplest form presented here) that according to Gillespie (1965) only 32 per cent of the lowest income groups receive net gains when one would have predicted a percentage greater than 50. The 32 per cent is not, however, inconsistent with Hochman–Rodgers. Thus, on balance, and recognising that the evidence is extremely thin, it appears that their hypothesis of caring performs rather better than Downs' hypothesis of selfishness, which is a rather pleasing (if unexpected) result for economists tentatively to assert.

The Positive Politics Approach

Gordon Tullock's positive theory of income redistribution is based, as are the previous theories we have outlined, upon a stylised conception of the democratic process but has more in common with the Downs theory than with Hochman–Rodgers in assuming that politicians behave in broad correspondence with the wishes of a *majority* of the electorate. The Downs theory postulates that the n per cent of families with the lowest incomes (where $n > 50$) are able to use their majority to take incomes from the top $(100 - n)$ per cent of families. Tullock asks, however, why we should not postulate that the top n per cent ($n > 50$ again) should not remove some of the incomes from the bottom $(100 - n)$ per cent of families, since in at least the simple versions of these models only the number of votes cast is relevant in determining the redistributive—or any other—policy of governments. Consequently, one would expect the middle $(2n - 100)$ per cent of voters to control actual policy choices. For example, if a simple majority were sufficient for a policy decision in an electorate of 100 people, $n = 51$ and the middle 2 per cent of voters would be able to effect a redistribution from either end towards themselves—in general, there would be a presumption that redistribution would tend to favour the middle income classes.

Several modifications to this very simple prediction can be made while remaining within the simple overall view of the democratic process. The chief modification arises out of the obvious fact that the relatively rich have more money. As a result of this, the higher the number of rich persons included in any coalition intending to transfer money from the rest of the population the smaller the amount of money that can actually be transferred—the cost of admitting a rich person to the coalition is higher than the cost of admitting a poor person. Consequently, it is most likely for coalitions aiming at higher redistribution to contain persons none of whose incomes are higher than any person's not in the coalition—the dominant coalition is likely to consist of the poorest n per cent of the population. Remembering, however, that the middle $(2n - 100)$ per cent are the marginal coalition members, the question arises of how the coalition of n voters will share the spoils taxed off the remaining $100 - n$?

If n is 51 and we suppose that 'the poor' constitute the bottom two deciles of the income distribution, this 20 per cent is only about 40 per cent of the dominant coalition. Of course, if more than 51 per cent of voters were needed to support a policy before the government felt sufficiently confident to implement it, then the poor would constitute an even smaller percentage of the dominant coalition. It thus appears that the middle and lower-middle classes (defined in terms of the family income distribution) would dominate the dominant coalition, so while one would predict that some redistribution would go to the poorest people, the theory suggests that the lower-middle and middle income brackets would fare best. The upper-middle and upper income classes would not gain at all from redistribution—they would lose from it.

The broad pattern of redistribution suggested by Tullock's theory is thus that the flow would be from the best off to the worst off, but that the lower-middle percentiles would tend to gain more than the very worst off.

Two factors might work to moderate these tendencies. First, to the extent that middle income groups are generous, the relative shares of the gains from redistribution among the dominant coalition will shift in favour of the really poor. Second, if the broad pattern of redistribution is as the theory implies, one would expect individuals at the *extremes* of the distribution to want to form a coalition. This would be in the interests of the very rich, for the really poor could by such an arrangement obtain more transfers and at the same time, by terminating transfers to the middle groups, the rich would also be better off. It would also be to the advantage of the poor, who would receive more under such an arrangement and hence be persuaded to leave the dominant coalition. The paradoxical result is thus obtained that the poor may recognise that their interests are more coincident with those of the very rich than with those nearer to them in income.

The data, such as they are, do not appear to support the Tullock prediction that the bulk of the gains will accrue to lower-middle income groups, though they are consistent with the modified version. Even in the absence of caring, it may be that the interests of the rich in minimising the burden of the inevitable redistributive tendency of democracy are coincidental with the interests of the poor in maximising receipts.

Finally, we may note that neither the Downs nor the Tullock theory is based upon the necessary existence of non-specific caring instincts on the part of any section of the population, though neither approach necessarily rules out such motives (which, of course, form the whole basis of the Hochman–Rodgers approach). Common to all three theories, however, is the assumption that the relatively poor are not averse to gaining through the redistribution of incomes. Although ignorance and the costs of acquiring information can be, and have been, introduced into such analyses, the possibility that the poor prefer not to receive handouts through the state or via any other means has not been incorporated. In practice, as we shall see, one of the problems of obtaining a desired (by someone) redistribution lies in the reluctance of at least some of the poor to benefit from it. To the extent that this is true, one would *not* expect the poor to be as strongly interested in a coalition with the very rich as may otherwise be the case. Moreover, neither would they be expected to form a very vocal minority even of the dominant coalition. Both effects intensify the fundamental redistributive implications of the basic Tullock hypothesis even though it is not supported by the evidence to date. Tullock does provide, however, a theoretical explanation for the widespread view among empiricist students of social policy that most redistribution takes place among the middle income groups even though systematic evidence on this point is still lacking. Given the data difficulties emphasised, it is clearly premature to reject or accept decisively any of the theories that have been discussed. On current evidence, the Hochman–Rodgers hypothesis appears to do best by a short head, but further refinement of both methodology and data may turn up something better than casual evidence that is more consistent with one of the other theories. As we find so often in the economics of social policy, there are many fascinating beginnings but few firm conclusions. It is a highly researchable area indeed! When you have studied chapter 5 and perhaps done some empirical investigations of your own, it would be profitable to return to this section to re-evaluate the relative merits of these rival theories.

Equality or Minimum Standards?

The redistribution arguments with which this chapter has thus far been concerned have had it in common that the poor and the rich are both objects of policy—redistribution is from the relatively rich to the relatively poor not only because the former have more to transfer but because the relative positions of the two groups are themselves important. The political argument (deriving from the principles of liberalism) for this more or less symmetrical treatment is that great inequalities of purchasing power also imply inequalities in political power. Redistribution is thus seen not only as the likely *consequence* of democratic politics (as the positive theories discussed above imply) but also as a probably *necessary condition* for democratic politics to exist.

As we shall see in chapter 6 when problems of policy are discussed, relative equality is only a part of the problem, albeit the more general part, for in societies where the greatest inequalities have been removed the emphasis has tended to shift away from the question of relative inequality towards safeguarding the economic well-being of those in the lowest percentiles of the income distribution. In this context, the question of guaranteeing minimum standards for all citizens—the avoidance of poverty—acquires prominence. Policy interest becomes less concerned with how progressive the tax structure is or should be and more concerned with how many people or families fall below a certain standard and what that standard should be. The search for a technological definition of subsistence has proved futile and the poverty line used officially has itself varied over time and varies between countries. In fact, the minimum standard cannot be defined without value-judgements. While these might be a part of a theory of social justice, here we shall focus on preferences—as we have throughout this chapter.

The economics of minimum standards can conveniently be explored using a variant of Figure 4.6 above, as in the accompanying Figure 4.7. Let us suppose that A, a middle-class professional, has £10,000 a year and B, a poor man, has no income at all. If we exclude the possibility that B may steal from A, or may use the state to expropriate income from him, we ask how will the minimum standard for B be determined? The answer, not surprisingly, turns out to depend crucially upon what is meant by a 'minimum standard'. According to one view, the minimum standard of guaranteed income is determined by what is regarded as being necessary for a 'decent' life for B and his family. What is 'decent' will depend upon A's views on this subject rather than B's, but B will, of course, normally be able to influence A's views by bringing various facts to his attention, or by having pressure groups operating on his behalf (for example, the Child Poverty Action Group) bring them to his attention. According to this view, we suppose that A's marginal valuation of reduction in B's income

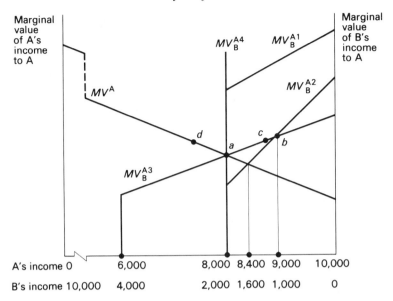

FIG. 4.7 Minimum standards when there are preferences about income distributions.

deficiency falls steadily as the deficiency is removed but, once the decent minimum is attained, that A places no value on further transfers to B. Given such a minimum, A will value attaining it but will not wish to go beyond it. The minimum is thus associated with a 'kink' or discontinuity in A's MV of B's income. MV_B^{A1} is such a marginal valuation curve, with £2,000 per year being regarded by A as the decent minimum for B. Given the configuration of the two curves MV^A and MV_B^{A1} in Figure 4.7 we may say two things. First, the minimum income of £2,000 *ought* to be guaranteed to B. Secondly, we may assert on the positive side that (assuming that the free rider problem is somehow solved and that the political system works efficiently) it actually will be guaranteed.

The meaning and relevance of the minimum standard are not quite as simple as this, however. Consider the possibility that, with the *same view of the minimum*, A's marginal valuation curve for rectifying B's income deficiency were to be that indicated by MV_B^{A2}. In this case the amount that ought to be transferred (and that would be if no 'imperfections' existed) would be only £1,600. A would not be prepared to bring B up to the 'minimum standard'. This difficulty could be avoided if we defined the minimum standard to mean the maximum A will contribute (viz. £1,600 in this case) but this clearly is not what is usually meant by the minimum. At one time it was thought (by Rowntree) that the minimum ought to be that sum of money that would enable a person to operate *physiologically* at an efficient level. Subsequently, it has become much broader than that, but is still couched in terms of the 'necessities' of a decent existence—if not a decent life—defined without reference to the balancing of subjective gains *and losses* on the part of A. Consequently, the possibility arises of a minimum standard—even a generally recognised minimum standard—that no one, save B, will want to achieve. We shall meet the empirical counterpart of this analytic problem in chapter 6 when we come to discuss the poverty line.

Finally, consider two other possibilities. MV_B^{A3} has it as an implication that the amount by which B's poverty is to be alleviated is £2,000—the same as in the case of MV_B^{A1}. In this case, however, A values further transfers to B (up to £4,000) but will not actually transfer more than £2,000 because it is not 'worth' it to him. MV_B^{A4} has it as an implication that, whatever the subjective costs to A, B will get his £2,000—but not more. In this case, we might say that B was, in A's eyes, *absolutely* in need—he should have the £2,000 regardless of its cost.

Sorting out which of these four possibilities is the true meaning of the minimum is clearly not easy. Let us dismiss MV_B^{A4} as a likely possibility, for it is very odd in implying that A's desire to help B is the same no matter how high the cost to A and no matter *how* badly off B is. MV_B^{A1} is also somewhat odd, in that it implies that A would continue to transfer the same £2,000 even if the last *thousand* of his own income had no value to him at all! The most plausible possibilities must, by this process of elimination, be MV_B^{A2} and MV_B^{A3}, but in neither of these cases is the 'minimum' agreed the minimum that will be met—or that should be met. In fact, the kinks in the MV curves have neither positive nor normative significance. The degree to which poverty is alleviated will be determined not by what is 'decent' for a man and his family, but by whatever the community, in the light of its desire to help and what it must forgo to do so, decides. This conclusion will be of great help in disentangling the vexed problems to be met in chapter 6 concerning the relevance for social policy of the poverty line.

Another important implication emerges from this. To the extent that concern is with the poor in particular rather than with equality in general, and to the extent that MV_B^{A1} and MV_B^{A4} are unlikely descriptions of A's concern for B, the amount that A will make available to alleviate B's poverty will depend, given his preferences in this regard, upon the costs of doing so. If, for every £1 sacrificed by A only 50p goes to B, B will receive less than if B received the full £1. We may see this readily on the diagram, for now £1 buys only one half as much poverty alleviation. Consider the curve MV_B^{A3}. When A has lost £2,000, B has gained only £1,000 and A's marginal valuation of the income in his own use is given by a and his marginal valuation of the income received by B is b. Clearly, b is higher than a, so by transferring more to B's use from his own A will gain. In fact, he will continue to gain until his marginal valuation in each use is once more equal, i.e. at *d* and *c*. Thus with uniformly declining marginal valuations (which seems not unrealistic) the greater the administrative and other costs of making transfers, other things equal, the less will be received. This has the convenient implication that both the A's and the B's in the real world will seek to make transfers as efficient as possible. It also implies that tax relief on charitable donations will increase the value of receipts, and that if people were equally concerned about a disaster in their own country and a similar disaster in Africa, they would give less to a representative African than to their own.[5] That they tend to give less to those in need who are far away indicates, of course, that people are less concerned about distant catastrophies.

Equal Treatment for Equal Cases

A final important implication of this analysis is that individuals in 'like circumstances' should be treated alike. The meaning of 'like circumstances' is largely a matter of subjective judgement for the observer, but analytically it can mean none other than 'imposing a like externality'. The normative implication that like cases should be treated alike can be derived with the help of Figure 4.8. MV^A once again indicates A's marginal valuation of his

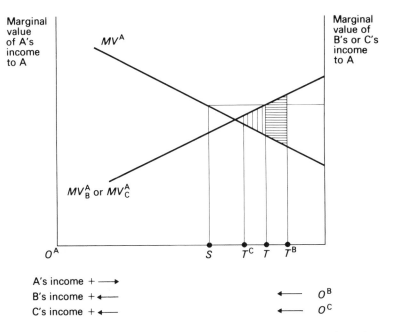

FIG. 4.8   Equal treatment of equals when there are preferences about income distributions.

income in his own use and M_B^A and MV_C^A indicate his valuation of its use for B and C. If B and C impose a like externality—most likely when B and C are 'statistical' individuals (e.g. single pensioners with so savings of their own, unmarried mothers or fathers, *etc.*) and are not known personally to A—then MV_B^A and MV_C^A are identical. Social welfare is then maximised where $MV^A = MV_B^A = MV_C^A$, i.e., where A transfers $O^B T$ to B and $O^C T$ to C, with $O^B T = O^C T$, himself sacrificing $2(O^B T)$ or $2(O^C T)$, retaining $O^A S$ for his own use. If A transferred, say, $O^B T^B$ to B and $O^C T^C$ to C, it is readily seen that by equalising the transfer he would gain the horizontally shaded area and lose the vertically shaded area. The same principle applies when there are large numbers of persons such as A and more recipients than merely two.

NOTES

1. Some readers may be confused by our various discussions dealing alternately with households, families and individuals. In this chapter, individuals are the basic unit of analysis because individuals make choices, either alone or in groups. Since it appears to be the case that prime concern is over redistribution of incomes between *families*, one is really asserting that individuals are concerned more about the economic status of families than about other individuals. For *analytical* reasons it is highly convenient, nevertheless, to treat families *as if* they were individuals. In empirical work, however, families must be carefully distinguished from individuals—if our presumption is correct that individuals are concerned mainly about families.
2. In fact, this was not an application only of the law of diminishing marginal utility since this law alone said nothing about the *relative* marginal utilities enjoyed by different people.
3. The coercion referred to is not the coercion that may be readily agreed to by the generous in a Hochman–Rodgers world as a solution to the free rider problem, they will face (see pp. 31–34 for a reminder of the nature of this problem); it is the imposition of the will of one section of the community upon another section.
4. The Downsian theory does not really require politicians to turn with the political wind like weathercocks on every occasion. A politician may be successful simply because he is a sincere believer in particular causes and is consistent in his beliefs. He may also be successful in getting votes by *leading* opinion rather than by merely following it. Either way, however, there are tendencies for politicians who do not 'please the people' not to win votes and hence to have a lessened influence on policy. All politicians must seek one or another way of avoiding this contingency save those possessing those monopolies known as 'safe seats'.
5. We have implicitly assumed non-negative 'income' or (as better termed here to avoid confusion) 'welfare' effects in this analysis. Indifference curves provide a more general way of discussing the issues. Suppose A's opportunity set to be bounded by AB representing the postulate that £1 sacrificed by A is received by B. Suppose A (assumed non-selfish) prefers point E_0 on this line where an indifference curve is tangential. AC represents the boundary of the choice set with transaction costs, taxes on gifts, etc. If the new indifference curve is tangential along Aa, A will give less and B receive less; if tangency occurs between a

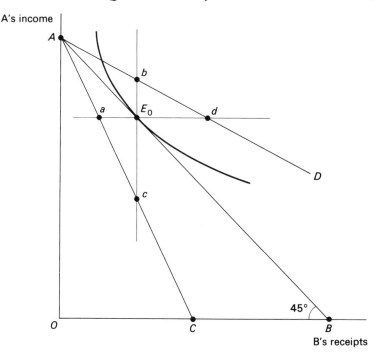

FIG. 4.9 Indifference curve analysis of gifts when there are preferences about income distributions.

and c, A will give *more* but B still receive less. If tangency occurs between c and C, A will give more and B will receive more. If 'welfare effects' are everywhere positive we can rule out the section cC as a final resting place for A since the negative substitution effect is reinforced by the negative welfare effect, and he may settle anywhere on Ac.

Putting the same argument into reverse and starting again from E_0. Let gifts now be subsidised. If welfare effects are positive, the new tangency of an indifference curve with the new boundary to the choice set AD will lie either on bd when A gives less but B receives more, or on dD when A gives more and B of course receives more. The evidence of the relationship between income and charitable donations is of some relevance here and it is positive, indicating welfare effects of the sort assumed.

QUESTIONS ON CHAPTER 4

1. Distinguish between the positive and normative approaches to income redistribution.
2. Is identity of tastes a necessary condition for equality of incomes to maximise average utility?
3. Do the conclusions reached in using Figure 4.3 apply when M and M' intersect one another?

4. What is the Lerner theorem?
5. What is Sen's maximin theorem?
6. What is an *efficient* redistribution of incomes?
7. When will an efficient distribution also be an equal distribution of income?
8. Outline Downs' theory of income redistribution.
9. Outline Tullock's theory of income redistribution.
10. Which positive theory of income redistribution best accords with any facts you may have researched?
11. Distinguish between vertical and horizontal redistribution.
12. Is a minimum income needed by anyone? What is your criterion of need? What others may there be?
13. Should 'like cases be treated alike'? Why?
14. What can be deduced about the best distribution of income using *only* the proposition that marginal utility of income always falls and a clearly stated welfare objective?
15. What kind of coercion may be voluntarily decided upon to resolve free rider problems?
16. Should taxation be progressive?
17. Should utility be 'taxed' rather than income (or wealth)?
18. Is there a uniquely efficient distribution of income?
19. Is there a uniquely just distribution of income?
20. Suppose redistribution reduces the national income. Does your preferred degree of equality depend upon the sacrifice it may necessarily entail?

FURTHER READING

Blum, W. J. and Kalven, Jr., H. (1953) *The Uneasy Case for Progressive Taxation.* Chicago: University of Chicago Press.

Breit, W. and Culbertson, Jr., W. P. (1970) Distributional equality and aggregate utility: comment. *American Economic Review, 60,* pp. 435–41.

Buchanan, J. M. and Tullock, G. (1965) *The Calculus of Consent.* Ann Arbor: University of Michigan Press.

Tullock, G. (1971) The charity of the uncharitable. *Western Economic Journal, 9,* pp. 379–92. Reprinted in A. A. Alchian, *et al. The Economics of Charity.* London: Institute of Economic Affairs, 1973.

Dalton, H. (1920) *Some Aspects of Inequality of Incomes in Modern Communities.* London: Routledge.

Downs, A. (1957) *An Economic Theory of Democracy.* New York: Harper.

Friedman, M. (1947) Lerner on the economics of control. *Journal of Political Economy, 55,* pp. 405–16. Reprinted in M. Friedman *Essays in Positive Economics.* Chicago: University of Chicago Press, 1953.

Hochman, H. M. and Rodgers, J. D. (1969) Pareto optimal redistribution. *American Economic Review, 59,* pp. 542–57.

Lerner, A. P. (1944) *The Economics of Control.* London: Macmillan.

Lerner, A. P. (1970) Distributional equality and aggregate utility: reply. *American Economic Review, 60,* pp. 443–3.

Little, I. M. D. (1950) *A Critique of Welfare Economics.* London: Oxford University Press.

Meyer, P. A. and Shipley, J. J; Musgrave, Richard A; Goldfarb, Robert S; Hochman, H. M. and Rodgers, J. D. (1970) *American Economic Review, 60,* pp. 988–1002.

Pigou, A. C. (1932) *The Economics of Welfare* (4th edition). London: Macmillan.
Sen, A. K. (1969) Planners' preferences: optimality, distribution and social welfare. In J. Margolis and H. Guitton (eds) *Public Economics: An Analysis of Public Production and Consumption and their Relations to the Private Sector*. London: Macmillan.
Sen, A. K. (1973) *On Economic Inequality*. Oxford: Clarendon Press.
Stigler, G. J. (1970) Director's law of public income redistribution. *Journal of Law and Economics, 13*, pp. 1–10.

CHAPTER 5

Measurement of Distribution and Redistribution

In the previous chapters we have examined some of the reasons deriving either from considerations of efficiency or considerations of justice why societies may wish to alter the distribution of income, wealth and specific types of consumption. In the next chapter we shall examine some of the policy debate about why inequality arises and how redistribution of income and wealth might best be effected. In the present chapter we shall be engaged with three main issues: the measurement of inequality, specific studies of the measurement of the distribution of health care and education benefits to illustrate the problems of measuring benefit incidences, and the measurement of the redistribution of income generally. The general aim in this chapter is to identify the main problems one encounters in talking about distribution. The next chapter is more substantive and policy-oriented.

A. MEASURES OF INEQUALITY

Figure 5.1 is a histogram showing the proportionate distribution of post-tax incomes in three countries: the UK, the USA and the Federal Republic of Germany. It shows the proportion of total income accruing, after income tax, to each decile of the population of households in the three countries. Thus, the lowest ten per cent of households (first decile) received, after tax, 1.5 per cent of total income in the USA, 2.5 per cent in the UK and 2.8 per cent in Germany. The richest decile (top ten per cent) received, after tax, 26.6 per cent in the USA, 23.5 per cent in the UK and 30.3 per cent in Germany.

Table 5.1 shows a distribution of income for taxable units (i.e. a married couple or single person, not households) in the UK in 1975–76. These data are unsatisfactory as a representation of the distribution of income as we shall see in the next chapter when we come to discuss policy. These official statistics are used here solely for illustrative purposes. Now that the distribution is not in deciles, as was the case in Figure 5.1, the data display more

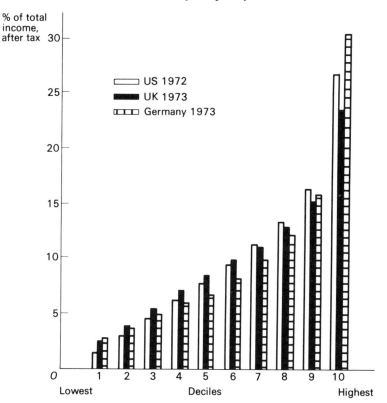

FIG. 5.1 Proportionate distribution of post-tax income in the USA, UK and Federal Republic of Germany, 1972–73.

dramatically the difference between the lowest (and really there should have been some *negative* incomes for those businessmen, etc., who made losses in 1975–76) and the highest. The definition of income includes, incidentally, pensions (public and private), employers' National Insurance contributions and imputed rent of owner-occupied dwellings. Thus there were about 1.8 million units with incomes less than £750 per year and 46,000 with incomes over £20,000 (all before tax).

Column (b) shows that most units are located in the middle: 46 per cent of units had incomes between £2,000 and £5,000, with an average over the whole distribution of £2,869 before tax. Comparison of columns (c) and (d) shows the *progressivity* of the tax structure: a higher proportion of reported taxable income going in tax the higher the income. One measure of progressivity is the elasticity of after-tax income with respect to income, also known as *residual income progression*.[1] This takes a value of 1 for a proportional tax and < 1 for a progressive tax. The elasticity is .98, or very nearly proportional between incomes of £634 and £890, but falls to .41 for

TABLE 5.1 Incomes in the UK, 1975–76

(a) Range of income (£ per annum)	(b) Number of income units (1,000s)	(c) Mean income before tax (£)	(d) Mean income after tax (£)	(e) % of total income units	(f) % of total income before tax	(g) % of total income after tax
Under 750	1793	634	632	6.3	1.4	1.7
750+	2471	890	883	8.7	2.7	3.3
1000+	2368	1129	1090	8.4	3.3	4.0
1250+	2194	1377	1288	7.7	3.7	4.3
1500+	1771	1626	1457	6.2	3.5	4.0
1750+	1389	1876	1598	4.9	3.2	3.4
2000+	2801	2251	1886	9.9	7.8	8.1
2500+	2580	2748	2257	9.1	8.7	8.9
3000+	4537	3486	2823	16.0	19.5	19.6
4000+	3188	4445	3526	11.2	17.4	17.2
5000+	1598	5434	4208	5.6	10.7	10.3
6000+	1002	6779	5093	3.5	8.4	7.8
8000+	322	8823	6261	1.1	3.5	3.1
10000+	127	10843	7102	0.45	1.7	1.4
12000+	90	13033	8156	0.32	1.4	1.1
15000+	64	16938	9188	0.23	1.3	0.9
20000+	46	31500	12391	0.16	1.8	0.9
Total	28,341	2869	2305	99.76	100.00	100.00

Source: National Income and Expenditure 1967–77. London: HMSO, 1978, Table 4.8.

incomes between £16,938 and £31,500, indicating that a rise of x per cent in pre-tax income implies a $0.98x$ per cent rise in post-tax income at the lower level but only $0.41x$ per cent at the higher level.

One dramatic way of displaying the distribution pictorially is given in Figure 5.2. This is Pen's Parade (Pen, 1971). Here you imagine a parade of

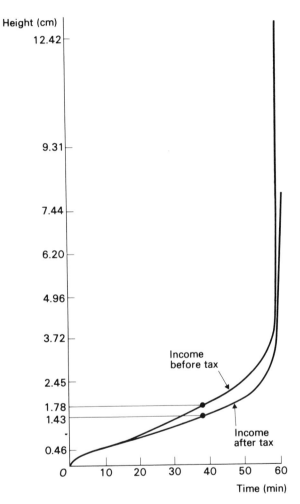

FIG. 5.2   Pen's Parade for the UK, 1975–76.

tax units marching past you where the height of each marcher is proportional to his income and the parade will have passed in exactly one hour. The average tax unit of £2,869 in 1975–76 is a marcher of average height, *viz.* 1.78 m high. Thus, first to pass in the parade are some dwarfs less than half a metre high (mostly pensioners), then the very low paid (mostly female). The parade will have gone on for nearly 40 minutes (two thirds past) before the average person passes by, then the giants take over. In the last 5 minutes some gigantic freaks pass: the tallest of them disappearing off the top of the chart at a height of 19.5 metres. But that is, of course, only the average of those in the final income bracket (over £20,000). If Pen is right in putting J. Paul Getty last in the parade you would—for a micro-second—just have got a glimpse of his towering 15 kilometres! (For comparison, Pen's Parade of post-tax income units is also shown in Figure 5.2.)

In this section of the chapter we shall be looking at some summary measures of the degree of inequality. Suppose one asked, with reference to Figure 5.1, whether post-tax income is distributed more unequally in one country than another. After looking at the figure in closer detail you may conclude that, since in the UK the lower deciles always received a higher share than in the USA, and the higher deciles a lower share, post-tax income was more equally distributed in the UK than the USA. The judgement is harder to make in the comparison, say, between the UK and Germany, for in Germany the bottom three deciles and the top decile each received a higher share than in the UK, while the middle deciles received a higher share in the UK than in Germany.

This illustrates one difficulty in judging the extent of inequality: making a *general* statement, or inventing a summary statistic, about the extent of inequality may not be as obviously easy as one may at first suppose. A further difficulty—or set of difficulties—arises when one tries to *quantify* by precisely (or even approximately) how much more one distribution is unequal than another and how *responsive* one measure is compared to another when the distribution is changed in specified ways. In the first part of this chapter we shall examine some common—and some less common— measures of dispersion that have been—or could be—used to summarise the extent of inequality. As we shall see, in the last analysis it will not prove possible to make a judgement about the appropriateness of rival measures without making *value* judgements based on ethical principles or inferred as being the distributional externalities characteristic of a society. We shall not consider *all* possible measures, nor even all those that have received some attention in the literature. We shall, however, include the most obvious candidates as well as some sophisticated non-obvious ones.

The Range

An obvious starting point is to consider the range (the difference between the highest income household and the lowest, or the difference between the top 10 per cent and the bottom 10 per cent.) We might take either the range of absolute income or the range of the shares. Thus, using the latter, one may calculate from Figure 5.1 that the range in the share going the top 10 per cent and the bottom 10 per cent (i.e. the difference between the maximum and the minimum) is 21.0 percentage points in the UK, 25.1 in the USA and 27.5 in Germany. (To obtain a standardised measure one might divide each by the mean, but this is only desirable if one is taking the range of the absolute levels of income.) But regardless of which variant of the range one uses (another possibility would obviously be to use quartiles rather than deciles in the range of shares), the limitation of this method is plain enough: it focusses exclusively on the tails of the distribution. Thus if, for example, it were the case that income is more equally distributed over the middle deciles in Germany than the UK (as it is) then we may wish to say that, in general, Germany is more egalitarian than the UK. Suppose, for example, that it was the case that all deciles other than the first and tenth had the *same* share in Germany (as it is not), then one would very probably judge Germany to have a more equal distribution.

The Variance

The variance includes *all* the differences between households in the distribution and thus does not suffer from the disadvantage noted above of the range. The variance is defined as

$$V = \sum_{i=1}^{n} (\mu - y_i)^2 / n$$

where μ is the mean household income, y_i is the income of the ith household and n is the number of households. As can be seen from the definition, the variance is the sum of the squares of the differences between a household's income and the mean, all divided by the number of households. Squaring the difference between the mean and household incomes implies that the extremes will receive a greater weight than incomes close to the mean. Any transfer from a richer household to a poorer will reduce the variance, but transfers from the richest to the poorest will reduce V by more than transfers from the next richest to the poorest. Amartya Sen has dubbed the feature that transfers from poorer to richer or from richer to poorer increase or decrease V the 'Pigou–Dalton' condition for a satisfactory measure of inequality since both eponymous gentlemen made this point.

A problem with the variance arises, however, if one is comparing two distributions having different means. It is, therefore, possible for one distribution with a lower mean household income than another, but having a higher *relative* variation, to show a lower variance. In such a circumstance one might well wish to describe the distribution of income having the lower mean as the *less* equal distribution, even though it had the lower variance.

This could be overcome by using the *coefficient of variation*:

$$C = \sqrt{V}/\mu,$$

which is clearly independent of the level of the mean household income.

A difficulty remains, however, with these more sophisticated measures of dispersion: they give equal weight to *any* difference between two incomes that is the same in absolute terms. Thus, a transfer of £100 from the richer of two households to the lower will receive the same weight so long as the initial income difference between the two is the same, regardless of where they are in the distribution. For example, £100 transferred from A to B when A's income is £10,000 and B's is £9,000 receives the same weight as when A's is £4,000 and B's £3,000. Moreover, why weight according to the *squares* of the differences? And why weight by reference to the mean as in *V* and *C*?

Lorenz Curves and the Gini Coefficient

Easily the most frequently used measure of inequality in income distribution studies is the Gini coefficient. This is most usefully explained using the Lorenz curve. If we rank households by income from the lowest to the highest along the bottom axis of Figure 5.3 and, along the vertical axis, measure the *cumulative* share of total income received by the households in question, a Lorenz curve is traced out. Zero per cent of the population has zero income and 100 per cent have 100 per cent, so the curve runs in a north easterly direction. If everyone has the same income, the curve will simply be the straight diagonal line, but if the lower households in the distribution have a proportionately lower share of total income, then the Lorenz curve will be below the diagonal. Figure 5.3 shows the diagonal (line of absolute equality) and Lorenz curves for the UK, USA and Germany based on the data of Figure 5.1.

The Lorenz curves show very clearly the problem we noted in connection with Figure 5.1, namely that whether one regards Germany as more or less unequal than the UK or the USA depends upon how one wishes to weight the shares going to the poorest and the richest. If the share of the poorest gets sufficiently high a weight, then Germany will be judged less unequal—despite the relatively high share of income going to the rich. Only if the Lorenz curves do not intersect can we conclude unambiguously that the distribution is more unequal in one country than another.

The Gini coefficient is the ratio of the difference between the line of absolute equality in Figure 5.3 and a Lorenz curve to the triangle below the diagonal shown as *OAB* in the figure. This will take a value of zero when incomes are equally distributed (i.e. the Lorenz curve is coincident with the diagonal) and a value of 1 at the other extreme when the Lorenz

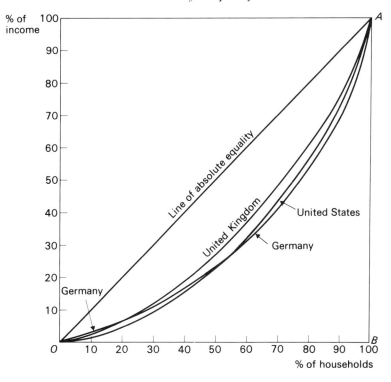

FIG. 5.3   Lorenz curves in the UK, USA and Federal Republic of Germany.

curve has a ⌐ shape and all the income accrues to just one household. For the countries in the figure, the Gini coefficients were 0.318 in the UK, 0.381 in the USA and 0.383 in Germany: virtually the same in the USA and Germany despite the fact that the bottom 20 per cent of households in Germany had 6.5 per cent of all income compared with 4.5 per cent in the USA. The Gini formula is

$$G = \frac{1}{2n^2\mu} \cdot \sum_{i=1}^{n} \sum_{j=1}^{n} |y_i - y_j|,$$

where n is the number of households, μ the mean household income, and y_i, y_j are any two of the n households.[2]

It is obvious that the Gini coefficient emphasises the absolute differences in household incomes rather more than relative differences (say, relative to the mean) and that comparisons between every possible pair of households are also made.[3] A handy way of interpreting a Gini coefficient is that if one chooses two households at random from the income distribution and takes the absolute difference between their incomes as a proportion of the mean income, then on average this difference will be twice the Gini coefficient.

For example, a coefficient of 0.38 means that the *expected* difference between any two randomly selected households' incomes will be 76 per cent of the mean income.

It will by now be obvious that there is no single satisfactory measure of the degree of inequality, for a satisfactory measure must incorporate those aspects of distributions that people think are important, or ethical principles suggest ought to be taken into account. All the summary formulations thus far provide essentially arbitrary weighting solutions to these normative problems.

Atkinson's Measure

A. B. Atkinson (1970, 1975) has proposed a method for directly confronting the issue of arbitrary weights, and a measure that explicitly incorporates value judgements relating to the degree of inequality. His approach is to consider two income distributions: one that is the actual distribution across households and another that is an *equal distribution of a lower total income*. He invites the following conceptual experiment: what is the lowest total income that, if equally distributed, would be regarded as equally acceptable to the present distribution? Thus, if one would accept the sum over all individuals of what Atkinson terms 'the equally distributed equivalent income' (per head) as being 80 per cent of the actual total income, then one would regard the 'value' of an equally distributed income as 'worth' sacrificing 20 per cent of current income to attain. His measure of inequality is:

$$A = 1 - \frac{y_e}{\mu},$$

where y_e is the per capita income in the equally distributed equivalent income. A must lie between 0 and 1. If income is already equally distributed, then no sacrifice can be made to make it more equal, y_e therefore equals μ and $A = 0$. If income is not equally distributed, then the more one is prepared to sacrifice to attain equality, the lower is y_e relative to μ and the closer A approaches 1. Thus, if the per capita income under the equally distributed equivalent income were 80 per cent of the mean of the actual distribution, then $A = 0.20$. Alternatively, the value of redistributing to bring about equality would be equivalent to raising total income by 20 per cent.

The sharp distinction between this quite explicitly normative concept of measurement and the more descriptive measures discussed before can be brought out by considering two alternative distributions in a two person world. Let one distribution be (0, 10) and the other (5, 5). Few would have any hesitation in describing the former as (a good deal) more unequal than the latter, for the latter is a manifestly perfectly equal distribution. But suppose further that one were not prepared to sacrifice any income at all to make (0, 10) more equal, then $y_e = \mu$ (just as $y_e = \mu$ for the equal distribution) and the Atkinson measure of inequality has the same value (zero) for each distribution.

Plainly, therefore, just as the earlier measures were not *normatively* much use, so this measure is not *descriptively* much use. What the Atkinson measure *does* tell us is (granted its value content) whether there exists any *normatively interesting* inequality. If $A = 0$, then plainly we need not worry about any inequalities that the descriptive measures may suggest exist.

You may wonder what the person with zero income in the (0, 10) distribution is thinking about all this! The answer is that it does not matter what he thinks *unless* he is the (or a) person involved in the selection of y_e. Whether he is, or should be, is not a matter we need enquire about in this discussion of the meaning and interpretation of measures of inequality. It is, however, clearly an important political issue whose values *should* be reflected in y_e.

B. Measurement of Benefit Incidence

The problems discussed above in interpreting inequality in terms of a summary statistic suggest that, at best, such statistics should be treated as just that: (crude) summaries. More thorough interpretation and evaluation can only be satisfactorily made by a disaggregation of aggregate data. In chapter 3, we argued that a major concern seems to be that most people find less acceptable wide divergences in the consumption of certain specific goods and services than the same divergences in general purchasing power. If this is indeed the case then it would seem to follow that the distribution of consumption of specific social services will be a crucial element in this disaggregation. In chapter 7 we shall investigate in more detail some possible forms that the social concern, or externality, may take. In the present section, however, we shall focus on two such specific investigations: the distribution of health service benefits in England and Wales and the redistributive impact of education benefits in California. Rather than present summary statistics such as the Gini coefficient or Atkinson's A, we shall present the actual distributions—as best as is empirically possible—and relate them to what chapter 3 suggests may be an approppropriate benchmark: need.

Distribution of Health Service Benefits in England and Wales

The principal kind of redistribution that takes place in health care systems, whether financed out of voluntary insurance, compulsory insurance or general taxation, is from the relatively well to the relatively sick—at least in so far as the sick receive services and the well do not. If average health care expenditure per household experiencing sickness is H, on average each household in the community must contribute pH, where p is the probability of using up H. Healthy households thus pay, on average, pH, while households experiencing sickness receive $H - pH = (1 - p)H$. This is a straightforward transfer of income, which may or may not, depending on whether true insurance is being provided, also provide gains from risk-pooling and insuring against risk.

In assessing the incidence of benefit we need, therefore, to know who the sick are. Table 5.2 shows how the prevalence of conditions causing limited long-standing illness varies by socio-economic group in England and Wales: in all diagnostic categories except for eye disease, semi- and un-skilled manual workers have a higher prevalence than any other social class. This is, moreover, true of mental illness and heart disease—often thought to be the special hazards of the managerial and professional classes. In general, the trend is clear: the lower down the socio-economic scale one goes, the higher the prevalence of sickness.

TABLE 5.2 *Variations in the Average Rate of Sickness Causing Limited Long-Standing Illness by Socio-economic Group, England and Wales, 1971*

Condition	Average rate per 1,000	Professional, employers and managers	Intermediate and junior non-manual	Skilled manual	Semi-skilled & unskilled manual
Mental disorders	11.0	59	65	95	175
Diseases of nervous system	8.7	75	87	79	156
Diseases of eye	7.3	97	112	77	105
Diseases of ear	7.7	56	70	110	142
Heart disease	24.4	83	91	85	141
Other circulatory diseases	10.5	85	70	86	150
Bronchitis	16.9	47	69	106	167
Other low respiratory diseases	13.5	78	96	93	141
Diseases of digestive system	11.4	71	78	101	148
Arthritis and rheumatism	27.5	73	90	79	161
Other disease of musculo-skeletal system	9.3	76	101	99	122
Fractures, etc.	6.3	67	57	105	170
Other injuries	9.5	59	102	100	146

Source: The General Household Survey—Introductory Report. London: HMSO, 1973, Table 8.13.

It would not be surprising, particularly since the proportionate distribution of sickness within each socio-economic group seems broadly the same, to find that the lower social groups are more intensive utilisers of the National Health Service. Table 5.3 shows the proportion of NHS spending by social groups in 1972, as calculated by J. Le Grand (1978), compared with prevalence of illness, and shows that although the lower social groups took a higher proportion of spending, their share was less than proportionate to their share in reported sickness spells. The benefits are attributed to socio-economic groups by taking the expenditure on hospitals, GPs, etc. and allocating it to the groups in proportion to their utilisation. Had health spending been proportionate to sickness prevalence, the percentages in columns (5) and (6) of Table 5.3 would all have been 100. Clearly, however, there is a steady decrease in spending per reported sickness spell.

TABLE 5.3   *Distribution of Health Spending in England and Wales, 1972, by Social Class*

| | % reporting either limiting long-standing illness or acute sickness | | Share of spending as a % of health care expenditure | | % of share in sickness | |
| | (1) | (2) | (3) | (4) | (5) | (6) |
	Actual	Age/sex standardised	Actual	Age/sex standardised	Actual	Age/sex standardised
Professional, employers and managers	13.9	14.8	16.8	18.8	120.9	127.0
Intermediate and junior non-manual	19.7	19.4	22.5	20.5	114.2	105.7
Skilled manual	34.5	36.7	33.4	34.6	96.8	94.3
Semi-skilled and unskilled manual	31.9	29.1	27.3	26.2	85.6	90.0

Source: Le Grand (1978), Table 2.

The principal explanation for these results is that, even though the money price of health care in the UK is zero, utilization rates by the sick in lower socio-economic groups are lower than those for the sick in higher groups. Since a principal objective of the NHS has been to increase utilisation by those whose need can be met by it, this is a major problem itself requiring explanation. There seem to be several major candidates (which are not mutually inconsistent): (a) 'time' prices are higher for the lower groups; (b) the value of health is higher for the higher groups; (c) educational attainment is lower for the lower groups; and (d) discrimination by health service staff.

'Time' prices are the major costs of using the NHS: time spent travelling to the medical centre, time spent waiting in waiting rooms, etc. (including waiting in inpatient beds), time spent in treatment and convalescence, time of other family members in home nursing, etc. In each case these costs tend to be higher for the lower groups; they have fewer cars and telephones and so will tend to spend more time travelling and may travel in ways that involve higher money costs too; they also tend to live further away from medical facilities; working time lost by a wage earner is often associated with earnings losses, which is less frequently so with salaried workers; other family members of lower groups are more likely also to be wage earners who may incur earnings losses for home care. All these factors lead us to predict a lower demand for care for persons in lower social groups having the same clinical condition, even if they have the same basic 'taste' for health care.

The value of health for the higher groups is higher in terms of the value of working time. Since the effects of a health improvement are normally expected to persist over a longer period of time than the costs of acquiring and receiving care (at least, this may be said of acute health services), then the differences in employment contracts between wage and salary earners become less important. Educational attainment is also higher in the higher socio-economic groups, and this affects both the demand for health as well as the (derived) demand for health care. In each case there are broadly three ways in which higher educational attainment affects these demands. First, the better educated are usually better informed and so are more aware of links between life-style and health states: fewer smoke, more have better diets (better balance, lower sugar, saturated fat, and calorie intake, etc.). This helps to explain both the better health status of higher social groups and also their higher utilisation when sick, even though they will be sick less frequently. Secondly, the better educated are better able to combine the resources of the household so as to promote health. Thirdly, the better educated tend to have higher earnings, which not only increases the value of healthy time in work but also increases their command over health-promoting resources other than health services themselves (better housing, better neighbourhood environment, etc.).

Finally, the better-off tend to have a better rapport with professionals in the health service since they come from similar social backgrounds. The average time spent by a GP with middle-class patients is higher than with lower-class patients. Doctors tend to know more about middle-class patients' backgrounds and are able to treat more completely the 'whole' patient. Higher social class patients are also better able to 'work' the system, and are more articulate in explaining and insisting upon their 'rights'.

All of this is, of course, to say that the demand for health care is determined by many more factors than money price alone. To increase utilisation by the relatively lower social groups will require more positive actions than are currently being undertaken. A menu of possibilities suggested by the theoretical considerations of the preceding paragraphs would include: improved local availability of health services to the lower groups to reduce time prices; financial compensation for lost earnings (patients' time is invariably treated as a free resource in all health care systems!); improved health education; and care that a hostile, 'middle-class', value system does not dominate the service in its relations with the lower groups.

These issues emerge only, of course, with the examination of disaggregated data of the sort in Tables 5.2 and 5.3. In so far as they relate to a correctly perceived set of externality relations in the community, they enable a more precise development and a more constructive critique of social policy in the distributive area than the summary statistics discussed earlier.

Redistributive Impact of Education Benefits in California

Another kind of redistribution study, which is relevant to the evaluation of distributive efficiency where there are externalities, or which is also relevant to distributive justice (whichever view one takes), attempts to assess the *re*distributive impact of a specific programme of public spending. We noted above that a publicly financed health care system, or health insurance programme, tends to redistribute from the well taken as a whole to the sick taken as a whole, though there may be a regressive pattern of receipts of benefit when one looks at income or socio-economic classes. Clearly, then, another kind of study might look more explicitly at the total redistributive effect by focussing not only on receipts of benefit but on finance as well. Such a study was made for the redistributive effects of public higher education in California by Hansen and Weisbrod (1969) as amended by Pechman (1970) for the year 1965.

Although in a study such as this the benefit side is reasonably unambiguous, the same cannot be said for the tax side. Taxes are rarely earmarked for specific purposes, so one of the first problems is to establish (a) which taxes are to be taken as the financial source of the benefits and (b) what proportion of these taxes is to be taken as spent on the specific service in question (in this case, higher education). In this study, the *state* taxes asserted (apparently arbitrarily) to contribute to higher education were personal income tax, sales, cigarette, alcoholic beverage and gasoline taxes and the *local* taxes were local sales and property taxes. Omitted taxes included, for example, state corporation tax and the state estate and gift taxes. In the calculations it was further assumed that 40 per cent of the cost of junior colleges was borne by local governments and 60 per cent by the state of California. Costs of state colleges and the University of California were assumed to be borne by the state of California entirely. Although there is free tuition in California, not all the costs of *education* are covered by taxes. The most notable exception is, of course, forgone earnings, which are borne solely by the family. Total tax payments were then adjusted by a factor equal to the ratio of higher education spending to total taxes (of the set specified) so that the total tax take attributed to higher education equalled expenditures on higher education. On this basis column (a) of Table 5.4 was completed by income class.

TABLE 5.4   *Average Net Subsidy or Tax Payment for Californian Higher Education by Income Class, 1965*

Income class ($)	(a) Average tax ($)	(b) Average subsidy Assumption (1) ($)	(c) Average subsidy Assumption (2) ($)	(d) Net subsidy(+) or tax (−) Assumption (1) ($)	(d) Net subsidy(+) or tax (−) Assumption (2) ($)
0– 3,999	66	56	83	−10	+17
4,000– 5,999	77	122	139	+45	+62
6,000– 7,999	88	129	143	+41	+55
8,000– 9,999	112	126	122	+14	+10
10,000–11,999	142	179	160	+37	+18
12,000–13,999	175	167	155	−8	−20
14,000–19,999	229	229	181	0	−48
20,000–24,999	348	271	252	−77	−96
25,000+	974	291	235	−683	−739

Source: Pechman (1970), Table 3.

The distribution of benefits is made on two alternative assumptions. The first (assumption 1) is that used by Hansen and Weisbrod, namely that the dollar value of benefits was distributed by income class according to the distribution of families with parent-supported children in colleges or the university. Assumption (2) is that benefits were distributed by income class according to the distribution of *all* families having children in college or university (i.e. including self-supporting students).

The results indicate a broadly *progressive* structure of redistribution. On assumption (2) the progressiveness is quite smooth, with all families having an income over £12,000 paying net taxes and those below receiving a net subsidy. On assumption (1) one reaches much the same conclusion save for the very poorest, who were were net losers.

Caution is due in the interpretation of these numbers not only because of the *empirical* assumptions made to enable their calculation but also because of some major conceptual issues. Pechman (1970), for example, argues that the most important aspect of the redistributive effect of higher education is not so much in terms of taxes paid and tax-cost of resources received, but really in whether the *lifetime earnings* of recipients are made more or less equal. This question's answer is bedevilled not only by problems (which we discuss later) concerned with measuring rates of return to educational investment but also with the vexed question of intergenerational equity: how does one compare the sacrifices of one generation with the benefits they make possible but that accrue to a later generation? Clearly, a concept of intergenerational equity is required.

Before leaving these issues and turning to the assessment of the wider redistributive impact of the whole of public spending, we should look briefly at some technical issues involved in making incidence assumptions of the sort embodied in the two studies we have described.

Distributing the Benefits of Public Goods

Both studies, and they are typical in this respect, attribute benefits on the basis of a head count of these known directly to receive the service. There are two sets of reasons why this procedure is arbitrary, the first relating to externalities and the second to incidence problems.

As far as externalities are concerned, it is clear that, in so far as one is concerned in such studies to measure the distribution of benefits of public expenditure, the procedures described above treat the consumption of such goods as education and health as *purely private goods*. The *only* benefit is the benefit received by the individual, household, or family in question. Yet, since in each case described above the analysis was of a public service provided without charge, it is perfectly clear that (assuming that the systems are not entirely irrational) there must be substantial external effects associated with their consumption.

A potential adjustment for this feature can be illustrated by making the extreme (and unrealistic) assumption that the benefits of the public service in question are *purely* public. This is the precise opposite of the assumption in the studies reported above. Thus, in a two-person world, if A receives a benefit of cost £100, then B receives the same benefit of cost £100. In an interesting study Aaron and McGuire (1970) have shown a way of proceeding to assign benefits to individuals.

To explain their proposal it is necessary first to recall the distinction made in chapter 2 between the marginal utility and the marginal value of consumption, where

$$MV_x = MU_x/MU_m$$

and MV_x is the marginal value of X, MU_x is its marginal utility and MU_m is the marginal utility of money income. With this distinction in mind, let us recall the necessary condition for an optimal rate of public goods provision, namely

$$MV_x^A + MV_x^B = MC,$$

taking X as the public good in question, and A and B are two individuals. If we now assume that A and B are equal in their ability to enjoy income (an assumption we have earlier frowned on) and also equal in their ability to enjoy the public good, then if A and B have different incomes we may write

$$MU_m^A \neq MU_m^B$$

and, since they each receive the same amount of the pure public good,

$$MU_x^A = MU_x^B.$$

Assume further that X is produced at a constant per unit cost so that

$$MC_x = AC_x,$$

then the total cost of X will be $X \cdot AC_x$ and we can write

$$MV_x^A \cdot X + MV_x^B \cdot X = MC_x \cdot X = AC_x \cdot X = £100$$

using the optimality condition for public goods provision and the constant cost assumption. Recalling again the relation between MV_x and MU_x we may rewrite this as

$$\frac{MU_x^A}{MU_m^A} \cdot X + \frac{MU_x^B}{MU_m^B} \cdot X = £100.$$

Using the $MU_x^A = MU_x^B$ assumption and letting $MU_x^A = MU_x^B = k$ we may in turn write

$$k \left[X \cdot \frac{1}{MU_m^A} + X \cdot \frac{1}{MU_m^B} \right] = £100.$$

What this expression says is that the costs of the public good (£100) may, on our assumptions, be allocated between A and B according to the reciprocal of their marginal utilities of income.

Thus, if we wish to allocate the benefits of, say, the *availability* of spare health care capacity in the NHS (a public good, since if it is available for A it is also available for B and at zero money price) then provided one can accept the assumption that the optimal spare capacity exists (for treating, say emergency cases) and are prepared to accept that each person has the same marginal utility at the level provided, then the allocation of the costs to the beneficiaries depends on postulating some appropriate form of the utility function of income.

Although some of these assumptions may strike you as implausible, note that the assumption that all benefit *equally*, so the £100 should be distributed on a straight *per capita* basis, implicitly makes the *additional* assumption that $MU_m^A = MU_m^B$. The great virtue of the Aaron and McGuire approach is that it lays bare the assumptions underlying any attempt to allocate the benefits of public goods to individuals. The problems in making such an attribution of benefit, such as determining what part of a service is public and what private or comparing different marginal utilities, are not problems only of the Aaron and McGuire analysis but of *all* distributional studies that attempt to allocate the benefits of public goods. Merely assuming *public* goods to be *private* is, of course, no solution at all.

Final Incidence of Costs and Benefits

The second set of arbitrary elements in these redistribution studies arises from their incidence assumptions. Le Grand assumes that the receipt of health benefit has no further 'second round' effects on income and consumption. Pechman, Hansen and Weisbrod assume not only that receipt of educational benefits does not have similar effects but that tax payments have no incentive or disincentive effects on the propensity to earn income and hence on the pattern of consumption. It is clearly arbitrary to cut off consideration of second round—and further round—effects.

Consider a two-person community in which, after a redistribution has taken place, A has £2,000 income and B £1,000. The redistribution, we shall suppose, has taken the form of £500 taken in income tax from A and given as an income deficiency payment to B (that is, we assume that the 'government' (a) operates costlessly, (b) balances its budget, (c) has no other functions). It would almost certainly be false to say that A is £500 worse off and B £500 better off as a result of the redistribution. It will almost certainly be false to say that total income after the redistribution (£3,000) was the same as the income previously available for redistribution. If the £500 tax on A is to imply that his income would be £2,500 had no redistribution taken place, then it must be assumed that his choice of amount of work to do to earn the income is independent of what he expects to take home. On the face of it, that is unlikely. But if he works less for the same wage after the tax than he would have without tax, then he is (a) losing more than £500 to B (though he is only paying £500); (b) gaining some benefit by not working as much as he did before, thereby reducing his loss; (c) reducing his contribution to the total value of physical output in the economy. Conversely, consider B. If we are to infer that his no-redistribution income would have been £500 we must also be assuming that his choice of working hours is independent of money receipts. Suppose, however, that after the redistribution he also works less than he would have if no redistribution took place, then he is (a) gaining in net money terms less than the £500 transferred from A; (b) gaining more leisure than he would have otherwise have had; (c) reducing his contribution to national output.

Similar problems relate, of course, to other forms of taxation. The redistribution effects of £500 taken from A and given to B as an income deficiency payment will, it is to be expected, vary according as the £500 is removed from A by income tax, wealth tax, excise tax, a reduction in educational expenditures on A's children, etc. Moreover, in complex societies, there is a large number of complicated interrelationships among the decisions made by a single individual and also between the various individuals in the society. With benefits that are given in kind, there is a problem of valuing their worth to those who receive them. Enough has surely been said, however, to convince the reader of the great complexity of the analysis and measurement of the incidence of income tax and subsidies.

Another example will illustrate the kind of issue involved in trying to pin down the true incidence as distinct from the apparent incidence of taxes on goods. Consider the tax side only and suppose that a benefit is being financed by an indirect tax. Figure 5.4 shows in panel (a) the supply and

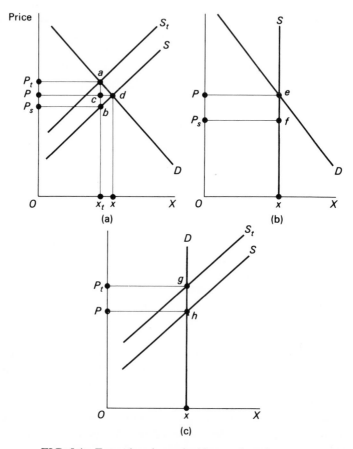

FIG. 5.4   Formal and true incidence of a sales tax.

demand curves for a good X. The initial price of X is P. A constant per unit sales tax is now placed on X equal to $P_t - P_s$. In panel (a) the price rises by $P_t - P$ (less than the amount of the tax), quantity consumed falls to x_t from x, and total tax paid is $P_t ab P_s$. Consumers pay $P_t ac P$ of this tax and, in addition, lose acd, which is the excess value of the X they no longer consume over and above what they would have paid for it at the old price. Producers pay $Pcb P_s$ and, in addition, lose cdb which is the extra they would have received at the old price less what it would have cost them to produce it. Clearly, the assumption that the tax 'take' represents the cost of providing the service is a special one: if the demand curves slope down (as they do) and supply curves slope up (as they often do) then the tax 'take' *understates* the cost of public provision. Moreover, if demand elasticities differ as between income groups, and different goods vary in the amount and type of labour they employ, then the reduction in consumption and in employment may have important redistributive effects that are not included in the analysis.

Panels (b) and (c) illustrate cases where these problems do not arise. In panel (b), supply is wholly unresponsive to price changes so price to suppliers falls, after the tax, to P_s but demand remains at x. The tax 'take' is $PefP_s$ but output and price remain the same. In this case the tax is paid entirely by the suppliers of the taxed commodity. The tax 'take' measures the loss to suppliers correctly and there are no unemployment, etc., consequences. In panel (c), demand is wholly unresponsive to price changes. In this case the tax 'take' $(P_t ghP)$ again measures the cost (but this time borne entirely by consumers paying the higher price) and there are, again, no output effects on employment. It thus becomes clear that implicit in the treatment of incidence in the studies described are embodied some strange and highly unrealistic assumptions.

C. Redistributive Effects of the Whole Public Sector

It will be obvious that the difficulties discussed above in connection with relatively limited studies of redistribution are going to be substantially amplified in more comprehensive assessments of the redistributive impact of the entire government budget. An obvious major one consists in the fact that such an exercise is essentially comparing the existing post-tax–post-expenditure distribution with one imagined to exist *in the absence* of a public sector. Whichever way one conceives of doing this—either assessing the effect of introducing a public sector into a purely private economy, or removing a public sector from an economy that already includes it—it is clear that one is in part writing conjectural history. For many economists, this alone is sufficient to dismiss the exercise as valueless. Why, then, this section? There are basically two answers to that. First, such studies continue to be made and a complete account of work in the redistributive field must therefore take account of them. Second, the question such studies seek to answer never fails to be asked. Therefore, if one is to deny its answerability, it is as well to be acquainted with the method used in attempts that have been made to answer it.

A fully comprehensive treatment of redistribution in modern societies ought properly to start with the analysis of what determines the *pre-tax/subsidy* distribution of income and wealth among families. This, for reasons of space rather than any issue of principle, will not be covered here. Moreover we shall continue not to be concerned with the redistribution of wealth, but rather with personal incomes. This latter approach is adopted primarily because of the nature of the data with which we shall be dealing and because our aim in this chapter continues to be the analysis of techniques rather than the detailed analysis of actual distribution and re-distribution in any one country. But the procedure remains, in principle, undesirable because of the close connection between income and wealth. It can also lead us seriously astray in our interpretations if we concentrate on the redistribution of incomes received during a time period (usually a year), for even a person who owns little physical capital may have human capital of considerable value with a relatively low flow of current income in the time period considered. For example, it is generally the case that annual incomes of educated employees in employment rise steadily to a peak at the age of 55 but may begin (at the age, say, of 21) at a lower level than less trained or educated manpower of the same age. Suppose, now, that a prime concern of social policy was to reduce the inequality of economic power between individuals (or families). By looking only at current earnings one might conclude as a result that incomes ought to be redistributed from the older to the younger individuals with similar job qualifications, and from the less educated to the more educated for younger persons of similar ages. Both inferences would be false, because on average the human wealth of the young is greater than that of the old with similar job qualifications and the human wealth of the young educated person is greater than that of the young less-educated person. Ideally, one should take expected lifetime earnings, suitably discounted in the case of future earnings to allow for the lesser value people place on future income relative to the here and now, as one's unit of measurement as suggested above by Pechman (1970). Unfor-tunately, in practice this is at present not possible. In using current income data, whether earned or 'unearned', the reader is therefore warned about the inherent dangers in making inferences about the direction of the desired distribution. Present value calculations of future earnings, however, could also mislead even if they were possible since lower income groups are far more constrained in the extent to which they can borrow against future income.

Another set of difficulties arises in connection with the kind of redistrib-ution considered. In modern societies, the redistribution of incomes is an exceedingly complex business. Flows from individuals into the budget of government can occur through income and wealth taxation, through indir-ect taxation, through the sale of government produced goods and services, through inflation[4] and through several other means as well. Similarly, the benefits provided by the government go to special pressure groups (e.g. farmers, intellectuals); to special interest groups (the sick, the old); to everyone out of necessity in the case of mostly public goods (such as defence, law and order). In short, resources are collected from and distributed to a motley collection of individuals, both horizontally and vertically with respect to income classes. Moreover, the form in which resources are redistributed, though mostly in money on the revenue side, takes the form of both money and of goods and services in kind on the expenditure side. Clearly the task of identifying the individuals who contribute and who receive, and the respective amounts contributed and received, is a formidable one.

Yet further difficulties relate to the concept as well as the measurement of the changes that occur in the economic position of individuals as a consequence of redistribution. In any society, either a set of redistributive results occurs or it does not. If it does, one naturally seeks to assess what its effects have been and to do so one needs to know what the distribution of incomes would have been if the redistribution that took place had not taken place. But this is by no means a simple task. One of the functions of government, as has been seen above, is to provide public goods and these certainly have redistributive impact. But the pre- and post-redistribution comparison is not as simple as imagining that currently publicly produced public goods were previously produced in the private sector. It may not be possible for them to be produced in the private sector, or not on the same scale. But if this is so, then redistribution cannot be considered to take place out of a constant total community income—redistribution cannot be considered apart from production. Moreover, even supposing this problem had been solved somehow and supposing also that a definition of 'income' to be used had been decided upon, one would still require, as we saw above, first a theory and measurement of the incidence of taxes and, second, a theory and measurement of the incidence of expenditures.

Finally, there remains the problem of defining the basic units of analysis—income and the unit receiving the income. The definition of income most commonly employed by economists is that it is 'potential consumption' in the sense of the value of consumption that is possible in any time period without reducing the value of his wealth. This definition has the advantage of measuring the total potential increase in a person's wealth during the time period (if he consumed nothing it would be his actual increase), or his 'economic power'. It has, however, the disadvantage of not corresponding to the Inland Revenue definition, which, for example, excludes unrealised capital gains.

As far as the income unit is concerned, the natural unit to take is that within which incomes are shared. The basic unit is naturally the nuclear family of adults and their children but the question arises as to how far to include other household members (where a household is defined as in the Family Expenditure Survey as persons 'living at the same address having meals together and with common housekeeping') such as married children, elderly persons, or lodgers living with the nuclear family. If the fundamental concern in redistribution or poverty is with 'economic power', the choice would seem to depend upon the extent to which incomes were actually shared within households. If they were not shared very extensively, poverty among e.g. the elderly will be understated by using the household as the unit. In general the best definition seems to be the nuclear family. Intra-household 'transfers' outside the nuclear family should therefore be treated as separate sources of income for those additional household members. In practice, however, one must often take households or tax units as the unit since that is the basis on which data are available.

In investigating empirically the redistributive effects of the government at the most general level, the effects of all government activities would be considered. For example, ideally one would include an assessment of the distribution (by family income class) of expenditure on defence, roads, agriculture, museums and art galleries. Alternatively, even though all these government activities have—and are sometimes intended to have—redistributive effects, one might take a narrower view and assess the redistributive effects of 'social policy', in which case, of course, one faces the problem of defining the activities that are held to constitute 'social policy'.

Income Redistribution in the UK, 1977

The concept of income used by the British Central Statistical Office (CSO) in its studies of redistribution is derived from the Family Expenditive Survey of about 7,000 households. Original income is household income in cash and kind before the deduction of those taxes and before the addition of those state benefits which are included in the analysis. It excludes all of the employers' social security contributions (treated as an indirect tax), all corporation tax and capital gains. Income in kind included consists primarily of an imputed value of income from housing for people in rent-free and owner-occupied accommodation. The data for original income in 1977 are shown by decile in Table 5.5.

The assumptions implicitly made about the incidence of taxes and benefits were rather extreme and were as follows: income tax was assumed to fall entirely upon the individual taxpayer; employers' social security contributions to fall entirely upon consumers; indirect taxes on final and intermediate goods were assumed to be passed on fully in higher prices (and thus to consumers). On this basis the figures in row 4 of Table 5.5 were derived showing how the amount of tax paid rises with income.

On the benefit side, a far more restricted set of items of expenditure was included in the CSO study, viz. family allowances, pensions and other cash benefits such as educational scholarships; imputed values of state education services, the National Health Service and welfare foods, and indirect benefits such as housing subsidies. The cash benefits were what respon-

TABLE 5.5 *Income, Taxes and Benefits, and Redistribution, UK, 1977* (£)

	Lowest 1	2	3	4	Deciles of original income 5	6	7	8	9	Highest 10
1. Household original income	20	392	1442	2703	3607	4411	5194	6096	7392	11079
Tax payments										
2. Direct Taxes[a]	1	15	168	461	660	893	1060	1306	1637	2749
3. Indirect Taxes[b]	277	328	514	673	755	857	966	1056	1242	1557
4. Total	278	343	682	1134	1415	1750	2026	2362	2879	4306
Benefits										
5. Cash[c]	1358	1186	1002	553	370	285	251	238	219	219
6. Kind[d]	387	414	483	571	609	669	671	670	755	805
7. Price Subsidies[e]	226	143	135	129	102	101	100	86	90	94
8. Total	1971	1743	1620	1253	1081	1055	1022	994	1064	1118
9. Fiscal Residual (8–4)	+1693	+1400	+938	+119	−334	−695	−1004	−1368	−1815	−3188
10. Income After Taxes and Benefits	1713	1792	2380	2822	3273	3716	4190	4728	5577	7891

Source: Central Statistical Office *Economic Trends*, January 1978, Table 3, p. 116.

[a] Taxes on income only. Corporation tax, taxes on wealth and gifts excluded.
[b] Rates, import duties, taxes on beer, wines and spirits, VAT, oil and other intermediate taxes such as employers' contributions to national insurance.
[c] Includes child benefit, pensions and unemployment and other direct cash benefits.
[d] Includes education, health and welfare funds.
[e] Including subsidies on council houses, rail travel and food.

dents stated the households received over a twelve-month period. Educational benefits in kind were valued at cost according to the type of education being received and according to the number of persons receiving it in each household. Benefits from the National Health Service were also valued at cost to the health services and were allocated among households according to (a) children born during the period, (b) number of children, (c) adults below retirement age, and (d) adults over normal retirement age ((a) being based on the current cost of maternity services, and (b), (c) and (d) according to rough estimates of the extent to which different age groups make use of the service). School meals and other welfare foods were allocated according to the number of children and the cost was calculated net of household contributions. Housing subsidies (the difference between current expenditure by local authorities on housing and the rents paid by tenants) were estimated separately for each local authority dwelling in the sample.

The aggregate effect of these benefits is shown in row 8 of Table 5.5 and reveals a far less strong relation with original income. The net redistributive effect is presented in row 9, showing an apparently quite strong progressive element in the net redistribution, with the richest 10 per cent of households losing, in net terms, 29 per cent of their original income and the poorest 10 per cent gaining, in net terms, 85 per cent on theirs.

Figure 5.5 shows two Lorenz curves for the pre- and post-redistribution

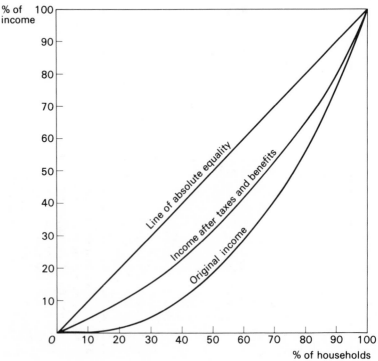

FIG. 5.5   Lorenz curves pre- and post-redistribution, UK, 1977.

data of Table 5.5. The Gini coefficient of the pre-redistribution incomes is 0.425 and that for the post-redistribution incomes is 0.258 indicating a substantial move toward equality. Inspection of Table 5.5 indicates that cash benefits were chiefly responsible. The most significant element here is the high proportion of retired households in the lowest decile who are wholly dependent upon state pensions.

Table 5.5 also shows how apparently regressive are benefits in kind. As will be recalled from earlier discussion, not all desired redistribution is vertical. Horizontal redistribution, in response to special needs (often cor-related with the number of children in the household), is clearly indicated in row 6 of Table 5.5.

The average original income in 1977 was £4,234 whereas the average post-redistribution income was only £3,808. A major reason for this discrepancy is that while the calculations embrace a large part of the tax side of the budget, a substantial part of the expenditure side is omitted. This demonstrates the limited coverage of this CSO study, which attempts only to cover the redistributive effects of 'social services' narrowly defined, plus cash transfers to persons, on the one hand and personal taxation on the other.

There are clearly good reasons why one may be concerned to assess the *overall* impact of government policy on the distribution of incomes. The chief of these is that it is the net result of all policies, taken together, for individual families or households that is normally the object of concern in redistribution. One may also, however, be concerned to assess the redistrib-utive impact of policies that are designed to be redistributive or that are defined as falling within the sphere of 'social' policy. The area of 'social' policy has smudgy edges (if it has any at all), which will tend to vary from commentator to commentator and does not, accordingly, commend itself. The identification of policies that are, in part or in whole, designed to be or regarded as redistributive is, perhaps, less difficult. The best approach, on this view of the purpose of the exercise, would probably be to examine each policy individually to discover the extent to which it contributes to redis-tribution and whether it is progressive or regressive. What the CSO study has done, in effect, is to combine all policies that are thought to have—or that ought to have—strong redistributive effects, and to assess their joint effect. It concentrates on the deliberately redistributive effects of the state. Redistribution in its broadest sense might properly include transfers that take place in the private sector, especially if the redistributive effects of 'social' policy are being considered (which might include, for example, private and occupational pension schemes).

For some purposes it may be desired to construct a 'social welfare budget' in which the redistributive effects of the social services (or 'social' policy) are examined in connection with the means that are used to finance them and only them. The social welfare budget implies, since most taxation is general and not earmarked for specific spending purposes, that some assumptions must be made about the proportion of tax proceeds being devoted to the categories of spending being considered. An obvious assumption of this sort is to suppose that social services are financed out of total taxation (net of earmarked taxes) in the same proportions that their costs (net of earmarked receipts) occupy in total expenditure. Presumably, the social welfare budget would be balanced or unbalanced as the total budget was balanced or unbalanced. Alternatively it could be adjusted to balance, with the rest of the government's budget bearing the whole of the overall surplus or deficit.

Whatever solution is adopted to these problems there still remain the two great conceptual difficulties mentioned before of studies of this kind. The first concerns the possibility of more realistic estimates of the incidence of taxes and benefits. The second is the more fundamental one and is, to some, decisive in rendering results such as those in Table 5.5 meaningless, namely that the conjectural history involved in supposing what things would be like *without* the budget is simply not capable of relevant quantification. Caution in interpretation is therefore the order of the day.

Income Redistribution in the USA, 1960

The problem of 'conjectural history' is not capable of resolution. It is, however, possible to make sensible adjustments based upon research into the empirical estimation of the incidence of taxes and benefits. A classic and pioneering study of this sort was Gillespie's (1965) analysis of redistribution in the USA for 1960. This work, together with his more recent analysis of income redistribution in Canada (Gillespie, 1976) are models for how to proceed with such analysis.

Gillespie used a variety of income concepts for measuring the changes in the economic position of families. The concept of income used in the results reported here was hypothetical income in the absence of a public sector, comprising family money income plus capital gains and retained earnings, part of corporation profits tax, part of the employers' social security contribution and imputed rental values of owner-occupied homes, plus own produce consumed by farmers, less all personal transfer payments. In common with other empirical students of income redistribution, Gillespie ignored the logical difficulties in assuming that abolition of the public sector does not affect the private sector's ability to produce the same goods, but some of the dangers inherent in simple arithmetical manipulations were met, so far as possible, by using the results of incidence studies of corporation tax and employers' social security payments. Thus, some studies have indicated that the effect of the imposition of corporation tax is partly to raise prices (shifting some of the burden of the tax on to consumers) and partly to reduce shareholders' incomes. Consequently, Gillespie allocated an estimated one-third borne by consumers to taxpayers according to the distribution of consumption expenditure by income and the rest to taxpayers according to the distribution of dividend earnings by income class. One-half of the employers' social security contribution was distributed among wage earners and the other half (through its effect on prices) was distributed among taxpayers according to consumption by income class. Individual income tax was assumed to fall entirely on the individual paying tax; excise taxes were assumed to be passed on entirely to consumers and sales taxes were assumed to be shifted to consumption goods.

On this basis, the percentage figures in rows 3, 4 and 5 in Table 5.6 were derived, showing that both federal and especially state and local taxation are in general remarkably regressive—the proportion of income taken in tax falls as incomes rise. The regressivity arises mainly from the highly regressive incidence of social security contributions and indirect taxes. Frequently, however, a regressive tax structure is unavoidable at the lower end of the income distribution. For example, a family living entirely on income transfers (which are excluded from our income base) will pay some tax (e.g. sales tax on purchases of consumer goods), which could be an infinite proportion of original income! Consequently, it is sometimes misleading to look only at the progression of the tax side of the budget—an overall view must be taken, including expenditures.

TABLE 5.6   *Percentage Income Paid in Tax, Received in Benefit and Net Change, USA, 1960*

	Under $2,000	$2,000 – $2,999	$3,000 – $3,999	$4,000 – $4,999	$5,000 – $7,499	$7,500 – $9,999	$10,000 and over	Total (weighted)
				Family money income brackets				
1. Families	14	9	9	11	28	15	14	100
2. Family money income	2	4	5	8	28	20	33	100
Tax payments								
3. Federal	37.8	42.0	33.6	28.1	20.8	15.7	26.6	23.9
4. State & local	26.2	25.1	18.0	17.4	12.4	7.1	5.3	9.8
5. Total	64.1	67.2	51.6	45.5	33.2	22.8	31.9	33.7
Benefits								
6. Federal	174.7	56.4	34.6	22.0	17.1	15.7	15.3	20.9
7. State & local	126.1	52.9	25.7	18.3	12.2	8.5	5.4	12.8
8. Total	300.8	109.3	60.3	40.3	29.3	24.2	20.7	33.7
9. Net change in original income	+236.7	+42.1	+8.7	−5.2	−3.9	+1.4	−11.2	0.0

Source: Gillespie (1965) Tables 3, 5, 6 and 11.
Note: items may not add to totals due to rounding.

Benefits from public expenditures were valued at cost and divided up among the various income classes as follows: highway expenditures were allocated among consumers of passenger travel, consumers of transported goods and non-users (such as adjacent property owners); education expenditures among the families of pupils and students according to the stage of education completed; public health and housing expenditures were allocated according to presumptions about who benefited from them—for example, immunisation expenditures (which are largely public goods) were allocated according to family distribution, and sewage control by a weighted average of owner-occupied and rented housing units; social security benefits were allocated according to the distribution of the income classes of recipients; agricultural support expenditures according to the estimated incidence of these benefits—for example, partly to consumers (a negative gain), partly to farmers (positive gain), partly to the nation (as the value of surplus production) and partly to taxpayers (another negative gain). General expenditures (such as national defence) were allocated according to the distribution of original income. The possibility that, in a society with no public sector, the private sector might increase the rate of its own transfer expenditures was ignored.

The net result of the various calculations implied by the foregoing produced the distributions shown in rows 6, 7 and 8 of Table 5.6, which are quite strongly progressive in their effects (in the sense that benefits fall as a proportion of income as the latter increases). The net effect on redistribution of governmental activities is shown in row 9, from which it appears that the redistribution produced net gains to those with incomes up to $3,999 and net losses to those in higher income classes, with the exception of those in the $7,500–9,999 group. The main redistribution would appear to have taken place from the richest 14 per cent of families (having 33 per cent of total family money incomes) to the poorest 23 per cent (who had 6 per cent of total money oncomes). A striking oddity is that not only was the net incidence of redistribution regressive in the $4,000–10,000 brackets but that those 15 per cent of all families, with 20 per cent of all money incomes, in the $7,500–$9,999 bracket actually received net gains from redistribution.

Total tax collection in 1960 amounted to $134,147 millions with expenditures of $133,595 millions. The existence of this small budget surplus, with not all collections being disbursed, implies that the post-redistribution of incomes was lower (at least over some ranges) than it would have been with a balanced budget. Had the surplus been distributed proportionately, would the post-redistribution distribution over all income simply have been shifted upward? Would a similar effect have occurred if the excess taxes had not been collected, on a proportionate basis? The answer depends upon the effect that budget surpluses and deficits have upon the price levels of different commodities subject to tax and the level of employment that changes earned incomes for different classes, an analysis of which is beyond the scope of the study. In general, however, one would not expect a mere vertical shift of the post-redistribution distribution. One would expect it even less in view of the improbability that the surplus would have been spent in the same proportions as the original distribution.

NOTES

1. The formula is

$$\frac{(Y_1 - T_1) - (Y_0 - T_0)}{(Y_0 - T_0)} \cdot \frac{Y_0}{Y_1 - Y_0}$$

where Y_0 and T_0 are lower levels of income and tax and Y_1 and T_1 the higher levels.

2. For purposes of calculation, the following version of the formula is easier to handle:

$$G = 1 + \frac{1}{n} - \frac{2}{n^2\mu}(y_1 + 2y_2 + 3y_3 + \cdots + ny_n)$$

where y is the highest income, y_2 the next highest, etc.

3. The sensitivy of the Gini coefficient depends not on the size of the household income levels but on the number of households lying between the two being compared. As Sen (1973) shows, if A has an income of £2,000 and B of £1,900, and if A is the 1,000th richest household and B the 1,100th richest, then £1.00 to B is taken as equivalent to £1.10 to A since the weights are the rank order of the household in the distribution. But if some 100 new immigrants now get incomes between £1,900 and £2,000, then the Gini coefficient would give the same weight to £1.00 of A's income as to £1.20 of B's.

4. An illuminating discussion of the effects of inflation upon redistribution is by Alchian (1968). He argues persuasively that inflation *per se* does not discriminate among social or economic classes of persons (though the manner in which it is generated may do so) but that it discriminates against *all* net monetary creditors.

QUESTIONS ON CHAPTER 5

1. What criteria would you employ to decide whether one distribution was more equal than another?
2. What is Pen's Parade?
3. Define the variance and the coefficient of variation. What are the advantages and disadvantages of these summary measures of distributions?
4. Define the Gini coefficient and explain its relationship to the Lorenz curve.
5. Define Atkinson's measure of inequality.
6. What is the relation between socio-economic status and the prevalence of sickness in the UK (or some other country)?

7. Is a 'time price' a fairer allocation device than a money price?
8. What is the relation between income class and the consumption of education in California (or some other place)?
9. How would you allocate the benefits of public goods in a study of distribution or redistribution?
10. When will a 10 per cent tax on a commodity cause its price to rise by 10 per cent?
11. Who pays social security contributions: employees, employers, or both? What factors determine the answer?
12. Do redistribution studies necessarily involve the writing of conjectural history? If so, how serious a problem does this create?
13. What unit is best used in redistribution studies: individuals, families or households?
14. What incidence assumptions do the CSO studies make?
15. What incidence assumptions does Gillespie's study make?
16. How does inflation affect the distribution of income?
17. Which is more important: the distribution of income, wealth or specific types of consumption?
18. If education makes people richer than the average over their lifetimes, is it fair to subsidise it?
19. Is the distribution of income becoming more or less equal in your country?
20. Who benefits most from public spending on:
    (a) defence
    (b) law and order
    (c) education
    (d) roads
    (e) cleaner air?

FURTHER READING

On measures of inequality:

Atkinson, A. B. (1970) On the measurement of inequality. *Journal of Economic Theory*, 2, pp. 244–63.
Atkinson, A. B. (1975) *The Economics of Inequality.* Oxford: Clarendon Press.
Cowell, F. A. (1977) *Measuring Inequality.* Oxford: Philip Allan.
Pen, J. (1971) *Income Distribution.* London: Allen Lane, The Penguin Press.
Sawyer, M. (1976) Income distribution in OECD countries. In *OECD Economic Outlook Occasional Studies.* Paris: OECD.
Sen, A. K. (1973) *On Economic Inequality.* Oxford: Clarendon Press.
Stark, T. (1977) *The Distribution of Income in Eight Countries.* Royal Commission on the Distribution of Income and Wealth, Background Paper No. 4, London: HMSO.
Wiles, P. (1974) *Distribution of Income: East and West.* Amsterdam: North-Holland.

On benefit incidence:

In view of its importance, the literature is depressingly thin. The best pieces are probably:

Aaron, H. and McGuire, M. (1970) Public goods and income distribution. *Econometrica, 38,* pp. 907–20.

Hansen, W. L. and Weisbrod, B. A. (1969) *Benefits, Costs and Finances of Public Higher Education.* Chicago: Markham.

Judy, R. (1970) The income distributive effects of aid to higher education. In L. H. Officer and L. B. Smith, (eds) *Canadian Economic Problems and Policies.* New York: McGraw Hill.

Klein, R., Barnes, J., Buxton, M. and Craven, E. (1974) *Social Policy and Public Expenditure 1974.* London: Centre for Studies in Social Policy.

Le Grand J. (1978) The distribution of public expenditure: the case of health care. *Economica, 45,* pp. 125–42.

Pechman, J. A. (1970) The distributional effects of public higher education in California. *Journal of Human Resources, 5,* pp. 361–70.

Rein, M. (1969) Social class and the utilisation of medical care services: a study of British experience. *Hospitals, 43,* pp. 43–54.

On budget effects:

Alchian, A. A. (1968) Inflation and distribution of income and wealth. In J. Marchal and B. Ducros (eds) *The Distribution of National Income.* London: Macmillan.

Central Statistical Office (1979) The effects of taxes and benefits on household income, 1977. *Economic Trends,* January, pp. 97–130.

Gillespie, W. I. (1965) Effect of public expenditures on the distribution of income. In Musgrave R. A. (ed.) *Essays in Fiscal Federalism.* Washington DC: Brookings Institution.

Gillespie, W. I. (1976) On the redistribution of income in Canada. *Canadian Tax Journal, 24,* pp. 419–50.

Michelson, S. (1970) The economics of real income distribution. *Review of Radical Political Economics,* Spring, pp. 75–86.

Mieszkowski, P. (1969) Tax incidence theory: the effects of taxes on the distribution of income. *Journal of Economic Literature, 7,* pp. 1103–24.

Musgrave, R. A., Case, K. E. and Leonard, H. (1974) The distribution of fiscal burdens and benefits. *Public Finance Quarterly, 2,* pp. 259–312.

Nicholson, J. L. (1964) Redistribution of income in the UK in 1959, 1957 and 1953. In C. Clark and G. Stuvel, (eds) *Income and Wealth,* series X. London: Bowes.

Peacock, A. T. (1977) The treatment of government expenditure in studies of income redistribution. In W. Smith and J. Culbertson, (eds) *Public Finance and Stabilisation Policy,* Amsterdam: North-Holland.

Peacock, A. T. and Shannon, J. R. (1968) The welfare state and the redistribution of income. *Westminster Bank Review,* August, pp. 30–46.

Prest, A. R. (1967) The budget and interpersonal distribution. *Public Finance, 23,* pp. 80–98.

Titmuss, R. M. (1962) *Income Distribution and Social Change.* London: Allen and Unwin.

CHAPTER 6

Poverty and Income Maintenance

A. CONCEPTS OF POVERTY

There are, as the externality discussions of chapter 3 would lead one to expect, two broad views as to what poverty is: that it relates on the one hand to the *absolute* rate of consumption by some set of individuals and, on the other, that it relates to the *relative* deprivation of individuals. The majority view, at least in Britain, is 'that poverty is a condition under which people are unable to obtain subsistence, as the basic necessities of life, or is a condition which applies to particular low-income minorities, such as pensioners or the unemployed' (Townsend, 1979, p. 914). Townsend goes on: it is 'a severely limited conception of need, fostered by motives of condescension and self-interest as well as duty by the rich' (p. 914).

Put (unflatteringly) like this, it is clear that the source of the concept of poverty is an externality: some individuals (the relatively rich) prefer that others should not live at a particular low standard. It is a matter of the *preferences* of the relatively rich. But there is also an alternative view, independent of the predilections of any class in society, which would seek the definition of poverty in the idea of social justice: poverty is the standard of life that it is unjust that individuals should have to tolerate. For example, in a Rawlsian conceptual experiment, if all would come to the same conclusion behind the 'veil of ignorance' that certain minima (which may be relative to an average standard of life, or to the standard enjoyed by the wealthiest) ought to be guaranteed each member of society, then anyone falling below such a level may be described as being in poverty.

The definition of poverty may therefore be founded in preferences or in ethics. But it must, inescapably, involve *values*: whether values based on preferences or values based on ethical principles. It is no part of our task here to take sides in any of these issues. Given the political heat, however, that discussion of policy towards poverty can engender, it is as well to be aware that fundamental differences of perspective do exist as regards poverty's absoluteness or relativity and as regards its source, whether in a theory of social justice or in the preferences of members of society. As we noticed in the discussion of need, policy probably reflects both types of concern.

The search for a minimum subsistence level of income in any technical sense has proved unproductive. Even for fundamentals such as food, individuals' requirements for 'efficient' work depend on the nature of the work, their age and a diversity of other factors. The analysis of previous chapters suggests, however, that even had it been possible to identify technical 'needs' in this way, and to administer the exceedingly complicated schedule of benefits that would have resulted, these 'needs' would not necessarily have been the subsistence level that society would, in the event, have accepted for its minimum standard. To be sure, such information would have been of help to people making up their minds as to what the level ought to have been, but the truth is that a technological (or biological) approach to what is a social problem is not, of itself, enough. The resolution of a social problem depends upon the resolution of conflicting views (values, if you like) of what and how much ought to be done to alleviate hardship.

For practical purposes, those seeking to escape postulating their own preferences or appealing to their own preferred theory of justice to obtain a definition of poverty often take, as an *objectively revealed* definition, the levels of benefit embodied in social security programmes by government. They are objectively revealed, but they are revelations (doubtless imperfect) of some aggregated general view held *subjectively* by members of society and interpreted, in democracy, by politicians pursuing their own interests.

There are several estimates of the number of persons in poverty in the UK, using Supplementary Benefit (SB) criteria (or the National Assistance that preceded it). Among early pioneering studies, Brian Abel-Smith and Peter Townsend (1965) estimated 3.8 per cent persons and 4.7 per cent households in 1960 (0.9 per cent and 1.3 per cent respectively had incomes below 4/5ths of the Scale). A. B. Atkinson (1969) has estimated 3.4 per cent persons below the line in 1969. These estimates are all, owing to their reliance on Family Expenditure Survey data, likely to be underestimates, being based on household units and a concept of 'normal' rather than current income (people out of work for less than three months are considered to receive their 'normal' income).

Table 6.1 shows some estimates based upon Inland Revenue data. The data are likely to be overestimates owing to incentives to underreport income; despite being based on the nuclear family, a number of assumptions had to be made about, e.g., unchanging family composition during the financial year.

More up-to-date information about the types of household in poverty in Britain was provided in the report of the Royal Commission on the Distribution of Income (1978b) based on the General Household Survey in 1975. This shows that the most important category of those in poverty, using either the SB level as a benchmark or 20 per cent above this level, were the elderly. In 1978 about 25 per cent of the British population lived at or below 140 per cent of the SB level of income.

TABLE 6.1   *Families and Persons with Incomes below National Assistance Scales*

Year	Families[a] with incomes below NA Scales '000s	%	Persons with incomes below NA Scales '000s	%
1954	3,800	14.8	6,294	12.3
1959	2,584	10.0	4,607	8.8
1963	3,103	11.7	5,077	9.4

Source: Gough and Stark (1968), Table IV and footnote 1 on p. 179.
[a] Families are Inland Revenue Tax Units adjusted so far as possible to include the head, spouse and dependent children only—i.e. the 'nuclear' family.

TABLE 6.2   *British Household Types in Poverty in 1975 ('000s)*

	Income at or below SB level No.	%	Income between SB level and 120% SB level No.	%	Income between SB level and 140% SB level No.	%
Elderly						
couple	620	13.5	860	19.5	710	14.6
single man	200	4.4	160	3.6	110	2.3
single woman	1,370	29.8	680	15.4	410	8.4
Married couples						
no children	230	5.0	160	3.6	310	6.4
1 child	120	2.6	280	6.3	450	9.2
2 children	350	7.6	590	13.3	980	20.1
3 children	280	6.1	440	10.0	780	16.0
4 children	230	5.0	360	8.1	280	5.7
5 or more children	220	4.8	280	6.3	260	5.3
Single parents	670	14.6	340	7.7	210	4.3
Single households						
man	140	3.1	110	2.5	140	2.9
woman	160	3.5	160	3.6	230	4.7
Total	4,590	100.0	4,420	99.9	4,870	99.9

Source: Maynard (1979), Table 12.1.

At this level (140 per cent of SB rates), note also that couples with two or three children accounted for over one quarter of poor households and, together with the elderly, made up over half of the total number of poor households.

More detailed information is available from Townsend's 1979 study of poverty in 1968–69, based upon a sample survey. Table 6.3 gives his estimates for each of three definitions of poverty: the SB definition, a relative income standard and a deprivation standard. The relative income standard defines the poverty line as being 50 per cent of the mean net disposable income of the household for each of fourteen household types.[1] The deprivation standard is harder to define. Townsend compiled an index of household characteristics such as: has not had a week's holiday from home in the past year, does not have fresh meat for as many as four days a week, has no refrigerator, does not usually have a cooked Sunday joint. While these characteristics may vary from one ethnic group to another, Townsend found some evidence that below certain income levels, the total index score increased 'disproportionately' and this critical income was the deprivation standard.

TABLE 6.3 *Households and Persons in Poverty in UK, 1968–69*

	% households	% population	Number of households (millions)	Number of (non-institutionalised) population (millions)
SB standard in poverty (100% or less of SB rates)	7.1	6.1	1.34	3.32
on margin of poverty (100–139% of SB rates)	23.8	21.8	4.50	11.86
Relative income standard in poverty (50% or less of mean income for household types)	10.6	9.2	2.00	5.00
on margin of poverty (50–79% of mean income for household types)	29.5	29.6	5.58	16.10
Deprivation standard in poverty	25.2	22.9	4.76	12.46

Source: Townsend (1979), Table 7.1

As would be expected, the number of households in poverty rises as one moves from the relatively ungenerous absolute standard of the SB rates through the relative income standard to the deprivation standard, with the latter standards increasingly reflecting caring preferences over the absolute requirements of social justice.

What is one to make of these various definitions? It is not for the social scientist to engage in advocacy as to what the proper definition *ought to be*. Our role as social scientists must be to explore and define the conceptual issues that are raised and to construct explanatory models giving an account of the causes of poverty and how it may be removed or reduced most effectively. Before turning to the causes of poverty and policy to combat it, let us therefore first examine some further central issues of concept. We shall select two for particular investigation: the construction of an index of relative deprivation, and the development of 'equivalence scales' of income for households of varying size. One thing common to both is that each is heavily imbued with value judgements—if we can isolate these for explicit consideration by policy makers, at least one substantial step forward will have been taken.

Relative Deprivation Index

There are three quite fundamental value judgements involved in the construction of an index of this type, which we shall take to be entirely based upon caring preferences:

(a) the choice of characteristics in which deprivation is to be measured, and their scaling;
(b) the *relative* valuation of combinations of the characteristics;
(c) the assigning of an index score to those combinations judged to be equivalent.

It is not, of course, usually the social scientists' job to assert any particular value judgements of his own. Few would (one hopes!) subscribe to the view of Ralph Turvey (and few—one hopes again—would wish to substitute for 'economists' other experts like 'social administrators', 'political scientists', 'sociologists' ...):

> My personal feeling is that the value-judgements made by economists are, by and large, better than those made by non-economists! ... The point is simply that the people who are experienced at systematic thinking about a problem are usually those who make the best judgements about it. Thus, whatever their theory of aesthetics, most people are prepared in practice to accept the judgement of an art critic about the merits of a painting. [R. Turvey, Present value versus internal rate of return. *Economic Journal, 73*, p. 96.]

Choice of characteristics in terms of which deprivation is to be measured is equivalent to listing those attributes of individuals (households, etc.) that are regarded as undesired—that impose an adverse externality on caring members of the population. Besides involving values, it is also a technical question, in the sense that some items may be left off the list of characteristics if they are highly correlated with others. For example, if two characteristics are 'at least one day without cooked meat in last two weeks' and 'no fresh meat most days of the week' (which are two of Townsend's listed on p. 1173) and households having the one characteristic also usually have the other, little is added to the index by having both. But the fact remains that the selection involves major value judgements—even if it also involves other kinds of judgement (such as a social scientist might properly make). The nature of the value judgements involved here is complex, for it involves not only views about what is undesirable, but also views about what may be undesirable for particular sections of the population (e.g. vegetarians are not 'deprived' by virtue of not eating fresh meat). This suggests that it may be desirable sometimes to construct class-specific or, more generally, culture-specific indexes, or else to select characteristics so basic to all cultures for the problem not to arise.

Scaling each characteristic (e.g. one meatless day in the last 3 weeks, 2 weeks, 1 week) is less a matter of values than of convenience. The value aspect of scaling really comes in at the next stage when degrees of deprivation are compared in each characteristic. Relative valuation of characteristics is required if they are to be combined in a single index. Often this stage is only *implicit* in the work of those who construct indexes. But it is worth considering *explicitly* in order to tease out the value issues involved. It is easiest to see these issues if we take a numerical example. Let us take two of the characteristics used in Townsend's index of deprivation: no week's holiday in last year, 2 years, 3 years, 4 years; and no fresh meat 2 days, 4 days, 6 days in the week. These characteristics and their associated scale points are shown in Figure 6.1. Individuals may be classified in any of

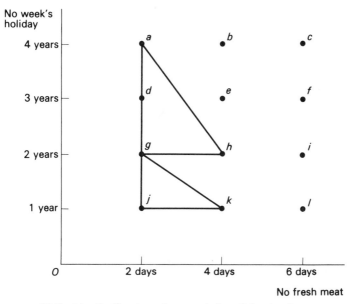

FIG. 6.1   Scaling two characteristics of deprivation.

the various combinations of these characteristics labelled *a*, *b*, *c*, etc. The value judgement that has to be made concerns the *relative* importance attached to these combinations: we want to partition the space in Figure 6.1 into combinations regarded as worse or better than others, with equivalent combinations lying on the borderline between. With larger numbers of characteristics and finer scaling of each, the greater the opportunity for identifying equivalent combinations.

Let us suppose that *g* is regarded as equivalent to *k*. We may safely assume that *h* is worse than either *g* or *k* by virtue of the fact that an individual at *k* is worse off in one dimension and is no better off in the other. More difficult is the relative valuation of *incremental* changes. Consider: if *g* and *k* are equally bad, then a change in deprivation from *j* to *g* or *j* to *k* will be equally deplorable. Now consider a move from, say, *g* to *d* or *h*. Given that *g* and *k* are equally bad, will a move from *g* to *d* be regarded as equally bad as a move from *g* to *h*? Not, of course, necessarily so: *d* may be regarded as either better or worse than *h*. Let us suppose that in fact *a* is regarded as equivalent to *h*. What does this imply? That two more days without meat per week are regarded as just as bad as no holiday for a second year when two days without meat and one year without holiday are the state of deprivation, but just as bad as *two more years without a holiday* when two years without holiday and two days without meat are the state of deprivation. In other words, in this case, the degree of importance attached to *further* deprivation increases as individuals are increasingly deprived.

This is a value judgement, but a subtle one. It implies that if the importance attached to incremental deprivation is not constant, one cannot assign numbers to the degrees of deprivation measured on the axes and simply add them up. In economic jargon, the rate of trade-off, as indicated by the triangles in Figure 6.1, varies with the amount of deprivation. (Compare the analysis of Figure 2.1.)

Assigning an index score is the final stage. Suppose we assumed, as in the second stage, that the equivalences were between *a* and *h* and *g* and *k*. We can now rank the following combinations:

$$a = h > g = k > j$$

and, of course *a* > *d*, therefore *h* > *d*, *d* > *g* as well as *c* > *b*, *c* > *f*, etc. These *ordinal* comparisons now need numbers to be attached to indicate *how much worse a* and *h* are compared with *g*, etc. Each of the pairs *a* and *h* and *g* and *k* will get the same number since they are equally bad. Once a number has been assigned to each combination, we shall have derived a *cardinal* index of deprivation incorporating a three-stage process of making value judgements. The index will not be 'objective'. But it will embody in *quantified* form the social value judgements made by whomever has compiled the index.

All such indexes embody these value judgements. They are inescapable. The important questions to ask when one comes across such indexes include: Were the value judgements clearly identified? What were they? Who made them? Were they the 'right' ones? Who *should* make them? The last two questions do not have answers in social science and are inherently controversial. But they cannot be properly asked, let alone answered, without answers to the first three questions—which *are* in the province of social science. Of course, the selection of particular values of the index as indicating poverty, whether by making an absolute judgement or by comparing the index with income levels and noting, as Townsend does, the 'kinks' in the relationship, involves the making of yet further value judgements, which are, perhaps, more transparently obvious than those we have more carefully teased out in this analysis and which are rarely explicitly brought out in statistics of deprivation.

Equivalence in Incomes and Consumption

Households are heterogeneous. The problem then arises of what income is equivalent in the sense of affording households of different sizes and composition (and possibly facing different prices of consumer goods) an equal standard of living.

The analysis of an index of deprivation shows the necessity for making value judgements about which combination of different degrees of deprivation in different dimensions are regarded as equivalent. Another kind of equivalence judgement is required in comparing households or families of different sizes or composition: for example, what level of income, or food consumption, is regarded as 'adequate' for a married couple aged 25 years and what for a middle-aged couple with five children?

In principle this judgement could be made by a direct interpersonal comparison by an external observer, whose own value judgements would be applied in much the same way as they are in the construction of an index of deprivation. Other attempts have included some to calculate minimal biological requirements of protein, calories, etc., for various types of person, to which reference has already been made, and a more interesting set of attempts, which we now briefly look at, to obtain estimates of what, behaviourally, is the equivalence between families and households of different size.

Let us consider the conceptual problems raised by this question by taking a concrete example. Consider two households differing only in size and composition. One is a married couple, the other a married couple with a child. Assume that a child consumes half as much food as a married couple but that no additional housing is needed by the child. These assumptions do not correspond exactly to reality but serve to illustrate

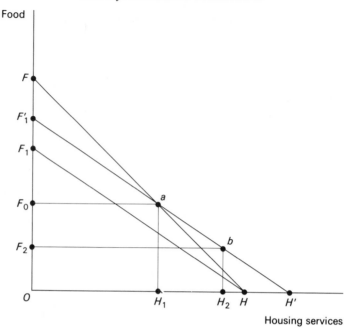

FIG. 6.2   Equivalent food and housing services consumed by childless couple.

problems arising from the fact that some household consumption is independent and additive while other consumption is joint. Figure 6.2 shows the combination of food and housing services consumed by the childless household. For convenience we assume that all income is spent on these two items of consumption only. Thus, given the average prices of food (p_f) and housing services (p_h) with a given income (Y_0), the maximum food purchasable is $Y_0/p_f = OF$ and the maximum housing services are $Y_0/p_h = OH$. With given prices, any point on the household budget line FH is attainable. We assume that the married couple has selected a, consuming OF_0 food and OH_0 housing services.

For the married couple with a child, the purchasing power of income over housing is the same as for the childless couple, but household food costs 50 per cent more, implying that with the same income only 2/3 of the *equivalent food consumption* is possible: OF_1 in Figure 6.2. The household budget line effectively becomes $F_1 H$ instead of FH. At this higher price of household food consumption we now ask what income would enable the larger household to consume at the same level as the childless couple. The answer is that income whose budget line $F_1' H'$ would enable the household to consume at point a in Figure 6.2.

But would the larger household, if given an income supplement equivalent to the childless household's income in purchasing power (budget line

$F_1' H'$), actually consume at point a? In general, we would expect not, for the relatively higher cost of food would cause some substitution away from food towards housing—to a point such as b to the south east along $F_1' H'$. The combination b cannot be regarded by the household as inferior to the combination a, for they could choose a if they wish. The combination OF_2 food and OH_2 housing for the larger family is not therefore inferior to OF_0 and OH_0 for the smaller (assuming them to have the same tastes for food and housing). In fact, we shall regard them as equivalent bundles.

Using this analysis we have thus shown that it is possible to identify (a) equivalent commodity consumption bundles for families of different composition and (b) equivalent incomes.

More generally, the amount of income that is equivalent, at the relatively high cost of food, to the income when family food costs were lower is the lower income multiplied by a Laspeyres, or base-weighted, quantity index:

$$Y_0 \times \frac{\sum P_1 Q_0}{\sum P_0 Q_0}$$

where Q_0 is the consumption bundle of the smaller family and P_1 and P_0 represent the prices of household consumption of each item for the larger and smaller family respectively. Thus, in Figure 6.2, if the income of the childless couple was 100, and p_f, p_h were 10 and 20, whereas prices of consumption for the larger household were 15 and 20, then the equivalent income can easily be calculated to be 120: 20 per cent more. This income does in fact correspond to budget line $F_1' H'$. Equivalent incomes can be quite easily computed, given the costs of acquiring equivalent consumption levels for each household.

Household consumption patterns, assuming similar basic preferences, can be seen from Figure 6.2 to consist of two basic components:

(a) the substitution effect causing a shift away from the relatively costlier items towards the cheaper (e.g. from a to b on $F_1' H'$) and
(b) the income effect caused by a generally lower or higher purchasing power if goods have become generally more or less expensive (e.g. from a point chosen on $F_1' H'$ to one on $F_1 H$).

If these two effects can be estimated (for example, by cross-sectional regression models) then equivalent consumption bundles corresponding to the coordinates of a and b in Figure 6.2 can be estimated.

McClements (1978) has calculated equivalence scales for fifteen commodities. Table 6.4 shows the equivalent consumption for a married couple with one child at various ages compared with a married couple without children. The numbers are interpreted in the following way. Consider the food scale: a couple with a child aged 0–1 will consume, at its equivalent income, 5 per cent more food; or with a child aged 17, 42 per cent more.

This is, of course, after allowing for substitution effects (note that a household with a baby consumes 3 per cent more tobacco!) and for economies of scale in household 'production' of meals, etc.

TABLE 6.4 *Estimated Commodity Equivalent Scales by Age of Child (married couple = 1.00)*

| Commodity | Age of child in years | | | | | | |
	0–1	2–4	5–7	8–10	11–12	13–15	16–18
Housing	1.17	1.17	1.22	1.20	1.21	1.18	1.22
Fuel	1.12	1.16	1.17	1.18	1.14	1.19	1.15
Food	1.05	1.18	1.24	1.25	1.28	1.30	1.42
Alcohol	1.00	1.05	1.05	1.04	1.01	1.99	1.07
Tobacco	1.03	1.02	1.03	1.03	.98	1.99	1.09
Clothing	1.08	1.17	1.26	1.31	1.34	1.42	1.50
Durable	1.24	1.28	1.28	1.34	1.36	1.40	1.40
Other	1.07	1.22	1.21	1.28	1.32	1.37	1.48
Transport	1.15	1.23	1.24	1.29	1.33	1.33	1.50
Services	1.10	1.23	1.23	1.29	1.36	1.41	1.53

Source: McClements (1978), Table 5.1.

These results—and too much should not be claimed for their accuracy—reflect the *actual behaviour* of households. The fact that substitution takes place as the relative cost to different types of household of various types of consumption changes must be lived with so long as we are concerned with policies directed at *income* maintenance. If it is the view that, for example, increases in (say) tobacco and alcohol consumption are *not* a part of the policy objective, then emphasis must shift from redistribution in cash towards redistribution in (non-tradable) kind, for if income supplements are given in cash, and recipients have discretion as to how they shall be spent, some will unquestionably be spent on such items of consumption.

Note also the judgement that individuals may be taken as being equally well off if they consume the equivalent commodity scale. As a factual matter this is hard to test, though it is counter-intuitive (typically people's tastes vary). As a value judgement, that people should be treated *as though they had the same tastes*, at least for certain basic types of consumption, it may be more acceptable.

B. CAUSES OF POVERTY

To answer the question 'who are the poor?' is to provide some clues as to the underlying causes of poverty. Table 6.2 provides some indication that old age is an important characteristic of a sizeable number of the poor. From Townsend's survey we may conclude that middle-aged professional and managerial workers who were fully employed and living either alone, in married couples, or with small families, were least likely to be poor by any of his measures. Elderly people who had been unskilled manual workers and children in the families of young unskilled workers, especially those with experience of substantial unemployment, sickness or disability, or in one-parent families, were most likely to be poor. About one third of those in poverty by the SB definition were in income units in which someone had been substantially unemployed: half of these came from income units where someone was earning less than 90 per cent of the mean for their sex. Another third were in income units where someone was disabled or had recently been ill for five or more weeks. Another third belonged in income units where someone was retired and of pensionable age. About one tenth were in income units where someone had been unemployed for a week or more during the year and another tenth were from one-parent families. (These percentages do not add to 100 because some people were in more than one category.) The proportion of people in poverty was higher in the non-white population than in the population as a whole. Fifteen per cent of married couples with four or more children were in poverty.

In summary, it seems that poverty may arise for the following two main reasons: low earning power when in employment and lack of employment. Low earning power tends to be mainly associated with lack of opportunity, low skill level, disability and personal characteristics such as race or sex. Lack of employment as a cause chiefly embraces the long-term unemployed, the single-parent family and retirement pensioners. In addition, large families account for a sizeable proportion of all in poverty.

Before turning to policy to combat poverty, we shall discuss in greater detail some of the economic aspects of earnings differences, disability, non-productive discrimination in employment, unemployment and pensions. The treatment of each will necessarily be summary.

Skill Differentials

To focus exclusively on this cause of inequality and poverty let us make some sweeping assumptions: that the labour market is completely open so that each individual can choose whatever occupation he wishes and acquire whatever skills he thinks worthwhile; that employers are wealth maximisers so that all they care about is the value of output contributed by employees; that there are differences in talents: intelligence, etc.; that access to the capital market is equal for all; that neither employers nor employees are organised in monopolies. We shall relax these later. Meanwhile, we can focus on the *human capital* explanation of earnings differentials.

Recall from chapter 2 (p. 38) that individuals, in acquiring costly skills, will consider it worthwhile (when the benefits of the skills extend over a long working life) to pursue such investments until

$$\Delta E = rK,$$

where ΔE is the earnings differential that *just* compensates for the costs K, and we assume that such investments in skill are undertaken only for the earnings advantage they give (no non-pecuniary benefits of more skilled jobs). Such training need not, of course, be formal schooling. Much training takes place on the job. In such cases it is useful to make a distinction between *general* and *specific* on the job training.

If a firm provides an opportunity for individuals to acquire skills that have value outside the firm, the other firms could compete such individuals away from the firm who trained them by offering them an appropriate wage. Such *general* skills will consequently usually be financed not by the firm but by the worker. In training (as, say, an apprentice) the worker accepts a lower wage—lower than his actual productivity warrants; when training is complete he receives a higher wage reflecting his new productivity. Thus, the worker has paid the cost of the training and receives the return on it. In the case of *specific* skills that have no, or little, value outside the firm, the training firm faces no such competition and if it, rather than the worker, chooses to bear the costs of training, then *it* will later be able to recoup them by keeping wages lower than the value of the worker's contribution to output in the firm.

We thus see that earnings differentials are predicted by human capital theory to arise mainly in the area of general skills that have wide marketability.

Of course, this theory only explains a part of the inequality of earnings. For example, many professional groups have succeeded in establishing an occupational monopoly: entry to the profession is restricted enabling higher returns to be sustained than our equation implies by virtue of keeping out many of the new entrants who would otherwise flock in. For other groups, non-pecuniary considerations may outweigh pecuniary ones (e.g. the priesthood). Basic abilities also differ. Nevertheless, Mincer (1976) reports a study in which 71 per cent of the variation in wage differentials is explained by a statistical model based on human capital theory. (As we shall see later in the chapter, this estimate is higher than most and a good deal higher than some.)

Unequal Opportunities

As mentioned above, monopolistic practices can create unequal opportunities that account for a greater inequality in earnings than the human capital theory alone would lead one to expect. Another major inequality in opportunities arises in access to the capital market. If employees are to bear the cost of skill acquisition, then they must somehow finance it. In a perfect capital market, the expected yield could be used as a pledge against loans, rather in the way that a building society lends to an owner occupier against the security of the house itself. Typically, however, society makes rules against this type of transaction in human capital: ownership of the present value of the skills is not permitted to be alienated from the possessor of the skills by, for example, long-term indenture or by species of slave contracts. This has two consequences: loans made for acquisition of skills tend to be riskier, so that interest rates become relatively high, especially for those who have no other, non-human capital, to borrow against; secondly it introduces inequalities between social classes since they differ in the extent to which they own non-human capital that can be used either to secure loans for human investment or to be run down as human capital replaces non-human.

In addition to these and other market inequalities of opportunity, there are also differing opportunities owing to differing abilities and aptitudes among people. More 'able' people, for example those with higher measured IQ or those whose social and personal upbringing has imbued them with values oriented towards high achievement in the work situation, will tend to have a higher return to skill acquisition, are more likely to stay on at school after 16, to be accepted into colleges of further education, universities, etc. In any case, more able people are also simply more able—for two people having had equal training, we are not surprised if the more able of the two has higher earnings. Finally, some abilities are more valued than others. Independently of the training received, intellectual skills, musical skills, persuasive skills, charm, etc., all command different premiums in the market place.

Clearly the *combination* of training and ability is a powerful advantage. Many of the poor are those who have had little training and who possess few natural abilities of great value in the market place.

Disability and Discrimination

Not all disabilities are earnings-relevant. A one-legged professor earns as much as two-legged professors. But for those that are, the source of the low earnings lies either in the relatively low productivity of disabled workers, or in the relatively high cost of training them to comparable productivity levels with other employees and adapting the work-place in suitable ways, or both.

The most obvious indicator of discrimination against particular categories of worker, whether on grounds of disability, race or sex, is often thought to be the proportion of workers of that category in a particular occupation at a given wage relative to the proportion in the population as a whole. If the ratio is less than 1 it is often thought that there is *prima facie* evidence of discrimination. Low-productivity workers are a case we have already discussed. Let us therefore consider workers whose labour time is in fact perfectly substitutable. If employers are wealth maximisers, they will be perfectly indifferent as to which workers' labour time is used: whether, say, black or white. If, then, the proportion of blacks employed in a particular firm is smaller than the proportion in the total labour force having the relevant occupational skills, it must arise, not from the employers' side but on the supply side of labour. In particular, it may arise because of differing supply elasticities. Imagine a labour force of equal numbers of black (B) and white (W) workers of equal skill. Wealth-maximising employers will (assuming away complications arising from union wage-setting) employ each type up to the point at which the wage is equal to the value of additional output (the demand curve for labour time).

In Figure 6.3 S_{B+W} indicates the combined supply of labour time from

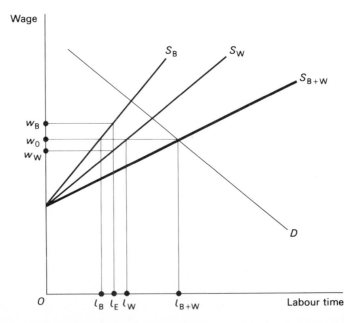

FIG. 6.3　Wage discrimination with different labour supply elasticities.

blacks and whites. Given the firm's demand D, an equilibrium wage Ow_0 is expected, under free entry and competition in the labour market, to be established. This wage per hour will accrue to both types of labour. But if the supply elasticities differ, as they do in Figure 6.3, then even though the numbers in the total population are (by assumption) equal, blacks will supply less labour time and will, as a group, take home a lower share Ol_B/Ol_{B+W} of the wages bill. As can, indeed, be seen in this example, for equal shares in employment to occur out of the same total (Ol_E/Ol_{B+W}), blacks' wages would have to rise to Ow_B and whites' to fall to Ow_W. In such a case, the blacks' share of wages would be larger than the whites': there would be reverse discrimination— and a differential not sustainable under competition.

The above example is not, of course, employment discrimination as it is commonly meant. It merely illustrates the danger of inferring too much from the 'obvious' indicator of relative employment rates of equally skilled workers from different social groups. More relevant are persisting wage differentials between equally skilled groups. This is stronger evidence both of discrimination and of the *absence* of wealth-maximising behaviour by employers.

If employers have different demands for equally productive workers, for example D_B and D_W in Figure 6.4, and we assume both that the supply

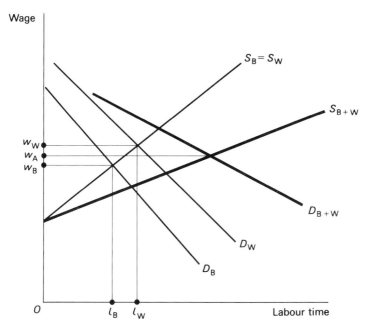

FIG. 6.4 Wage discrimination without different labour supply elasticities.

characteristics of blacks' and whites' time are the same and that they are equal in number $(S_B = S_W)$, then not only will fewer blacks be employed than their numbers in the workforce would lead one to expect but also they will receive a lower wage. In Figure 6.4, Ow_A is the (weighted) average wage received by all workers: the whites' rate of pay is higher than this and the blacks' lower. The difference, $w_W - w_B$, is the monetary measure of the marginal disadvantage of employing an equally productive black worker to a (racially) prejudiced employer.

This analysis focusses on discrimination by employers. Other types include, in particular, discrimination by fellow employees (especially when unionised) but this is not discussed here. The analysis of employer discrimination seems, however, consistent with much of the evidence. For example, Becker (1957) finds relatively lower employment than expected of blacks in the Southern USA in monopolistic industries than in competitive. Duncan *et al.* (1968) and Blinder (1973) found, after standardising for family background, education, seniority in occupation and various other factors, that about 40 per cent of the difference in pay between blacks and whites in given occupations could be attributed to outright discrimination.

Of course, in addition to discrimination *in* the job market, there is also discrimination that denies some jobs to particular minorities and that denies them the *opportunity* (via, for example, education) to acquire skills comparable to those attainable by members of a majority group of equal 'basic' ability.

Unemployment

Poverty among the unemployed is chiefly the consequence of rates of social security benefit. At present levels of unemployment, substantially exceeding 1 m in Great Britain, an *average* person can expect to be unemployed for four months once every six years—but the expectation is, of course, highly skewed. The unskilled, the young, women and the frequently sick are far more subject to unemployment than others. Although the unemployed as such are a relatively small proportion of all those in poverty, *among* the unemployed the incidence of poverty is relatively high.

Although enough is not known of the household/family circumstances of the unemployed (who may benefit from shared incomes from other household members), the problem is basically one of low benefit levels. In Britain, only one-sixth of the unemployed receive the earnings-related supplement and less than a half receive the basic National Insurance benefit for various reasons, some for 'industrial misconduct' but chiefly because of the exhaustion of entitlement owing to being unemployed for more than a year. Supplementary Benefit, which in principle should lift anyone's real income up to levels specified in the benefit scale, is not claimed by about 20 per cent of those unemployed entitled to it (Royal Commission on the Distribution of Income and Wealth, 1978, p. 94).

One of the great stumbling blocks to more generous provision of benefit to the unemployed seems to be less the cost than the alleged disincentive effects it would have. The ratio of net resources out of work to that in work is termed the *replacement ratio*. This can be close to 100 per cent or even in excess, indicating that the person is better off out of than in work, particularly when account is taken of means-tested benefits such as free school meals, clothing allowances and the like.

In 1977, it has been shown (Atkinson and Flemming, 1978) that replacement ratios of 100 per cent or more occur almost entirely among those who in work had the very lowest weekly earnings (£35 or less in a year when average weekly earnings were about £75) and who were unemployed for more than 28 weeks (the maximum period for which earnings-related supplements were payable) or who had a dependent wife and four or more children. Only a *minority* of the unemployed satisfy these conditions. It is important, therefore, not to exaggerate the frequency of high replacement rations as a disincentive to work. It is also important to bear in mind that little is known *in fact* about the response of either the employed or the unemployed to high or changing replacement ratios. What we have is a lot of hypothetical examples, quite a lot of prejudice, but very little hard fact.

Pensions

Pensions can be, and have been, viewed in either of two ways. The first of these is the investment/insurance model; the second is the intergenerational transfer model. Each of these can be illustrated using a simple example. Let us suppose that a 'representative' individual works for 40 years from age 25 and retires at 65. He will die at age 75 we suppose—unless he has died before. To keep the arithmetic simple, let us suppose that if he commences work he will survive until age 65, and if he commences retirement he will survive until 75. He may therefore die at age 65 with probability d and at age 75 with probability $(1 - d)$. We thus have a simple life-cycle of two stages: work and retirement. The question is how best to provide an income for retirement.

The investment/insurance model works like this: if the individual makes an annual payment of £C at the end of each year of his working life, and it is invested at an interest rate i, he would accumulate a fund F, equal to[2]

$$F = C[(1 + i)^{40} - 1]/i$$

for each pound of his contribution made annually over the 40 years of his working life. We now ask what annual pension, A, this accumulated sum would enable him to enjoy for a ten-year period. The answer to this is that each pound of an annuity for ten years, also at interest rate i, will cost a price of:[3]

$$P = \left[1 - \frac{1}{(1 + i)^{10}}\right] \Big/ i.$$

The maximum pension is, of course, $A = F/P$: the maximum annuity obtainable per pound of the accumulated contribution.

However, the individual, if he contributes at all, may not live to enjoy his pension. Actuarially, there is a probability d that he will contribute but not live to receive benefit. The actuarially fair contribution (C') would therefore be $C' = £(1 - d)C$, entitling the worker, if he survived, to a pension of £A.

Let us take a numerical example. Suppose there are 100 employees. Let $d = 0.4$ and $i = 0.1$. Suppose each earns £6,000 per year and pays an actuarially fair premium $C' = £50$ of annual income before tax, over a working lifetime of 40 years, each worker will contribute a total F of £22,130 at 10 per cent interest and the total fund for a cohort of 100 employees of the same age starting their contributions at the same time will evidently be £2,213 m. On our assumptions only 60 of the cohort will live to enjoy their pensions, and each will live for ten years. The annual annuity for ten years that this accumulated fund will support is a total of £360,150 or £6,002 per employee. Thus, each employee is able to enjoy approximately the same pre-tax income in retirement as in employment.

Putting it the other way round, if each wants a pension of £6,002 per year, and insurance companies know d to be 0.4, then at 10 per cent interest the formula

$$C' = (1 - d)\frac{AP}{F}$$

gives the appropriate annual premium (C'), where the symbols have the same meaning as before.

It is natural to interpret this investment/insurance model in market terms—even though by assuming actuarially fair premiums we have assumed that insurance companies operate at zero cost. One can conceive of a variety of contracts to suit different demands for pensions, dependants' benefits, etc., with premiums adjusted to reflect length of period of contribution, size of contribution and probability of survival in work and in retirement according to individual circumstances. This model of pensions is concerned essentially with redistribution of an individual's income *over his or her life-cycle*.

The intergenerational transfer model of pensions is, by contrast, concerned essentially with interpersonal transfers from those in work to those in retirement. The pure intergenerational transfer model needs no funding nor is it actuarially calculated according to life expectations. In its simplest form it consists of flat rate compulsory contributions by employees and employers and flat rate benefits to the currently retired. As far as the employer is concerned, his contribution is a wage cost. Effectively, the employee has a full wage of $w + p$, where w is the pre-tax wage and p is a payroll tax paid by the employer, and he has a net wage of $w - c$ where c is the employee's contribution.

Because income typically grows through time, $p + c$ also grows, and so does b, the flat rate benefit. Effectively, the government, at any point in time, selects a point such as e in Figure 6.5 such that $p + c$ per worker is transferred in part to retired workers. In Figure 6.5, $b < (p + c)$ to allow for the disincentive effects that flat rate contributions may have, especially

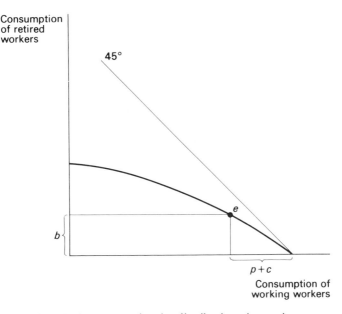

FIG. 6.5   Intergenerational redistribution via pensions.

on low-paid workers whom this regressive form of tax may be expected most particularly to deter from work. (We ignore the administrative costs of such schemes, as we did before in discussing the investment/insurance model.)

Viewed as an investment, the pay-as-you-go system seems an unattractive proposition. Ignoring interest payments, weekly employee's and employer's contributions totalling, at current rates in Britain, £16.50 for a working life of 50 years, give a lifetime contribution of £38,610; the basic component of the retirement pension for a married couple is, by contrast, £28.00 per week, which amounts to £14,560 over ten years, which, for a person not expecting to experience unemployment, long-term sickness, etc., represents a negative return. But this is to misconceive the nature of this kind of pension arrangement in which the contract is not an insurance or investment contract based on actuarial principles, but an implicit contract such that, in exchange for maintaining current pensioners at a level not usually supportable by current contributions alone (the balance coming from general taxation), the contributor expects that *future governments* will impose taxes sufficient to maintain workers presently employed but then in retirement at a level appropriate in the wealthier society expected at that time. By contributing *now* he expects a public obligation later to be discharged when he too retires.

In practice, private insurance schemes reflect some aspects of social security systems and social security systems also reflect some elements of insurance. A flavour of the controversy concerning the role of the state in pensions can be got from the Further Reading to this chapter.

From the perspective of this chapter, we can now see, however, that neither model of pensions ensures immunity from poverty. The true social insurance model, here termed the investment/insurance model, will give low pensions to those whose contributions are low whether through low wages, frequent unemployment, etc. and will also give a low yield when, as has recently been the case, nominal rates of return on investment barely exceed, and often fall short of, the rate of inflation. The social security model, here termed the intergenerational transfer model, will give low pensions according to political factors.

C. SOLUTIONS TO THE POVERTY PROBLEM

The reader will be left to analyse the particular policies available to governments and individuals in any particular place or time for him or herself. Here we concentrate on the general characteristics of the alternatives.

There are two basic approaches to solutions in mixed economies, which, although they are not logically mutually exclusive, often appear so in the context of controversy over reform. The first is a *set* of policies aimed at eradicating specific sources of poverty or mitigating the consequences for specific categories of the poor. The second approach is for a grand scheme to maintain incomes.

Specific policies may be inferred from our foregoing discussion. They might include subsidies for the acquisition of skills, removal of monopoly practices, outlawing of discrimination, employment subsidies, minimum wages in low-pay industries, more comprehensive 'equivalence' in benefit levels, more generous benefits for the long-term unemployed, more generous pensions. .

The grand schemes are basically two-fold in a mixed economy: a national minimum wage and social dividend or negative income taxation.

A National Minimum Wage

The proposals for NMW are really less for its introduction than for extending and raising the present arrangements in many countries that already apply in a number of industries. (In Britain these are Wages Boards in agriculture and Wages Councils in some other industries such as Button Manufacturing.) The objective is therefore to extend the NMW to all industries and to legislate it at such a rate that those families where the wage earner is in employment would have their incomes raised to at least the poverty line. The NMW is only a partial solution to the problem of poverty—it does not tackle the problems of poverty in old age, among the self-employed, casual workers or the disabled, nor does it directly tackle poverty in families where the usual earner is unemployed.

Three effects of the NMW are worthy of special attention, all of them requiring a substantial application of positive, as well as normative, economic analysis. The first of these consists in the possibility that, because minimum wages are legislated in monetary, not real, terms (though the intention is, of course, to raise real incomes), the intention of the NMW will be frustrated, or partially frustrated, through its impact upon the general price level via raising production costs in general and through the reaction of other workers (and employers) raising money wages in an attempt to maintain their own real wages. If the NMW were to apply to female workers, for example, the impact on the price level is likely to be quite marked (as well as leading probably to substantial female unemployment). In so far as the poor tend to consume goods produced labour-intensively by the relatively unskilled, the effect will again be more pronounced.

The second consists in the incidence of the costs of financing the NMW. The costs will be borne, in varying proportions, by the producers and consumers of goods and services, but the precise incidence of the costs will depend, among other things, upon the elasticity of substitution of minimum wage labour and other factors of production, upon product demand elasticities and upon the consumption patterns of different income groups in society.

The third consists in the fact that NMW concentrates its benefit upon those who remain in employment while, at the same time, tending to drive others out of employment or into low-productivity self-employment as efficient firms substitute other factors of production for higher cost labour and/or reduce rates of output. If, however, the NMW is applied effectively (i.e. set at a rate higher than current wages) only in some sectors, rather than in all sectors, while on the one hand there need be no long-term unemployment (provided workers are prepared to move between industries) any gains made in the earnings of workers who retain employment in the NMW industries will be offset, in varying degrees, by losses to other workers and to workers who are compelled to leave NMW industries. For example, a National Minimum Wage in the relatively labour-intensive sector of the economy causes prices in that sector to rise relative to other sectors' prices, so that output from other sectors will expand and that of the labour-intensive sector fall. The capital–labour ratio in the capital-intensive sectors must fall and the (marginal) productivity of workers in these sectors must fall thereby tending to make these workers relatively worse off than they would otherwise have been.[4]

The significance of the various factors discussed here for the desirability of the NMW depends crucially upon the size of the NMW relative to current low wages, upon the empirical assessment of the appropriate elasticities and upon one's evaluation of the fairness of the incidence of its costs. Even making the crudest assumptions that characterise some discussions of the NMW, e.g. that all elasticities are zero, so that only consumers of the products produced by NMW sectors bear these costs, some assessment still needs to be made of the extent to which NMW earners consume the products of their own industry.

Social Dividend and Negative Income Taxation

Social Dividend (SD) and Negative Income Taxation (NIT) are, as we shall see, formally identical, so they are treated together. The emphases placed upon them by their various proponents have been, in a historical sense, slightly different so there is some virtue in regarding them as separate proposals. The SD is, in general, a scheme that guarantees a weekly payment (let us suppose, set at the poverty line) for everyone and is paid by the state. A proportional or progressive tax rate is then applied to family income (excluding guaranteed income) above some minimum exemption level. By building a basic floor below every family's income it is clear that SD is paid regardless of need. Consequently, it is more 'universal' than 'selective', though some selectivity in, say, the form of Supplementary Benefit in Britain would have to be retained in cases of special needs not allowed for in the basic guaranteed income needed by the 'average' poor.

Let us take a highly simplified example of an SD plan. Suppose every two-person family were guaranteed an annual income of £2,000 and a proportional tax rate is applied to all other income[5] at $33\frac{1}{3}$ per cent. Tax payments would equal SD receipts for persons with incomes of £6,000, which is usually known as B, the break-even point. The relationship between the (proportional) tax rate t_s, guaranteed minimum income Y_g, and the break-even point B, are rather obviously seen to be

$$B = Y_g/t_s.$$

After B, a progressive tax rate, t_p may apply.

The emphasis in NIT is placed upon the break-even point rather than the minimum guaranteed. B in the NIT literature has tended to be equated with the exemption level of income E. If a person's income exceeds the exemption level, he pays (say) a progressive income tax t_p. If his income is below E he receives an income maintenance payment equal to some (usually supposed to be constant) proportion of the shortfall between actual income and exemption income. This proportion t_n is the negative income tax rate. Thus, if his income is Y, he receives $t_n(E - Y)$ if Y is less than E. The exemption level and the tax rate together determine the level of income below which no one can fall—guaranteed income Y_g. Obviously, if ordinary income Y is zero, then

$$Y_g = t_n E.$$

The similarity of SD and NIT is obvious, for if the break-even and exemption levels are the same $(B = E)$ and the same tax rates apply $(t_s = t_n)$, then

$$Y_g = t_s B \qquad \text{or} \qquad B = Y_g/t_s.$$

Figure 6.6 shows diagrammatically the relationship between pre-tax and post-tax income under NIT. Along the 45° degree line through the origin the two are equal. Along $Y_g e$, we see how much will be *added* to pre-tax income at the rate t_n to yield post-tax incomes in the range between Y_g (the minimum possible) and E, the break-even point. Along ey, we see how much will be *subtracted* at the progressive rate t_p from pre-tax income to yield post-tax income. Under SD, everyone is given a social dividend of Y_g and any other income is taxed at the proportional rate t_n up to level B and the progressive rate t_p thereafter.

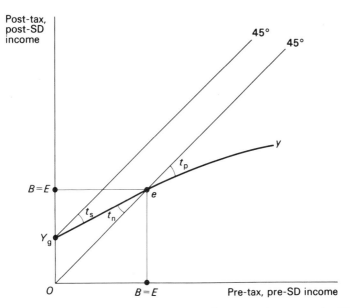

FIG. 6.6   Relationship between pre-tax and post-tax income under NIT.

The effects of NMW on employment and prices, as we have seen, have been the cause of much concern. With SD/NIT concern has chiefly centred upon the effects it may have on individuals' willingness to work and upon the periodicity of payment.

The disincentive effects that new taxes and benefits and changes in their rates can have seem mainly to be of concern for the odd and Puritan reason that the nature of the externality is that it is all right to raise the real income of the poor so long as they do not persist in taking it in the form of leisure.[6] Let us therefore suppose that any reduction in effort *is* to be regarded as a disadvantage to be weighed against the benefits of the schemes we are discussing. Disincentive effects fall into two broad classes: total and marginal. A total effect exists in the choice between whether or not to work at all. This choice must evidently be affected to some extent by the amount of income available in and out of work. A marginal effect operates in the decision to work more or to move to a higher paid job and here the marginal tax rate (the resulting change in tax divided by the causative change in income) is the significant variable.

We have discussed the 'total' disincentive effects above in connection with the replacement ratio. The standard economic analysis of the effect of marginal tax payments (and/or benefits forgone) on incentives to work is that there is an 'income effect' and a 'substitution effect' usually working in contrary directions. The income effect reduces take-home pay and hence provides an incentive to work more to maintain living standards. The substitution effect reduces the price of leisure relative to the rewards of work and hence encourages more leisure.[7] Which dominates cannot be told *a priori* (the theory is mainly of use to counter those who argue *a priori* that increases in tax rates always have a disincentive effect). The empirical evidence on this point (see Further Reading) is patchy but gives no firm evidence that marginal tax rates have any serious disincentive at least for the lower income groups. The evidence from NIT experiments in the USA (e.g. Pechman and Timpane, 1975) is that there are identifiable disincentive effects but their magnitude is rather small. It is tempting therefore not to worry about high marginal rates, at least from the incentives point of view. As for the total effect of guaranteed incomes on those who are not in work, one would expect to see a disincentive effect operate most keenly if the system were one that offered both a high level of benefit relative to earnings in employment and a high aggregate marginal tax rate on income. Once again, there is little evidence that the long-term unemployed who are in receipt of benefit are reluctant to work (if they can find it, and if they are not otherwise handicapped).

We have so far failed to relate this discussion of incentives (assuming that they are in principle a rational source of concern) to the SD/NIT proposals. The reason why will now be clear. What little evidence exists suggests that in practice disincentive effects are not likely to be very important. The really interesting (and costly) exercise of testing the behaviour of people when faced with different benefit/tax opportunities—even of working out the theoretical probabilities in a comprehensive way—remains to be done in Britain.[8] This is another stretch of the uncharted waters in the economics of social policy. Nevertheless, at least in principle, the implicit marginal rates in most SD/NIT schemes can be adjusted to avoid most of the sharp breaks that occur with many of the means-tested benefits that are currently available in Britain.

NOTES

1. The household types are: man aged 60 or over; man under 60; woman 60 or over; woman under 60; man and woman; man and woman and 1, 2, 3 or 4+ children; three adults; three adults plus children; four adults; other households without children; other households with children.

2. Recalling the kind of present value arithmetic of chapter 2, $F = C + C(1 + i) + C(1 + i)^2 + \cdots + C(1 + i)^{39}$ is the amount of the fund amassed by putting away C at the end of each year and investing it at i per cent. Multiply through by $(1 + i)$ and subtract the above equation from the new one thus:

$$F(1 + i) = \qquad C(1 + i) + C(1 + i)^2 + \cdots + C(1 + i)^{39} + \cdots + C(1 + i)^{40}$$

$$-F = -[C + C(1 + i) + C(1 + i)^2 + \cdots + C(1 + i)^{39}]$$

$$Fi = \qquad -C \qquad\qquad\qquad\qquad\qquad\qquad + C(1 + i)^{40}$$

Whence $F = C[(1 + i)^{40} - 1]/i$

3. $P = \dfrac{A}{1 + i} + \dfrac{A}{(1 + i)^2} + \cdots \dfrac{A}{(1 + i)^{10}}$

   is the present value of an annuity stream equal to A each year for ten years at i per cent, assuming again that the sum accrues at the end of each year. Multiply through by $(1 + i)$ and subtract the above equation from the new one thus:

$$P(1 + i) = A + A/(1 + i) + A/(1 + i)^2 + \cdots A/(1 + i)^9$$

$$-P = \quad -[A/(1 + i) + A/(1 + i)^2 + \cdots A/(1 + i)^9 + A/(1 + i)^{10}]$$

$$Pi = A \qquad\qquad\qquad\qquad\qquad\qquad - A/(1 + i)^{10}$$

   Whence, $P = A[1 - (1 + i)^{10}]/i$,
   and the price of an annuity of £1 is as stated in the text.

4. For a possible exception to this general expectation, see the article by Harry G. Johnson (1969).

5. In practice, progressivity is probably preferable and the taxation of small incomes is anyway very costly by comparison with the revenues obtained. Whether positive tax rates are applied to all incomes or only beyond an exemption income level does not affect the break-even point.

6. An alternative specification of the externality such that taking more leisure would definitely detract from the welfare of the rest of society would derive from

making the size of GNP the maximand of social and economic policy. The reader will not need reminding that, in this book, the far more sensible maximand 'social welfare' is adopted, not social wealth—though our maximand includes wealth. So long as any reduction in effort is marginal to the economy as a whole, even though output must necessarily fall, social welfare will not.
7. A more complete approach treats the individual as combining time with other things to 'produce' consumption goods. For example, this leads to the complication that to enjoy leisure one must earn income to acquire the other things that make leisure different from mere idleness. See, e.g., Gary S. Becker (1965) 'A theory of the allocation of time', *Economic Journal*, 75, pp. 493–517.
8. For a review of US experiments with negative income taxation see Pechman and Timpane (1975) and Haveman and Watts (1977).

QUESTIONS ON CHAPTER 6

1. Does policy towards poverty reflect mainly preferences or ideas of social justice? Justify your view.
2. What is poverty?
3. Is poverty increasing in your country? (Are people poorer or are there more poor people, or both?)
4. What is Townsend's deprivation standard?
5. What value judgements are involved in computing a deprivation index?
6. Is a deprivation index cardinal or ordinal? Explain.
7. What is meant by equivalence of household incomes?
8. What is a Laspeyres index?
9. Who are the poor?
10. How far can human capital theory explain earnings differentials?
11. How would you test for the presence of racial discrimination in the labour market?
12. Does social security increase unemployment?
13. Is pensions policy concerned with redistribution of an individual's lifetime consumption or with redistribution from working to the retired generations?
14. What annual sum invested for each of 40 years will yield you an annual income of £1000 for the subsequent 10 years (assume a 10 per cent interest rate)?
15. Can someone deserve to be poor?
16. What is the main cause of poverty?
17. What are the effects of minimum wage laws?
18. What is the negative income tax?
19. Could NIT abolish poverty if its rates were set appropriately?
20. Are the poor necessarily always with us?

FURTHER READING

On poverty:

The best general source is:

Townsend, P. (1979) *Poverty in the UK*. Harmondsworth: Penguin.

Other very useful sources include:

Abel-Smith, B. and Townsend, P. (1965) *The poor and the Poorest*. London: Bell.
Atkinson, A. B. (1969) *Poverty in Britain and the Reform of Social Security*. London: Cambridge University Press.

Atkinson, A. B. (1972) *Unequal Shares*. London: Allen Lane.

Atkinson, A. B. (1975) *The Economics of Inequality*. Oxford: Clarendon Press.

Atkinson, A. B. (ed.) (1976) *The Personal Distribution of Incomes*. London: Allen and Unwin.

Atkinson, A. B. and Flemming, J. S. (1978) Unemployment, social security and incentives. *Midland Bank Review*, Autumn, pp. 6–16.

Beveridge, Sir W. (1942) *Social Insurance and Allied Services*. Cmd 6404, London: HMSO. The *locus classicus* of British social security.

Bruce, M. (1968) *The Coming of the Welfare State*, (4th edition). London: Batsford.

Gough, J. and Stark, T. (1968) Low incomes in the UK. *Manchester School, 36*, pp. 173–83.

Meade, J. E. (Chairman) (1978) *The Structure and Reform of Direct Taxation*. London: Allen and Unwin, chapter 13.

Mincer, J. (1976) Progress in human capital analysis of the distribution of earnings. In Atkinson (1976). *op. cit.*

Prest, A. R. and Stark, T. (1967) Some aspects of income redistribution in the UK since World War II. *Manchester School, 35*, pp. 217–44.

Rowntree, B. S. (1901) *Poverty—A Study of Town Life*. London: Macmillan.

Rowntree, B. S. (1941) *Poverty and Progress*. London: Longmans.

Rowntree, B. S. and Lavers, G. R. (1951) *Poverty and the Welfare State*. London: Longmans.

Important British official sources include:

Ministry of Pensions and National Insurance (1965) *Financial and Other Circumstances of Retirement Pensioners*. London: HMSO.

Ministry of Social Security (1967) *Circumstances of Families*. London: HMSO.

Royal Commission on the Distribution of Income and Wealth (1978a) Report No. 6, *Lower Incomes*. Cmnd. 7175, London: HMSO.

Royal Commission on the Distribution of Income and Wealth (1978b) Background Paper No. 5, *The Causes of Poverty*. London: HMSO.

On equivalence scales:

McClements, L. D. (1977) Equivalence scales for children. *Journal of Public Economics, 8*, pp. 191–210.

McClements, L. D. (1978) *The Economics of Social Security*. London: Heinemann, chapter 5.

McClements, L. D. and Muellbauer, J. (1979) Exchange of Notes in *Journal of Public Economics, 12*, pp. 221–44.

Muellbauer, J. (1974) Household composition, Engel curves and welfare comparisons between households: a duality approach. *European Economic Review, 5*, pp. 103–22.

Prais, S. J. and Houthakker, H. S. (1955) *The Analysis of Family Budgets*. D.A.E. Monograph No. 4, London: Cambridge University Press.

On discrimination:

Arrow, K. J. (1973) The theory of discrimination. In O. Ashenfelter and A. Rees (eds) *Discrimination in Labor Markets*. Princeton: Princeton University Press.

Becker, G. S. (1957) *The Economics of Discrimination*. Chicago: University of Chicago Press.

Blinder, A. S. (1973) Wage discrimination: reduced form and structural estimates. *Journal of Human Resources, 8*, pp. 436–55.

Chiplin, B. and Sloane, P. J. (1976) *Sex Discrimination in the Labour Market.* London: Macmillan.
Department of Employment (1973a) *The Quota Scheme for Disabled People.* London: HMSO.
Department of Employment (1973b) *Sheltered Employment for Disabled People.* London: HMSO.
Disablement Income Group (1972) *Creating a National Disability Income.* London: DIG.
Duncan, O. D., Featherman, D. L. and Duncan, B. (1968) *Socioeconomic Background and Occupational Achievement.* Washington, DC: US Department of Health, Education and Welfare.
Haber, L. D. (1973) Social planning for disability. *Journal of Human Resources, 8,* pp. 33–55.
Phelps Brown, H. (1977) *The Inequality of Pay.* Oxford: Oxford University Press, chapter 5.
Wiseman, J. and Cullis, J. G. (1975) Social policy towards disabled people. In A. J. Culyer, (ed.) *Economic Policies and Social Goals.* London: Martin Robertson.

On pensions:

Arthur, T. G. (1978) Pensions: the role of the state. *National Westminster Quarterly Review,* August, pp. 36–46.
Asimakopulos, A. and Weldon, J. C. (1968) On the theory of government pension plans. *Canadian Journal of Economics, 1,* pp. 699–717.
Boskin, M. J. and Hurd, M. D. (1978) The effect of social security on early retirement. *Journal of Public Economics, 10,* pp. 361–78.
Browning, E. K. (1973) Social insurance and intergenerational transfers. *Journal of Law and Economics, 16,* pp. 215–38.
Buchanan, J. M. (1968) Social insurance in a growing economy. *National Tax Journal, 21,* pp. 386–95.
Cohen, W. J. and Friedman, M. (1972) *Social Security: Universal or Selective.* Washington, DC: American Enterprise Institute.
Diamond, P. A. and Mirrlees, J. (1978) A model of social insurance with variable retirement. *Journal of Public Economics, 10,* pp. 295–336.
Feldstein, M. (1978) Do private pensions increase national saving? *Journal of Public Economics, 10,* pp. 277–94.
Prest, A. R. (1969) Comments on 'Social Insurance in a growing economy: a proposal for radical reform'. *National Tax Journal, 22,* pp. 554–6.
Sheshinski, E. (1978) A model of social security and retirement decisions. *Journal of Public Economics, 10,* pp. 337–60.

On minimum wages:

Brozen, Y. (1962) Minimum wages and household workers. *Journal of Law and Economics, 5,* pp. 103–10.
Colberg, M. R. (1960) Minimum wage effects on Florida's economic development. *Journal of Law and Economics, 3,* pp. 106–17.
Department of Employment and Productivity (1969) *A National Minimum Wage: An Inquiry.* London: HMSO.
Johnson, H. G. (1969) Minimum wage laws: a general equilibrium analysis. *Canadian Journal of Economics, 2,* pp. 599–603.
Leffler, K. B. (1978) Minimum wages, welfare, and wealth transfers to the poor. *Journal of Law and Economics, 21,* pp. 345–58.

Mincer, J. (1978) Unemployment effects of minimum wages. *Journal of Political Economy*, 84, pp. S87–S104.
Petersen, J. (1957) Employment effects of minimum wages. *Journal of Political Economy*, 65, pp. 412–30.
Stigler, G. J. (1946) The economics of minimum wage legislation. *American Economic Review*, 36, pp. 358–65.

On social dividend and negative income taxes:

Brown, C. V. and Dawson, D. A. (1969) *Personal Taxation, Incentives and Tax Reform*. London: Political and Economic Planning.
Brown, C. V. and Jackson, P. M. (1978) *Public Sector Economics*. Oxford: Martin Robertson, chapter 14.
David, M. and Leuthold, J. (1968) Formulas for income maintenance: their distributional impact. *National Tax Journal*, 21, pp. 70–93.
Friedman, M. (1962) *Capitalism and Freedom*. Chicago: Chicago University Press.
Green, C. and Lampman, R. J. (1967) Schemes for transferring income to the poor. *Industrial Relations*, 6, pp. 121–37.
Haveman, R. H. and Watts, H. W. (1977) Social experimentation as policy research: a review of negative income tax. In V. Halberstadt and A. J. Culyer (eds) *Public Economics and Human Resources*. Paris: Cujas.
Lees, D. S. (1967) Poor families and fiscal reform. *Lloyds Bank Review*, no. 86, pp. 1–15.
Pechman, J. A. and Timpane, P. M. (eds) (1975) *Work Incentives and Income Guarantees: the New Jersey Negative Income Tax Experiment*. Washington, DC: Brookings.
Prest, A. R. (1970) The negative income tax: concepts and problems. *British Tax Review*, no. 6, pp. 352–65.

On incentive effects:

Many of the foregoing discuss disincentive effects, especially:

Atkinson, A. B. and Flemming, J. S. (1978) *op. cit.*
Pechman, J. A. and Timpane, P. M. (eds) (1975) *op. cit.*

In addition, and more generally:

Albin, P. S. and Stein, B. (1968) The constrained demand for public assistance. *Journal of Human Resources*, 3, pp. 300–11.
Barlow, R., Brazer, H. E. and Morgan, J. N. (1965) A survey of investment management and working behaviour among high-income individuals. *American Economic Review*, 55, pp. 252–64.
Break, G. F. (1957) Income taxes and incentives to work: an empirical study. *American Economic Review*, 47, pp. 529–49.
Brem, C. T. and Saving, T. R. (1964) The demand for general assistance payments. *American Economic Review*, 54, pp. 1002–18.
Brown, C. V. (1968) Misconceptions about income tax and incentives. *Scottish Journal of Political Economy*, 15, pp. 1–21.
Fields, D. B. and Stanbury, W. T. (1970) Incentives, disincentives and the income tax. *Public Finance*, 3, pp. 281–318.
Godfrey, L. G. (1975) *Theoretical and Empirical Aspects of the Effects of Taxation on the Supply of Labour*. Paris: Organisation for Economic Co-operation and Development.

Maynard, A. K. (1979) The economics of social policy. In D. H. Gowland (ed.) *Modern Economic Analysis*. London: Butterworths.

Metcalf, D. (1977) Unions, incomes policy and relative wages in Britain. *British Journal of Industrial Relations*, 15, pp. 157-75.

PART III

The Welfare State

CHAPTER 7

Are the Social Services Different?

A. WITH WHAT SHOULD POLICY BE CONCERNED?

The answer to the question that forms the title of this chapter is 'Yes and No', which we shall elucidate. The reason for posing it is, however, more obvious. We shall, in subsequent chapters, be applying economic analysis to problems of specific social policies and social services and, in so doing, shall be treating the policy objectives and the services as economic goods and services. To do so implies the very reasonable question—is this valid? As an example of the kind of problem encountered, consider 'education' in university. Universities teach, they develop and preserve culture (they 'warm the air'), they train people for productive activity, they turn out 'good' citizens and so on. Many would take a more Socratic view of what university education is, for example that it is essentially the pursuit of a universal object—learning—of intrinsic value as an end in itself, the other things being extrinsic accidents distinguishable from the essence and not necessarily associated with it. In short, is it not both naive and possibly dangerous to treat this phenomenon of education, of the profoundest concern to philosophers from time immemorial, as an 'economic' good? Does this not imply concentrating on the accidents and ignoring the essence thereby possibly destroying what is ultimately good about it?

Or, consider 'health'. What constitutes good health seems less of a philosophical question than the meaning of 'education' and yet the official definition suggested by the World Health Organisation—a state of complete mental, physical and social well-being—is evidently discussible in much the same terms as 'education'; though the view of 'education' that sees its essence as the individual pursuit of *universal* objects cannot readily be applied in health, for ultimately it is the individual who *possesses* health but no one can sanely claim to *possess* philosophy, history—or even economics!

Consider a tricky good that is less an end in itself than a means to the end of better health: human blood. There is clearly something abhorrent about considering this exceedingly useful therapeutic agent as an economic good—and indeed it has been asserted not to be one. *Ought* we therefore to apply our economic apparatus to it? More generally, ought thinking about social policy to be trammelled by cultural, as well as logical, constraints?

We are not, of course, always (perhaps, usually) aware of the cultural limitations of our thinking, but if ever we are, then we fail to pursue the logic of our thought beyond the bounds of 'reasonableness' only at our peril. To say that education, health and blood are beyond the 'economic' is to say also that they are beyond the realm of social policy, for only economic goods need to be allocated, whether according to principles of efficiency, or justice, or fairness, or anything else. It is to say that education—the pursuit, perhaps, of an ideal—cannot have policy decisions made about it. Since this is obviously false, we must find some reconciliation between the policy decision-making aspect and the essentialism that one feels inescapably drawn to when considering the nature of many of the social services.

It may sometimes be the case that the concern of social policy is *not* with essences but with accidents. For example, it may be of overriding concern to the scholar to establish the value *per se* of learning, but social policy may be concerned principally with the *training* of qualified personnel. With blood, the principal concern may be less to do with its intrinsic (and symbolic) qualities than with ensuring its adequate supply in good condition as a medical life-saving input.

At the same time there is no general presumption that social policy is concerned solely with an instrumental view of education, blood and ethics. Social policy is concerned with *all* of the things that are of concern to society. This need not imply conflict (for example, the promotion of training is not necessarily inconsistent with 'education'—subjects pursued as ends in themselves are not necessarily useless for all other purposes—but it sometimes does. Thus, an effective method of ensuring adequate blood supplies may involve buying and selling it, which may discourage people from giving it—and acts of giving may be regarded as an essentially good thing in blood supplies).

In all this there is no division between the economic and the non-economic. Choices have to be made, priorities settled, means decided and so on. What is exceedingly difficult in the field of social policy is frequently the *quantification* of some of the most important characteristics that ought to shape policy. How does one quantify the output of the National Health Service? How does one quantify the values to be placed upon that output? How does one quantify the relationship between the output and the various costly inputs that create it? Some people argue that not only is quantification of such things impossible but also inherently undesirable.

As we shall see, these problems of quantification are receiving economic attention but even were it impossible to quantify the end outputs and their social value the scope for useful economic analysis would not be exhausted. We shall consider briefly some of the ways in which this is true. Later chapters will discuss some of these applications in much greater detail. One possibility in normative economics is to apply the techniques of cost-effectiveness in order to establish which of two alternative policies (considered to be, say, equally desirable in themselves) involve the least social cost. (Even if they were not considered equally desirable, the costing of the options would reduce the area of uncertainty for decision takers.) A positive use would be to make assertions about the probable effects (i.e. based on economic prediction) of different policies or different organisational frameworks in terms of the direction in which important variables are expected to move. At the least, such qualitative statements are useful in refuting naive prejudices. As we have seen in chapter 6 the economic analysis of the response of labour supply to changes in tax rates does not unambiguously yield a disincentive effect, as is frequently thought.

The major danger with *any* public policy is that the perfectly proper public requirements of accountability and control may tend to give emphasis to those dimensions of social policy that are readily quantifiable at the expense of those, possibly more important, dimensions that are not. It is easier to calculate the social class of students attending university than it is to measure the effects of attendance on 'education'. It is easier to cost a year's stay in hospital for a chronically ill patient than it is to measure the social value of keeping him there a year. It is easier to devise a new plan for paying for health insurance than it is to assess its cultural consequences in terms of the social environment. These dangers are inherent in the world we live in—a world of ignorance and uncertainty but where decisions must be taken. They are, however, not inherent in economics. Indeed, as we shall see, economics has something exceedingly important to say about the form of institution that is appropriate for minimising these dangers.

Economists are frequently confronted with the charge that they try to 'add up' non-additive and highly disparate entities[1] and, moreover, that they try to extend this arbitrary adding-up procedure to *every* variable relevant to a policy decision by putting money values on everything. If anything, such strictures are more likely to be made in the context of social services than of, say, the siting of an airport. We should, therefore, be clear about what the economic approach really does imply.

First, to the extent that the Welfare State is a response to the existence of caring externalities based upon the preferences of members of the community, we have seen that there is an all-pervasive element of choice: there is no unique *imperative* based upon either biological factors or considerations of social justice. This requires, in turn, that benefits in the Welfare State be evaluated in relation to their cost; in short, that the whole panoply of the Welfare State be subject to efficiency analysis. This requires in turn the making of conceptual distinctions between inputs and outputs, the study of the various means by which inputs are transformed into outputs, and the assignment of values (termed costs and benefits according as they apply to inputs or outputs). In addition to the analysis of means and ends, and the links between them, analysis is also required of the ways in which values (preferences) are expressed and the effectiveness of market institutions, political processes, and so on, in revealing them. It also requires the exercise of analytical imagination in the invention of new ways in which such values may be better expressed or inferred.

Even if we were to suppose that the Welfare State is largely a response to a moral imperative not rooted in caring preferences, much of this agenda remains intact: we would still need to study effective means of attaining the moral ends sought, to measure and monitor inputs, outputs, and so on. What we would no longer be required to do is to cost them, for a moral imperative is to be obeyed regardless of cost. But costs of a sort reappear if there is any conflict between various moral imperatives (for example, between 'freedom' and 'minimum subsistence' and 'privacy') such that achieving one required the sacrifice of some of another.

On either view, it is neither always possible nor even desirable to assign a money value to the (say) outputs, even if the various dimensions in which output has been measured are indeed 'added up' into an index of deprivation, as in the preceding chapter, or an index of health or education, as discussed in the next chapters. Thus, in determining the overall balance of public expenditure between health, education or housing, it may not be of great help to assign a money value to the total outputs of these sectors, even if the outputs can be measured, since the balancing of benefits at the margin has to be done at the political level, where caring preferences and views about social justice acquire reality by being expressed by those whose task it is to interpret the will of members of the community. But at less aggregate levels it is very frequently helpful to have benefits valued in money terms for comparison with cost. At this level, cost–benefit analysis comes into its own (see chapter 11).

As we shall see when we look in greater detail at health, education and housing, there is a large research agenda under the heads discussed above. Since the bulk of social policy in the Welfare State proceeds as though its objectives are fundamentally to satisfy preferences (both selfish and caring), the fixed elements in the system being more the result of administrative and political inertia and/or vested interests than of ethical absolutes, the scope for the application of political economy is very wide indeed, and, with the steady growth of the public sector, has been growing yet wider.

Returning, therefore, to the original question 'are the social services different': clearly they are different in the trivial sense that pensions and health services are not the same thing as a violin recital or a ton of metallurgical coke. But they are not different in the sense that they require allocation and institutions to allocate them. Clearly they are different in the sense that they are allocated and often produced within the public sector— but coke gets produced in the public sector and recitals in the private. But they are not in the sense that *individuals* ultimately do not make the decisions concerning their production and allocation. Very important, they are *not* different in the sense that economic problems do not exist concerning their production and allocation, and in the sense that they are so disparate that only arbitrary methods exist of valuing their costs and benefits. Equally important, they *are* different in so far as they embody the concern that one set of individuals may have for another. Indeed, the one important sense in which it appears they *are* different lies in the postulated fact that caring externalities exist in relation to them and not to most other things. No discussion of the efficiency of the social services can therefore be complete without a consideration of caring externalities.

B. MODELS OF EXTERNALITY

But this is not the end of the story, for having established the *prima facie* case for their not being different in the one important sense that matters for our purposes, there remains a major problem in identifying the nature of the specific distributive concerns underlying the social services. Depending upon what they are, the appropriate nature of policy responses can be very different. In externality terms, the problem consists in identifying the nature of the caring externalities in the provision of social services.

We shall now examine four externality models of the social services. First we shall assume that the caring externality relates to the *absolute* amount of service received (*size* of pension, *years* of schooling, health *services* received, and so on). In the second, we shall assume that it is the *relative* amount that matters (pension *relative to*, say, average earnings, schooling of the poor *relative to*, say, some minimum standard laid down, health services consumption of the poor *relative to*, say, the rich). The third and fourth models assume that the externality relates to the *effects* that social services may have on the characteristics (nutrition, educational attainment, skill levels, dependence on others, health status) that they are intended to alter. This can be divided into a concern with absolute characteristics of individuals, or with their characteristics relative to one another or to standards.

We thus have a two-way classification describing our four basic types of externality. These are shown in summary form in Figure 7.1. The bulk of the economic literature has concerned itself with type I externalities. There has been some discussion of type II externalities. Types III and IV are only just beginning to be discussed seriously by economists and social administrators. This discussion is long overdue since types III and IV seem to approximate most closely to reality. Also, as we shall see, the distinctions made here enable us to go some way towards disentangling the underlying issues that divide the so-called 'selectivists' from the so-called 'universalists'.

	Absolute levels	Relative levels
Services consumed	I	II
Characteristics to be changed	III	IV

FIG. 7.1   Four types of externality in social services.

Type I Externality

Consider the widespread view that the consumption of social services confers external benefits of the first kind, relating to the absolute amount, or rate, of the service. Figure 7.2 contains the basic geometry for analysing some welfare consequences of this externality. Let us assume initially that the service in question (say housing, education or health) is bought and sold in market transactions without any public intervention.

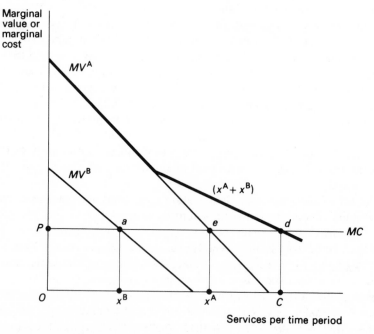

FIG. 7.2.   Efficient output and consumption in the absence of externality.

MV^A and MV^B represent the marginal valuation (or demand) curves of two individuals, A and B, for service. The sum of their demands at each price is denoted by the heavy curve $(x^A + x^B)$. For convenience, assume that services of a specified sort are available at a constant cost OP. In the absence of any externalities, at a price OP, B demands Ox^B and A demands Ox^A, a total of OC. Given the demands, the cost curve and the absence of external effects, these rates of consumption are Pareto optimal.

Now suppose that A considers that B is not getting enough service, that is he would value B's greater consumption. Suppose, more precisely, that in Figure 7.3 this concern of A for B is represented by the curve MV_B^A: the

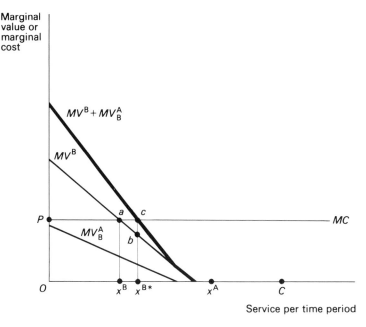

FIG. 7.3. Efficient output and consumption with type I externality.

marginal value to A of B's consumption (or A's demand for B's consumption). The marginal *social* value of B's consumption is now the value to B *plus* the value of B's consumption to A, found, as we have previously seen, by summing vertically the two curves MV^B and MV_B^A. This gives the new curve $MV^B + MV_B^A$. Note that this intersects the marginal cost curve at c, *to the right* of the previous point a. In the presence of externalities of this kind, therefore, B ought to consume more than he chooses (can afford) in isolated purchases of his own. The overall consumption of services will be too small if left only to market forces.

Figure 7.4 completes the story. Here we add at each price the *social* demand for service for B $(MV^B + MV_B^A)$ to A's demands (his individual

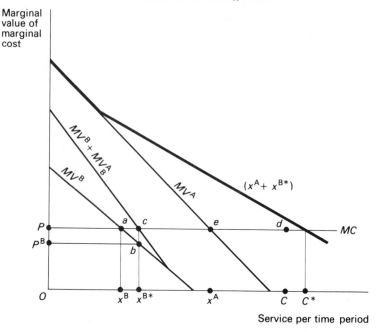

FIG. 7.4   Efficient price subsidies under type I externality.

demand is the social demand since no externalities apply in his case). This horizontal summation gives us the new heavy curve $x^A + x^{B*}$. The new optimal total care to provide is C^* rather than C—the difference being the amount more that B gets. Note that, at the optimum, A would still prefer to see B consume more (MV_B^A is positive) but he does not value B's additional consumption sufficiently to make it worth either his or B's while to incur further costs of providing care.

We can now see that, if a type I externality exists, a simple market solution to the allocation of the service with a uniform price will lead to inefficiency. In particular, efficiency requires B to consume x^{B*}, but at price OP he will consume only x^B. Several solutions are, in principle, possible. One is for A to make available the *extra* units of care ($x^B x^{B*}$) at a price OP^B. This would cost A the rectangle bisected by the diagonal ab since he would have to pay the difference between cost and price on the extra units. Another is to make each additional unit available to B at the price equal to the height of MV^B between a and b on a sliding charge, that is to try to get B to pay as much as he is willing for each additional unit. This would cost A the triangle abc. In practice each of these solutions is likely to pose difficulties, particularly in identifying the demand curve between a and b and in administering the subsidies. The simplest solution (but also the costliest in terms of subsidy) is to charge B an across-the-board price of OP^B for all service. The clear policy implication, however, is that the service should be subsidised for at least some consumers.

In a more realistic world with many potential recipients of subsidised service new complications emerge. If MVs vary—as they are bound to—then optimal subsidies will also vary. It is widely believed that the demand for social services varies directly with income. If this is the case, and assuming that the external part of the social demand for each person's service is the same across all persons, then the more precise policy implication follows that the subsidy ought to *vary inversely with income.*

In Figure 7.5, MV^E is the external demand for any person's service.

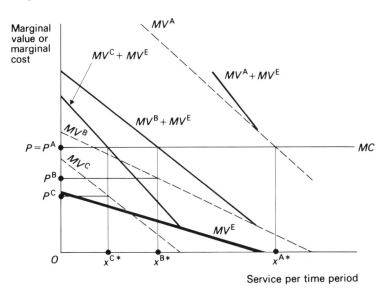

FIG. 7.5   Price subsidies are universely related to income under type I externality.

MV^A, MV^B and MV^C are the demand curves for each of three individuals, shown as dotted lines. Demand curves to the right are successively for wealthier persons (i.e. we assume social services are a normal good). Optimal consumption by each is given by the intersection of the sum of MV^E and each person's MV with the marginal cost and is Ox^{C*}, Ox^{B*} and Ox^{A*} for each, involving a subsidy of PP^C per unit for C, PP^B per unit for B and zero for A. In A's case, while some consumption rates yield external benefits, at his chosen level, x^{A*}, the marginal external benefit is zero, so the internal individual optimum is the social optimum. In C's case, note that without the subsidy he would actually consume no service at all.

Arguments for selective subsidy, of the type just discussed, can frequently be heard, though put less formally, in public and political debate. They form a basis of the efficiency arguments of those preferring 'selective' to 'universal' systems of social benefit. (Why give services to those who do not 'need' them?) Sometimes there is the temptation to suppose that those holding the opposite view to oneself in the argument about whether social services should be selectively or universally provided are either fools or knaves. The truth, however, is more likely to be that the views of each group are the logical implication of some basic value judgement that they make or that they attribute to the bulk of the population such as, for example, that people care only about absolute consumption of certain specific services. Because passions may be deeply felt about these issues and because the argument just considered has a substantial amount of persuasive power, it is as well to emphasise the two crucial assumptions that have been made so far. First, we have assumed that the externality concerns the *absolute* amount of consumption, rather than the consumption of one person relative to another. Second, we have assumed that the externality concerns *consumption*, rather than the *effects* the consumption is expected to have. Changing these assumptions can have dramatic effects on the policy conclusions.

Type II Externality

There are obviously lots of ways in which the type I model could be adapted to cater for relativities—presumably any of the measures discussed in chapter 5 could be candidates for inclusion, and there are, for this reason, many potential subdivisions of the type II externality. For expository purposes here, we shall suppose that the nature of the externality is that *equality* of service is wanted for individuals with similar characteristics so that it is *deviations* from equality that may be worth removing. Equal treatment for equal need is one interpretation of what the Welfare State should aim to do. But here the emphasis on equality is different from that discussed earlier. For example, in chapter 4 we noted that equal treatment of those who have the same *general* external effects (and for whom the marginal costs of transfer were the same) was implied by a policy of efficient distribution of income. In the discussion of externality type I above it was an implication that those imposing the same *specific* external effects should likewise be treated the same. In these cases, equality of treatment is an implication of efficiency. In the case we are about to discuss, however, it is a prior desideratum. This leads to some different policy implications.

In Figure 7.6 we have two individuals, A and B, with A consuming $Ox^A - Ox^B (= x^B x^A)$ more than B. This difference might be reduced in four ways.

(a) The sacrifice method: A throws away his own consumption. The cost to A is the value to him of his consumption, which is shown by the height of MV^A. For example, to reduce his consumption from x^A to x^B would cost him $x^A dfx^B$—the whole area under his MV curve between x^B and x^A. This method assumes he has already bought or is otherwise entitled to Ox^A consumption.

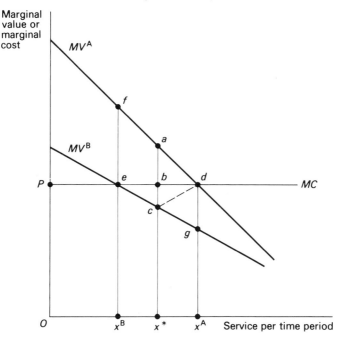

FIG. 7.6 Alternative policies under type II externality.

(b) The gift method: instead of sacrificing what he has already bought, X could be transferred from A to B and, since B would gain what A lost, this method is twice as effective in reducing absolute differences as the sacrifice method and must therefore be cheaper. In fact it would cost A only $x^A dax^*$—he would lose x^*x^A and B would gain the same amount x^*x^B.

(c) The abstention method: A abstains from, or is denied, marginal purchases of services. The cost to him in this case is the difference between the value of the extra forgone and what its cost would have been. In Figure 7.6, the cost of abstaining from $x^B x^A$ consumption is *edf*—otherwise known as the consumer's surplus on these units of consumption.

(d) The subsidy method: according to this method, B is paid the difference between his MV and the price. For example, the minimum amount he must be paid to increase consumption from x^B to x^A is *egd* in Figure 7.6.

Which method will be used? Working on the presumption that individuals will seek to minimise the cost of achieving equality, one can immediately see that the sacrifice method will not be used since it is more costly than any other method involving, as it does, the acquisition but non-use of services.

Of the four possibilities, therefore, the first (the sacrifice method) can unambiguously be ranked below the other three. We therefore rule this out as a rational method of obtaining equality. Of the three remaining, it is

clear that the cost to A of reducing his consumption by giving to B
($x^A dax^*$) must be larger than a suitably chosen *combination* of abstention
and subsidy (*bda* + *ebc*) producing equality at the same level Ox^*. We may
therefore infer that the combination of abstention and subsidy will be
preferred (by A; B, whose preferences count only in so far as A is not
permitted to compel consumption of the service against B's will, is in a
'take it or leave it' position in this model).

But it is quite easy to show that there exists a better combination of
abstention and subsidy than that portrayed in Figure 7.6. This can be seen
by noting that the marginal cost of abstention (= *ab*) is higher than the
marginal subsidy cost (= *bc*). The least cost combination of the two
methods for A is where the marginal costs are equalised. This is shown in
Figure 7.7, where *hi* = *ij* and where at a lower cost to A (and less absten-

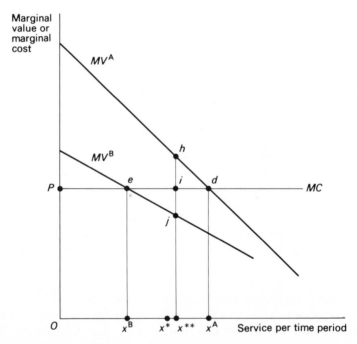

FIG. 7.7   Efficiency output and consumption under type II externality.

tion) equality is attained at a higher level of average consumption than
hitherto.[3] We thus see that in this case the subsidy pattern is *not* only
related to income (if demands are income elastic) but that *rationing* of
potential high demands is implied: the nature of the externality postulated
affects the efficient method of internalising it. In this case, not only should
the method of provision be such as to make social services cheaper to the
relatively poor (or anyone with low demand) but it should compel the

relatively rich (or anyone with high demand) to curtail demand by rationing at going prices. This is not implied by the argument underlying the normal selectivists' case or by externality type I, but may form the logical basis for the view that argues for subsidised services and reduction of 'privilege' by, for example, prohibiting private schools or hospitals where people may otherwise purchase 'more' than those receiving, say, state services.[4] Note, moreover, that this rationale is not based upon some moralising elite imposing *its* view of the 'good society' upon others. What it says is much more powerful than that; it is this: that if the externality takes the form postulated (viz. that it relates to relative consumption of services) it is in the interest of those who care in this way to moderate their own demands. Prohibition is a form of voluntarily accepted coercion adopted to overcome the free rider problem in this case and has a rationale similar to that of compulsory taxation in cases we have met earlier.

Types III and IV Externalities

If we now alter the object of concern from the consumption of services themselves to the characteristics of individuals that such services should change, then entirely new considerations come into play, which mark off types III and IV externalities sharply from types I and II. For this reason we shall consider types III and IV together. We are, in types III and IV, concerned with absolute and relative *characteristics* of individuals such as their state of health or educational level. For example, health services are required because they can make sick people well, museums and art galleries are required because they awaken cultural awareness and appreciation, schools and universities because they change the individuals who pass through them in ways thought to be significant by members of society as a whole.

The focus in these models is upon what we may call the *social service production function*, which may be schematised as in Figure 7.8. In this

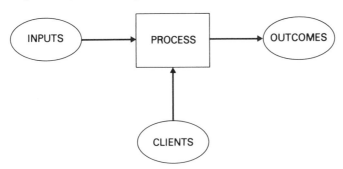

FIG. 7.8   Social services production function.

figure, the actual services, which are the end-focus in the other models, are the *inputs* (physical and human) that, when combined with *clients* of the system, produce outcomes. Teachers, buildings and equipment (inputs) are used with pupils (clients) to produce skills embodied in people (outcomes); doctors, nurses, buildings and equipment (inputs) are used with patients (clients) to produce healthier individuals (outcomes); home visitors and adaptive aids (inputs) are used with elderly housebound individuals (clients) to produce greater mobility and less dependence (outcomes).

This view leads to yet another pattern of subsidies, etc. Since the *effectiveness* of a process in transforming inputs into outcomes is a technical matter, it has to be left in large part to the professionals: teachers, doctors, social workers, etc., though the resources with which they are endowed will presumably be now determined by how policy makers view the productivity of those resources in producing desired outcomes. But if what should determine receipt of service is the extent to which the recipient's intellect will be usefully sharpened, his health improved, his pain relieved, his mobility increased, his dependency reduced, and so on, then his *willingness to pay* becomes an irrelevance. Instead, the professionals must decide where, at the margin, the greatest outcomes are to be had—given a resource budget to which they must keep.

It is this approach that underlies the concept of the need for specific social services and that not only forms the basis of analysis of each of the social services to come in remaining chapters, but that also underlies cost–benefit analysis and programme budgeting, also to be discussed later. We may summarise the difference between types III and IV and types I and II by noting the following implications:

(i) Social services *may* be seen as consumption goods like any other. The private sector exists to give reality to such demands;

(ii) externality relationships depend upon a perception that an individual's characteristics could be improved by social services;

(iii) the link between inputs provided and outcomes is an 'engineering' type relationship requiring professionally skilled judgement;

(iv) in the *public* sector, therefore, appropriate services (a technical judgement) should be given to those whose characteristics society as a whole wishes to maintain or improve (a value judgement);

(v) in the *public* sector, while the services given to individual clients will be determined by the exercise of professional judgements by experts, decisions determining the amount of inputs to be made available for the use of particular professionals or groups of professionals in schools, universities, hospitals, local authorities and so on, will be made by taking a collective view concerning the effectiveness of the process, the cost of its inputs and the value of its outcomes.

(vi) a further implication is that, in the *public* sector, positive prices would become a complete irrelevance: services would be allocated according to a combination of judgement about what was 'needed' and what was 'effective' (given the resources available).

C. REQUIRED INFORMATION

The way of thinking suggested by types III and IV externality is encouraged not only by this micro-economic focus on individual agents, processes and consumers. There has also been a growing tendency since the 1950s, especially in the USA, towards the publication of books attempting to assess the 'state' of contemporary society—books such as Vance Packard's *The Status Seekers* or J. K. Galbraith's *The Affluent Society*. The authors may be social Pollyannas or Cassandras (usually the latter) and the features they seize upon in commenting upon the 'state' of society may accordingly be seen as vindicators or indicators. One thing, however, is clear and this is that, like the Paretian concept of social welfare, these authors emphasise that the accretion of material, and priced, wealth—the growth of Gross Domestic Product (GDP)—gives a wholly inadequate description of the welfare of a society, especially of the relatively wealthy societies. While the indicators used by these popular authors, and the interpretations put upon them, tend to reflect the particular values of the authors themselves, the social scientist would seek a set of indicators both more comprehensive and whose importance might be more generally recognised. The 'social indicators movement', as it has become known, shares the fundamental belief that many of the most crucial areas for social decision making need to have a great deal more attention paid to them.

Just as output budgeting (or PPBS) was principally a development within the US Department of Defense and was subsequently applied (rather too hastily for success) in a broad range of governmental activity, so the development of social indicators grew specifically out of another vast, costly and highly technological area of expenditure—the US space programme. The social impact of much modern technology was recognised to be inadequately measured by the conventional 'economic' indicators such as incomes, prices and employment or unemployment rates. Exactly the same is true, of course, with many of the areas of social policy. We have in this book frequently noted the inadequacy of many prices as indicators of social value; frequently prices are altogether absent; we have also noted the difficulties inherent in conceptualising, let alone measuring, the output of many social policies. Sensible social policy would clearly be much

improved if it were possible to measure more accurately (even if not perfectly) the social value of various policy alternatives, the 'real' consequences
of social policies and the relationships between the means (inputs) and the
ends (outputs).

The basic urge driving many members of the 'social indicators movement' is to measure things like 'educational deprivation', 'social inequality',
'health', 'need' or—most ambitious—Durkheim's notions of 'average moral-
ity' and 'individualism'. But this basic desire to make more rigorous any
discussion or measurement of the dimensions of a social 'problem' or of
social policy is not enough to enable one to proceed very far and can lead
to peculiar results if careful thought is not put in at the fundamental level
of designing *appropriate* indicators. It is not, for example, impossible to
find accurate looking numbers among the social policy literature that purport to describe, say, the *urgency* of a social problem. Thus, studies exist
that rank areas and regions along a scale that has been derived by adding
such phenomena as numbers of unemployed, malicious woundings, occupied males in skilled and unskilled jobs, numbers of households with a
density greater than $1\frac{1}{2}$ persons per room, deaths from bronchitis and
dividing all these by the population. How could one use such an indicator
of social deprivation or need? Why should the components of such an
indicator receive equal weights? How would the indicator be affected by
policies that are supposed to affect it? Is the indicator specific, or comprehensive enough? What social theory has been used to decide what to
put into the indicator and what to leave out? Likewise, examples abound
whereby the success of social policy is measured by the deployment of
resources rather than by the impact of the resources deployed on the
ultimate policy objective. *Input* measures (such as beds) or *throughput*
measures (such as deaths and discharges) abound in the health policy
literature and although they may be valid social indicators for some purposes they are not measures of output or of urgency of need or of effectiveness in meeting needs. These and related problems are evidently highly
pertinent and must be tackled before the measurement exercise ever gets
under way. In short, a theory of the relationship of social indicators and
social policy is required. One must be ever-conscious that blind
quantification—quantophrenia—may be as dangerous—and is probably
more dangerous—than no formal quantification at all.

To make a rational choice in social policy, knowledge is required about
the four key constituent elements in any social choice. Each of the four is
necessary and together they are sufficient for rational policy making. These
are, first, a measure of the objective or *outcome* of a policy (or collection of
policies). It is, for example, of little use to embark upon a set of policies
designed to promote educational equality or equality of life opportunity
unless one has some fairly unambiguous indicator that enables one to
monitor the success of one's policies. The second need, in view of the

multiplicity of the objectives of social policy, is the necessity to rank them in order of priority, to place social valuations upon them or 'shadow prices'. One has to be able to trade off various objectives such as equality of educational opportunity and increasing the nation's health and to be able to identify areas where objectives are mutually complementary—where one policy increases two outputs. In short, one requires an indicator of *social need*. Third, there is the need to understand the technology of policy: one requires a model that relates the increases in one objective to the necessary reductions in another. With either given or growing national resources it is equally necessary to know these 'production function' relationships, which set a limit to what *can* be done, which relate the real inputs in social policy to feasible outputs. Fourth, one needs to know the social costs of the policy.

Although information is needed about only these four things, they are a formidable quartet. The most fundamental of them in logic is the output indicator, for an indicator of need is naturally cast in terms of the output indicator: after all it is the output, or effects of the policy, that is needed. Similarly, production possibilities indicators relate one output to another. Output indicators are also, however, of importance purely for their own sakes in providing information about the state of society and the ways in which it is changing. It is in this sense that the term 'social indicator' has become most widely used, though it is a sense that can easily lead to misleading results unless the quartet of types of indicator is borne clearly in mind. For example, indicators of hospital throughput are sometimes proposed as measures of ill-health but they may vary as inputs in the system change. Thus, a planned reduction in psychiatric beds from 2.5 per thousand population to 0.5 per thousand would falsely indicate an improvement in the nation's mental health. This proposed indicator fails to make the kind of distinction emphasised here.

The relationships can be easily illustrated in a diagram. Figure 7.9 depicts our by now familiar conceptualisation of a social choice problem. The priorities indicator measures the social value of increments in the output indicator, and is equivalent to an MV schedule. The technical indicator measures what must necessarily be forgone of other outputs in increasing the indicator in question. The money value of direct inputs in a programme will normally be an inadequate guide to the height and shape of this schedule for it is not merely the expenditure on, say, manpower in the health service that is to be recorded here but the social value of that manpower in its most socially valuable alternatives use—say, in primary school education. This indicator is conceptually equivalent to a marginal social cost schedule. For each of them one dimension is easily seen to be the output indicator itself and the other is some numéraire system by which numbers are attached indicating relative priorities—money units are usually the most convenient. Clearly, the better the information the more

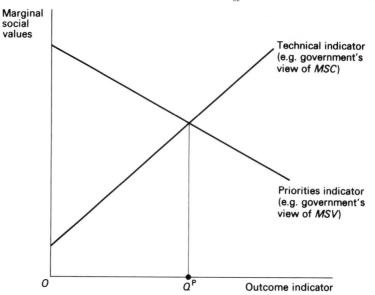

FIG. 7.9   Social indicators as marginal social value and cost under type III and IV
externality.

likely policy makers will be able to approach the optimal programme size
at Q^P.

Output indicators, in an ideal world, would correspond to the programme headings of an output budget, which is discussed in detail in
chapter 12, and would be more or less aggregated according to the purposes of the output budget. For some very specific purposes, not usually
identified in a broad output programme, one requires very specific output
measures. To illustrate, let us suppose that one is concerned with a cost-
effectiveness study of care for the elderly wherein one compares the effect of
residential homes with that of domiciliary care on the health and welfare of
elderly persons. Clearly, the required output indicator would attempt to
measure as accurately as possible the health and welfare of such persons.
The dimensions in which this can be done are, in principle, infinite and
include such aspects of their well-being as: ability to dress themselves;
mobility; ability to feed; ability to cut toenails; mental state; and so on.
Some of these dimensions will be highly correlated with others, enabling us
to eliminate some of them. Expediency will also compel one to restrict the
list and at this point the impossibility of having an entirely objective
indicator becomes clear. Not only must a choice be made about which are
the most important dimensions of 'output' for inclusion, but those that are
eventually included must be weighted according to one's view of their

importance in contributing to a person's general state of well-being. For example, it is possible to score an elderly person's state of mind on a scale of, say, 1–3 and also his ability to cut his toenails, but it is obviously not possible for the scores to be added up as they are. Not only may they be not entirely independent of one another but one may be regarded as being much more significant than another. (Recall our discussion of an index of deprivation in chapter 6.) An element of subjectivity creeps in. Whose subjective values should be used?

For more general purposes, output indicators may be more aggregated. For example, periodic surveys of the nation's 'health' may be taken that would be even cruder than specific output measures but that would raise essentially similar conceptual problems.

The difficulties of devising reasonable output indicators are enormous. The most advanced work in this area to date has taken place in the health field. There has also been a long-standing tradition (but mostly outside official circles) of measurement of the distribution of resources (but not much of the distribution of outputs). In the education field, however, output measurement has not yet got much beyond the crude basis of counting the heads of individuals in various stages of education—a throughput measure rather than an output measure. There has been no attempt to date to seek the ultimate outputs of education policy, to measure them and to adjust for quality. The reasons, of course, are not hard to find, for the task is very demanding. It may be that in some areas of policy, ultimate outputs will remain elusive and secondary indicators will always have to be used based upon some hypothetical relationship between the notional true output and its surrogate. In the short run the use of secondary indicators is inevitably more widespread, for in many cases neither the conceptual nor the practical problems of final output measures have been solved. In short-run compromises, however, it is of utmost importance that the long-run objectives—with all their *organisational* consequences—should not be lost from sight.

The twin problems of developing usable short-run compromise indicators while simultaneously tackling the long-run development of proper output indicators can be illustrated by the problems confronted in health service policy. At present there is scarcely any information about the final outputs that measure the success of the health and personal social services in improving the nation's well-being, notable exceptions being in the maternity and general health programmes where the level of infant and maternal deaths and handicapping conditions arising at birth are known and the incidence of certain diseases subject to preventive measures is measured. Other output data are at best patchy or difficult to interpret (e.g. hospital inpatient waiting lists and times) or not based on random sampling (e.g. The Royal College of General Practitioners' morbidity surveys).

There does exist, by contrast, a relative abundance of secondary measures relating to:

(a) numbers of cases treated;
(b) ratios of inputs (staff, equipment, expenditure, etc.) to clients;
(c) balance of care, i.e. the range and mix of services being delivered to different client groups.

Thus, it is possible by using these secondary measures to measure success in terms of the extent to which specific targets are obtained. But these secondary indicators—whose relationship with final outputs is far from clear—themselves need substantial improvement. For example, even such a well-known throughput measure as the number of cases relates to episodes of sickness rather than to individuals: for example, the same individual admitted twice to hospital counts as two cases. Outpatient events are not linked to inpatient events. It is not generally known whether the same elderly persons who receive 'meals on wheels' (hot meals supplied to the home) also receive home help (assistance with housework). A major improvement in these data will be to relate them to clients.

In an output budgeting context, secondary indicators with a satisfactory client base provide a valuable foundation for predicting future budgets— i.e. for forecasting future expenditures based on fulfilling anticipated health programmes. They also help to provide decision makers with an evolving picture of how policy in the health and personal social services is developing and help to identify problem areas worthy, perhaps, of special study.

Ultimately, however, the objective of health policy is not to provide certain ratios of inputs to outputs, to maintain or increase particular throughputs of clients or even to abolish waiting lists! It is, to the extent that concern is a type III or IV externality, to improve the health of the population. The other factors are relevant only in so far as they help (a) to identify the real outputs, (b) to locate their costs and (c) to enable decision makers to balance the relative (social) values of improved health as between different clients and enable higher decision makers to balance the relative value of improved health in general as against more education, higher pensions, less poverty, crime or broken homes. In short, the ultimate objective of genuine output measurement should never be lost sight of. Not the least important of the reasons for emphasising this is that only a genuine output-oriented approach can succeed in cutting across existing organisational lines and suggesting new ones, putting organisation in a more rational relationship with its end objectives.

Difficult though even the conceptualisation—let alone the operationalisation—of an appropriate definition and measure of health output is, the output of education establishments is, if anything, even harder to come to terms with. Educators, like the medical profession, are understandably suspicious of the economic approach, fearing that it will tend to emphasise quantity at the expense of quality, the easily identifiable rather than the subtle, the short-term effects rather than the long-term, the financial rather than the cultural. However, many educators are inconsistent in their attitudes, especially when pay claims are in the offing. Then the assertion that the output or productivity (output divided by input) of schools and universities cannot be measured objectively is contradicted by their unsubstantiated assertions that it has, in fact, increased since the last award.

There is no single objective or output of the education sector. Therefore any measurement of educational output, at whatever level, must be multidimensional. At its broadest, education alters the individuals being educated and the purpose of output measurement is thus to measure this 'value added'. Standardised tests to measure the transmission of knowledge and other attainments of pupils and students to test cultural awareness, creativity and moral or social values, have been devised by educational psychologists. Unfortunately systematic information, as compared with occasional experiments, has not been collected for any lengthy period of time or for the very long period (i.e. long-term effects on those who have been educated). At the moment, therefore, such measures as these are not available for examining the secular trends in education or for measuring productivity and cost-effectiveness.

We shall be returning to these issues in greater detail in the remaining chapters of Part III. In concluding this chapter, let us emphasise that the central feature marking the social services as 'different' from other services is the externality relationship. We have discussed several forms that it might take, and there is no general reason to suppose that only one form will be present in either society or any special field of policy. Indeed, it may be the case that a different type of concern is precisely what generates some of the principal differences between rival attitudes to the various areas of social policy. This will shape the nature of our subsequent discussion of the problems of production, finance and allocation in the major social service areas taken up in each of the following chapters. The application of *general* techniques such as linear programming, estimation of cost curves, cost–benefit analysis, cost-effectiveness analysis and output budgeting are discussed in Part IV. These generally raise problems and have a relevance that is not unique to specific social services.

In the three following chapters health, education, and housing are discussed with particular emphasis on their special features. In each case, where appropriate, we examine the nature of the production function, human capital aspects, measurement of output, externality relationships, and finance. While these areas of application cover most of the remaining areas of the Welfare State not discussed in Part II, viz. the services in kind, we have excluded some areas, notably employment services, training outside of schools and colleges, and other personal social services. However, the analysis that is presented is relatively easily extended to such areas and this, for reasons of space, is left to the reader.

NOTES

1. A persistent critic is Peter Self. See 'Nonsense on stilts: the futility of Roskill', *New Society*, 2 July 1970.
2. One approach, which effectively *defines* social services as being 'different', is the 'social rights' or 'welfare rights' approach used by some students of social policy and many social administrators. As we have seen in chapter 1, the arbitrariness of this approach is inconsistent with the Paretian method of analysis, for it permits statements such as 'I (A) think B ought to have a right to X and, moreover, C ought to pay for it'. The actual preferences of B and C need not enter the picture at all. We argued in chapter 1 that, while such utterances are perfectly legitimate statements of a personal viewpoint, they are unsatisfactory as the basis for a social science approach to social policy. However, our approach will include (at least in principle) whatever benefit A gets from transfers between C and B implied by giving B some particular right. Beyond that, no matter how noble A's motives are in one's opinion, we do not go. The matter is properly treated explicitly as a question of justice that must transcend individual preferences for various patterns of rights in society.
3. Make sure you understand why $(ebc + abd)$ in Figure 7.6 is larger than $(eij + hdi)$ in Figure 7.7. To check that you do, draw a figure showing the points in Figure 7.6 and those in Figure 7.7 making sure that $hi = ij$ and $eb = bd$. To show this we only need to show that $biha > cjib$ since triangles ebc and hid are common to both (eij contains ebc and abd contains hid). Since bi is a common side to these two areas and $ab > bc$, and we know $hi = ij$, therefore $biha > cjib$. Q.E.D.
4. The 'more' is in quotation marks to indicate that it may imply not necessarily more 'output' of such institutions, but more *input* (more teachers per pupil, more staff—or more senior staff—per bed, etc.) or more *quality* (often measured in the same way).

QUESTIONS ON CHAPTER 7

1. Should donors be paid for their blood? Should hospitals pay for blood?
2. What dangers are inherent in quantifying the consequences of social policies? How may they be overcome? Is quantification valuable even when they cannot be overcome completely?
3. Are social services different from other kinds of service? If so, in what way? If not, why is the state involved in their finance and production?
4. Outline the nature and policy implications of type I externalities.
5. Outline the nature and policy implications of type II externalities.

6. Outline the nature and policy implications of types III and IV externalities.
7. How would you set about establishing which model of externality best reflects prevalent attitudes in society?
8. Suppose that social justice (rather than preferences) related to the objects of concern in the four externality models. What difference for policy would that make?
9. What are the outputs of social policies?
10. Should social indicators measure inputs, throughputs, outputs, or all three?
11. Evaluate the routinely published data relating to either health or education in your country in terms of some desiderata (of your own choosing) of rational planning.
12. Do individuals have 'natural' or 'human' rights to social services?
13. What value judgements are embodied in the concept of output of social services?
14. What role should technical experts, politicians, consumers, voters, have in determining the output and the means of producing it in
    (a) education
    (b) health care?
15. Why should social services be produced (if at all) in the public sector?
16. What does history have to teach concerning the underlying reason for the current pattern of health services in your country?
17. Should public education spending be allocated on an equal per capita basis, or to maximise educational attainment, or to maximise the increase in education attainment?
18. How should social service outputs accruing to different individuals, regions, etc., be weighted?
19. Should social services be free of charge?
20. Should *ineffective* (in terms of their output) services be provided by the state when they are demanded by their clients?

FURTHER READING

On the nature of education:

Griffiths, A. P. (1965) A deduction of universities. In R. D. Archambault (ed.) *Philosophical Analysis and Education.* London: Routledge and Kegan Paul, pp. 187–207.

Hirst, P. H. and Peters, R. S. (1970) *The Logic of Education.* London: Routledge and Kegan Paul.

Newman, J. H. (1915) *On the Scope and Nature of University Education.* London: Dent.

Peters, R. S. (1965) Education as initiation. In Archambault, *op. cit.*, pp. 87–111.

On the meaning of health:

Culyer, A. J. (1978) Need, values and health status measurement. In A. J. Culyer and K. G. Wright (eds) *Economic Aspects of Health Services.* London: Martin Robertson.

Sigerist, H. E. (1941) *Medicine and Human Welfare.* New Haven, Conn.: Yale University Press.

World Health Organisation (1958) *Constitution of the World Health Organisation.* Annex 1, *The first ten years of the WHO.* Geneva: WHO.

Whether blood is an economic good:

Culyer, A. J. (1977) Blood and altruism: an economic review. In D. B. Johnson (ed.) *Blood Policy: Issues and Alternatives.* Washington, DC: American Enterprise Institute.

Cooper, M. H. and Culyer, A. J. (1968) *The Price of Blood.* London: Institute of Economic Affairs.

Cooper, M. H. and Culyer, A. J. (1973) *The economics of giving.* London: Institute of Economic Affairs.

Titmuss, R. M. (1966) *Choice and the 'Welfare State'.* London: Fabian Society. Reprinted as chapter 12 in R. M. Titmuss *Commitment to Welfare,* London: Allen and Unwin, 1968.

Titmuss, R. M. (1972) *The Gift Relationship.* London: Allen and Unwin. This controversy is best read in its chronological order.

Whether health care is 'different':

Culyer, A. J. (1971) The nature of the commodity 'health care' and its efficient allocation. *Oxford Economic Papers, 23,* pp. 189–211.

Culyer, A. J. (1972) On the relative efficiency of the NHS. *Kyklos, 25,* pp. 266–87.

Klarman, H. E. (1965) *The Economics of Health.* New York and London: Columbia University Press.

Lees, D. S. (1961) *Health Through Choice.* London: Institute of Economic Affairs.

Titmuss, R. M. (1963) Ethics and economics of medical care. *Medical Care,* pp. 16–22. Reprinted as chapter 21 in R. M. Titmuss *Commitment to Welfare, op. cit.*

Titmuss, R. M. (1966) Choice and the welfare state, *loc. cit.*

Office of Health Economics (1971) *Prospects in Health.* London: OHE.

On externality models (again, applied to health):

Culyer, A. J. (1971) Medical care and the economics of giving. *Economica, 38,* pp. 295–303.

Lindsay, C. M. (1969) Medical care and the economics of sharing. *Economica, 36,* pp. 351–62.

Pauly, M. V. (1971) *Medical Care at Public Expense.* New York: Praeger.

On vouchers (applied to education):

Center for the Study of Public Policy (1970) *Education Vouchers: A report on financing elementary education by grants to parents.* US Office of Economic Opportunity.

Friedman, M. (1962) *Capitalism and Freedom.* Chicago: University of Chicago Press, ch. 6.

Maynard, A. K. (1975) *Experiment with Choice in Education.* London: Institute of Economic Affairs.

Olsen, E. O. (1971) Some theorems in the theory of efficiency transfers. *Journal of Political Economy, 79,* pp. 166–76.

Peacock, A. T. and Wiseman, J. (1964) *Education for Democrats.* London: Institute of Economic Affairs.

Rowley, C. K. (1969) The political economy of British education. *Scottish Journal of Political Economy*, *16*, pp. 152–76.

State of New Hampshire (1973) *The New Hampshire Education Voucher Project.*

US National Institute of Education (1973) *Education Vouchers: the experience at Alum Rock.* Washington, DC: NIE.

Wiseman, J. (1969) The economics of education. *Scottish Journal of Political Economy*, *6*, pp. 48–58.

CHAPTER 8

Health Services

A. THE PRODUCTION FUNCTION

We shall examine more subtle measures of ill-health than mortality later in this chapter. To begin with, however, it is instructive to look at the historical evidence relating health services to mortality. In a nutshell, the remarkable fact seems to be that with the possible exception of smallpox vaccination (an exception that is hotly contested by some (Razzell, 1978)) only when the twentieth century was well into its majority did any evidence appear that the personal health services (that is, services or procedures actively supplied or 'done' to individuals) had any impact on health. There was an enormous population rise in Britain after 1700. Although the increase was relatively small from 1700 to 1750, after the middle of the eighteenth century population rose rapidly and steadily right through to the end of the nineteenth century. From 1750 to 1850 the best estimates indicate that population increased three-fold. Over the very long run, population in England and Wales was around 1.5 m at the time of the Domesday Book of 1086, 5.5 m in 1700, 18 m in 1851 and 49 m in 1971.

Since the early eighteenth century birth rates have exceeded death rates in every decade and both seemed to have declined fairly consistently throughout the period. Migration was, incidentally, relatively unimportant in determining population growth in England and Wales.

Now we are not concerned here with the historian's question 'What caused the population increase?' But we must examine the possibility that it may have been due to medical interventions, because it is quite clear that the cause in fact relates not to birth rates (which were falling) but to death rates.

Cause of death in Britain was first registered in 1838, and there is little doubt that the principal factor contributing to the population increase since and before that time was a decline in mortality rates due to a reduction in the number of deaths from communicable diseases. The main non-infectious contributors before the twentieth century were probably a reduction in infanticide and death from starvation, and since 1900 the dramatic fall in prematurity and other neo-natal non-infectious disease. Now, since mortality was falling and life expectancy was rising before these causes of death were properly understood, let alone treatable, it is difficult

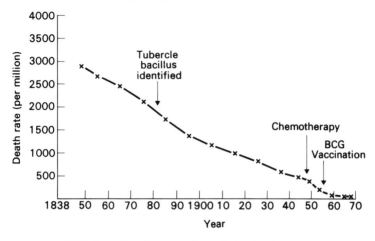

FIG. 8.1   Respiratory tuberculosis: death rates.

to attribute the immense improvement in the health of the British between 1700 and 1900 to personal health services.

Look at the pattern of decline for some major infections (Figures 8.1–8.6) as revealed by McKeown (1976). Respiratory tuberculosis was by far the largest killer in the mid-nineteenth century. Despite Koch's discovery of the tubercle bacillus in 1882, effective treatment with streptomycin began only in 1947—after seven-eighths of the reduction in the death rate had already occurred.

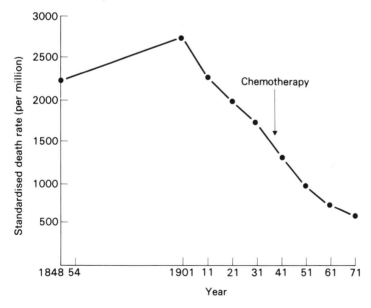

FIG. 8.2   Bronchitis, pneumonia and influenza: death rates.

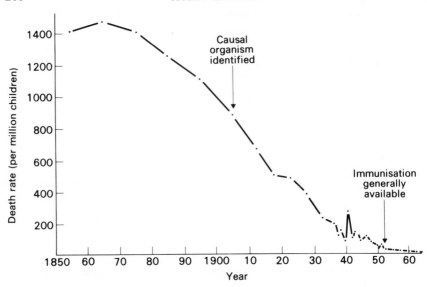

FIG. 8.3   Whooping cough: death rates of children under 15.

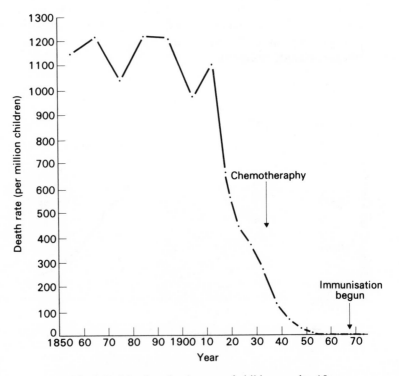

FIG. 8.4   Measles: death rates of children under 15.

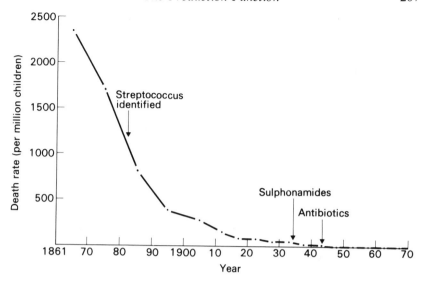

FIG. 8.5   Scarlet fever: death rates of children under 15.

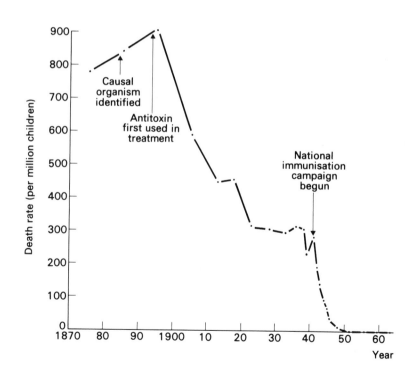

FIG. 8.6   Diphtheria: death rates of children under 15.

Bronchitis, influenza and pneumonia (the next largest cause, taken together) have to be taken together for data reasons. There is still no effective immunisation against bronchitis and 'flu. The effective therapy marked on the chart is the early sulphonamides which were effective against streptococcal infection, and sulphapyridine (later) against lobar pheumonia. The curve shows a slightly steeper slope after the mid-1930s, but the impact appears to have been relatively small. Whooping cough confirms the pattern—the greatest decline in mortality occurred over-whelmingly prior to effective medical intervention.

Measles, in the next chart, shows a decline in mortality only since 1915. But it was possible to control mortality, which is usually due to secondary infection, only after the drugs of the mid-1930s. Immunisation was only recently available. Similarly with scarlet fever, there was no effective treat-ment before prontosil in 1935—after 90 per cent of the improvement had already occurred.

Diphtheria shows some changes possibly attributable to effective use of antitoxin introduced around the turn of the century and to immunisation after 1941. However, other influences may have caused these declines, for in the USA some states experienced a decline in mortality in the 1940s with-out an immunisation programme.

Improved nutrition has been held to be a factor contributing to man's ability to resist disease. The trouble with this thesis is that although agri-cultural productivity rose after the agricultural revolution, it is not clear that per capita food consumption increased (though after the 1870s regula-tion improved the quality of food). In any case, the mortality of the aristo-cracy seems to have followed much the same pattern as that of the rest of the community.

The impact of the sanitary reforms of the nineteenth century is less ambiguous. Adequate drainage, refuse disposal away from publicly frequented places and the improvement of water supplies began to be generally introduced halfway through the century. The decline in mortality from intestinal infections such as cholera is alone an adequate indicator of their effectiveness.

Until this century, then, it would appear that, apart from any spontan-eous declines in the virulence of disease that may have occurred, the chief agents improving the health of the British people were (possibly) improved nutrition and (certainly) hygienic measures. The activities of the medics, whether the humble apothecary or the Fellows of the hugely prestigious Royal College of Physicians, were relatively insignificant.

During the twentieth century, entirely new developments in medical technology and especially in pharmacology made it possible for the first time for medical intervention to have a marked and indisputable impact on the natural history of disease. The principal causes of death today are cancers, heart disease, cerebrovascular disease, pneumonia and bronchitis;

all of which strike at older persons. Mortality rarely occurs before the age of 45 and is even then unlikely to be caused by infection or contagion from another diseased person—such a death is more likely to have been caused by a road accident. There has also been a remarkable reduction in the severity of spells of morbidity. Effective treatments now exist for pernicious anaemia, high blood pressure, juvenile diabetes, rheumatic disease, allergies and respiratory diseases, and mental illness. Simple surgical repair work on hernias, haemorrhoids, prolapsed wombs, etc., is now a matter of routine with only minor risks attached. The wonders of modern surgery have become effectively applicable only in the last two decades with the development of anaesthesiology, which has made long and complicated operations on the vital organs both safer for the patient and easier for the surgeon. Compare this with mortality rates for common surgery, such as amputation, of between 50 and 90 per cent in the largest English hospitals at the end of the nineteenth century.

Today, the diseases from which people die in wealthy countries are chronic and their onset insidious. The major impact of the pharmaceutical revolution on bacterial infections and spirochaetal diseases such as syphilis (stemming mainly from the antibiotics) and on virus diseases (mainly preventive rather than curative) is possibly over. Once again the biggest contributors to further reductions in morbidity are probably environmental. But while once it was an environment of poverty that killed, today it is an environment of wealth. Traffic accidents, smoking, obesity and the laziness of urban living are among the principal causes of mortality and morbidity.

This, then, appears to have been the broad pattern. Until the 1930s the chief causes of improvements in health were improvements in the environment. From the 1930s to the 1950s the chief contributors to better health were drugs and new surgical techniques. In the 1960s the revolution in psychotropic drugs took place and really effective treatment of mental illness became possible for the first time. The same period saw the introduction of really effective drugs against high blood pressure. Today, the major sources of further improvement appear once more to be environmental. The wheel has turned full circle.

While this evidence should most certainly not lead us to suppose that the impact of health services on health is small, it does serve to warn us that it may not be so large, particularly at the margin, as is sometimes supposed. Moreover, it reminds us that the output 'health' or 'longer life' is produced in a production function that includes environmental elements as well as health services. Further evidence against the invariable productivity of *more* services comes from cross-sectional data. The last two columns of Table 8.1 rank health service spending as a proportion of GNP and the number of doctors per 10,000. It is not easy to identify much correlation between them and the other columns. Indeed there is none, positive

TABLE 8.1 *Ranking of Seven Countries by Selected Indicators, 1971*

Country	Mortality rank order							Other rankings	
	Perinatal	Infant	Maternal	Males 34–44	Males 45–54	Females 35–44	Females 45–54	Health expenditure as % GNP	Physicians per 10,000 pop.
Sweden	1	1	1	2	1	2	1	3	4
Netherlands	2	2	2=	1	2	1	2	4	6
England and Wales	4	3	2=	3	4	5	6	7	7
Canada	3	4	4	5	5	4	4	2	3
Italy	7	7	7	4	3	3	3	6	5
France	5	5	6	6	6	6	5	5	1
USA	6	6	5	7	7	7	7	1	2

Source: A. L. Cochrane (1975) World health problems. *Canadian Journal of Public Health, 66,* no. 4.

or negative, that is statistically different from zero. Of course, mortality is a very crude indicator of effective impact of medical care, particularly in this stage of the twentieth century and especially in the developed world. But even judged at the less aggregate and more specific level of diseases in terms of remission, or prolonged life, many treatments have been shown to be ineffective or harmful, while even more have never been subject to systematic scientific evaluation.

One may be shocked at the assertion that treatment can be ineffective or harmful. Yet it is true. According to the US National Institutes of Health's Clinical Trials Committee many treatments remained in medical practice too long and often at very high cost and to the detriment of patients. The list includes gastric freezing for peptic ulcer, colectomy for epilepsy, potassium arsenite for treatment of leukemia, bilateral hypogastric artery ligation for pelvic haemorrhage, mercury for the treatment of syphilis, portacaval shunt for hepatic cirrhosis, renal-capsul stripping for acute renal failure, sympathectomy for asthma, internal mammary artery ligation for coronary artery disease, the 'button' operation for ascites, adrenalectomy for essential hypertension, complete dental extraction for a variety of complaints thought to be the result of focal sepsis, and wiring for aortic aneurysm. Amongst apparently ineffective procedures still used (not to mention many unproven ones) are using drugs to reduce blood cholesterol to prolong life after recovery from heart attack, treatment of older coronary victims in intensive care units, treatment of severe viral hepatitis with corticosteroids, cervical smear tests for the presymptomatic diagnosis of cancer in women, tonsillectomy, lengthy hospital bed rest in treating tuberculosis (Cochrane, 1972; Ederer, 1977).

There is also variation and uncertainty in diagnosis and treatment. It is now increasingly difficult to distinguish unambiguously between a healthy and a diseased state using technological measurements. For haemoglobin levels, blood pressure, blood sugar levels, and several other testable indicators, a decision has to be taken as to how far above or below average a measure must read before action is warranted. Observer error exists, notably in the reading of X-ray photographs, but also in the measurement of blood pressure. Even among the most experienced hospital doctors, diagnosis can vary quite markedly. One study compared the diagnoses made by consultants in a major hospital with the final diagnosis reached, usually after surgery had taken place. For one common condition, appendicitis, only 75 of the 85 cases were correctly diagnosed by the most experienced men in the hospital. Overall, they were 80 per cent correct in their diagnoses.

Appropriate treatment is likewise far from being as easy and unambiguous to identify as may be popularly thought. There is generally a choice of treatment. In an appendix to the Sainsbury Committee's report on the pharmaceutical industry in the UK (Committee of Enquiry, 1967) it was reported that 455 general practitioners prescribed over 30 different prescriptions for each of five common illnesses. Only 8 out of a total of 2,275 prescriptions were found to be unacceptably toxic or ineffectual, but the cost variation was substantial. For painful osteo-arthritis, for example, 11 per cent of GP's recommended Indocid at a prescription of 180 old pence, while 10 per cent recommended aspirin at a cost of 2d.

Hospital practices can also vary widely. For example, despite strong evidence that bed rest is unimportant in the treatment of pulmonary tuberculosis, the mean length of stay in hospital is falling only slowly and is very variable from specialist to specialist. (In one case nearly 20 per cent of male patients were discharged in under a month and all within three months. In another 10 per cent were discharged in under a month and over 20 per cent were still in hospital after a year.)

The effects of several standard treatments on the normal course of disease is unknown or in dispute. Tonsillectomy, for example, is the commonest cause for the admission of children to hospital and the operation has a positive (if small) mortality. Yet there is evidence to suggest that the best medical treatment may be superior, or not inferior, to surgery. Certainly, admissions for tonsillectomy vary enormously per head of population from region to region in Britain (from 234 per 100,000 population in Sheffield to 410 in Oxford in 1971, of which 81 per cent of the cases were aged 14 or less). The treatment of mature diabetes is in doubt, as compared with diabetes in the young for whom insulin appears effective. Modern psychiatry is replete with therapies whose theoretical foundations are in dispute and whose effectiveness remains very largely untested in any systematic way.

The production of health by health services is, for so important an area in terms both of cost and potential consequence, remarkably underresearched. While this poses problems for economists seeking efficient ways of allocating the nation's resources, it is not of course particularly their role to remedy the deficiencies. Epidemiological research into these questions is fortunately growing apace and is beginning to provide some of the basic data concerning production functions for health upon which policy may come eventually to be based.

B. HEALTH AS INVESTMENT

On purely clinical criteria, there is a vast potential yet for new demands on the health service. An early attempt to identify the magnitude of the so-called 'iceberg of sickness' found in the late 1930s that over 90 per cent of more than 3,000 people examined had some identifiable sickness, but only 26 per cent were aware of being sick and only 8 per cent had been receiving medical attention (Pearse and Crocker, 1949). Similar studies at intervals since the Second World War have come up with similar findings.

Social class, income, education, the price of health care, all are known to affect the demand for health care by the patient. It is tempting to treat the demand for health services in an *ad hoc* fashion by just listing the factors that seem to be relevant. And yet there is no need for *ad hoc* theorising about these phenomena. There is a general theory to account for them, a theory based on the proposition that individuals to a large extent choose the state of their health: a theory based on the theory of human capital.

The demand for good health is the demand for an investment good—one that yields services over a period of time. The services yielded by a person's 'stock' of health are basically two: the direct 'utility' of feeling well and the indirect benefits derived from the increased amount of healthy time available for productive use both in work and non-work activities. At any point of time, an individual can be imagined to own a particular stock of health that is subject to depreciation as time passes and that, if depreciation goes far enough, falls low enough to result in death. Like other capital stocks, the stock of health can usually be increased by investment. The investment production function for any individual can be regarded as dependent upon the amount of time he puts into improving the stock. Key variables involved here are diet, exercise, housing, consumption habits and environmental factors such as public health provision and education—health education naturally affecting the efficiency with which other inputs in the production function are combined. Finally, a potentially important input is, of course, consumption of medical care.

Since many of these variables are under the control of the individual, he may be regarded up to a point as choosing his preferred stock of health, or rate of investment, subject to constraints, which are principally the amount of time available to him and the value of his time in work (i.e. his wage).

The theory is due to Grossman (1972a, 1972b). This theory is not so much a specific theory of the demand for health *care* as a general theory of the demand for *health*. Although he misleadingly speaks of two reasons for demanding health, as a consumption and as an investment determining the amount of healthy time available for market and non-market activities, it is clear that a better terminology would identify direct and indirect sources of utility.

The basic idea is that at time t each individual has a stock of health (H), measured in imaginary units, such that without further action, depreciation will take place between t and $t + 1$. Thus:

$$H_{t+1} = H_t - dH_t,$$

where d is the rate of depreciation of the stock H. With investment in the stock at time t (I_t),

$$H_{t+1} = H_t + I_t - dH_t,$$

or

$$H_{t+1} - H_t = I_t - dH_t$$

where the right hand side is net investment.

The question is, what determines the amount of investment in any time period? The empirical measure used in this analysis to represent the marginal product of the health stock is defined in terms of the number of healthy days. Thus, without getting into the difficult question of the measurement of the stock of health itself, the value of increments in it is the number of additional healthy days (generated by investment to improve health) multiplied by the wage rate. If, for simplicity, we ignore the nonpecuniary return, that is, the sheer joy at being less sick than otherwise, then one may assume that the individual will devote resources to increasing his stock of health up to the point at which the marginal cost of the gross investment in period 1 is equal to the present value of the future additional healthy days:

$$C_0 = \frac{GW}{1+r} + \frac{(1-d)GW}{(1+r)^2} + \frac{(1-d)^2 GW}{(1+r)^3} + \cdots + \frac{(1-d)^{n-1}GW}{(1+r)^n}$$

where C_0 is the cost of additional investment and the right hand side is the present value, net of depreciation, of the healthy days gained, with G representing the additional days, W the wage rate and r the marginal rate of time preference.

By multiplying this equation through by $(1 + r)/(1 - d)$ and subtracting the above equation, we derive the following:[1]

$$C_0 \left[\frac{1+r}{1-d} - 1 \right] = \frac{GW}{1-d} - \frac{(1-d)^{n-1}GW}{(1+r)^n},$$

which by rearranging, and letting n become distant, yields[2]

$$\frac{GW}{C_0} = r + d.$$

How is this to be interpreted? GW/C_0 is the value of additional healthy time per unit of investment undertaken, or the marginal value of investment or again, as more commonly termed, the marginal efficiency of capital (MEC). As the stock of health (H) increases, one would expect the marginal product (G) of capital to fall (due to diminishing returns). Hence, GW/C_0 will fall as H increases. The 'cost of capital' is $r + d$, being the sum of the rate of time preference and the depreciation rate. This does not depend on the size of the stock of H. We are now in a position to draw Figure 8.7. Here we see a negatively shaped MEC curve (due to diminishing returns in G) and a given $(r + d)$. We have already shown that the individual will invest in health capital up to the point where (ignoring the

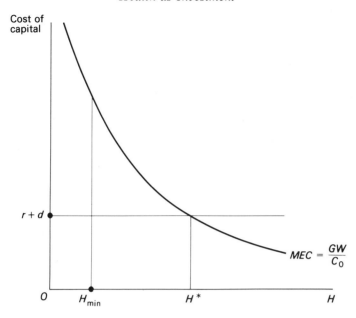

FIG. 8.7 Marginal efficiency of health capital.

direct utility of feeling well) $MEC = r + d$. In the figure, this occurs at H^*—the chosen stock of health. H itself has not explicitly entered the model at all, yet we are now in a position to make some—admittedly qualitative—propositions about it. Let us first note two things. First, since a person's stock of health cannot be sold on the market, gross investment must always be positive. Second, the stock of health cannot fall below a certain minimum level, marked in Figure 8.7 as H_{min}, which we take to correspond with a stock so low that death ensues.

Now consider the effects of aging and income changes. Taking age first, to consider its effects alone, assume that wages (W), the marginal product of the stock (G) and the marginal cost of gross investment (C_0) are independent of age. Let us now postulate, as seems eminently reasonable, that d (the rate of depreciation of the stock) varies over the life-cycle: for example that it falls during early stages and increases beyond a 'certain' age. The latter at least is plausible since the depreciation rate is in part a reflection of biological processes and aging is, of course, associated with loss of physical and mental strength and increasing incidence of (often multiple) chronic disease. An increase in d then implies (other things constant) that over the life-cycle the demand for health will fall: older people, even after investments in their health, will nonetheless be less healthy.

In considering the effect of changing wages on health, we must also consider the marginal cost of gross investment C_0. Higher wages clearly raise the marginal efficiency of health capital since they reflect an increase in the value of both leisure and work time.[3] But they also affect C_0. The cost of gross investments does of course include the money costs of acquiring medical care but it also includes a time-cost of the patient—which must rise with wages. Moreover, medical care is only one costly way of increasing the stock. By devoting time (and other resources) to hygiene, to creating stable and loving family relationships, to obtaining information on life-style conducive to better health, living in healthier (and usually more costly) physical environments, and in a host of other ways, individuals may also—at a cost—engage in what is, in terms of this model, gross investment. Clearly then, rising wages will increase the cost as well as the return. What will be the net effect on GW/C_0 if both W and C_0 rise in these ways?

We can say unambiguously that the ratio will rise if the individual's time is not the only factor in C_0. Let us, for example, suppose C_0, the marginal cost, to have two components: a time cost, T (valued at W), and other costs, K, valued at their price p. We now have

$$MEC = \frac{GW}{TW + Kp}.$$

From this it is easy to see that a given increase in W must cause MEC to rise. Indeed, if T is very small then MEC will rise by the same proportion as W. The effect of a rise in W is therefore to shift the MEC curve upward causing a higher health stock to be chosen at any given rate of time preference and depreciation.

Grossman also explored the role of education in the demand for health and argued that general education raised the marginal product of time in the non-health service ways of promoting health as well, of course, as specific health education, just as education (see next chapter) is argued to increase the productivity of time in work. The effect of this rise in productivity is to reduce the unit cost of gross investment, again leading to an upward shift in the MEC curve and, hence, an increase in the desired stock of health. To the extent that education also increases W, this will further intensify the effect. Note that increases in the demand for health need not always be associated with increases in the demand for health care services. For example, if improved education raises the productivity of non-medical inputs in the health production function more than that of medical care inputs, it would induce some substitution away from medical care consumption. Conversely, decreases in the demand for health can also cause increases in the demand for care.

Some empirical results for the USA that are consistent with the analysis are shown in Table 8.2. The signs of the relationship between mortality rates and income and education are particularly striking.

More speculatively, we might conceive the demand for health as being complementary to other dimensions of the 'good life'. It has been widely noted that age-adjusted mortality rates are much higher for widowed and

TABLE 8.2 *Percent Changes in US Age-Specific Mortality Rates Resulting from a Ten Per Cent Change in Several Variables*

| | Variables (10% change in): | | | Per capita |
	Income	Education	Cigarette consumption	health expenditure
% change in mortality	+2.0	−2.2	+1.0	−0.65

Source: R. Auster *et al.* (1972) The production of health, an exploratory study. In V. Fuchs (ed.) *Essays in the Economics of Health and Medical Care.* NBER, Columbia University Press, Table 8.3, p. 145.

divorced men than for single men. It is surely not implausible to suppose that this is because they lack some other dimensions of life that make good health valuable. Some evidence in support of the hypothesis is that death rates for the widowed and divorced men are much higher from suicide, motor car accidents, cirrhosis of the liver and lung cancer, where 'choice' is more possible, than from vascular lesions, diabetes or cancer of the digestive organs, where it is less possible or, at least, where the relationship between life-style and health status is somewhat obscure. Married persons, generally, have better health and live longer. In addition to the demand effect discussed above, there may also be a 'production effect' here—good health is possibly produced more efficiently in a marriage or with cohabitation (persons with a natural propensity to ill-health may also be discriminated against in the marriage/cohabitation market!).

It is thus clear that both the demand for health and the demand for health care services depend upon a complexity of factors, only one of which is, of course, the monetary price of purchasing inputs (including the price of medical care) and only one of which is the external environment of viruses and other hazards to health. The investment model of health may seem a heavy-handed way of drawing some rather unremarkable conclusions. Yet its importance should not be understated. For one thing, it represents the only currently available attempt by economists to model the demand for health itself, rather than the demand for services, and it focusses attention on the non-service aspects of individual choice. Second, it is relatively new. It is never wise to 'write-off' new ideas merely on the grounds that their full implications have yet to be drawn out and tested.

A striking difference between health treated as investment and education treated in the same way is that the latter application of the analysis has led—as we shall see in the next chapter—to a large number of empirical studies to calculate the rate of return, whereas there have been—apart from Grossman's initial tentative empirical work—as yet no further studies of the empirical returns to health investment. The principal use to which such calculations are put is when *social* rates of return are computed to indicate whether there is evidence of under- or over-investment: if the rate of return exceeds the social opportunity cost of borrowing (or the social rate of time preference) then the inference would be that there was under-investment; or if the computed rate were less, then over-investment.

The difficulties in so doing are fairly obvious. First, computed rates of return would omit the utility gains from better health and hence understate the full private return. Secondly, in so far as there are externalities of the sort discussed in chapter 7, the social rate will also be understated. Consequently, at best one would be able to diagnose only *under*-investment, for if the return net of these factors exceeds the opportunity cost of funds, then *a fortiori* returns will exceed the opportunity cost if they include the omitted factors. But with a rate of return less than the opportunity cost of funds, nothing much can be said—the omitted factors may or may not make up the short-fall.

Imperfections in the market for human capital lead one to expect under-investment, when considered alone, since the value of additional healthy days accruing in the future cannot be used to secure loans to finance the investment (in the absence of slavery) and one would particularly expect under-investment in the case of the relatively poor who have little physical wealth to pledge.

Against this must be set some reasons to expect the contrary result: in most developed countries health care is available either at highly subsidised prices (mostly zero price in Britain) or under insurance, which makes the effective price at the point of consumption zero. This tends to encourage health care consumption beyond the level at which price equals the marginal cost.

Given these conflicting factors, which are in varying degrees difficult to compute, it is scarcely surprising that the policy debate over how best to finance health care has been acrimonious. Ultimately, however, the issues are not theoretical but *empirical*. The problem—as yet unresolved—is to quantify the hitherto unquantified.

C. Output and Externality

From the positive economics of the demand for health we are moving to normative questions to do with externality. In the British National Health Service health care is available at a money price that is effectively zero. One reason for this was undoubtedly because of a widespread feeling that the risks of having to bear substantial costs of medical care should be pooled across the whole community and paid for by 'premiums' (taxes and National Insurance contributions) that were related to ability to pay rather than the probability and cost of sickness. We shall return to this question in the next section. But a further reason was also that individuals manifestly care about the health of others in the community and it was widely felt that inability to pay directly for care, or for insurance, should not be allowed to deter consultation for medical care. We focus on this here.

As we saw in chapter 7, in our discussion of externality types III and IV, the argument suggests a low or zero price at the point of utilisation. In addition, however, the externality argument suggests that, if the feeling is widespread that people care about the health of others, the appropriate kind of non-price rationing to use in eliminating excess demand by, on the one hand, rationing existing resources to patients and, on the other, deciding what resources to make available in the first place, would be to *not* provide care of dubious or no effectiveness in its impact on health status.

Thus, while in Britain today one can still occasionally hear arguments for the imposition of consultation charges or hotel charges (in hospital), policy has mostly focussed on (a) establishing which procedures are of demonstrable effectiveness, (b) identifying the least cost method of providing effective services, and (c) allocating resources by geographical area so far as possible in proportion to the professionally judged need for effective care in each area.

Prices are thus not of great help. There is the danger that money prices on top of time (etc.) prices will tend to discourage consultation and hence the early detection of dangerous disease, while the predictable exemptions for special categories (children, maternity cases, pensioners, those in receipt of supplementary benefit, etc.) are likely to cause substantial administrative costs as well as to to stigmatise those exempted and to lock the poor even more solidly into the 'poverty trap'. Nor do prices offer much in the way of an additional source of revenue: whatever is raised over and above administrative costs can easily be offset by a reduction in public expenditure out of taxation by governments committed both to controlling its rate of growth and to a balance of resources as between health, education, housing, etc.

Efficient resource allocation in matters relating to health (which have to embrace factors affecting health but lying outside the health services) clearly requires as a central and vital piece of information, knowledge of *health status*, since this is plausibly the object of concern to society, is presumably also of no little importance to the individual receiving care and constitutes, of course, the output (more strictly, *changes* in health status constitute the output) of health service production functions.

Suppose we follow the usual practice and set about defining health status in terms of ill-health. We might postulate, as in the discussion of the deprivation index in chapter 6, that it comprises several dimensions—ability to function physically (e.g. climb stairs, write letters) and mentally (solve problems of particular kinds), degree of anxiety, degree of pain. The selection of these dimensions involves, as we saw in chapter 6, judgements of value. It is not the job of economists to specify whose value judgements they should be, but it is economists who, for the most part, have been more aware than others (such as medical or social workers) that the judgements here are not 'objective' or scientific but are 'subjective' and value-laden. It is also for economists to say, if the externality models III and IV are indeed appropriate idealisations of the rationale of a public system like the NHS, that at some stage in the making of these value judgements a role must be found for those who are to be seen as the agents of the public—who interpret the public's concern for the health of others.

The dimensions, once chosen, can be measured on a scale. This is usually an ordinal scale having relatively few (say, from 3 to 10) points on it, each of which is descriptive of a degree of incapacity, pain, etc. In Figure 8.8 two

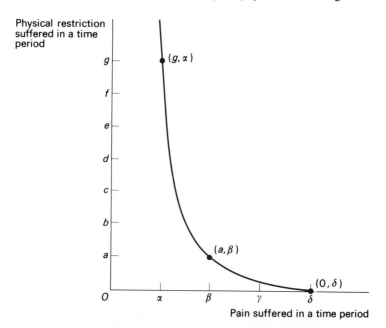

FIG. 8.8   Trading off two dimensions of ill-health.

such dimensions have been marked on the axes. One is measured in terms of increasing intensity on the scale a, b, c, d, e, f, g. The other is measured on the scale $\alpha, \beta, \gamma, \delta$. The point α may correspond to a state of having a mild headache (for which one might take aspirin), β would be a more severe pain needing more powerful analgesics, γ may correspond to, say, a severe migraine, and δ may correspond to the kind of pain for which morphine would be prescribed. The choice of scale points is in part a question of experience and convenience. It does not involve any value judgements other than the important ones in identifying one state as being more severe than another.

To compare individuals, diseases, areas, client groups, etc., again, as we saw earlier, one has to combine these dimensions. This involves us asking questions like: is the combination $g\alpha$ more or less severe than $a\beta$ or 0δ? Implicitly, by making comparisons of this kind, the space in Figure 8.8 can be partitioned off by 'indifference curves'. These curves need not be concave because the axes measure *order* of severity only. One such curve has been drawn in for illustration. Identifying the order of severity of the *combinations* involves further difficult but essential value judgements. Finally, it will often be desired to ascribe numbers to the indifference contours to indicate *how much* worse one level is compared with another. This again involves value judgements of a very different kind.

Now in all this, economic analysis does not give policy makers 'answers' to policy questions, But it does accomplish two quite crucial things. First, we have been able to distinguish quite easily and clearly several value judgements that must be made. This is important, partly because people are notoriously bad at distinguishing value judgements from other kinds of judgement, and partly because the qualifications one requires for scientific, professional or technical judgements are not necessarily those required of people who must make value judgements. It is also important because, by identifying the need for different kinds of value judgement, one may alert people to the possibility that it may be desirable to have different kinds of 'experts' making them.

Secondly, breaking the problem down in the way we have enables one to avoid crudities that may other wise be perpetrated (or if one still perpetrates them, then at least one is aware of what one is doing). As an example, it is very common (for example in social work) to use a points scoring system to decide the most urgent needs. The points a, b, c, etc. correspond to numbers such as 2, 4, 6, etc. describing how much worse b is than a, c is than b, etc. The points α, β, γ correspond to another set of numbers such as 4, 6, 12, describing their relative severities. The severities of combinations are the simple sums of the points. This system is equivalent to supposing that all indifference curves are straight parallel lines sloping down in a south-easterly direction.

This characteristic arises from the fact that this method of assigning numbers to the combinations assumes (a) a constant rate of trade-off along any contour, and (b) that the severity with which one characteristic is regarded is independent of the other characteristics that may be associated with the patients, areas, etc. Thus pain α adds the same amount to the overall score regardless of whether an individual is perfectly mobile (O on the roman letter scale) or completely bed-bound (14 on the scale). Besides identifying issues such as these that must be resolved—preferably explicitly—economic analysis also provides some empirical methods of deriving an index of health. We leave space here for but one illustration using some analysis based upon that used in chapter 2 to analyse uncertainty.

The Standard Gamble and Health Measurement

Suppose we wish to compare the health status of various individuals in a hospital. We assume (as it is realistic!) that the information we have available is far from ideal but we must make do with it as there are no funds for a sample survey. The data we have simply attach a diagnosis to each patient. The problem we shall consider is whether there is any systematic way of assigning a severity weight to each diagnostic category.

For judges we shall use doctors, since we require people with experience (even if vicarious) of many different diseases. With each doctor we shall play the following game: select any two of the diagnostic categories on the list, say diseases A and B. Now we ask the doctor to put them in the order of severity he regards as most appropriate. Suppose he puts them in the order: most severe A, least severe B. We (the researchers) now arbitrarily assign numbers to A and a third condition Z, 'perfect health', such that A's number is larger than Z's. Since these are going to be our weights, let us call A's weight $W(A)$, B's $W(B)$ and Z's $W(Z)$. Suppose the numbers we assign them are $W(A) = 2$, and $W(Z) = 1$. We now use a crafty method of assigning a number to diagnostic category B.

We offer the doctor the following hypothetical choice: he can either suffer condition B or he can take a pill out of a bottle that will either cure him completely (condition Z) or else give him A. Only we, the researchers, know which pills will cure and which will cause A, but we will tell him how many of each there are; and we juggle around with the relative number of each until the subject doctor is indifferent to the choice between continuing to suffer B and taking a pill out of the bottle. At indifference, the weight he is attaching to B is the sum of the weights of A and Z adjusted by the probabilities of either occurring:

$$W(B) = pW(A) + (1 - p)W(Z).$$

Since we know $W(A)$ and $W(Z)$, having assigned arbitrary numbers to them, and have discovered p by experiment, we may now calculate $W(B)$. Suppose he became indifferent when $p = 0.4$, then:

$$W(B) = 0.4(2) + 0.6(1) = 1.4.$$

We proceed to find similar numbers for diseases C, D, E, . . . always keeping $W(A) = 2$ and $W(Z) = 1$. For diseases more severe than A, A is replaced in the equation. For diseases less severe than A, B is replaced in the equation.

Although this procedure begins by arbitrarily assigning numbers to two conditions, all the other numbers are far from arbitrary. Indeed, whatever the original numbers assigned (in our example, 2 and 1) the relative position of all other numbers will be the same. The measure we have obtained is precisely analogous to that used to measure temperature: either Centigrade or Fahrenheit will do. We cannot say that 100°C is twice as hot as 50°C (the equivalent temperatures on Fahrenheit are 212°F and 122°F, and the one is obviously not double the other). But relative increases are independent of which measure is used. Thus, if we raise temperature from 50°C to 100°C and then increase by the same increment to 150°C, the same increment on the Fahrenheit scale will produce an identical increase in temperature: the original increase was $212° - 122° = 90°F$. The next is by 90°F to 302°F. But $302°F = 150°C$.

Thus, supposing that we initially assigned $W(A) = 2$ and $W(Z) = 1$ and that:

$$W(B) = pW(A) + (1 - p)W(Z)$$

with $p = 0.4$, and

$$W(C) = pW(A) + (1 - p)W(Z)$$

with $p = 0.2$, then we derive the numbers in column (a) of Table 8.3 But if, instead, we had made $W(A) = 101$ and $W(Z) = 3$—different numbers but preserving the same rank order—then we would have obtained (as you should check for yourself) the numbers in column (b). Or had we chosen $W(A) = 72$ and $W(Z) = 71$—again preserving the order—we would have obtained the numbers in the column (c) (again check). And now you can readily check that:

$$\frac{W(A) - W(B)}{W(B) - W(C)} \quad \text{or} \quad \frac{W(A) - W(Z)}{W(B) - W(Z)}$$

are always the same whether we use scale (a), (b) or (c).

TABLE 8.3 *Weights Assigned to Diseases by the Standard Gamble Method*

Disease	(a)	(b)	(c)
A	2.0	101.0	72.0
B	1.4	42.2	71.4
C	1.2	22.6	71.2
Z	1.0	3.0	71.0

We thus have a method of putting health states on a scale—a scale moreover whose increments remain constant in proportional terms—and so one can speak meaningfully, when using such a scale, of increasing or decreasing marginal severity of disease. If one would take the further step of associating the severity of illness with the *need* for care, then one has a way of formalising, and summarising, the value judgements embodied in the idea of 'need' or 'health status' in an operational method of measurement.

The method we have just described is often termed 'the standard gamble' method of deriving an index of preference. It is not the only way and others are reviewed in Culyer (1978b). It does, however, illustrate again how theory can be specifically applied to quantify what may seem at first sight to be hopelessly subjective value judgements. We remarked in the first section of this chapter how crude mortality rates were used as measures of the effectiveness of health services. Once again, the development of techniques such as the standard gamble is still in its infancy. These techniques do offer, however, a promising line of attack on the difficult problem of deriving more subtle and sensitive measures of ill-health than death itself.

Using the standard gamble method, Wolfson (1974) in Canada derived the severity weights (on a scale of 0–1) for a set of diseases of which some are shown in Table 8.4. Using a related technique, Torrance (1970), who was concerned with evaluating values placed upon TB treatment at home and in sanitaria, and upon alternative 'qualities of life' for patients with chronic renal failure under kidney transplantation, home or hospital dialysis, found that the mean scores (again on a scale of 0–1) were as in Table 8.5, which again represents a quantification of what would otherwise have to remain a subjective and somewhat inarticulate value judgement. Incidentally, it is worth noting that in each of these illustrated cases the judges by no means wholly agreed in their judgements, indicating that there may well be no *unique* solution to these problems—the results will indeed depend upon who is selected to make the judgement.

Quantification does not, as will be clear, remove the necessity of making value judgements. On the contrary, it shows their necessity in a very precise way. In a world where human capital markets are highly imperfect,

TABLE 8.4 *Severity Weights of Selected Diseases*

Disease	Weight
Leukaemia	.7700
Tetanus	.6996
Multiple sclerosis	.4311
Cerebral haemorrhage	.1366
Polio	.1013
Hypertensive disease	.0652
Peptic ulcer	.0252
Osteoarthritis	.0091
Cystitis	.0064
Haemorrhoids	.0024
Influenza	.0005
Impetigo	.0001

Source: Wolfson (1974).

TABLE 8.5   *Relative Values of Care*

	Home confinement in TB	Sanatorium confinement in TB	Kidney transplant	Home dialysis	Hospital dialysis
Average score of 11 judges	.57	.37	.85	.66	.57

Source: Torrance (1970) App. 1, Exhibit 9.

where it seems there are large external effects, where decisions about health care are often made by doctors acting as agents for patients, and where the effective rationing function of price is destroyed by insurance or subsidy, the necessity for facing up to such value questions is inescapable. Who should decide? That is left to the reader!

D. HEALTH INSURANCE—THE MARKET OR THE STATE?

The debate over the role of the state in the finance of health care has been, at times, furious (see Further Reading). Analysis can, however, often reduce passion by showing that antagonists in any argument each have *some* truth on their side. Often, the real issues may turn out to be *empirical* rather than ideological. And so it is with the debate over health care finance.

Let us begin by considering the case for an insurance system operated in the market by private agents. We shall assume that it is the financial cost of care against which insurance is taken out. The disutility *per se* of sickness is not insured against. We also assume (unrealistically perhaps) that sickness does not itself affect the ability to enjoy income. These assumptions do not much affect the major conclusions to be drawn. Figure 8.9 plots utility against income and is essentially a reproduction of Figure 2.7 in chapter 2. Let I_0 on the horizontal axis represent income expected next year. If the individual were to fall sick and have to spend H of his income on health care, then his income would (net of health care expenditure) amount to $I_0 - H$. The utilities of his net income in either case are indicated on the vertical axis as $U(I_0)$ and $U(I_0 - H)$ respectively. If the probability of the event causing H to be spent is known to be p, then the individual's expected income next year is $I_0 - pH$. This is marked on the horizontal axis for $p = 0.4$. The expected utility of this uncertain income is labelled $pU(I_0 - H) + (1 - p)U(I_0)$ on the vertical axis, which says the expected utility is the sum of the expected utility of income if sickness occurs and the expected utility if it does not. The probability of the former is p and of the latter clearly $(1 - p)$. With $p = 0.4$, the expected

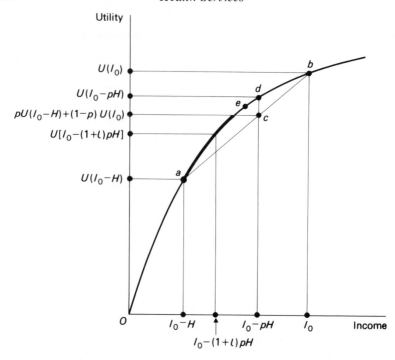

FIG. 8.9 Efficiency of health insurance with loading.

utility lies four-tenths of the way between $U(I_0)$ and $U(I_0 - H)$, which can alternatively be found by drawing the straight line ab and noting its height four-tenths of the way south-west along it. This is the expected utility of the uncertain prospect of losing income (it does not, to repeat, measure in any way the expected utility loss due to ill-health *per se*). If we now compare this with the utility of the certain loss of an insurance premium equal to pH, the utility of $(I_0 - pH)$ must lie on the utility of income curve above c, namely at d. Thus any individual with a diminishing marginal utility of income will prefer a certain loss, monetarily equal to pH, to the uncertainty of the greater loss H with the probability p. The individual in short is risk averse. So much is familiar from chapter 2.

In financial terms, the following equation holds:

$$p(I_0 - H) + (1 - p)I_0 = I_0 - pH.$$

If insurance companies incurred no cost of administration, earned no profit, etc., so that the premiums they charged were actuarially fair, then the appropriate premium for an event costing H with a probability of occurrence p would obviously be pH. The right-hand side of the equation can now easily be seen to represent the situation where the individual is insured against event H, and the left-hand side the situation where he is not.

The natural question to ask next is whether insurance, the advantages of which are clear, is best provided via the market or by the state. Notice that in a 'perfect' insurance market, if it were felt that some were taking 'too little' insurance, their premiums could be subsidised by the state, and a minimum level of insurance could be made compulsory for all households or families on the externality grounds discussed above. The issue here does not concern externalities, but the relative efficiency of the market and the state in providing insurance itself. The choice rests chiefly on the outcome of three arguments concerning (a) 'loading charges', (b) 'adverse selection', and (c) 'moral hazard': quaint terms, but around which an immense debate has centred, particularly in North America and Australia, where the choice between private and public insurance is by no means as firmly resolved as it seems to be in Britain. A fourth argument also becomes inextricably combined with the others, This is whether compulsory health insurance is desirable and, if so, whether it should be designed in a public insurance system or a private one.

Loading charges arise, as we saw in chapter 2, because insurance companies incur costs of running their business. There may also be inflated charges due to monopoly, or higher than necessary charges due to inefficiency where competitive forces are weak. For convenience, let us suppose, as in chapter 2, that loading charges are a proportion l of the premium pH. The premium now becomes $pH + lpH = (1 + l)pH$ and the certainty outcome $I_0 - (1 + l)pH$ leaves a lower net income than formerly, with $I_0 - pH$. This is shown in Figure 8.9 as a point to the left of $I_0 - pH$.

The question for the individual is now whether insurance at actuarily unfair premiums is preferred to 'self-insurance' (i.e. no insurance). Insurance will, by definition, be preferred so long as $U[I_0 - (1 + l)pH]$ exceeds $pU(I_0 - H) + (1 - p)U(I_0)$. Equally clearly, l could rise high enough to ensure this is not the case. In the diagram, the utility of the loaded premium is clearly lower than the utility of self-insurance. Indeed, any l large enough to bring the individual on to the heavy curve below the horizontal line through c will be less preferred.

The first conclusion, then, is that if through economies of scale, etc., a system of public insurance can have lower loadings than private insurance offering the same benefit, it will on this ground be preferable. The reverse argument applies, of course, if public systems have higher loadings. Once again, the argument has nothing to do with subsidies. A public system with low premiums and run at loss should be compared only with a comparably subsidised private system.

Adverse selection arises when purchasers of insurance know better than insurers the probability of their falling sick. In particular, if an insured person believes his p to be higher than the insurance company believes it likely to be on the basis of less reliable information than that known to the customer, then such individuals will face an actuarially unfair premium that may be too low. Certainly, to cover disbursements and costs, companies will have to raise premiums overall—making the premiums to other insured persons (more) loaded. 'Bad' risks will be over-protected and good risks relatively under-protected. For example, take a population of 100 individuals, 50 of whom expect to have to pay out £100 on medical fees and 50 of whom expect to pay £300. The insurance company does not know, we suppose, these different expectations of the individuals. All the company knows is the overall risk. If they all purchase insurance, the actuarily fair premium based on the experience of all 100 will be £200, since £20,000 will just cover benefits paid out (50 × £100 + 50 × £300). But this will seem excessive to those expecting only to pay £100 who will, unless they are all *very* risk averse, take out less insurance. The insurance company will be left with an expected pay-out of £300 per person, instead of £200. The actuarially fair premium will thus become £300—an even greater disincentive to the 'good risks'—and the company will tend to insure only the very worst risks at an appropriately high premium. Public insurance may also suffer from adverse selection of this sort, but if the public insurance scheme is compulsory this will also clearly help to reduce adverse selection; compulsory private insurance would not, of course, so long as more than one company was competing for business.

Moral hazard is of two kinds. The first arises when the insured person falls sick and seeks care. Since he no longer faces a price that he must pay, he will tend to move down his demand curve for more (or better) care (more nursing, a longer hospital stay, more convalescence, better food, better qualified surgeons, etc.). This increases *H ex post* and, unless companies anticipate or control it, will reduce the supply of insurance for price-elastic services or raise premiums above the actuarially fair (and *ex ante* preferred) amount. Reverting to Figure 8.9, if *l* now represents a mark-up to cover moral hazard, again it can be seen that the advantages of insurance are eroded completely at sufficiently high rates of *l*. Alternatively, controls may be used such as deductibles (the insured pays the first £*x* of medical expense), which have no effect on the demand for care other than via income effects, unless the £*x* is larger than the total expenditure. Coinsurance (the insured pays *x* per cent of the medical bill) clearly reduces moral hazard, but it also reduces the value of insurance. One might also set a limit to the insurance benefit. Up to this limit moral hazard would be unchecked. Beyond it demand would become relatively inelastic—an unfortunate state of affairs in the event that some *H* should exceed the policy limit and the person's income.

The second kind of moral hazard affects the probability of the insured event occurring. To the extent that the occurrence of the insured event is affected by the behaviour of the insured person, the fact of having insurance protection reduces his or her incentive to take steps to prevent the event from occurring. One feels less reluctance to report sick if one has insurance against earnings lost through sickness. One feels less incentive (though not none) to keep fit and take care if the costs of one's medical care will be borne by someone else. Once again, then, *l* rises. Both deductibles and coinsurance increase one's incentive to reduce the probability of sickness occurring and hence reduce *l*. But they also reduce the value of being insured. In some insurance systems, higher premiums are payable by smokers, drinkers and those with hazardous occupations or hobbies. This has the advantage of reducing some of the costs while preserving the value of insurance. However, there are also costs of screening out the low-risk classes of person and of making sure that their undertakings not to smoke, etc. were not fraudently made, or that their occupational (etc.) circumstances do not change during the life of an insurance policy.

Moral hazard of the first type is in principle more easily controlled in a system of publicly owned medical care institutions, since much of the elasticity of demand for care is supplier-induced (by doctors) rather than demander-induced (by patients), and in public systems payment to doctors is less likely to be on the basis of fee-per-service (which clearly encourages the supply of more service by those who advise the patient what his demand should be). The case here, therefore, is more for the control of the suppliers of the service rather than the insurers. Moral hazard of the second type requires risk-discrimination for effective control. Note that in a 'free' system such as the British National Health Service (NHS), the moral hazard problem is complete: doctors must develop a non-price rationing system to choke off the excess demand in the event that supply is not (it never is) increased sufficently to meet all demands at zero price, and no one has as yet seriously suggested that individuals whose life-styles are more hazardous to health should pay higher contributions towards the cost of the NHS.

Compulsory insurance has the advantage that it may assist in realising scale economies and in internalising externalities. Compulsion, however, implies that some people will be taking insurance involuntarily: their utility will fall without being compensated. The usual value judgements of welfare economics provide no means of telling us whether these losses are or are not offset by corresponding gains elsewhere. It is to be noted, however, that the reduced loading charge that may be possible under a compulsory scheme implies that more people will prefer compulsory public health insurance than voluntary private insurance. In Figure 8.9, if private insurance enables individuals to attain point *e*, then any public shceme enabling them to attain a point along the section of the curve *ed* will be preferred by all those previously insuring. It will also be preferred by some of those previously self-insuring. The remainder will have to be coerced.

The NHS is, of course, effectively equivalent to a system of compulsory public insurance, with government ownership or employment of the majority of health care institutions and factors such as hospitals, GP and welfare services, etc. These are supplemented by other services, some free (such as charitable welfare work) and some provided in the market (such as private care and private insurance). In the NHS we thus have a completely subsidised system. Moreover, it is subsidised directly. Its clients are not given subsidies with which to purchase insurance or care (or anything else). We have direct provision in kind. The economic reasons for such a system lie in the arguments discussed in this and the previous sections: capital market imperfections, the nature of the externality and the relative costs of different methods of pooling risks. This is not a complete description of the issues, for it omits (for example) any discussion of the countervailing monopsony power of government in dealing with monopoly sellers such as the medical profession or the drug industry, and it also omits any discussion of the relative behavioural differences to be expected as between non-profit and for-profit institutions. But despite this the discussion should enable you to perceive some of the central issues and to apply a dispassionate and non-partisan analysis where more frequently passion and partisanship are the rule in debates over health service organisation and finance. Chapter 11 contains some application of common economic techniques such as cost–benefit analysis to health problems, including efficient production and efficient levels of insurance cover. For other empirical issues such as the measurement of demand elasticities, health indexes and health service effectiveness, the reader is referred to the Further Reading.

NOTES

1. Thus:

$$C_0\frac{1+r}{1-d} = \frac{GW}{1-d} + \frac{GW}{1+r} + \frac{(1-d)GW}{(1+r)^2} + \frac{(1-d)^2GW}{(1+r)^3} + \cdots + \frac{(1-d)^{n-2}GW}{(1+r)^{n-1}}$$

$$-C_0 = -\left| \frac{GW}{1+r} + \frac{(1-d)GW}{(1+r)^2} + \frac{(1-d)^2GW}{(1+r)^3} + \cdots + \frac{(1-d)^{n-2}GW}{(1+r)^{n-1}} + \frac{(1-d)^{n-1}GW}{(1+r)^n} \right|$$

$$C_0\left|\frac{1+r}{1-d} - 1\right| = \frac{GW}{1-d} \qquad\qquad -\frac{(1-d)^{n-1}GW}{(1+r)^n}$$

2. As n becomes indefinitely large, $(1-d)^{n-1}/(1+r)^n$ tends to zero, so we have

$$C_0\left|\frac{1+r}{1-d} - 1\right| = \frac{GW}{1-d}.$$

Multiplying through by $(1-d)$ gives

$$C_0[(1+r) - (1-d)] = GW,$$

which, when simplified, becomes

$$\frac{GW}{C_0} = r + d.$$

3. Implicitly we are considering wages after income tax. Even if an individual responds to higher net wages by reducing his work in the market and substitutes more leisure, that leisure (per hour) cannot be worth less to him than the wage (per hour)—otherwise he would have chosen to work the extra hour(s).

QUESTIONS ON CHAPTER 8

1. What is the impact of health services on health?
2. Distinguish between the demand for health and the demand for health care.
3. 'Countries spend what they can afford on health services'. Discuss.
4. What, in Grossman's model, may cause an increase in the demand for health?
5. How would you measure health status
   (a) in testing Grossman's model
   (b) in planning health service investments in the public sector?
6. Describe and evaluate the standard gamble method of assigning weights to components of a health index. Compare it with any *two* other methods discussed in your reading.
7. Should health insurance be
   (a) comprehensive
   (b) compulsory
   (c) subsidised?
8. How may moral hazard be reduced or overcome in a health insurance system?
9. Should all health needs be met?
10. Should private practice coexist with publicly financed health services?
11. How would the behaviour of proprietory (profit-making) hospitals be expected to differ from non-profit hospitals?
12. Of what is there the greatest shortage: nurses, renal dialysis machines, hospital beds, or doctors? Justify your answer.
13. How would you value the output of health services relative to, say, education services, or defence?
14. Is life of infinite value?
15. What factors have statistical studies found to be important determinants
   (a) of mortality rates
   (b) of health spending?
16. 'Health care is a merit good'. Discuss.
17. How should doctors be paid? Predict the consequences of the following systems:
   (a) salary
   (b) capitation
   (c) fee-per-service.
18. Should medical education be subsidised?
19. Are waiting lists for admission to hospital evidence of inefficiency?
20. Is there any limit to the demand for health at zero price?

Health Services

FURTHER READING

On epidemiology and health services:

Alderson, M. (1976) *An Introduction to Epidemiology.* London: Macmillan.
Cochrane, A. L. (1972) *Effectiveness and Efficiency: Random Reflections on Health Services.* London: Nuffield Provincial Hospitals Trust.
Committee of Enquiry into the Relationship of the Pharmaceutical Industry with the NHS (1967) *Report.* London: HMSO.
Ederer, F. (1977) The randomized clinical trial, In C. I. Phillips, and J. N. Wolfe, (eds) *Clinical Practice and Economics.* London: Pitman.
Feldstein, M. S., Piot, M. A. and Sundaresan, T. K. (1973) *Resource Allocation Model for Public Health Planning: a case study of T.B. control.* Geneva: World Health Organisation.
McKeown, T. (1976) *The Modern Rise of Population.* London: Arnold.
Morris, J. N. (1975) *Uses of Epidemiology.* Edinburgh: Churchill Livingstone.
Pearse, I. H. and Crocker, L. H. (1949) *The Peckham Experiment.* London: Allen and Unwin.
Razzell, P. E. (1977) *The Conquest of Smallpox.* Firle: Caliban Books.

On health economics generally:

Cooper, M. H. (1975) *Rationing Health Care.* London: Croom Helm.
Cullis, J. G. and West, P. A. (1979) *The Economics of Health: an Introduction.* Oxford: Martin Robertson.
Culyer, A. J. (1976) *Need and the National Health Service.* London: Martin Robertson.
Culyer, A. J. (1979) *Expenditure on Real Services: Health,* Unit 9 of course D323 'Political Economy and Taxation'. Milton Keynes: Open University Press.
Culyer, A. J. and Cooper, M. H. (eds) (1973) *Health Economics.* Harmondsworth: Penguin.
Culyer, A. J. and Wright, K. G. (eds) (1978) *Economic Aspects of Health Services.* London: Martin Robertson.
Fuchs, V. R. (ed.) (1972) *Essays in the Economics of Health and Medical Care.* New York: Columbia University Press.
Fuchs, V. R. (1974) *Who Shall Live?.* New York: Basic Books.
Klarman, H. E. (ed.) (1970) *Empirical Studies in Health Economics.* Baltimore: Johns Hopkins.
Lindsay, C. M. (1980) *National Health Issues: the British Experience.* Nutley, NJ: Roche Laboratories.
Maynard, A. K. (1975) *Health Care in the European Community.* London: Croom Helm.
Newhouse, J. P. (1978) *The Economics of Medical Care: A Policy Perspective.* Reading, Mass.: Addison-Wesley.

On health as investment:

Grossman, M. (1972a) On the concept of health capital and the demand for health. *Journal of Political Economy,* 80, pp. 223–55.
Grossman, M. (1972b) *The Demand for Health: a Theoretical and Empirical Investigation.* New York: Columbia University Press.
Grossman, M. and Benham, L. (1974) Health, hours and wages. In M. Perlman (ed,) *The Economics of Health and Medical Care.* London: Macmillan.

Mushkin, S. (1974) Health as investment. *Journal of Political Economy, 70*, pp. 129–57. Reprinted in Culyer and Cooper, (1973) *op. cit.*

On output and externality:

Culyer, A. J. (1978a) *Measuring Health: Lessons for Ontario.* Toronto: University of Toronto Press.
Culyer, A. J. (1978b) Need, values and health status measurement. In Culyer and Wright (1978) *op. cit.*
Culyer, A. J., Lavers, R. J. and Williams, Alan (1972) Health indicators. In A. Shonfield and S. Shaw, *Social Indicators and Social Policy.* London: Heinemann.
Guttman, L. (1944) A basis for scaling qualitative data. *American Sociological Review, 9*, pp. 139–50.
Katz, S. *et al.* (1963) The index of ADL: a standardised measure of biological and psychosocial function. *Journal of the American Medical Association, 185*, pp. 914–19.
Patrick, D. L. *et al.* (1973) Methods of measuring levels of wellbeing for a health index. *Health Services Research, 8*, pp. 229–44.
Rosser, R. and Watts, V. C. (1972) The measurement of hospital output. *International Journal of Epidemiology, 1*, pp. 361–8.
Torrance, G. W. (1970) *A Generalized Cost-Effectiveness Model for the Evaluation of Health Programs.* Hamilton: McMaster University, Faculty of Business.
Williams, Alan (1978) 'Need'—an economic exegesis. In Culyer and Wright (1978) *op. cit.*
Wolfson, A. D. (1974) *A Health Index for Ontario.* Toronto: unpublished.
Wright K. G. (1978) Output measurement in practice. In Culyer and Wright (1978) *op. cit.*

On demand and insurance:

Andersen, R. and Benham, L. (1970) Factors affecting the relationship between family income and medical care consumption. In Klarman (1970) *op. cit.*
Arrow, K. J. (1963) Uncertainty and the welfare economics of medical care. *American Economic Review, 53*, pp. 941–73. Reprinted in Culyer and Cooper (1973) *op. cit.*
Beck, R. G. (1974) The effects of copayment on the poor. *Journal of Human Resources, 9*, pp. 129–42.
Cairns, J. A. and Snell, M. C. (1978) Prices and the demand for care. In Culyer and Wright (1978) *op. cit.*
Evans, R. G. and Williamson, M. F. (1978) *Extending Canadian Health Insurance: Options for Pharmacare and Denticare.* Toronto: University of Toronto Press.
Feldstein, M. S. (1973) The welfare loss of excess health insurance. *Journal of Political Economy, 81*, pp. 251–80.
Lees, D. S. and Rice, R. G. (1965) Uncertainty and the welfare economics of medical care: comment. *American Economic Review, 55*, pp. 140–54.
Newhouse, J. P. and Phelps, C. E. (1974) Price and income elasticities for medical care services. In M. Perlman (ed.) *The Economics of Health and Medical Care.* London: Macmillan.
Pauly, M. V. (1968) The economics of moral hazard. *American Economic Review, 58*, pp. 231–7.
Rosett, R. (ed.) (1976) *The Role of Health Insurance in the Health Services Sector.* New York: Columbia University Press.
Scotton, R. B. and Deeble, J. S. (1968) Compulsory health insurance for Australia, *Australian Economic Review*, 4th Quarter, pp. 9–16.

CHAPTER 9

Education

A. THE PRODUCTION FUNCTION

Given our remarks at the beginning of chapter 7, it is scarcely surprising that the absence of a measure of the elusive 'output' of educational institutions (let alone the wider, less formal, educational processes of society in general) has seriously hampered research into the efficiency of production. Nor is it surprising, in an area where widely differing expectations are held of the education system, that policy should be riven with controversies of long standing. But it is not just that it is unclear what to list as outputs, or how to weight them (for example, establishing the relevant weights to put on vocational training, cultural awareness, creativity, scholastic achievement, good citizenship, and so on), it is also that we lack systematic *evidence* (as opposed to assertion) about the extent to which teachers of varying degrees of skill, books, visual aids, programmed-learning machines and books, family background, inherited characteristics, ability of peers, etc. affect any one of these 'outputs'. As Blaug (1972), in his review of the whole field, puts it:

> we face a pervasive ignorance about the production function of education, that is, the relationship between school inputs, on the one hand, and [even] school output as conventionally measured by achievement scores, on the other ... the technology of the industry is imperfectly understood. The inputs are complex: the physical facilities of the school, the quantity and quality of teaching services, a variety of materials and equipment and a 'raw material', students' time, through which other inputs, such as environmental influences on learning outside schools, are transmitted. It is not that we lack piecemeal evidence: the psychological and sociological literature on the educational process is so vast that few of us could command it in one lifetime. The difficulty is that of reducing the mass of evidence to systematic generalizations. What we lack is a framework for organizing all the bits and pieces that we know. [p. 269]

Added to this pervasive ignorance is the curious resistance to believe what *does* seem well established. As Harris (1962) has remarked:

> over the years we have had hundreds of experiments testing the effectiveness of teaching in small and large classes. Despite the fact that in the vast majority of instances these tests show either that the advantage (as shown by tests) lies with the large class or that there is no significant difference, the folk-lore of the small class persists. [p. 530]

Moreover, passions wax hot over the meaning and extent of social divisiveness in different types of school, over equality of opportunity, over the legitimacy of parental and student choice, the perpetuation of social class differences, and so on.

We are thus at once profoundly ignorant and also profoundly optimistic in what we believe education may do for individuals.

In this chapter we shall not survey the literature of education as it relates to classroom methods, use of aids, size of classes, etc. What we shall do is explore the role that education has been held to play in the promotion of economic growth, examine the implications of treating education as investment, discuss the measurement of output and externality and alternative methods of finance. These topics encompass the principal areas in which economics has been applied to date.

The most famous studies of the relationship between education and economic growth are those by Denison (1962, 1967). Denison's approach can be best interpreted as an application of the Cobb–Douglas production function applied at an aggregate level to the whole economy (though this is only implicit in his work). The characteristic of constant returns to scale of the Cobb–Douglas function seems to be a close approximation to reality (see, e.g., Psacharopoulos 1973, ch. 6). This has an important implication for interpreting the sources of economic growth. Recall the Cobb–Douglas function:

$$Q = aN^{\alpha}K^{\beta} \qquad (\alpha + \beta = 1)$$

where N is person-hours of labour and K is machine hours of capital. Now it is a fairly easy matter to show that α and β are not only the elasticities of output with respect to changes in N and K, but also measure the relative shares in output taken by N and K—provided that inputs receive as payment their marginal products.[1] The Cobb–Douglas has the further handy property that the relative shares of N and K remain constant whatever the rate of output Q (assuming a not to change) since, as N increases (say) so its wage falls so as to compensate exactly for any rise in K times its price. If, moreover, any long term changes in a, reflecting technical progress and other factors, do not affect the relative marginal products of N and K (so-called 'neutral' technical progress) then it is clear that α and β are constant through time, as are factor shares in the national income (as has commonly been noted in the empirical literature).

Now, with these assumptions that the real world of aggregate production can be represented by the Cobb–Douglas function together with neutral technical progress, some remarkable results were derived by Denison. Putting the Cobb–Douglas function in logarithms, the rate of growth of national income (where a dot over a variable indicates its rate of change) is

$$\dot{Q} = \dot{a} + \alpha\dot{N} + \beta\dot{K}$$

where α and β are the shares of labour and capital in income. The rates of change in Q, N and K can be computed, and hence $\dot{a}$, the 'residual' in economic growth not accounted for by $\dot{N}$ and $\dot{K}$, can also be computed. Table 9.1 shows some results for the USA and Western European countries in 1950–62. As can be seen, the proportion of growth 'unexplained' by growth in labour and capital is about two thirds on average.

TABLE 9.1   *Contributions to Growth of Real National Income in Nine Countries, 1950–1962*

	$\dot{Q}$	$\dot{N}$	$\dot{K}$	α	β	$\dot{a}$	$\dot{a}/\dot{Q}$
Belgium	3.2	.55	2.61	78.0	22.0	2.2	.7
Denmark	3.5	.93	5.06	78.3	21.7	2.4	.7
France	4.9	.11	4.17	77.8	22.2	3.9	.8
Germany	7.3	2.00	6.37	74.4	25.6	4.2	.6
Italy	6.0	.56	3.50	74.2	25.8	4.7	.8
Netherlands	4.7	1.05	4.72	76.4	23.6	2.8	.6
Norway	3.5	.18	4.23	74.2	25.8	2.1	.6
UK	2.3	.65	3.35	81.1	18.9	1.1	.5
USA	3.3	1.14	3.58	82.0	18.0	1.7	.5

Sources: Denison (1967), Tables 2-1, 4-2, 15-2.

Denison believed that a large part of this residual could be attributed to increased education of the labour force. An improvement in the productive quality of labour is, of course, bound to affect the growth of national income more than similar improvements in capital because α, the elasticity of output with respect to labour, is so much larger than β.

There have been many studies which, at a more disaggregated level than Denison's have sought to identify the role of education in explaining earnings differences between individuals. The list of potential factors, other than education, that may conceivably affect earnings differences is, of course, enormous. A short list of such factors might include, for example, genetic or inherited 'ability'; parental socio-economic status and income (independently of its effect on access to education); colour, race and sex; degree of unionisation of the workers in question; age; experience; motivation; risk preference; 'luck'. In assessing the contribution of education it would clearly be desirable to hold these other influencing variables constant.

The main reason why Denison believed that a high fraction of the residual could be accounted for by education was his examination of the work of Wolfle and Smith (1956), from which he concluded that about two-thirds of the (gross) earnings differentials of college and high school graduates could be statistically attributed to the additional schooling, after allowing for differences in father's occupation, rank in high school class and IQ (Denison, 1964). Similar conclusions were reached by Becker (1964, p. 87). Blaug (1972, p. 52) dubs this fraction 'the alpha coefficient' (not the same as α in our Cobb–Douglas function) and recommends its use for adjusting gross earnings to obtain the return to education (more on this later). In fact, Denison ascribed 6 per cent of earnings differentials to rank in high school class, 3 per cent to IQ, and 7 per cent to father's occupation. Inherited IQ nearly always appears with a small coefficient in empirical studies. Bowles (1973) ascribed 4 per cent to inherited IQ, 57 per cent to socio-economic background and only 39 per cent to education. Jencks (1972) attributed only 20 per cent of earnings differences to education. Psacharopoulos and Layard (1979, p. 495) found, on the other hand, that 46 per cent of earnings differences were attributable to education. The more recent results of this type of study seem to indicate that approximately one-third of the variation is attributable to schooling.

It is clearly an important policy matter to establish the extent to which earnings differentials are attributable largely to social background or to education. The debate is by no means over and it is important, given the differences of methods used and in results obtained by various researchers, to be alert to the sources of difference—particularly those arising from the nature of the specification of the earnings function and those unmeasured determinants that may have been omitted.

The foregoing suggests that although there is doubt about the precise extent to which education enhances earnings, the debate centres on the empirical problem of measuring what is expected to be a positive contribution. There is, however, an alternative view that holds that even if there is an empirical association between (say) years of schooling and subsequent earnings, this is not so much due to the enhancing effect that education has on the productivity of individuals as to the fact that selection for education, or survival in a course of education, is a surrogate for an underlying 'ability'. On this view, education—especially higher education—is not so much a question of investment in specific and general skills as a *screening* device that identifies for employers those individuals having relatively high productive potential. According to the 'screening hypothesis', education—to the extent that it has any value in production—is a signalling device that helps to place the right individual in the right job.

Suppose, to polarise issues, that schooling has no effect on productivity (Arrow, 1973), but that ability as judged by educationalists is highly correlated with ability as judged by employers. Then one would expect to see a correlation between earnings and schooling by virtue of the education system acting as a 'filter' screening out less able individuals. In a less extreme form one is, of course, concerned to find out the extent to which the investment and the screening components contribute respectively to earnings differentials.

It has proved difficult to devise discriminating tests of this kind. One possibility is to suppose that, if the screening hypothesis has some truth in it, higher earners will be numbered chiefly amongst those who successfully *complete* their course and have a certificate as evidence. Drop-outs would, therefore, not be 'filtered' through. Unfortunately for this interpretation of the screening hypothesis, drop-outs earn at least as much as those who complete courses. Another implication of the screening hypothesis might be, as employers acquire first-hand experience of employees and can employ a finer and more specific filter of their own, that the effect of schooling on earnings differentials will fall as years of job experience increase. Again, however, the evidence does not support this aspect of the screening hypothesis. Finally, one may note that to use schooling as a filter is an exceedingly costly mechanism: surely, if a filter is all—or mostly all—that education is to employers, it would have paid someone to develop less expensive screening procedures, aptitude tests, and the like to use instead of rather than in addition to education? Since this has not happened on any great scale one's belief is strengthened that the educational process *itself* enhances productivity.

The issue remains controversial but the evidence to date is not strongly in support of any extreme version of the screening hypothesis—a thought to comfort those who believe that education is a major means of enhancing individuals' lifetime opportunities and a major means (though not the only one) by which individuals can escape from the drudgery of much unskilled work both in and out of the labour market.

B. EDUCATION AS INVESTMENT

If education increases earnings, as the foregoing clearly implies, it is scarcely surprising that the human capital model of investment has been frequently applied in this territory. The typical assumptions made in the literature include the following:

(a) That individuals maximise lifetime earnings. This has two main implications: first, since education also brings non-monetary benefits, that estimated returns will *underestimate* (*ceteris paribus*) the true returns; second that hours worked are determined outside the model by some convention (it is clearly implausible to suppose that individuals would rationally choose to work the number of hours per year that maximised earned income—there are *other* good things in life too!). One of the minority of studies taking account of variability in hours worked according to training is Lindsay (1971).

(b) That in the absence of further training after school (for example, on-the-job training) the age–earnings profile will be flat. How seriously this assumption would lead one to qualify results is hard to tell. Many educated workers are on incremental salary scales, and many others who are not expect a rising real income with the passage of time.

Sometimes attempts are made to allow separately for the effects of post-school training and 'experience', for example by adding a variable (age − years of full-time education − 5) in the estimating equation.

(c) That all individuals have equal access to capital markets and are of equal basic 'ability'. We have already seen earlier in this chapter, and also in chapter 6, that these assumptions are not strictly tenable; nevertheless, most rates of return analyses do not attempt to adjust for 'ability' or—except very crudely in, say, distinguishing returns for whites and blacks in the USA—for different degrees of access to the capital market for financing education.

(d) That during schooling no time is spent in the employed labour force and, after schooling, all time is spent in the employed labour force. This simplifying assumption is more likely to be seriously falsified in Britain than the USA since the British education system is more varied and, in particular, part-time education (especially vocational education for engineers, accountants, etc.) is much more highly developed. The usual assumption of rate of return studies that identifies 'education' with years completed of full-time education clearly fails to capture this important reality.

Under these (and other more specific) assumptions, the usual procedure has been to estimate the rate of return to an educational investment by a version of the equation already met in chapter 2 (p. 37). Suppose, for example, that we seek to find the average return on three years' additional (higher) education for an individual with an expected working life of 47 years. The rate of return is defined as the discount rate that will equate discounted net benefits to zero. If we know the direct costs of the education per year (C), the forgone earnings that could have been earned were the average individual not in school (E_f) and the higher earnings subsequently made possible (E_s) over the rest of his or her working life, then solving the following equation for r, the rate of return, yields the answer sought:

$$0 = \sum_{t=1}^{44} \frac{(E_s - E_f)}{(1 + r)^t} - \sum_{t=-2}^{0} \frac{(C + E_f)}{(1 + r)^t}.$$

The left-hand term on the right-hand side represents the present value of the earnings increment while the right-hand term represents the costs of the education. The latter are cumulated *forward* to year 0 and subsequent benefits are discounted back to the same date.

In exercises of this sort it is common to distinguish *private* from *social* rates of return. The former relate to the costs incurred and benefits received by the individual. E_f and E_s are therefore earnings *after* income tax in such an analysis; C is educational costs *net* of subsidies on tuition fees, gross of living allowances, etc. The social return includes taxes and subsidies paid.

Social rates as usually computed, however, do not take any account of whatever non-monetary externalities may exist. Private rates are important in considering the personal incentives individuals have for acquiring education and in considering interpersonal equity in financing education (on which more below). Social rates are important in the context of decisions concerning the social pay-off to educational expenditure.

Confusion sometimes exists as to whether the rates thus computed are *average* or *marginal*. They are usually average in the sense that they are estimated for classes of individual (e.g. university students) across whom there will be some variation and perhaps a large variation. But there is also another sense of average as distinct from marginal. For example, if we compute the rate of return to an *incremental* period of education, then the return is a marginal rate of return. On the other hand, if we compute the return on some education as distinct from none, then it is average. Clearly, when one is dealing with discrete time intervals in which training and educational experiences take place, there is a certain arbitrariness in the distinction—after all, some rather than none is itself an increment. The important thing to remember in all this is less whether the return is marginal or average (in our second sense), than the size of the increment of education to which it relates.

Most rates are actually estimated on cross-sectional data. For choices regarding current decisions to invest (whether private or social in the sense defined above) one ideally would need *expected* cost and earnings differentials. For evaluations of earlier decisions one would ideally have followed a cohort of individuals over their working lifetime. Evidently, then, the context in which cross-sectional results are interpreted ought to be made clear if the reasonableness of using current (or recent past) cross-sectional data is to be ascertained.

Table 9.2 indicates the computed rates of return for a variety of different forms of higher education in various countries in the late 1960s. Social rates of return are typically lower than private rates since the additional income tax paid by higher earners is less than the subsidy on education and because externalities (to the extent that they exist) are excluded. Nonetheless, the variation both across subject and across countries is striking. Readers interested in more details concerning specific countries, investments, etc. are referred to Blaug (1972), Psacharopoulos (1973) and Taubman (1975).

It is tempting to proceed by analysing alternative periods of time spent acquiring education by reference to a diagram similar to Figure 8.7 in the previous chapter (p. 215), where the horizontal axis would measure years of schooling and the *MEC* curve the rate of return. Unfortunately, schooling is not the homogeneous entity that H was and returns to incremental education do not always display a continuous fall as more education is

TABLE 9.2   *Social Rates of Return to Higher Education by Subject and Country* (%)

Subject	Great Britain	Norway	Sweden	Denmark	Belgium	India	Brazil
Economics	3.9	8.9		9.0	9.5		16.1
Business administration		16.6	9.0				
Accountancy	7.5						
Law		10.6	9.5	10.0	6.0		17.4
Medicine		3.1	13.0	5.0	11.5		11.9
Dentistry		8.8					8.4
Engineering	1.4	8.4	7.5	8.0		16.6	17.3
Agronomy		2.2					5.2
Architecture				9.0			
Applied Science	1.4			7.0			
Secondary school teacher training		6.0		9.0			
Primary school teacher training				7.0			
Overall higher	8.2	7.5	9.2	7.8	9.3	12.7	15.0

Source: Psacharopoulos (1973), Table 4.9.

experienced. Table 9.3 shows some examples of social and private returns to primary, secondary and higher education that make the point. Nonetheless, the general principle still applies that—provided one accepts the results for what they purport to be—the social (or private) desirability of various levels of education is given by their ranking in terms of the rates of return. Moreover, if the social (or private) return exceeds the social (or

TABLE 9.3   *Social and Private Rates of Return by Educational Level in Ten Countries* (%)

Country	Year	Social			Private		
		Primary	Secondary	Higher	Primary	Secondary	Higher
Canada	1961	—	11.7	14.0	—	16.3	19.7
Ghana	1967	18.0	13.0	16.5	24.5	17.0	37.0
Great Britain	1966	—	3.6	8.2	—	6.2	12.0
India	1960	20.2	16.8	12.7	24.7	19.2	14.3
Israel	1958	16.5	6.9	6.6	27.0	6.9	8.0
Mexico	1963	25.0	17.0	23.0	32.0	23.0	29.0
New Zealand	1966	—	19.4	13.2	—	20.0	14.7
Norway	1966	—	7.2	7.5	—	7.4	7.7
Puerto Rico	1959	17.1	21.7	16.5	>100.0	23.4	27.9
USA	1959	17.8	14.0	9.7	155.1	19.5	13.6

Source: Psacharopoulos (1973), Table 4.1.

private) opportunity cost of resources (that is, the return to be had from an alternative investment outside education), then one has evidence for the (economic) soundness of such expenditures in social (or private) terms. The converse is not true, as we have seen before (p. 238), by virtue of the fact that not all benefits are included in these analyses. In general, it has been found that the rate of return to investment in education is higher than that to physical capital in the poorer countries and lower in the developed countries, while rates to *both* human and physical investment are higher in the poorer countries. This seems consistent with one's intuition about the relative scarcity of *all* forms of capital in the poor countries and the tendency in the developed world to consider education to be worthwhile even if it shows a relatively low monetary return.

C. OUTPUT AND EXTERNALITY

So far we have treated the idea of education itself in a summary, not to say philistine, fashion. Manifestly, education is not to be equated only with years of schooling and its benefits are not only financial. Clearly some forms of education may involve negative monetary returns and yet be justified both privately and socially (for example, training for the priesthood). More important for our purposes, the fact that the amount, quality and availability of education are of universal concern in all societies indicates that social policy towards education is concerned with far more than only its contribution to growth of GNP or wealth, whether private or social.

As with externalities in other areas of social policy, economic opinion is divided both as to their existence and their size. Blaug's (1972) list of externalities in education was drawn from a trawl through some of the literature and included: income gains to others than those receiving the education in question: income gains to subsequent generations from a more educated present generation; provision of an effective mechanism for identifying talent; assisting occupational mobility of the labour force; provision of an environment that stimulates research and invention; encouragement of 'socially responsible' behaviour; encouragement of political stability through a more informed electorate and better-educated political leaders; transmission and nurturing of a cultural heritage; widening of intellectual and cultural horizons to enhance the value of leisure time. Blaug classifies the first four of these as 'economic spillovers' and the remainder as 'atmospheric' effects on the not altogether satisfactory grounds that the former are directly related to the production of (monetary) wealth while the latter are intangible and ultimately interpretable and even revealable only through the political process.

In addition to these factors one should probably add a set of distributional considerations that seem to represent widespread feelings in society: that all citizens ought not merely as of right, but as a matter of compulsion, attain certain minimum standards of literacy and numeracy so far as they are capable; and that access to attainments beyond this level should be voluntarily available to all capable of such attainments. These latter two may be seen either as basic rights derived from, say, Rawlsian considerations (see p. 63) and hence as elements in a socially just system of education, or alternatively as externalities in the sense that other persons' welfare is increased by the arrangements that make these rights available.

There is, as we have pointed out above, dispute about the significance of each of these factors—those regarding them as non-existent or small tending as a corollary to support private fee-paying education and those believing at least some of them to be important tending to favour free state education. Without taking sides in the debate, we may nevertheless identify four points that are very widely agreed:

(1) Minimum periods of schooling should be enforced on all children.
(2) Such coerced education consumption should be provided free.
(3) Such education should also comprise broadly defined curricula taught at not less than a minimum standard.
(4) In so far as any education at all is subsidised, the externality arguments alone do not justify *state* provision—only state subsidies on education (of the appropriate type) wheresoever provided.

There is no prospect in sight that this debate is likely to be ended. One reason for this is that there have been next to no attempts to quantify the 'atmospheric' effects or to set about inventing methods that might lead to their (even partial) quantification. Consequently, what is unquantified may conveniently be taken as small or large according to one's personal predilection. The second main reason is that there has been little attempt, analogous to the fairly advanced work in the health territory, to measure the true outputs of education, concern for which may underly types III and IV externalities in education (supposing such to exist). While in principle some of the techniques of health economics (and related disciplines) may be applicable here (see chapter 7), the economics of education remains sadly—and surprisingly—underdeveloped in this respect.

As we saw in chapter 7, there is no single objective or output of education and many educators are suspicious of attempts at specification and quantification. One of the troubles with this attitude is that one rarely gets beyond first attempts. These are invariably rather crude and therefore easily criticised so that those attempts that have been made tend to be stillborn.

Some interim estimates of the output of secondary schools and universities in the UK have been derived by Blaug and Woodhall (1965, 1968) based upon the crudest quantity indices, such as annual school leavers and graduating students. Since these basic measures manifestly fail to include any quality changes, methods of weighting the crude outputs were devised that went some way towards such an adjustment.

In the case of secondary education the procedure was as follows. The first weighting system tried was an 'economic' quality adjustment based on the assumption that, on average, differences in relative earnings after leaving school over working lifetimes reflect the vocational value of different types and levels of secondary schooling. Owing to data deficiencies, only rough adjustments according to estimates of the present value of earnings were possible, leading to the time series of output in column 2 of Table 9.4.

TABLE 9.4   *Indicators of Secondary School Output, 1950–1963 (1950 = 100)*

School year	Unweighted no. of school leavers	'Economic' indicator	'Educational' indicator	'Academic' indicator
1950–1	100.0	100.0	100.0	n.a.
1951–2	97.2	97.1	97.2	n.a.
1952–3	102.0	102.5	102.3	n.a.
1953–4	102.5	103.6	103.2	100.0
1954–5	99.9	102.2	101.1	100.3
1955–6	95.1	n.a.	97.0	99.6
1956–7	102.6	n.a.	104.3	107.5
1957–8	109.4	n.a.	111.5	115.1
1958–9	116.4	121.9	118.9	124.0
1959–60	117.6	125.2	121.5	132.5
1960–1	119.9	128.7	122.6	136.7
1961–2	143.6	152.5	148.0	159.4
1962–3	134.9	149.1	142.0	161.8
1963–4	129.8	146.3	138.7	167.6
Average annual increase in output	2.0%	2.5%	2.6%	4.7%

Source: Blaug and Woodhall (1968).

The unadjusted number of school leavers is shown in column 1, showing that the adjusted indicator raised the annual growth rate of output from 2.0 to 2.5 per cent. A second 'educational' weights system used the period of schooling on the grounds that this reflects an acquired taste for learning. If many pupils drop out of school at or soon after the statutory school leaving age, output is considered, on this criterion, to be of lower quality than if they stay on. The result of this calculation is shown in column 3 of Table 9.4, raising the annual growth rate to 2.6 per cent. Finally, an 'academic' output indicator was devised where the weights were based upon 'O' and 'A' level examination scores. This indicator is shown in column 4 of Table 9.4, and shows the fastest growth rate. Clearly, on all four indicators, education output has been rising—and the quality of output (as measured by these three methods) has been rising even faster (though productivity per teacher was actually falling).

For the university sector a similar exercise has been performed. The basic quantity unit was the number of students completing a course and this was adjusted by a similar 'economic' quality weights system and an 'educational' adjustment based upon the length of a course leading to a degree. The third method of weighting in this case was a 'cultural' adjustment, which reversed the 'economic' set of weights and, in fact, used their reciprocal (a rare exhibition of economic masochism!). The results are shown in Table 9.5 for the three years for which data were obtainable.

TABLE 9.5 *Indicator of University Output, 1938–1962 (1952 = 100)*

Year	Unweighted no. of graduates	'Economic' indicator	'Educational' indicator	'Cultural' indicator
1938	61	60	60	60
1952	100	100	100	100
1962	140	144	143	142

Source: Blaug and Woodhall (1965).

Perhaps the most remarkable feature of both exercises—especially in the case of universities—is the way in which the crude output data completely dominate the trends: the adjustments for quality add noticeably little to the overall picture. The reader is left to draw his or her own conclusions from these facts.

D. EDUCATION FINANCE

Nearly every education system has been criticised for not going far enough in discriminating in favour of the relatively poor on the one hand (by compensating them partially for loss of earnings) and for discriminating relatively too much in favour of the relatively rich. Student fees in the whole of British higher education account for less than 10 per cent of recurrent expenditure, while in primary and secondary education no charge at all is made. Thus, students are heavily subsidised. Indeed it can be argued (and has been) that in so far as better-off families would purchase substantially more education than poorer, subsidies are given to internalise distributional externalities that do not exist. Of course, the full subsidies are not actually given in cash to the beneficiaries. Instead they are given to the institutions, which then allow entry with nominal fees, as in higher education (these fees themselves being subject to the variable subsidy), or else with no charge at all.

One possibility, therefore, would be to change the current system so that the entire grant (or part of it) was given to the student (but graduated according to family income) who received compulsory primary and secondary education and to those receiving voluntary sixth form or higher education provided they attended their institutions. Such a system could avoid both the gratuitous gift to those who impose no, or little, externality and, if the voucher's value exceeded the cost of a place, the penalisation of those for whom even free places are excessively costly.

Education Vouchers

A related, and much debated, proposal has been to give every family a lump sum payment for spending on education that would be normally sufficient to cover the full cost of an 'average' institution of a particular type for a specified period (presumably a term or academic year). A convenient way of ensuring that the cash is spent for its specified purpose is to award each eligible individual a coupon or, as it is popularly called, a voucher, entitling him or her to a prescribed money's worth of education. The purchasing power of the voucher could (if it were so desired) again be inversely related to family income and its maximum value be less than the average cost of education—the balance being payable in cash. Clearly there is a wide varity of possible vouchers (see Maynard, 1975).

The voucher is thus an earmarked benefit and would necessarily (if the benefit is to be graduated) be supplementable out of family income. At the primary and secondary school levels, voucher proposals have also been coupled with the suggestion that they be used in both private and public sector schools and that parents sending children to state schools should be able to choose whatever school they wish provided it meets the minimal educational standards implied by the externality. This complementary proposal implies according to its advocates that, in addition to efficient subsidising, there would be a greater variety of educational institutions (for example, placing different emphasis on scholarship, sport, discipline, free expression, social integration, religion, internationalism, political education); it would increase school responsiveness to parental values and concerns; stimulate competition among schools and hence quality; promote innovation; encourage parental initiative and, indeed, parental involvement in education; and finally, increase total resources spent on education (Peacock and Wiseman, 1964).

The literature on vouchers is more to be noted for counter-assertions about these claims and for counter-statements of value judgement than either for rigorous analysis of the plausibility of the implications of the scheme alleged by either side or for closer examination of the value judgements that are involved. For example, the counter-arguments run that variations in quality and of type of education are undesirable anyway; that parents would be the dupes of misleading advertising; that minimum standards would turn out very low; that variety would not promote common social values; that social divisiveness would increase; that the cheapest schools would be ghettoes for the children of the very poor and for problem children; that the extra expenditure would go only to the children of the well-to-do and that, anyway, there may be no increase in the resources spent on education at all.

A little careful economic analysis can help us to sort out some, at least, of these conflicting claims. First, the question of variety, choice and common values. In general, if parents do have different preferences regarding the kind of education they would like for their children, then any increase in choice enabling them to suit their preferences better would increase their welfare. At least the parties are agreed on the probable increase in diversity that would result from greater competition. The problem arises in comparing the welfare gains to parents who get their preferred choices with the welfare losses of those other parents (and non-parents) who do not approve either of the type of education chosen by these parents or of the fact that different value systems may be inculcated in society by different types of education. In short, variety and freedom of choice per se impose an adverse externality on them. Now while the existence of this adverse externality is indisputable, its status is in doubt. Although we did not explicitly incorporate this point in our discussion of economic efficiency in chapter 2—for it requires an additional value judgment—it would certainly be in keeping with the spirit of Pareto to exclude some externalities from consideration in social welfare. For example, if I like my bedroom walls pink and you like my bedroom walls blue, provided you are not my wife, it would seem not unreasonable to suppose that the externality imposed on you by the offensive colour of my walls should be ignored—'it's none of your business'. Perhaps the fact that I wish my child to have an education devoid of any religious instruction whatever but thoroughly imbued with the military virtues in an environment that excludes meat-eaters, while you wish *my* child *not* to have such an education, is such an externality that could be agreed, in a kind of 'social contract', not to be included in the calculus. If so, then the case for homogeneity and the inculcation of common values loses some of its strength. Remember, of course, that certain minimum standards would be laid down in any case. A similar argument could be made (or rejected) in the case of the 'ghetto' objection to vouchers. If it were the case that certain schools remained, or more of them became, ghettoes of a particular social class, ethnic group, or educational ability, it is at least not obvious that I should internalise the adverse externality I feel by forcing my middle-class friends to send their children there, even in the event that I shall send mine. In any case, should the ghetto phenomenon prove serious, it may be possible to avoid either side bulldozing the other side into accepting its values by taking appropriate measures to improve the quality of the education and environment in such schools by supplementary—and institutional—subsidies to these educational priority schools and areas.

The claims made by some voucher proponents to the effect that total resources in education would increase are not unambiguous in theory. For example, if vouchers would produce a total expenditure that is closer to the optimum (as they may do) it is not clear that this would necessarily be a larger expenditure than is current. It is perfectly possible for the education lobby, in the imperfect political mechanism, to have secured a larger than optimal quantity of resources. The extent to which wealthier families would secure 'better' or more education than others by supplementing their vouchers so as to make their total spending higher than the value of a maximum-valued voucher would depend upon a variety of factors including the basic voucher value, their taste for education and the minimum educational standards set. If, as seems likely, they would on average secure 'better' or more education for their children (as, indeed, they can—in their own view—at the moment by sending them to some of the private schools) this would give them a welfare gain. If others resent this advantage they suffer a welfare loss and there is no obvious way of comparing these gains and losses to indicate an unambiguous direction of change in social welfare. Those, however, who would deny the exercise of this advantage to the rich (and to the not-so-rich who value a particular education so highly that they make great sacrifices to give it to their children) should recognise that in their view there can be no private sector education at all.

In short, once we get beyond the empirical implications that variety will certainly increase and that expenditure in total may or may not, the economic framework (unless modified) cannot help very much to indicate whether the voucher proposal is a good one or not. As professional economists we simply cannot say. The ultimate decision pro or con will go to those who can mount the most effective political power, since the one thing that is not agreed in this debate is to let each family 'do its own thing': one set of views must be imposed upon the other set. In this issue it is the liberal order itself that is in question. For some, liberalism must reluctantly be sacrificed to ensure that the educational values they so passionately hold be embodied in the society's educational system. For the others, liberalism and education are too inextricably intertwined for it to be possible to conceive that they do not go hand in hand.

Student Loans

While the voucher proposal is not inapplicable to the financing of higher education, concentration on new forms of finance in this area has been much more on the proposals for a system of loans for students. Objections to the present grants system in Britain and elsewhere are made primarily on externality grounds. If it is the case that inequality of educational opportunity in the tertiary sector imposes an externality, then the current system is inefficient twice over: first, because about half of the student awards go to students from families where the earning parent earns more than the average annual income and, second, because the grants go to individuals themselves who have more wealth than average.

Since the latter proposition is not self-evident, yet forms the basis of the loans argument, we investigate it further. One of the effects of education is, as we have seen, to enhance the earnings of those who have been educated. In present value terms, therefore, the relative human capital of the educated exceeds that of the less educated. A loans scheme, it is argued, by which individual students were awarded repayable loans, would remove this inequity and would, at the same time, give low-income households access to the same educational opportunities by relating credit-worthiness not to household current incomes (which may also be exceedingly unstable) but to the expected future income of the loan recipient himself. Moreover, if it is desired to increase the flow of students through higher education, there is no reason why the loans' terms should not be subsidised in a variety of ways (e.g. lower interest rates and delayed repayment); nor need adverse distribution effects be suffered by those making educational investments that turn out, for one reason or another, to be financially unprofitable, for repayment can be made conditional upon reaching certain post-education income levels. Thus, persons whose wealth was not increased by education would not be disadvantaged. In effect, then, the mechanism would take a roughly similar form to income taxation. Indeed, such proposals have earned themselves the tag 'a graduate tax'.

Several arguments pro and con the graduate tax have been made. An argument against is that the present grants system has achieved an unparalleled (elsewhere) working-class participation in higher education and the loans scheme would work against this achievement. Against this it can be argued (a) that the loans scheme would enable students to overcome some of the present discrimination against students from low-income households and (b) that the proportion of working-class students in British universities has remained about constant since the 1920s (at 25 per cent) long before the present comprehensive grants system was introduced (in the 1960s).

For the scheme, it is argued that it would increase the amount of resources devoted to education since it would eventually result in large sums being paid into the Exchequer. Whether this is the case or not, however,

depends first upon the scale of the loans scheme (covering, e.g., maintenance and fees or the full cost); second upon the extent to which the middle-
class students, who presently gain a substantial bonanza from the current
system, would find higher education less 'profitable' and whose relative
numbers might fall; and third upon (a) whether capital sum repayments
and interest payments were treated as an earmarked tax to be devoted
entirely to higher education and (b) whether, even if they were, general tax
funds were regarded as substitutable for earmarked funds. In general, there
is no reason to suppose that the resources devoted to higher education
would not remain largely discretionary to policy makers, as they are now.

Two fallacious arguments against loans are (a) that people who 'brain
drain' would avoid repayments and (b) that those who do not emigrate pay
higher income tax anyway—so we already have an implicit 'graduate tax'.
The brain drain avoidance argument is easily met by modifications to
existing reciprocal tax arrangements between countries. The second argument confuses the general reasons for having a progressive tax system with
those for making the beneficiaries from short-term state assistance pay for
it in the long term.

A final question may be discussed here in connection with loans. If it is
the case that higher education is so very profitable, why has not the capital
market already stepped in to provide facilities? The reasons are probably
two-fold. First, since the future return is uncertain, capital markets characteristically require some collateral or security. In other areas this varies
from the ability to participate in the control of a firm in the case of equity
shares to the pledging of a life insurance policy as collateral. Low-income
households in particular find it difficult to use the capital market in
general, as do some high-income households, especially if they depend
heavily on overtime earnings and want a mortgage. In the case of student
loans absence of collateral is likely to prove a problem for some. Second,
there has always been, in view of the externalities, a degree of charity in the
financing of students. Even ignoring state subsidies, private individuals and
institutions with an interest in education have made grants and
scholarships—typically to the most promising students who have,
presumably, the highest rate of return. Consequently, the 'cream' of the
market has been skimmed off. Most of the loans schemes now proposed
are not 'commercial' schemes. It is envisaged either that they be administered by the government or, if operated by private agencies, that the
government would subsidise the terms of the contract.

The principles and problems associated with subsidies to reduce the
market price (possibly to zero) or to place purchasing power in the hands
of consumers in the form of cash grants, vouchers or loans are similar
throughout the whole of the social services. The extension of the voucher
system to health care—enabling individuals to purchase insurance against
ill-health—has, for example, most of the familiar pros and cons, value

disputes and predictive disputes that characterise vouchers for education.

At least part of the general problem of assessing the relative desirability of the broad basis of approach—subsidising producing institutions that make services available at a lower price (possibly zero) or consuming individuals who buy at the market price—depends upon how one evaluates the relative merits of the two implied methods of discrimination between competing client groups. The use of market prices is advantageous to the extent that these prices reflect the true value of additional resources in their most socially valuable alternative use and to the extent that the subsidies in question can be strictly tied to the consumption of the externality-creating activity (and that once the additional consumption desired by society is secured it cannot be resold). In education, while the latter two conditions are fairly easily met, it seems unlikely that the former (least cost production and, to a lesser extent, allocation to those who value the service most) are very perfectly met. Indeed, given the preponderance of non-profit institutions in education, where managements have relatively small incentives to be as efficient as they would have to be in a profit regime, it seems most unlikely.

The use of institutional subsidies is advantageous to the extent that they are used efficiently to increase output and quality and to the extent that the short-fall in supply in zero price cases is rationed out according to principles consistent with the nature of the externality. If the subsidised institutions are not publicly owned, once again relative inefficiency is to be expected unless they are for-profit institutions. But if they are publicly owned, a far greater use of the economic tools of efficient organisation is required if their operation is to be markedly more efficient than non-profit private institutions. As far as discrimination between the excessive number of potential clients is concerned, unless every identifiable qualified individual is to receive the service (as in compulsory education up to the age of sixteen), huge problems exist in defining who shall receive the education and in ensuring that those who carry out the day-to-day rationing procedures act in the social interest. High prices can always be overcome by giving the user enough resources to pay the price. Discretionary rules, however, are less easy to deal with and also place a great burden of responsibility upon those who do the allocating. How would *you* decide whom to admit to university? Examination scores are notoriously poor predictors of ultimate academic accomplishment. References may not always be relied upon. The temptation is irresistible to fall back upon subjective criteria whose validity is largely untestable. The interview is a classic example.[2]

NOTES

1. The marginal product of N is

$$\frac{\partial Q}{\partial N} = \alpha a N^{\alpha-1} K^{\beta}$$

and the marginal product of K is

$$\frac{\partial Q}{\partial K} = \beta a N^{\alpha} K^{\beta-1}.$$

The total amount of Q received by N, if each person-hour is paid its marginal product, is:

$$N \frac{\partial Q}{\partial N} = \alpha a N^{\alpha} K^{\beta} = \alpha Q = \text{labour's share}$$

and the amount going to owners of K is similarly:

$$K \frac{\partial Q}{\partial K} = \beta a N^{\alpha} K^{\beta} = \beta Q = \text{capital's share.}$$

Since $\alpha + \beta = 1$, $\alpha Q + \beta Q = Q$ and the shares of labour and capital exhaust the total product available.

2. Would you let your friend 'jump the queue'? How about your boss? Your boss's son? Your enemy?

QUESTIONS ON CHAPTER 9

1. Assess the contribution of education to ecnomic growth.
2. Is higher education best seen as an investment in or a filter of talent?
3. Distinguish between the private and social return to educational investment. Why do they differ?
4. What externalities exist in education?
5. What policy implications flow from a finding that the social return to education
   (a) exceeds the alternate rates of return that could be had
   (b) falls short of the alternate rates?
6. Have we over-invested in education?
7. What is the output of
   (a) kindergartens
   (b) secondary schools
   (c) universities?
8. Do imperfections in the human capital market imply the desirability of education subsidies?
9. Is voluntary long-term indenture
   (a) inefficient
   (b) unjust?
10. 'It may be just, but it is certainly inefficient to educate women as much as men.' Discuss.
11. Should education up to any given age be compulsory as well as free?

12. Who would gain and who lose from
    (a) giving university students a grant to cover their living expenses and university fees, and
    (b) giving them a loan to the same amount?
13. What differentiates the consequences of an education voucher from a cash grant of the same value? (Assume that the recipient takes (a) neither more nor less education with the voucher than with the grant (b) more education with the voucher.)
14. 'Grants to students are grants to the relatively rich, judged in terms of lifetime earnings. Grants are therefore unjust.' Discuss.
15. Why does the state own schools and employ teachers rather than merely subsidise and regulate them in the private sector?
16. Is there a shortage of teachers?
17. Why not sell degree certificates?
18. Should there be more investment in the acquisition of skills outside school and college and in, for example, the work-place?
19. What is 'good' education? Can it be best supplied in the market? By the state?
20. Is there a difference in the kind of educational investment needed in developed countries compared with the Third World?

FURTHER READING

Arrow, K. J. (1973) Higher education as a filter. *Journal of Public Economics, 2*, pp. 193–216.

Becker, G. (1964) *Human Capital.* New York: Columbia University Press.

Blaug, M. (1972) *An Introduction to the Economics of Education.* Harmondsworth: Penguin.

Blaug, M. and Woodhall, M. (1965) Productivity trends in British university education 1938–52. *Minerva, 3*, pp. 483–98.

Blaug, M. and Woodhall, M. (1968) Productivity trends in British secondary education. *Sociology of Education, 41*, pp. 1–35.

Bowles, S. (1973) Understanding unequal economic opportunity. *American Economic Review, 63*, pp. 346–56.

Denison, E. F. (1962) *The Sources of Economic Growth in the US and the Alternatives before Us.* New York; Committes for Economic Development.

Denison, E. F. (1964) Measuring the contribution of education (and the residual) to economic growth. In J. Vaizey (ed.) *The Residual Factor and Economic Growth.* Paris: Organisation for Economic Co-operation and Development.

Denison, E. F. (1967) *Why Growth Rates Differ.* Washington, DC: Brookings.

Griliches, Z. (1970) Notes on the role of education in production functions and growth accounting. In W. L. Hansen (ed.) *Education, Income and Human Capital.* New York: National Bureau for Educational Research.

Griliches, Z. and Mason, W. (1972) Education, income and ability. *Journal of Political Economy, 80*, pp. 574–5103.

Harris, S. E. (1962) *Higher Education: Resources and Finance.* New York: McGraw Hill.

Jencks, C. *et al.* (1972) *Inequality: A Reassessment of the Effect of Family and Schooling in America.* New York: Basic Books.

Layard, R. and Psacharopoulos, G. (1974) The screening hypothesis and returns to education. *Journal of Political Economy, 82*, pp. 985–98.

Lindsay, C. M. (1971) Measuring human capital returns. *Journal of Political Economy*, 79, pp. 1195–215.

Maynard, A. K. (1975) *Experiment with Choice in Education*. London: Institute of Economic Affairs.

Peacock, A. T. and Wiseman, J. (1964) *Education for Democrats*. London: Institute of Economic Affiars.

Prest, A. R. (1966) *Financing University Education*. London: Institute of Economic Affairs.

Psacharopoulos, G. (1973) *Returns to Education*. Amsterdam: Elsevier.

Psacharopoulos, G. (1977) Family background, education and achievement. *British Journal of Sociology*, 28, pp. 321–35.

Psacharopoulos, G. and Layard, R. (1979) Human capital and earnings: British evidence and a critique. *Review of Economic Studies*, 46, pp. 485–504.

Taubman, P. (1975) *Sources of Inequality in Earnings*. Amsterdam: North-Holland.

Taubman, P. and Wales, T. J. (1973) Higher education, mental ability, and screening. *Journal of Political Economy*, 81, pp. 28–55.

West, E. G. (1965) *Education and the State*. London: Institute of Economic Affairs.

Wiseman, J. (1959) The economics of education. *Scottish Journal of Political Economy*, 6, pp. 48–58.

Wolfle, D. and Smith, J. (1956) The occupational value of education for superior high-school graduates. *Journal of Higher Education*, 27, pp. 201–13.

CHAPTER 10

Housing

The organisation of this chapter differs from that of the two preceding chapters since this area of social policy is a good deal more involved with market *intervention* than with its substantial *replacement* by other resource allocation procedures. Accordingly, we begin with an analysis of the fundamental economics of the housing market and then move to the externality rationale for government intervention and a discussion of governmental policy towards housing. Housing policy is an immense area and we shall touch only on some central issues.

A. HOUSING AS A STOCK AND FLOW

A frequent concern in housing policy has been the existence of a 'shortage' of dwellings for the number of households. Figure 10.1 shows that, in England and Wales, the number of dwellings exceeded the number of households for the first time in the decade ending in 1971. However, such comparisons between dwellings and households can be misleading: for one thing the availability of dwellings itself helps to determine the formation of new households, so the two are not really independent; for another, some households wish to own more than one dwelling; for another, such aggregates can mask substantial regional variations; for yet another, 'shortage' (or 'surplus') really needs to be defined by reference to more carefully specified demand and supply factors, and with respect to any externalities embodying notions of what dwellings (and of what type) it is felt should be available for occupation. Summary statistics of total dwellings and household are manifestly inadequate representations of any relevant notion of 'shortage' or 'surplus'—relevant, that is, either to the wishes of existing and potential households themselves, or to some collective view of what ought to be.

In addition to the changes in the stock shown in Figure 10.1, there have also been marked changes over time in its tenure characteristics. Table 10.1 shows the distribution of the housing stock by type of ownership since 1914. This shows the three main kinds of tenure that dominate policy discussion in the UK: owner occupation, local authority rented accommo-

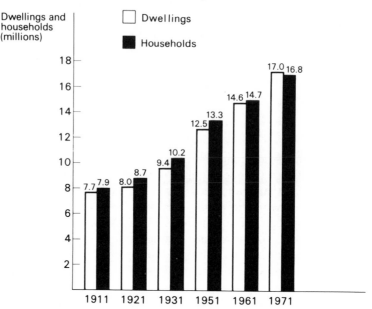

FIG. 10.1   Households and dwellings stock, England and Wales, 1911–1971.

dation and privately owned rented accommodation. The very large rise in the first, the emergence of the second and the substantial decline of the third are one of the most dramatic changes in way of life characterising British social history this century. These changes will be examined in greater detail later in the chapter.

TABLE 10.1   *Distribution of UK Dwellings by Tenure, 1914–1975 (%)*

	Owner-occupied accommodation	Local authority rented accommodation	Privately rented and other accommodation
1914	10	—	90
1947	26	13	61
1960	42	26	32
1975	53	31	16

Source: Donnison (1967), Table 10; Stafford (1978), Table 6.

One of the principal distinguishing features of housing is that it may be seen both as a *stock*, there being a given number of dwellings in existence at any one time, and as a *flow* where the flow can be interpreted in two senses: as changes per time period in the stock (e.g. additional dwellings built) or as the services yielded by a stock of dwellings or by an individual dwelling. Some idea of the durability of the dwelling asset can be given by

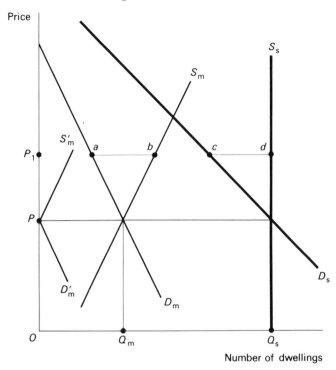

FIG. 10.2   Stock and market demand and supply of housing.

the fact that in Britain about one third of the stock existing in 1975 was built before 1918.

Let us begin by assuming that the stock is given in total. In Figure 10.2, the heavily drawn curves indicate the available stock of dwellings (S_s) that is all owned by individuals, corporate bodies, etc. D_s shows the demand for the ownership of stock, indicating that at lower prices a greater stock will be demanded and conversely a lower stock at higher prices. Abstracting from the fact that housing is a highly heterogeneous entity, the market-clearing price, OP, is the price at which the demand *to own* housing equals the available supply.

At any point in time, this stock will be owned by a given set of individuals and at each price the housing they own may be either too much or too little, depending on the price at which they can sell or buy and their preferences. At higher prices, owners will be more ready to sell (having 'too much') and at lower prices they will wish to buy. These amounts by which their ownership exceeds or falls short of their demands to own are shown in the finely drawn curves S_m and D_m. S_m shows the supply of housing on the market for sale at each price and D_m shows the demand for housing additional to that which each owns. The horizontal distance between D_m

and S_m is the same as that between D_s and S_s. Thus at price OP_1, $ab = cd$, since the difference between D_s and S_s at that price shows the excess of actual ownership over desired ownership, while the difference between D_m and S_m shows this same amount as the difference between what is currently on offer for sale and currently demanded for purchase. At the market-clearing price, OP, the amount offered for sale is just equal to the amount demanded for purchase: at higher prices would-be sellers cannot find customers and at lower prices would-be buyers cannot find sellers. If one could imagine that, at OP, everyone eventually owns neither more nor less housing than is wished, then of course no offers of sale or bids to buy would be made and the S_m and D_m curves intersect on the vertical axis—as indicated by S'_m and D'_m. Invariably, however, even at the market-clearing price, there will be positive amounts of housing offered for sale and demanded for purchase. Trade between buyers and sellers forces the S_m and D_m curves towards the vertical axis, but changes in personal circumstances (e.g. changes in income, household composition, job location) continuously occur so as to move S_m and D_m out towards the right.

This analysis of what is effectively a market in second-hand housing demonstrates that the underlying determinants of house prices when the stock is given are the total stock itself and the demand to own the stock. Market evidence, as exhibited by S_m and D_m, is determined by the *distribution* of the stock among owners. It is sometimes said that the price of housing is set by these market transactions and, since the actual exchange of housing is but a tiny proportion of the total stock in any time period, that 'the tail wags the dog'. This analysis shows, however, that the price is also determined—indeed *mainly* determined—by those who wish to own their housing and who are not 'in the market' to buy or sell. Even if there were no buyers or sellers there would (under the conditions described in Figure 10.2) still be a positive price of housing equal to OP, though this would not be revealed by any market transactions.

To this basic model of the housing market, whose main advantage is that it reveals the underlying importance of the idea of a demand for the stock of housing as distinct from the demand for housing for purchase, we may now add variations in the stock. We shall make this addition in a simple fashion at first, and discuss refinements later in the chapter. New housing will be constructed if price rises above a certain level and existing housing will disappear through unrepaired depreciation below a certain price. For simplicity we shall assume that these decisions to construct or allow to depreciate are made in response to current prices rather than—as is more realistic—in response to anticipated future prices. We shall also ignore the time-lags involved in construction and demolition of housing.

In Figure 10.3, panel (b) shows that the addition to the stock (S_h) will be positive above price OP^* and negative below. Adding this supply curve to the S_s curve in panel (a) in Figure 10.3 produces the new stock supply

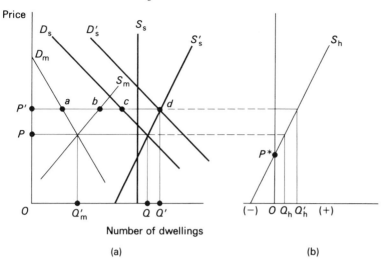

FIG. 10.3   Market and stock demand and supply of housing when the stock can
be altered.

curve S'_s, which again indicates the stock that will be owned at a variety of
prices where we now allow speculative builders, etc., to own some of the
stock. Once again an excess of the supply to own the stock over the
demand to own is equal to the excess of the supply for sale over
the demand for purchase ($cd = ab$), but now the S_m curve incorporates
the supply of new building (and demolition of old). At the market-clearing
price of OP, the total demand for the stock is OQ (including OQ_h newly
built stock), indicating that, over time, the stock is increasing in response
to increasing population, income, etc. OQ'_m shows the transactions in housing (including new housing) at the market-clearing price. D_m of course now
also includes any demand for ownership of the new stock by the building
industry itself (e.g. for speculative purposes).

Now suppose that an increase in the availability of mortgages, increase
in subsidy to house owners, or some such similar change in the environment, causes the demand for ownership of the stock to increase from D_s to
D'_s. A new market-clearing price of OP' is established. D_m moves to the
right and S_m to the left to establish a new quantity of trade in housing
somewhere along *ab* (not shown in Figure 10.3). Construction firms increase output to OQ'_h.

This simplified account of the workings of the market for both second-
hand and new housing not only emphasises that the supply of housing for
sale is the sum of both new building and offers of old stock, both of which
depend upon price, but also shows that the idea of a shortage can be given
at least one unambiguous intepretation: when buyers can buy all that they
want at the going price and sellers can sell all they want to sell there is, in

the most common economic usage, no shortage. Shortages arise when sellers wish to sell less than buyers wish to buy or, as we have seen, when the demand to own exceeds the available stock (including new building). Provided that prices can move in response to such shortages there is a continuing tendency for shortages to be eliminated *not only* via new building but also via the sale of older property. But there is also another very important concept of shortage to which we shall presently turn.

Before doing so it is necessary to complicate the preceding analysis somewhat by investigating more fully the nature of the price of a durable asset such as a dwelling and the nature of the commodity or service that is purchased.

Since housing is in fact more heterogeneous than the analysis thus far allows, it is common for economists to identify this heterogeneity in terms of the services yielded as a flow over time by an item of housing stock. These relate to characteristics such as space inside and outside the dwelling; number of rooms; heating; state of decoration and repair; garage; proximity to neighbours, schools, shops; social class of neighbourhood, etc. These could be combined into an index of the sort discussed in chapter 7, which in each period of time will have a rental value. If we denote this value as R, which is the price of a periodic (say annual) flow of services summarised by the index of characteristics, then the price (P) of the *stock* is the present value of these services net of depreciation (d) assumed (for convenience) to take place at a constant rate:[1]

$$P = R \left[\frac{(1 + i)^n - (1 - d)^n}{(i + d)(1 + i)^n} \right]$$

and for a dwelling that is expected to have a very long life, this is approximately by

$$P = \frac{R}{i + d}.$$

Thus the price of a dwelling is its annual rental value discounted by the sum of the interest and depreciation rates. Unlike the human capital equations with which we have dealt hitherto, however, the stock is itself a tradable commodity, hence the price of the stock can be seen reflected in actual market transactions. Trade can, however, also take place in the *services* of dwellings so that with a physical asset like a house or apartment it is possible either to buy the stock itself at a price P, which is tantamount to buying its services for its expected life, or alternatively to buy the services for a shorter period (say a year) at the appropriate rent R. Because P is large relative to most households' annual income, the choice between buying outright and renting is in part determined by the availability of loan finance and households' creditworthiness in the eyes of lenders. Given differential access to the capital market for persons of differing financial circumstances, it is scarcely surprising that those with few physical assets to offer as collateral, or with little human capital, or who are expected to have an unstable and uncertain income stream, who are more likely to be unemployed, etc., will tend to be constrained to the rented sectors of the housing market. Home ownership, in the absence of policies designed to overcome these financial disadvantages, will thus tend to be the prerogative of the middle and upper socio-economic groups.

B. EXTERNALITY AND HOUSING POLICY

The foregoing analysis can be the point of departure for a wide range of policy questions in housing: analysis of the construction industry, estimation of supply and demand functions, forecasting supply and demand, regulation of building standards, and so on (see Robinson, 1979, for a more comprehensive survey of issues than that undertaken in this chapter). Here we shall focus on a subset of such policy concerns all of which are a species of externality. These are basically three: a desire to increase the consumption of housing services by households beyond what they choose or can afford in an unregulated market; the desire to ensure that the financial burden of renting or buying accommodation is not 'too' high; and the desire, which is commonly found in many developed countries, to foster home ownership by the occupiers of dwellings. We shall investigate the fundamental economics of four commonly occurring problems: imposition of rent ceilings in the privately let sector; muncipal ownership and letting at subsidised rents in the public sector; subsidies to home owners in the private sector; and inner-city housing problems. Underlying all four areas of policy is the idea that in the absence of an appropriate set of social policies there would be shortage of dwellings of an adequate type either to rent or to purchase, where 'shortage' does not necessarily imply that at the going prices or rentals there are more potential buyers than sellers (the common economic definition mentioned above), but that at the going prices and rentals it is felt that more housing services (of either kind: rented or purchased) should be consumed.

Rent Controls

The imposition of ceilings on the rents of some types of privately let dwellings, together with controls over quality and the granting of security of tenure to existing tenants, has been held to account for the dramatic decline in this sector of the housing market in Britain and elsewhere. The analysis of rent controls in the form of a price ceiling can be conducted initially in terms of a figure such as Figure 10.3, by looking at the expected effects on the stock of housing. If in the starting situation the return to landlords from investing in dwellings to rent was competitive in the sense that no higher return could have been obtained by investing their wealth in other assets within the same risk class, then there will be a reduction in the amount of building to replace demolished stock. Taking, for example, D'_s and S'_s as the initial stock demand and supply and OP as the price when the rent is controlled, then building contractors will move down the supply curve of new housing (S_h). In addition, where possible, existing tenancies will not be replaced and some existing stock will be transferred to the unregulated rent sector or sold for outright purchase by home owners, thus shifting S_s to the left. This occurs because landlords—to the extent that they hold housing assets to generate income—will find relatively more attractive outlets for their savings and wealth elsewhere. These reductions in available stock will, of course, exacerbate the excess demand, or shortage in its usual economic sense, caused by holding prices below the market-clearing level.

If, however, returns to investment in housing exceed those available elsewhere, then there may be little effect—if indeed any at all—on new construction and little, if any, of the stock will be transferred to other tenure categories, for the highest return—though lower than before—will still be found in housing to let. Clearly, however, if the rent ceiling is sufficiently low, returns may yet be brought below the alternatives elsewhere available. The effect of a rent ceiling on the stock and supply of new dwellings therefore depends on the extent to which landlords' returns are above the normal returns available: if they are above it and the ceiling is not too low the worst that may be expected is a slower rate of new building.

In addition to the stock effects, it is interesting to explore the effects of rent ceilings on the services yielded by the stock (i.e. its quality). This analysis may be conducted in terms of Figure 10.4. The horizontal axis measures an index (on a ratio scale) of the services offered by the existing stock of accommodation for rent and it is these services that it is envisaged are demanded. The vertical axis measures the rent *per unit of service*. In an initial situation we assume that, at the rental OR_0, OQ_0 units of housing services are demanded at a total market rent of $OR_0 aQ_0$. We now suppose, say, that this rent is regarded as too high for the average tenant, and a price ceiling is imposed at the fraction OR_1/OR_0 of the original rent per dwelling $(= OR_1 bQ_0)$. This has two immediate effects. First the rents paid by tenants and received by landlords fall: a distribution of income towards tenants at the expense of landlords. Second, it creates an excess demand, or shortage in the usual economic sense, of $Q_0 Q_1$ since at the new rent the amount of service has remained the same (OQ_0) but the rent per unit has fallen to OR_1. The amount of housing services available from a given stock—even if the stock of dwellings itself remains the same size—is not,

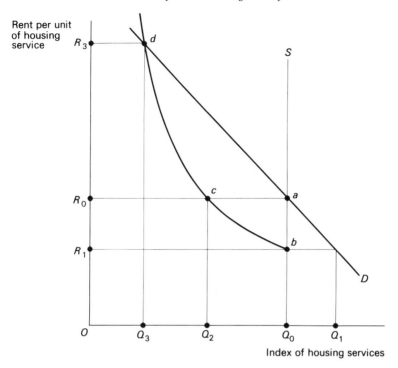

FIG. 10.4   Effect of rent controls on the quantity of housing services.

however, fixed at OQ_0. By allowing the stock to depreciate by reducing expenditures on repair and maintenance, landlords can reduce the amount of housing services. With the rental per dwelling fixed at $OR_1 bQ_0$, landlords can maintain the return on their stock by moving along the rectangular hyperbola *bcd* in Figure 10.4, at any point on which the rent per dwelling remains the same, viz. $OR_1 bQ_0$. Thus, by allowing the amount of service to fall to OQ_2, the rental per dwelling remains the same $(OR_0 cQ_2)$ whereas the *implicit* rental *per unit of housing service* has risen to OR_0. At this implicit rent per unit of service, demand will have been reduced from OQ_1 to OQ_0, but there will still be an excess demand for the services of the stock. Excess demand will be eliminated only when the implicit rental per unit of service has risen to OR_3, when the amount of services provided by the stock has fallen, as has the amount demanded, to OQ_3.

This adjustment takes time, of course, and it may be difficult in the short run for landlords to eliminate excess demand by a sufficient depreciation in the quality of services yielded by their stock of dwellings. In addition, policy measures are also adopted laying down minimum safety, health, etc. standards that may make it impossible for landlords to make the complete adjustment: under such circumstances, in so far as they adjust at all, they must then adjust the size of the stock.

Municipal Housing

Rent controls, such as were discussed above, offer an implicit subsidy to existing tenants but do nothing to increase the availability of accommodation. Indeed they may, as we have seen, have the effect both of reducing the services of tenanted housing and of reducing the total stock available so that existing tenants' subsidies become more apparent than real while the opportunity for potential tenants to acquire rented houses is reduced: a 'fair' rent at which one cannot obtain accommodation is indeed a privilege whose benefits are more apparent than real! These undesirable consequences arise because the subsidy to tenants is granted at the expense of the owners of the stock who may be expected to behave in a fashion such as to protect the value of their assets as much as possible. A policy that subsidised the rental to tenants, but that allowed owners to receive the going rent (including the subsidy), would not have these consequences. It is not altogether clear why this alternative policy is not more widely adopted in developed countries. One reason may be that a redistribution of wealth from landlords to tenants is a policy objective. Yet this seems unlikely since owners of accommodation to let have not characteristically been very wealthy people: in Britain, housing to let was a typical real investment for *small* savers in the nineteenth century and early part of the twentieth. More likely is that a subsidy policy that did not penalise owners would have created 'too' free a set of choices for potential tenants, entailing greater subsidy costs than may be possible with a system of municipally owned housing let at subsidised rents and not necessarily ensuing that the accommodation occupied by subsidised tenants was of an appropriate sort reflecting the externalities that generate the desire to subsidise in the first place.

While a full analysis has yet to be developed of the reasons for the failure to emerge of a subsidy policy that does not penalise landlords,[2] it remains the case that the municipalisation of housing has tended to be the preferred way out. Municipal authorities are not, of course, expected to behave like private landlords and so the adverse consequences of rent control policies in the private sector can be avoided.

In Britain, where municipal housing has been developed further than elsewhere, local authorities keep Housing Revenue Accounts that must balance on the cost side, of which interest charges are the largest single component (over 70 per cent of the total). The revenue side comes from rents received from tenants, specific subsidies made available by central government to the local authorities and, at the discretion of the local authority, transfers from local property taxation (known in Britain as local authority rates). Municipal housing rents are thus partly arbitrarily determined by the historical cost of building as reflected in inherited interest charge obligations and partly by specific subsidies determined by national and local interpretations of housing needs.

The remarkable expansion of 'council housing' in Britain is indicated in Table 10.1 (p. 256), though this expansion has not been sufficient to eliminate the excess demand for what is usually high standard accommodation (the so-called Parker–Morris standards for the building of muncipally owned accommodation were, while they were in force, higher than those in much private building). Local authorities consequently use supplementary criteria for allocating their stocks to tenants. Potential tenants signal their demand in the first instance by asking for their names to be added to a waiting list. Tenants are then usually selected by a combination of considerations: existing housing circumstances, length of time of residence in the area, length of time on the list, etc. Some authorities have points schemes such that the highest accumulation of points comes to the top of the list.

The system is subject to a number of criticisms. Most frequently heard are two: that labour mobility is reduced by the waiting list system for tenants who may wish to move between local authority areas; and that it is not possible to evict a household in good financial standing even though its 'need' for municipal housing may be small—and in particular less than that of many who may be waiting. This latter problem has given rise to pressure for the sale of municipal dwellings to sitting tenants at a less than market price for the dwelling. If a household is no longer in 'need', one way of measuring this is its willingness and ability to purchase the dwelling it occupies. Any price set above the present value of future rents net of maintenance and repair costs, and including the terminal site value of the property, implies a reduction in subsidy and hence a decrease in the municipal subsidy going to tenants able to afford to buy. Such a price is likely to be less than the market value of the dwelling, since rents are less than implicit market rents to owner occupiers, and hence may be both a rational policy for the municipal authority and beneficial to (some) tenants. To the extent that turnover of the stock from tenant to tenant is slow, a judicious policy of selling municipal housing need not be to the detriment of those who are waiting since such property would have been unlikely to have become available for reletting in any case. In the longer run, however, such sales must clearly act to their detriment.

Owner Occupation

Dwellings are capital. Their great expense relative to annual incomes implies that their purchase is normally made by taking out a loan. The principal specialised agency that has evolved in Britain for making loans to individuals for house purchase is the permanent building society. Credit normally takes the form of a mortgage loan whereby the money is lent to the purchaser on security of the property itself and the debt is paid off over a period usually lying between 18 and 25 years by an annuity payment: the amount borrowed, plus interest, is divided into equal monthly instalments. Initially, since none or little of the principal will have been repaid, the bulk of the monthly payment is interest, but as time passes and the outstanding debt is reduced, so the proportion of interest in the payment is reduced and the proportion of repayment of principal increases.

This system of finance places a relatively heavy burden on the young whose real incomes may be expected to rise but whose constant repayments represent a high proportion of income in the early years. Building societies are non-profit organisations and this, together with a pronounced risk-aversion arising from the fact that they lend money for long periods of time but borrow from lenders on short-term agreements (savings deposited with a building society can typically be withdrawn on demand or within days—at most weeks) tends to make them cautious both as to the type of property against which they will lend money and the type of person to whom they will lend. Thus older properties are less suitable as security against mortgage loans and manual workers with relatively unstable earnings tend to be discriminated against. They are also subject to pressure from central government to favour particular groups of buyers, such as those buying a house for the first time.

Because it appears to be an objective of housing policy to encourage home ownership, special tax advantages are available to the owner occupier. Thus, in Britain the interest component of the monthly payment to a building society is (up to a maximum) deductible from taxable income. To see the advantage this gives the dwelling purchaser as compared with the renter, consider an individual choosing whether to rent or purchase a house. For simplicity, assume that the price of the house is the present value of the annual rental and that the house will last indefinitely. Also assume that there are no maintenance and repair costs. Under these circumstances, if the price of the house is P and its annual rental R, the relationship between P and R is given by

$$P = \frac{R}{i}$$

where i is the interest rate. The annual payments if the individual chooses to rent will be iP, as may be seen by rearranging this equation.

Consider two individuals, a potential renter and a potential house purchaser, each of whom has wealth E to invest in either non-housing assets (the renter) or housing (the owner). If the price of the house is $P > E$, the purchaser must borrow $P - E$ to finance the purchase of his asset. In order to maintain comparability between the two let us also assume that the renter borrows $P - E$ to invest in other assets. He thus invests a total of P in non-housing assets. For the moment we also assume that interest payments may be deducted for income tax purposes on borrowings for either reason.

Denote the annual earned income each has as Y (the same for each) and their disposable income after net housing expenditures as Y_R for the renter and Y_P for the purchaser. For a (proportional) income tax rate of t we therefore have:

$$Y_R = (Y + iP)(1 - t) - i(P - E) - iP + ti(P - E)$$

where the first term on the right hand side of the equation is his annual post-tax earned and unearned income, the second term is the interest payments on his debt, the third term is rent paid to the landlord and the final term is his tax relief on borrowing.

Likewise, for the purchaser, we have:

$$Y_P = Y(1 - t) - i(P - E) + ti(P - E)$$

where the first term on the RHS is post-tax income, the second term is interest on his debt and the third his tax relief on borrowing.

The difference between the two is

$$Y_P - Y_R = t(iP)$$

which is the tax not paid by the purchaser on the imputed income of his house. If such imputed income is not a part of taxable income this, then, is the first financial advantage of home ownership over home renting.

Now suppose both that imputed income from home ownership is not taxable and also that interest payment relief is available only on debt taken out to finance house purchase. We now have

$$Y_R = (Y + iP)(1 - t) - i(P - E) - iP$$

which differs from the previous equation for Y_R by the removal of tax relief on debt, and

$$Y_P = Y(1 - t) - i(P - E) + ti(P - E)$$

as before. In this case the difference in disposable income is

$$Y_P - Y_R = t(iP) + ti(P - E)$$

which is the tax not paid on imputed income from house ownership plus the tax relief on the mortgage taken out to finance house purchase. If these two elements of subsidy exist (as they do in Britain) they clearly make home ownership an attractive financial option for persons with wealth to invest and borrowing capability, relative to renting their homes.

The extent to which the $t(iP)$ component of the subsidy on home ownership is regarded as a true subsidy depends upon the definition of income. Suppose one treated a house like other consumer durables (e.g. motor cars), then there would be no imputation of income from this source and the question of its being subject to income tax would not arise. To illustrate, suppose a car costs the same as a house (P) and that one individual rents his house and buys a car while the other buys his house and rents his car. Suppose the car has a rate of depreciation and maintenance cost of d per annum (while the house, as before, neither depreciates nor needs maintenance expenditure). Let there be no tax relief on interest payments for car purchase and no tax on the imputed income from ownership of cars or houses, then:

$$Y_R = Y(1 - t) - i(P - E) - iP - dP$$

where the first term on the RHS is post-tax income of the house renter, the second term is interest on his debt for car purchase, the third term is his annual rent paid to the landlord, and the final term is maintenance and depreciation of the car.

$$Y_P = Y(1 - t) - i(P - E) + ti(P - E) - (i + d)P$$

where the first term is post-tax income of the house purchaser, the second term is interest on his debt for *house* purchase, the third term is tax relief on borrowing for house purchase, and the final term is the rent of the car.

The difference between the two is:

$$Y_P - Y_R = ti(P - E),$$

which is the tax relief on the mortgage: housing viewed as a consumer durable receives no subsidy by virtue of exemption from tax on imputed income. The calculation of the relative subsidy on house purchase, in short, depends upon the nature of alternative investments available: if house renters having the same wealth as buyers typically invest in consumer durables that have no imputed income that is taxable, then house purchasers receive no subsidy on imputed income relative to house renters. Conversely, if income were imputed to *all* consumer durables and subject to income tax, there would again be no relative subsidy—other than the tax relief on borrowing for purchase.

Slums and Inter-City Decay

In the broadest terms there are two types of slum. One kind, commonly found in the older industrialised urban areas of Europe, consists of housing built for an increasing urbanised workforce in the nineteenth century and built to standards below those commonly adopted today (though arguably at least as high as those prevailing for the rural workforce in the last century). The combination of rising building costs and rising commercial site values with low incomes of the occupiers implies that this type of housing stock has depreciated without sufficient maintenance, low quality old buildings being relatively expensive both to maintain and to bring up to acceptable quality by today's standards. Rent controls on rented property have reinforced the decay in quality of such housing. This is not, of course, to say that letting slums is not profitable—on the contrary, the rental per unit of housing service is typically high in such property. However, the low incomes of occupiers, their frequent job-immobility and inability to afford travel expenses if they lived further away from the workplace, etc., imply that this kind of housing is all they can afford. One may suppose, indeed, that the existence of such slums is not in fact evidence of any imperfection in the housing market itself (as is occasionally argued): the problem is essentially one of low incomes, a perception by the better off that such conditions should not be allowed to continue (viz. an externality) and, which has been important historically, the public health hazards (another externality) of slum life.

The second kind of slum arises as high- and middle-income households move out from inner city dwellings in response to changing preferences for styles of residence (lower density, less urban, etc.) and rising maintenance costs on older property, cheaper transport, etc. The properties thus vacated become available, as their average price falls relative to newer housing in the suburbs and country, to lower-income groups. Developers may purchase such properties and subdivide them for sale or to let so entire areas have a marked change in their character: from genteel, even gracious, residences for the well-to-do they are transformed into more densely occupied, less well-maintained property for the relatively poor. This process of change in the function and use of older housing is termed 'filtering'. Multiple occupation and over-crowding further the process of depreciation and, in extreme cases, slums are the end product.

Policies towards the problems of slums have included rent regulation to protect tenants from gross exploitation by the more unscrupulous landlords, purchase and clearance by local authorities (with federal aid in the USA) with subsequent redevelopment (often in the form of high-rise building) and subsidies for improvement of specific properties, or the renovation of local authority purchased property. As is to be expected, given the traditional approach adopted in most countries, direct tenant subsidies tied to housing consumption has not been an adopted policy though, since the low income of slum dwellers is the principal reason why slums exist, this is arguably the most direct method, short of municipalisation, of tackling the problem. Indeed, subsidies either directly to tenants in the private sector or to poor owner occupiers of low-grade dwellings, or indirectly via municipalisation, are the only long-term effective means of abolishing slums. Urban renewal programmes without such an element of subsidy tackle only the symptoms and not the cause of the problem: households do not *seek* slum accommodation; rather they seek *cheap* accommodation and the mere replacement of poor with high-quality housing merely encourages filtering down elsewhere and the growth of new slums as the relatively poor look elsewhere for sufficiently cheap dwellings. Although there have been serious proposals for 'housing vouchers' or 'rent certificates' in the USA, which have been argued to be more effective in removing slums than municipal housing programmes (Olsen, 1969), they have not been subject to the same degree of analysis as have education vouchers. Here, then, lies an important area for future research in the political economy of housing policy.

Housing economics is, in general, poorly developed as yet and housing policy is complex and largely uncoordinated. Robinson (1979) quotes a recent British Secretary of State (A. R. Crosland) as saying in 1975:

> I was astounded to find, on taking over as Secretary of State, how flimsy was the basis on which housing policy was then built. No one had any clear idea of how many houses the country needed or where. No one seemed to have compared the help given to owner-occupiers on the one hand and tenants on the other . . . I am convinced that we need . . . to get beyond a housing policy of 'ad hocery' and crisis management and to find out precisely what needs to be done if we are to get on top of this desparate social problem once and for all. [Robinson, 1979, p. vii]

In this chapter we have, as with health and education, taken a rather general look at the analytical methods applicable to the special characteristics of housing policy. Cost–benefit analysis has, however, begun to be applied in the housing area (see next chapter) and there is an awakening of interest in the systematic analysis, rather than mere description, of housing problems. Future developments will lie largely with readers of a book such as this.

NOTES

1. As we have seen before, the present value of an asset which depreciates is given by:

$$P = \frac{R}{1 + i} + \frac{(1 - d)R}{(1 + i)^2} + \cdots + \frac{(1 - d)^{n-1}R}{(1 + i)^n}.$$

Multiplying this by $(1 + i)/(1 - d)$ and subtracting the above equation gives:

$$P\frac{1 + i}{1 - d} = \frac{R}{1 - d} + \frac{R}{1 + i} + \frac{(1 - d)R}{(1 + i)^2} + \cdots + \frac{(1 - d)^{n-2}R}{(1 - i)^{n-1}}$$

$$-P = -\left| \frac{R}{1 + i} + \frac{(1 - d)R}{(1 + i)^2} + \cdots + \frac{(1 - d)^{n-1}R}{(1 + i)^n} \right|$$

$$P\left| \frac{1 + i}{1 - d} - 1 \right| = \frac{R}{1 - d} - \frac{(1 - d)^{n-1}R}{(1 + i)^n}$$

Writing this as

$$P\left| \frac{1 + i}{1 - d} - 1 \right| = R\left| \frac{1}{1 - d} - \frac{(1 - d)^{n-1}}{(1 + i)^n} \right|$$

and multiplying by $(1 - d)$ gives:

$$P(1 + i) - P(1 - d) = R \left[1 - \frac{(1 - d)^n}{(1 + i)^n} \right]$$

whence

$$P(i + d) = R \left[\frac{(1 + i)^n}{(1 + i)^n} - \frac{(1 - d)^n}{(1 + i)^n} \right] = R \left[\frac{(1 + i)^n - (1 - d)^n}{(1 + i)^n} \right]$$

whence

$$P = R \left[\frac{(1 + i)^n - (1 - d)^n}{(i + d)(1 + i)^n} \right]$$

and, as n becomes infinitely large:

$$P = R \left(\frac{1}{i + d} \right).$$

2. For a voucher type subsidy proposal, see Olsen (1969).

QUESTIONS ON CHAPTER 10

1. Distinguish between the demand for housing as a stock and as a flow.
2. How would you identify a housing shortage?
3. Does Downs' theory of vote-maximising politicians explain the pattern of housing subsidies?
4. What is the relationship between the value of housing services and the price of a house?
5. In a free market would it be cheaper to rent or to buy?
6. What externalities, if any, exist in the housing market?
7. What are the effects of rent controls in the market for privately rented accommodation? Who gains and who loses from controls?
8. What is filtering down in the housing market?
9. How would you construct an index of housing services?
10. What role, if any, should the historical cost of building play in determining the rents charged for municipal housing?
11. How would you select tenants for municipal housing?
12. What subsidy do home purchasers receive?
13. Are municipal tenants more heavily subsidised than home owners?
14. What are slums and why do they exist?
15. Discuss proposals for a housing voucher.
16. In what ways (if at all) is the market for housing purchaser imperfect?
17. At what price, if at all, should municipal housing to sold to sitting tenants?
18. Why in Britain is most privately let accommodation let to relatively mobile persons?
19. Why is the housing of the rich subsidised?
20. What policy would you advocate to provide housing for the homeless?

FURTHER READING

General reviews:

Charles, S. (1977) *Housing Economics*. London: Macmillan.
Muth, R. F. (1969) *Cities and Housing*. Chicago: University of Chicago Press.
Needleman, L. (1965) *The Economics of Housing*. London: Staples Press.
Nevitt, A. A. (1966) *Housing, Taxation and Subsidies*. London: Nelson.
Robinson, R. (1979) *Housing Economics and Public Policy*. London: Macmillan.
  The most comprehensive recent account of the field.
Stafford, D. C. (1978) *The Economics of Housing Policy*. London: Croom Helm.
Wolman, H. L. (1975) *Housing and Housing Policy in the US and UK*. Lexington,
  Mass.: Lexington Books.

Other:

Aaron, H. (1970) Income taxes and housing. *American Economic Review*, 60,
  pp. 789–806.
Anderson, M. (1964) *The Federal Bulldozer: a Critical Analysis of Urban Renewal*.
  Cambridge, Mass.: MIT Press.
Black, J. (1974) A new system of mortgages. *Lloyds Bank Review*, January, pp. 9–16.
Cullingworth, J. B. (1966) *Housing and Local Government*. London: Allen and
  Unwin.
Donnison, D. V. (1967) *The Government of Housing*. Harmondsworth: Penguin.
Edwards, C. and Posnett, J. (1980) The opportunity cost of the sale of local author-
  ity rented accommodation. *Urban Studies*, 17, pp. 45–52.
Friedman, M. and Stigler, G. (1972) Roofs or ceilings? In F. A. Hayek (ed.) *Verdict
  on Rent Control*. London: Institute of Economic Affairs.
Fuerst, J. S. (ed.) (1974) *Public Housing in Europe and America*. London: Croom
  Helm.
Giertz, J. F. and Sullivan, D. H. (1978) Housing tenure and horizontal equity.
  National Tax Journal, 31, pp. 329–38.
Harrington, R. L. (1972) Housing-supply and demand. *National Westminster Bank
  Review*, May, pp. 43–54.
Kain, J. F. and Quigley, J. M. (1970) Measuring the value of housing quality.
  Journal of the American Statistical Association, 65, pp. 532–48.
Lowry, I. S. (1960) Filtering and housing standards: a conceptual analysis. *Land
  Economics*, 36, pp. 362–70.
Merrett, A. J. and Sykes, A. (1965) *Housing Finance and Development*. London:
  Longmans.
Olsen, E. O. (1969) A competitive theory of the housing market. *American Econo-
  mic Review*, 59, pp. 612–22.
Olsen, E. O. (1972) An econometric analysis of rent control. *Journal of Political
  Economy*, 80, pp. 1081–100.
Pennance, F. G. and West, W. (1969) *Housing Market Analysis and Policy*. Lon-
  don: Institute of Economic Affairs.
Ricketts, M. (1976) The economics of the rent allowance. *Scottish Journal of Politi-
  cal Economy*, 23, pp. 235–60.
Rosenthal, L. (1977) The regional and income distribution of council house subsidy
  in the UK. *Manchester School*, 45, pp. 127–40.
Rothenberg, J. (1967) *Economic Evaluation of Urban Renewal*. Wasington, DC:
  Brookings.
Wilkinson, R. K. and Gulliver, S. (1971) The economics of housing: a survey. *Social
  and Economic Administration*, 5, pp. 83–99.

PART IV

Techniques of Appraisal

CHAPTER 11

Economics and Planning in Social Policy

One of the major implications of earlier chapters was that, while qualitative analysis can establish some of the *general* characteristics of an optimal social policy as being dependent upon, for example, the nature of the externality, and can provide a rigorous mode of analysing often controversial issues without prejudging them, and can also underline the inconclusiveness of mere a priorism in deciding between overall methods of organisation, another major use is in forming the theoretical basis for *quantitative* analysis of specific social problems. This and the next chapter investigate further how this analysis can be used.

Until very recently there was very little planning based upon either the criteria or the methods implied by economics. Moreover, there has been substantial resistance to its introduction—though fortunately the techniques are being increasingly used today throughout the public sector and including social policy. Some of the resistance was based upon naive criticism of the basic theory. A hoary old example of this form of criticism is neatly summed up by the assertion that individuals and families are not precision calculating machines making explicit choices like 'Let's take Junior out of school—it's only yielding 8 per cent and we can get 9 per cent on fixing Grandma's broken thighbone'. As Harry Johnson once expostulated, one might as well object to the law of gravity on the basis of seeing a feather float more slowly to the ground than a lead bullet. Such misconceptions are encouraged by textbook writers who teach their readers that individuals 'consult their preferences' before acting—as though there is an imaginary hobgoblin sitting on everyone's left (or right) shoulder. It is true that economic analysis assumes a fundamental kind of rationality in human behaviour, but the basic theory does not purport to describe the thought processes that individuals go through. It asserts that they behave as if they went through these processes. And they do behave this way, though they may actually follow rules of thumb, convention, or copy their neighbours, for the conventions are successful conventions precisely because they produce results that are rational. A stupid convention is likely to be observed primarily in the breach. Sons' prior claims to education over daughters is not, for example, a stupid convention (though it may be an unjust one).[1]

The second kind of objection derives from the vested interests of selfish individuals with policy influence. No one likes being told he has been doing things all wrong (or partly wrong) and everyone would like, other things being equal, the basis of his policy decisions (especially if he is a politician) to be too obscure to be closely scrutinised. The techniques discussed in this and the next chapter are supposed first to make public decision makers behave explicitly in accordance with the rational calculus of maximising social welfare, second to provide a variety of means of finding quantitative answers to important questions of policy, and third to expose the decision framework to the public gaze so that elements that are largely matters of judgment can be seen as such and, if inconsistent with the general view, can be corrected by criticism and discussion.

The systematic use of welfare economics in social policy has been preceded by two basic alternative approaches to planning. One we shall term the 'arbitrary planning' method and the other is 'GNP fixation'. The unflattering labels indicate, of course, our disapproval.

A. 'ARBITRARY' PLANNING

'Arbitrary' planning can easily be illustrated by the common practices of manpower forecasting in education or health. Clearly, it is necessary to forecast future staffing 'needs' in education or health if only because of the length of time it takes to train professional people. Likewise, it is necessary to make budgetary allocations each year to, for example, teaching hospitals in the National Health Service in order that they are able to meet local and national 'needs'.

The first element of arbitrariness consists in the selection (or non-selection) of an objective. Manpower 'needs' and hospital 'needs' are meaningful only in relation to a policy objective. Government spokesmen, planners and (alas) many social scientists speak of 'needs'—whether of industry or society—as if they were self-evident. All too often the use of the word 'need' is a veil to special pleading—an attempt to lend a spurious objectivity to a purely personal point of view. For 'society needs', one should read all too often 'I think some individuals should get'. Rarely do the value judgements we have seen embodied in the concept of 'need' receive a thorough airing.

As with all economic problems there is a 'demand' side and a 'supply' side. Future supplies are dependent upon population growth, current students in training, future professional salaries relative to others both at home and abroad, facilities available abroad, and expected changes in the non-pecuniary characteristics of professional work (job satisfaction). Future demand depends upon population projections again, the demand for the services in which manpower is an input and the degree of substitution expected or planned between manpower and other inputs that affect the productivity of manpower.

Characteristically, the 'arbitrary' forecasters go astray in their population forecasts—a hazardous task for the long term (and for mistakes here they cannot really be held culpable: one has to make the best guess one can)— mistakes about net emigration movements, failure altogether to consider substitution possibilities and arbitrary specifications of the targets or objectives in terms of doctor/patient or teacher/pupil ratios. One of the chief snags of targets of this sort is that they do not measure outputs of the services in question but a ratio of inputs to clients (who are themselves, in a sense, also inputs). But these ratios as such do not enter the social welfare function. Entities in the social welfare function certainly include good education and good health but there is no general reason to suppose that these will vary now or in the future in direct proportion with the input ratios. Moreover, the input ratios may be altered in a variety of ways not only leaving the real output unchanged, but even increasing it! There is firm evidence that this is true of health, let alone education. Due to technical progress, however, the ways in which the ratios can alter themselves change. These factors make the specification of arbitrary needs in the future, based on current ratios, current technology and assuming current ratios to be 'efficient', completely meaningless.

Planning in social policy has, perforce, to take place under conditions of uncertainty and there can be no escaping the necessity for taking risks in the face of such uncertainty: no one can be sure what the size of the client population will be in ten or fifteen years time; no one can be certain how technology will change; no one can be certain what values will be held; no one can be certain what costs future decisions will entail. But, if one thing is certain it is that uncertainty will always be with us, another is that careful analysis of the present, or recent past, can give information that can help reduce some—if not all—of these uncertainties, or at least locate more precisely where the main imponderables lie. In planning future requirements of doctors or teachers, we can be reasonably sure that to assume the perpetuation of existing ratios of manpower to patients or students is erroneous and that the study of the marginal products of these and associated inputs can given clues as to how future needs may be most efficiently met. In planning the future housing stock, a knowledge of the relative expense of rebuilding old or constructing new property provides indicators of how projected demands may be cost-effectively met. In projecting demand, a knowledge of the determinants of the demand for services in the recent past, or cross-sectionally across societies having differing income and other characteristics, can enable both more informed projections to be made and the intelligent evaluation of such projections. In forecasting the take-up of places for the training of professionals, it is helpful to know what the returns to individuals may be from investments of particular kinds in their own human capital.

The general principle, then, is that one should not let the perfect (which is unattainable) become the enemy of the merely good. The studies described in the rest of the chapter provide illustrations of the techniques that have been developed and successfully applied in the pursuit of the 'merely good'.

B. GNP Fixation

'GNP fixation' attempts to assess the global productivity of resources in the social services, usually in terms of their contribution to a nation's growth rate. While having the virtue of a clearly defined objective—increasing GNP—and although we have described some of the work of this type in the chapter on education, this approach is a highly restricted one. For a start, the objective of social policy ought probably not to be (or only be) the maximisation of the growth rate of GNP. Secondly, such global estimates are not as a rule of any great help in the actual planning of health, education, social security, etc., programmes, though possible exceptions to these judgements exist in poor countries, where public health programmes can have a major impact on real incomes per capita and where increases in per capita wealth may have a higher weight in the social welfare function than in more highly developed societies.

One of the difficulties with the GNP approach is that different assumptions about the aggregate production function (the relation between all inputs, technical progress and GNP) can have drastic effects upon the contributions that health, education, and so on, are alleged to make to GNP. As far as we are concerned it seems far better to keep GNP firmly in its (important but subsidiary) place by treating the social services as having their own specific outputs rather than being mere inputs in the international game of keeping up in the growth rate league tables.

C. Microeconomic Planning

The most fruitful approach to the planning of social policy appears, at least for the immediate future, to utilise the basic conceptual apparatus outlined in this book. The empirical techniques derived from microeconomics are commonly referred to as production function, cost–benefit or cost–effectiveness analysis (with their corollaries, output budgeting and PPBS, which are investigated in chapter 12.)

Cost–benefit and cost-effectiveness attempt to apply to public decision making the rational calculus of welfare economics: cost–benefit by comparing all the social costs and benefits of rival plans and selecting those that contribute most to social welfare; cost-effectiveness by comparing the social costs of rival methods of achieving a stated objective and selecting the method that detracts least from social welfare. Clearly, the former is the more ambitious exercise since it attempts to evaluate community gains as well as losses, while the latter, especially valuable where the gains may be hard to estimate reliably, concentrates only on the costs of different ways of obtaining what is thought to be the same gain. Underlying both is the idea of the production function.

There exists an abundance of introductory material on these techniques (see previous references). It will be recalled that a major restraint (some would call it a strait-jacket) imposed on the social policy student in evaluating alternative methods of getting things done is that he should not judge changes from which some people lose and others gain as either good or bad in terms of social welfare (he can judge, of course, in terms of his own welfare). In practice this means strictly that only changes where losses are fully compensated can be evaluated. The working of market-exchange and costlessly operating, fully private property system provides the classic (but hypothetical) area in which the Pareto scheme can always be applied, for every loss imposed upon one individual by another individual will always be fully compensated, usually though not necessarily by the payment of a price.

In the real world, however, many losses are not compensated in this way because of externalities or because prices do not exist or do not properly measure marginal values and marginal social cost, with the consequence that, if one is to evaluate such changes, the (uncompensated) losses of some must be compared with the (uncompensated) gains of others. Any such comparison implies the use of the potential improvement criterion, which usually makes the assumption that each pound to each individual receives a weight of one.

The reasonableness of this procedure has been much debated. On the one hand it has been argued that use of unitary weights is optimal since the prevailing income distribution must be the socially preferred distribution—otherwise why has it not been changed?—and therefore that the weights thrown out by this distribution are the ones that ought to be used in a Paretian analysis of policy. On the other hand it has been argued that a more egalitarian criterion should be used—for example by weighting gains and losses to individuals by the reciprocal of the ratio of their income to average national per capita income.

The Paretian method of this book suggests that neither of these two approaches is likely to be the appropriate one. The first is unlikely to be appropriate since, even if the distribution of incomes is Pareto optimal, there is no general reason why the income weights that are optimal in general should be optimal for the specific purposes in hand. It may be that there is no way of further redistributing incomes that does not make someone worse off in welfare terms, but everyone may agree that some special weights are appropriate in individual social investment appraisals. Being more averse to differences in the consumption of specific goods than to the same differences in income or wealth is a case in point, which we have discussed above. The second is equally unlikely in that it merely asserts a specific weights system that may be preferred by egalitarians (or may not), but that is not necessarily the one preferred by society either in general or in specific cases.

In truth, it is not for the social scientist to decide what system of weights is socially preferred unless he has some means of knowing what society (that is, all the people comprising society) really does prefer. In practice, the choice of weights ought therefore to be made by an accountable authority acting for the collectivity. Analysts may experiment with some possible alternative methods of weighting gains and losses for different people, but if only one is to be used, pending a social (collective) decision about the proper weights, the simplest method is for the analyst to use provisional weights of unity. As such, they carry no normative significance. They are *purely* provisional. It may be, of course, that unitary weights turn out to be the ones preferred in a collective choice but this cannot be prejudged. *Pro tem* they are arbitrary and should be presented as such.

A second potentially important question of income redistribution in efficiency analysis concerns the fact that social investment itself changes the distribution of income. In some cases such changes may be sufficiently small for them not to be worth bothering about as redistributions. Even if they are important, however, it has been argued that the long-term distributional effects of numerous investments will tend to be randomised so that, on average, it is as if distributional effects were neutral. If neither of these arguments can be realistically sustained then it may become necessary to choose between the socially correct system of weights before the investment and the socially correct one after it. In practice, however, few investments are so momentous in their impact that they cause such substantial redistributive effects.

It is, of course, unusual for the economic adviser of government to have the preferred set of weights presented to him for his use. In practice he must either force decision takers to make their own choice or else he might offer them a menu from which to choose, including a whole range of plausible possibilities. His professional status, however, gives him absolutely no competence to choose for them, only a certain faculty for inventing some possibilities for consideration.

In what follows do not expect a detailed exposition of the methodology of cost–benefit or cost-effectiveness analysis. There are many nuances that are best explored using the Further Reading. What, however, we do hope to provide is an illustration of the kind of empirical results obtained by applying analysis of the sort introduced earlier. Of the various problems that have been tackled and that will illustrate the methodology (and its limitations), the following are illustrated in this chapter: A production function for acute hospitals—are they efficient? The marginal product of physician services—are there cheaper ways of getting the same output? The cost of higher education—what is the cheapest way of expanding higher education or where are the greatest savings from cutting back? The cost-effectiveness of kidney treatments—how should we treat patients with kidney failure? The cost-effectiveness of housing—rebuilding or renovation? The value of life—how much is it worth spending to save lives in the health services, on the roads, in home and factory? The value of library services—do decision makers have the right priorities? The net costs of health insurance—are the Americans overinsured? Eviction from council houses—should tenants in arrears be evicted?

The selection poses a reasonable variety of problems at various levels of both aggregation and importance. It also illustrates the very wide range of problems to which the basic analysis can—with suitably imaginative development—be applied. The first five examples deal with production function and cost-effectiveness studies; the next four deal with benefits and cost–benefit.

D. Illustrative Applications

A Cobb–Douglas Production Function for Acute Hospitals

Estimating a production function is a direct way of measuring the productive efficiency of an organisation: testing for the existence of economies of scale, efficient input combinations, and so on. A classic study by Martin Feldstein (1967) estimated a Cobb–Douglas production function for National Health Service acute hospitals of the form:

$$C = aM^{\alpha}B^{\beta}N^{\gamma}S^{\delta}$$

where the output (C) is taken as cases treated and the inputs are medical doctors (M), beds (B), nurses (N) and other supplies (S) respectively. Of the inputs, only B was in physical form; the others were weighted by wages (or prices) and therefore took the form of expenditure data. Table 11.1 shows the results of an ordinary least squares regression in the logarithms of the equation.

TABLE 11.1   *Coefficients of Cobb–Douglas Production for Acute Hospitals*

	α	β	γ	δ	Σ
(a)	.476	.414	.074	−.084	.880
(b)	.311	.500	.037	−.010	.858

Source: Feldstein (1967), Table 4.1.

These coefficients show, as we saw in chapter 2, the elasticity of output with respect to variations in each input. The first row of results (a) makes no adjustment for the important fact that different hospitals have different mixes of cases requiring different combinations of inputs (at varying cost). The second equation makes an allowance for this (using nine case types of the sort: proportion of cases in general medicine, ENT, surgery, gynaecology, etc.) and is the more reliable. As can be seen, the elasticity of output with respect to nurses and supplies is small (and not statistically significant). A one per cent increase in beds alone would enable a half of one per cent increase in cases, while a one per cent increase in doctors would enable a third of a one per cent increase in cases treated. Note that a one per cent increase in *all* inputs would enable an increase in output of .86 of one per cent. This indicates (recalling the discussion of chapter 2) that for the average size of hospital there are *decreasing* returns to scale; though too much emphasis should not be placed on this since the figures under the Σ column (indicating the sum of the elasticities) are not statistically significant. This study, as have many others since, failed to identify any significant advantages or disadvantages to larger (or smaller) size in acute hospitals.

Given the cost of each of the inputs it is next possible to calculate the most cost-effective proportions in which to combine inputs—assuming, of course, that the Cobb–Douglas specification here is the correct one. These have been calculated in Table 11.2 for an expanded set of inputs in which S (supplies) has been subdivided into drugs and dressings (D), catering (K), and other expenditure (X) not reported in the table.

Let us now let Feldstein speak for himself:

The optimum input ratios differ substantially from those observed. In the face of such large discrepancies, the reader may justifiably resist placing great confidence in the precise values of the estimated optimum ratios. But the table as a whole does indicate the directions in which budget allocations should probably be changed. Ignoring for the moment the possibility of altering the number of beds, we note that the current ratios of M/D and N/C are too high while M/N, M/C, D/N and D/C are too low. In short, too much is being spent on nurses, catering and other supplies and not enough on doctors, drugs and dressings. The government appears to have inappropriately limited the supply

TABLE 11.2 *Observed and Efficient Input Ratios in Acute Hospitals*

Input ratio	Observed average	Efficient ratio
M/D	2.5	1.5
M/N	0.4	13.3
M/C	1.6	7.6
D/N	0.2	9.1
D/C	0.3	5.1
N/C	1.5	0.6
M/B	128.6	749.0
D/B	53.1	511.0
N/B	300.3	56.0
C/B	204.3	100.0

Source: Feldstein (1967), Table 4.3.

of doctors and at the same time used its monopoly power to keep medical salaries substantially below their relative marginal productivity in the hospital service. Two implications emerge from this. First, the number of doctors in hospital should be increased even if higher salaries were needed to attract them. Second, until hospital medical staffs are substantially increased, the opportunity cost of the doctor's time should be evaluated at a shadow price which is substantially higher than that implied by current salaries.
The optimum number of beds depends on the annual capital cost at which beds can be obtained. For any plausible estimate of this, the ratios ... indicate that the N/B and C/B ratios are too high. A strict interpretation of these results would imply that expenditure on nursing, catering and other supplies should be decreased relative to the number of beds. But caution must be used in applying the results of a production function the form of which may not be wholly appropriate. [1967, pp. 100–1]

To that modest disclaimer we should also add that different conclusions might also be drawn if either the output measure were altered (say, to health improvement effected) or the case-mix evaluated for its 'appropriateness' in terms of the effectiveness of care of various types.

Feldstein proceeded both to investigate the effects of scale on the elasticity coefficients and to experiment with other forms of the production function. This further work amounted to a kind of 'sensitivity' analysis that strengthened some of the conclusions of the Cobb–Douglas function and qualified others. In general, however, there was strong evidence for slight but unimportant decreasing returns to scale, for the proposition that output would increase if a greater proportion of total expenditure were devoted to medical staff and less to nursing and housekeeping, and for the proposition that this last effect would be more pronounced in larger than average hospitals.

Marginal Product of Physician Services

Part of the folklore of social service provision is that 'important' inputs (like the services of highly trained professionals) are indispensable. This view underlies the 'ratios' approach to manpower planning. It is probably encountered most frequently in the medical sphere. Yet the question of the contribution to marginal output of one input (such as a physician-year) relative to another, or the question of how that marginal product itself changes with the amounts of other inputs, or the question of how much more of one input is needed to compensate for a reduction in the amount of another (keeping output the same), are *empirical* matters whose truth or falsity ought to be establishable by empirical estimation of production functions.

An attempt by Reinhardt (1972) to perform an exercise of this sort examined physicians' practices in the USA with a view to evaluating the efficiency of group practice and greater reliance on paramedical aides performing tasks previously done only by qualified doctors. The results were striking. In Reinhardt's own words:

> Our analysis leads to the conclusion that the average American physician could profitably employ roughly twice the number of aides he currently employs and thus increase his hourly rate of output by about 25 per cent above its current level. This figure takes on added meaning when it is recalled that a mere increase of 4 per cent in average physician productivity in the United States would add more to the aggregate supply of medical services than would the entire current graduating class from American medical schools. Looked at in another way, our results suggest that, in choosing his combination of practice inputs, the average physician in our sample appears to have priced out his own time at a value much below that implicit in his medical fees. On either interpretation, the results therefore support the thesis that American physicians tend to be wasteful in the use of their scarcest and most expensive resource. [1972, p. 55]

The procedure was to estimate the parameters of a variant of the Cobb–Douglas production function having both increasing and decreasing marginal returns to inputs as possibilities, and either increasing or decreasing returns to scale. It was thus more flexible than both the form discussed in chapter 2 and that used by Feldstein in the acute hospital study.

Since true output (health improvements) could not be measured practicably, several other measures of output were used of which the one reported here is *total weekly patient visits* (clearly this is, like Feldstein's measure of acute hospital output, really only a throughput measure). Inputs were weekly physician time in hours, capital utilisation, and number of nurses, technicians, and office aides. A dummy variable had the value 1 for single specialty practices and 0 for solo practices. Other variables included descriptive factors such as the doctor–population ratio.

As far as group practice is concerned, the regressions implied that physicians in group practices generated 4.5 per cent more patient visits than those in solo practice *after* allowing for the fact that they also had on average 17 per cent more aides per physician and put in 7 per cent more hours per week themselves.

The effect of adding paramedical aides in solo practice is shown in Table 11.3. The results represent the contribution of any of the three kinds of aide although the type of task done by each is in fact quite different. The marginal product of aides increases up to the level of about one aide per physician, then diminishes until marginal product of the aide falls to zero at around 5.5 aides per physician. (In the sample used by Reinhardt, the average number of aides was 1.81 per solo practice physician.)

The results (though they cannot be seen in Table 11.3) showed that the marginal product of physician hours increased up to about 25 hours per week and would fall to zero at (a not-observed) 110 practice hours per week.

TABLE 11.3 *Physician Output (patient visits per week) with Varying Physician Time Inputs and Aides in Solo General Practice, USA 1965–67*

Physician hours per week	Number of aides per physician							
	0	0.5	1.0	1.81[a]	2.0	3.0	4.0	5.0
40	85	96	107		128	146	159	165
60[a]	123	139	155	183[a]	185	212	230	239

[a] Sample averages.
Source: Reinhardt (1972), Table 3.

Although these results show that output would increase if solo physicians employed more aides, they do not, of course, imply that the value of the additional output would exceed the cost of the additional aides. At that time (1965–67) gross patient bills per visit were $6.60, or $5.60 net of incremental non-labour costs. The marginal cost of an aide is estimated as not exceeding (allowing for fringe benefits) $100 per week. Thus, had the average solo physician increased his aides from 1.81 to 4.0, the additional revenue ($263) would have exceeded the additional cost ($219). It would, therefore, have been *profitable* for the physicians to have increased employment of aides substantially, and output would have increased (with four aides) by 26 per cent.

In thus substituting their own time for that of aides, physicians not only reduce output (per physician) but *implicitly* treat the value of their own time as much less than they actually charge patients. Reinhardt estimated that the average fee charged by physicians was $17.50 per hour compared with the implicit marginal price put on their time of $9.00.

Given that American physicians have a rather long working week (60 hours on average), it is a nice question as to why they have failed to take advantage of the apparent productivity and *profitability* gains to them (and society in general). Reinhardt's speculations in answer to this puzzle are:

> One answer to this question may be that a good many physicians are simply not aware of the potential effectiveness of auxiliary personnel and of the apparent benefits of group practice formation. But it may also be the case that even a well-informed physician will prefer to remain in solo practice and to limit the size of his staff to levels below the optima suggested here. For example, our relatively low estimates of the shadow-price of physician time may simply reflect the fact that physicians attach certain psychic costs to the employment of aides. After all, a large auxiliary staff burdens the physician with administrative tasks which he may wish to avoid. Moreover, a physician may fear that extensive reliance on paramedical assistants will impair the quality of the services rendered by his practice, if not in fact, then at least in the eyes of his patients. Finally, it is conceivable that the physician's traditional penchant for privacy and professional independence carries over also to his attitude toward paramedical personnel. [p. 65]

Cost of Higher Education

Layard and Verry (1975) began their analysis of university cost functions as follows:

> What does it cost to educate an undergraduate or a postgraduate in a particular subject? The question is deceptively simple, since, like all questions about costs, it can only be answered when we know what alternatives are being considered. Suppose a government were wondering whether and how to provide university education for *x* more students. It should first decide where the students could be educated at least cost. If *x* were small, the government would answer this by simply comparing marginal costs in existing institutions. If *x* were large, new institutions might have to be considered and the extent of returns to scale would be crucial. Having determined the least incremental cost per student, the government would then perform a cost–benefit (rate of return) analysis to decide whether the expansion were warranted. The incremental costs would in all cases be evaluated holding other outputs like research constant, and would be compared with the value of the associated change in teaching output. [p. 54]

Economists are sometimes asked questions to which there can be no answer. One such would be 'How much does research contribute to university costs as against teaching?' This is an impossible question to answer because research and teaching are *jointly* produced in universities, much as mutton and wool are produced on sheep farms. There is no answer to the question 'Is the feed the cost of the wool or the cost of the mutton?' But often all that is really wanted is the cost of producing *more* wool, or *more* teaching. And to *that* question there *is* an answer.

In their analysis, Layard and Verry found—rather to their surprise—that there did not seem to be evidence of jointness in the production of teaching (especially graduate teaching) and research. This would have been indicated by the marginal cost of the one falling as more of the other was done. However, it did seem as though the total costs of teaching a given number of undergraduates and graduates, and of a given amount of research, were lower if some of each were done in each department, rather than only one of each being done in each department.

They accordingly set about estimating a simple linear total cost function, using cross-sectional data:

$$C = \alpha D + \beta U + \gamma G + \delta R,$$

where C is total cost, D is the number of departments of that type, U is the number of undergraduates of all departments in a subject group, G the number of graduates, and R the amount of research as measured by salary-weighted hours of time spent by staff on research.

Such an equation implies that the marginal cost (MC) of each 'output' is given by β, γ, etc. *Average costs* (AC) are:

$$AC_U = \alpha(D/U) + \beta + \gamma(G/U) + \delta(R/U),$$
$$AC_G = \alpha(D/G) + \beta(U/G) + \gamma + \delta(R/G)$$

and
$$AC_R = \alpha(D/R) + \beta(U/R) + \gamma(G/R) + \delta.$$

Thus it can be clearly seen that in this formulation marginal costs are dependent *only* on the rate of output, but that average costs depend upon the scale of operations of each output.

This procedure amounts to supposing that there are 'set-up' costs for each department in a subject group to which are added the other elements in proportion to the scale of output. Since marginal costs are constant with respect to outputs, returns to scale depend upon the magnitude of the fixed cost (α) in the manner shown by Figure 11.1.

The proxies chosen for the outputs illustrate the great difficulty of deriving precise output measures. To show that Layard and Verry were not unaware of the difficulties, we quote their own remarks on this problem:

> A fundamental problem involved in the estimation of university cost functions is the definition and measurement of output. Even though we concentrate on teaching and research outputs, ignoring universities' more intangible functions of preserving knowledge (rather than extending it), of providing a source of independent social comment and so on, we are forced to adopt second-best definitions. With regard to the teaching output, there are many characteristics of a graduate that are relevant. Some, such as cognitive skills and attitudes to change, mainly affect his capacities as a producer, while others mainly affect his capacities for enjoyable consumption. However, although we experimented with more ambitious measures [such as weighting degree classes, drop-outs, etc., by appropriate wage rates and subtracting from this a weighted (by appropriate wages) index of A-level scores, to derive an index of 'value added'] we

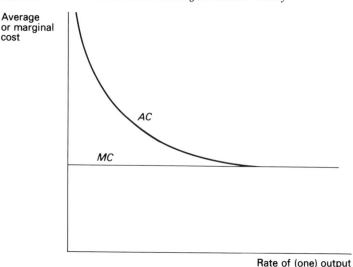

FIG. 11.1   Effect of fixed costs on marginal and average cost.

end up using the number of undergraduate and postgraduate student years
(U, P) as proxies for undergraduate and postgraduate teaching outputs.

Research is even more difficult to measure and although some results are
given using an alternative, publications-based, measure, for the most part we
use as a proxy for research output the annual, quality-weighted, hours spent by
staff on personal research. This is of course an input measure, and its use in
cost functions can only be justified as part of an attempt to obtain meaningful
estimates of the marginal cost of teaching, rather than research, outputs.
[pp. 57–8]

The main results are shown in Table 11.4.

TABLE 11.4   *Current University Marginal Costs, 1968–69 (£)*

Output	Arts	Social Sciences	Mathe- matics	Physical Sciences	Biological Sciences	English
Dept. set-up cost	2390	9310	830	1990	3103	6203
Undergraduates	310	310	350	480	550	680
Graduates	710	860	1470	2100	1580	1610
Research hours	5.24	3.17	6.08	7.71	6.11	4.80

Source: Layard and Verry (1975), Tables I and IV, regressions 2 and 11.

Of the estimates of departmental set-up costs, only the social science MC
is statistically significant and the overall picture is one in which returns to
scale are largely absent. (They note that in regressions *excluding* the
research variable, significant scale economies appear to exist in arts, social
sciences and mathematics.) The differences between the MC of undergradu-

ates and that of graduates is striking (it is much exaggerated if the research variable is excluded). The ratios of MC_U to MC_G varied from 2.4 in engineering to 7.6 in mathematics, and were substantially higher than the ratios at the time assumed by the University Grants Committee. In absolute terms the marginal cost of graduates was higher than commonly believed. The results conform to expectations that they would increase with the amount of technological hardware used—even though these data exclude building and capital costs in universities.

While the work of Layard and Verry marks a methodological improvement over the often arbitrary cost-slicing used in accounting types of approach (see, e.g., Bottomley *et al.*, 1972; Fox *et al.*, 1972), their claims for it remain modest:

> We believe that our methodology and results should be of interest both to those interested in the theory of multiple product non-profit organisations and to those more directly concerned with resource allocation in higher education. We stress, however, that all our estimates rest on heroic assumptions and are subject to substantial error, and that much progress is needed in the measurement of outputs and the modelling of university behaviour before the story of university costs can be fully unravelled. [p. 71]

There is obviously room for much more work of this kind—and not only on educational institutions.

Choice of Technique of Treatment for Chronic Renal Failure

While cost–benefit analysis attempts to compare rival projects, possibly of a very different nature, cost-effectiveness compares the social costs of attaining a particular objective and hence (since the social benefits will be invariant with respect to the means adopted) does not have to concern itself with benefit valuation. Clearly, to be validly applied, it is crucial that the 'output' that is not being valued really is invariant. Cost-effectiveness has two primary uses. First, where an objective has already been decided (on whatever grounds) such analysis can establish the socially least costly method of implementing it. This apparent cart-before-the-horse approach need not be as irrational as it sounds. For example, the objective need not be fully specified in terms of the size of output to be accomplished (e.g. patients treated) but merely in the sense that some will be produced (treated). Cost-effectiveness in this case might attempt the measurement of unit cost (cost per patient). Second, where benefits are extremely hard to estimate reliably, it is helpful to have cost data in order to discover the cost implications of obtaining some unquantifiable benefits. As we shall see in the later discussion (pp. 293–7) of the value of life, the knowledge that it would cost, say, £50,000 to give a patient an expected additional two years of moderately healthy life will give a framework for decision makers to place an implicit value on life (e.g. by saying 'it's not worth it', a life-year clearly is valued at less than £25,000).

Chronic renal failure due to kidney disease can be treated in three basic ways: by kidney transplantation, by haemodialysis (blood purification) by an artificial kidney at home or by one in a dialysis centre. In the USA it was estimated that a transplant costs $13,000, home dialysis $5,000 *per annum* and hospital dialysis $14,000 (1960 prices). Obviously home dialysis is the most cost-effective. Or is it?

To find out the answer, a common 'output' unit has to be identified, for if there is a 50 per cent chance of surviving a transplant for ten years and a 25 per cent chance of surviving home dialysis for five years, the outputs of the different treatments become important. Secondly, the flows of costs must be identified through time, so that those falling relatively more in the future (dialysis) are more heavily discounted compared with those falling mostly in the present (transplants). Thirdly, the treatments are not mutually exclusive. A rejected kidney can, for example, be replaced with another and the patient eventually be given dialysis. Finally, since relative costs vary through time, expectations of future costs must be included in the analysis.

In the study reported here, Klarman *et al.* (1968) estimated the probabilities of patients starting with one treatment moving on to others, estimated the cost flow through time, and used as the standardised output measure 'expected life-years gained'. The objective became to select the initial treatment that had the least social cost per expected life-year gained. An implicit value judgement in this was that one patient's life-year is as socially valuable as any other's. Using a 6 per cent discount rate, the USA data led to the results in Table 11.5.

TABLE 11.5   *Costs of Treating Chronic Renal Failure* ($'000)

Initial treatment	Present value of costs	Life-years gained	Cost per expected life-year
Hospital dialysis	104.0	9	11.6
Home dialysis	38.0	9	4.2
Transplantation	44.5	17	2.6

Source: Klarman *et al.* (1968).

Thus, the final results differed substantially from the crude expenditure data. As a matter of fact, some adjustment was made for the superior quality of life enjoyed after transplantation, but the differentials between the alternative methods are so sizeable that this element of arbitrariness and others, including omissions, are such as to be unlikely to alter the ranking of the three basic methods of treatment.

One important omission in the cost of the transplant, however, is the cost of acquiring the right organ at the right time. A major impediment to the wider use of transplanting is the chronic shortage of available 'spare parts' for suitable patients. This raises the interesting question of whether it would be a useful aid to policy to institute a system whereby living persons could be provided with incentives or compensation for bequeathing their organs at death for clinical purposes.[2]

In any event, the analysis established the prima facie superiority of transplantation and also indicated that machinery installed in a patient's home was less than half as costly as hospital dialysis. A shift to home dialysis would also reduce the cost of transplantation by virtue of the fact that a proportion of transplanted patients move on to dialysis.

Improving the Housing Stock

Most urban local authorities are the reluctant owners of sub-standard houses and slums. Local authorities have two means at their disposal for rectifying the problem: they may either demolish and build replacements at the socially approved standard or they may renovate existing dwellings. The socially optimal balance between rebuilding and renovation will be determined principally by the following factors: the density of redevelopment (scale economies are achieved when entire areas are dealt with); the direct costs of demolition and rebuilding or renovating; the expected life of new as against renovated dwellings; relative maintenance costs; and the relative value placed upon the services of each type of dwelling by tenants and the rest of society.[3]

Cost-effectiveness analysis can help in this difficult decision by incorporating the quantifiable elements of the problem into a single decision rule (Needleman, 1969). The principal unquantifiable element is, of course, the subjective valuations placed upon the units by tenants, which includes the positive benefits of better housing as well as the negative ones associated with community and family upheavals. Let us assume that the external benefit to the rest of society consists in getting housing up to whatever acceptable standards are set—as is implied by externality theory. Then we may further infer that since both renovated and newly built accommodation meet these requirements, the rest of society is indifferent about which type is made available, ignoring costs. This leaves unsettled the problem of tenants' valuations. Let us leave them undetermined for the moment and return to them later.

Renovation will be a less costly method of providing accommodation than rebuilding if the discounted present value of renovation costs plus the present value of the cost of rebuilding in *n* years' time plus the present value of the maintenance costs is less than the present value of rebuilding plus the present value of maintaining the new dwelling.

In practice, this calculation would prove quite complicated in view of the relationship, for example, between maintenance costs and age of dwelling. Moreover, scaling factors should be applied when large-scale redevelopment is undertaken and according to whether it is high rise or low density. For our purposes, however, the usefulness of the method can be illustrated with a simplified example of rebuilding or renovating a single three-bedroom dwelling unit.

Ignoring the value of the quality difference to tenants, therefore, our decision rule says renovate rather than rebuild if the following inequality holds:[4]

$$M + R_M \left[\frac{(1 + i)^n - 1}{i(1 + i)^n} \right] + \frac{B}{(1 + i)^n} < B + R_B \left[\frac{(1 + i)^n - 1}{i(1 + i)^n} \right]$$

where:

M = the direct cost of modernisation, assumed to fall in the present year;

R_M = annual maintenance costs of modernised dwelling, assumed constant in constant prices;

B = the direct cost of demolition and rebuilding in constant prices;

R_B = annual maintenance costs of rebuilt dwelling, assumed constant and in constant prices;

i = appropriate discount rate for the public sector;

n = expected life of property.

Rearranging the inequality, we get this rule: modernise if

$$M < B \left[1 - \frac{1}{(1 + i)^n} \right] + (R_B - R_M) \frac{(1 + i)^n - 1}{i(1 + i)^n}.$$

Suppose the average tender for a two-storey three-bedroom council house is £18,000 and the difference in maintenance costs between pre- and post-war properties is £75. Assuming that the renovated property would last 15 years before requiring demolition and replacement ($n = 15$), the critical value for M works out (using a 10 per cent interest rate) at about £16,700–so long as the cost of direct modernisation of such a property is less than this sum, renovation is the more efficient method of providing improved housing (at 6 per cent the critical sum is about £11,200).

Suppose that it cost £9,000 to bring a dilapidated property up to standard. The appropriate consideration for the local authority becomes whether the additional amenity to the tenant, which has been omitted from the calculation, is worth more than £7,700 (£16,700 − £9,000). Before jumping to the conclusion, however, that it is not and that there should be a massive switch to the renovation of substandard dwellings from new building, recall that rational policy would involve renovating those properties that are cheapest to renovate first. Other things being equal, the optimal balance (ignoring tenant amenity) is where the cost of a marginal renovated dwelling of this type has risen to £16,700. Further housing improvements should then be made by new building.

The Value of Life

The question of what value to place upon a human life in social policy decisions at once raises manifest difficulties of both concept and measurement. It is, nevertheless, important not to pretend that life is of *infinite* value (in the sense that anyone would be prepared to spend an indefinitely large amount of his resources in prolonging his or someone else's life by a given period) since countless decisions that we make affecting our own life chances imply clearly that this is not the case—otherwise who would climb mountains, smoke, over-eat, cross the street....? It is, however, no less important to avoid any crass materialism in approaching the question of what the value is or should be in social policy decisions. What does seem clear is that, across a broad range of policy decisions, the *implied* value placed upon saving a (statistical) life is extremely variable—perhaps because we are more averse to some ways of dying than others, or more averse to certain types of people dying than others or, more likely, simply because it is so difficult to keep a degree of detachment that we simply do not try to be consistent.

Gavin Mooney (1977), in a survey of British decisions made in the late 1960s and early 1970s, found that the following values were *implicitly* placed upon saving a life: £50 per avoided still birth in the maternity services, £1,000 per child's life saved by childproof drug containers, £94,000 per statistical life saved by slower motorway driving, £100,000 per agricultural worker's life saved by fitting cabs to tractors, £1m per sailor's life from improved trawler design, £20m per life saved by enforcing more costly building standards following the Ronan Point disaster. Regardless of the exactitude of these figures, which are typically based on the estimated maximum that the authorities were willing to pay to prevent the deaths, their range is so enormous (£50 to £10m) as to leave no doubt about the inconsistency of decision making in this matter. Strictly interpreted, and assuming that costs per life saved from any particular measure are constant, what this inconsistency implies is that for the cost of one life not saved by raising building standards we could have eliminated *all* still births and deaths from childhood drug abuse. This is not *quite* true, of course, since the marginal cost of preventing either kind of death approaches infinity when nearly all have been prevented. It nevertheless is true that when different values are applied in this way it would be possible to *reduce deaths* by reallocating the same expenditures among the life-preserving measures. So that is a measure of the importance of efficiency in this field and why it is important not to be squeamish and not to let emotion rule without reason's control.

Officially, the 1977 value placed upon a (statistical) life by the Department of the Environment in Britain was £63,330. This uses, as the basis of its calculation, the present value of expected earnings (gross of tax) for a representative individual and adds a notional allowance for 'pain, grief and suffering'. This 'human capital' approach has been the most popular method of estimating the value of life (see Mooney's survey). Various complications are usually allowed for (such as probability of unemployment, the need for deducting lifetime consumption) and much discussion has taken place concerning the value to place upon individuals (children, housewives, pensioners) who are not 'economically active' since, by inference, this method would value them at zero.

This latter problem clearly highlights the main defect of the human capital approach. At best it can be said to provide an estimate of what an average individual would be able to afford to prevent his certain death. But the value of preventing it (since this is the *limit* of his wealth) may be greater than this amount. Alternatively, the human capital measure can be said to measure an individual's contribution to GNP—his value is his contribution. In terms of what he *ought* to be valued at, this approach is subject to the same objections that we raised in discussing distribution according to desert in chapter 4. More generally, GNP is *not*, as again we saw earlier, the maximand in welfare economics. To treat it as the sole maximand is equivalent to treating people as carthorses or —worse still— slaves. Making an allowance for pain, etc., is—at least at present— essentially an arbitrary addition to an arbitrary sum.

Practically speaking, the usual social policy context in which the value of life has importance is in decisions concerning a *change in the probability* of death occurring. For consistency with the definition of economic efficiency, what we seek is *the marginal value of this change in the risk of death* (and, ideally, the marginal value of a change in risk not only to the individual in question but also to his family, friends, etc.).

The theory of this approach has been developed by Michael Jones-Lee (1976). The essence of the analysis can be put as follows. The individual will have a particular utility, given his wealth, if death is not expected during a time period and another utility if it is expected. Essentially, he has a utility of wealth function *conditional on surviving* through the period, $L(W)$, and another (lower) utility of wealth function *conditional on death* during the period, $D(W)$. These are charted for illustration in Figure 11.2, where at the level of wealth indicated by $\bar{W}$, the marginal utility of wealth conditional upon life (slope of $L(W)$) is lower than the marginal utility of wealth conditional upon death (slope of $D(W)$), implying that this individual would take out fair life insurance.

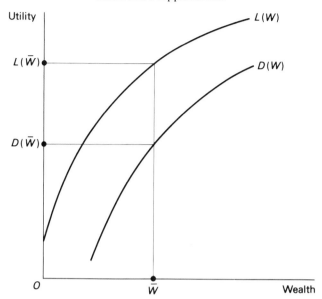

FIG. 11.2 Marginal utility of wealth conditional upon earlier or later death.

For an individual with wealth $\bar{W}$ and a subjective probability, $\bar{p}$, of death occurring in the time period, his expected utility is given by:

$$E(U) = (1 - \bar{p})L(\bar{W}) + \bar{p}D(\bar{W}).$$

We now allow that, at some cost, $\bar{p}$ may be reduced to some lower value denoted by p. Given that the marginal utility of wealth is always positive (both $L(W)$ and $D(W)$ slope upwards) and that the utility of wealth conditional on life is higher than when conditional on death $(L(W) > D(W)$ in the figure), then the individual will sacrifice some current wealth to reduce the probability.

In order to find the *value* he places on this reduction, we seek to find the *maximum* sum of money he will sacrifice (call it MV_{dp}) to obtain the reduction from $\bar{p}$ to p. This maximum sacrifice will, of course, leave him *just indifferent* to his original situation confronting $\bar{p}$, since the maximum he will pay will exhaust the whole benefit of reducing $\bar{p}$ to p. The following condition will then apply (recalling the earlier analysis of the economics of uncertainty):

$$(1 - p)L(\bar{W} - MV_{dp}) + pD(\bar{W} - MV_{dp}) = (1 - \bar{p})L(\bar{W}) + \bar{p}D(\bar{W}).$$

With this condition it is clearly possible to derive experimentally the empirical value of MV_{dp}.

In a population of n individuals, the marginal social value of risk change is the sum of the individual valuations, viz.

$$\sum^{n} MV_{dp},$$

and the average marginal social value is, of course,

$$\sum^{n} MV_{dp}/n.$$

This, as it happens, is also the appropriate value of a (statistical) life saved, as may be shown by the following line of reasoning. In a population of individuals, suppose probability $\bar{p}$ corresponds to the expected deaths of f individuals and p corresponds to the expected deaths of g individuals. Then the change in *objective* probability is s/n, where $s = f - g$. If the *subjective* probabilities $\bar{p}$ and p are the same as these objective probabilities, then the value of saving s lives is

$$s \sum^{n} MV_{dp}/n$$

and the *average* value of each life saved is therefore this divided by s, viz. once again:

$$\sum^{n} MV_{dp}/n.$$

In applying this method to middle-aged working academics, researchers and public employees of varying degrees of seniority, Jones-Lee derived estimates of MV_{dp} in 1975 varying between £12.5m and £0.05m with a mean and mode around £3m. This figure is dramatically higher than any of those previously used or suggested (e.g. by the human capital approach) and suggests not only that current practice systematically undervalues human life but also that methods not based securely on foundations of welfare economics impart a systematic bias to the methodology.

People are sometimes puzzled that the value of a death avoided can substantially exceed what anyone outside the top fraction of the highest percentile in the income distribution could possibly afford. The logic of the Jones-Lee approach may perhaps be best seen by considering the following example. Suppose there is a population of 100 individuals at risk. Suppose also that there is a procedure by which the risk that any one of them will die prematurely can be reduced from 2 per cent to 1 per cent, so that if the procedure is adopted one premature death is expected to be averted. We now use the Jones-Lee method to ascertain the value each of the 100 places on the reduction in risk. The sum of these values is the total value of the reduction in risk and, since the procedure is expected to save one life, that sum is also the value of the (statistical) life saved. Plainly this can exceed the whole wealth of even the wealthiest of the 100 individuals at risk.

Incidentally, you should note that the method developed by Jones-Lee implies a higher benefit for those having higher wealth if distributional weights of unity are used. As we have noted before, whether these or some others should be used is a moral question that cannot be *resolved* by the economics of social policy. In practice the question is likely to be settled in one way or another according to the nature of the interpersonal externalities that exist between members of that community. This implies settlement, of course, at the collective level.

What Are Library Services Worth?

Despite the fact that many outputs go unpriced, hence depriving decision makers of the most obvious basis (perhaps no more than this) for calculating social benefits, cost–benefit techniques are not necessarily rendered inapplicable, as we have seen. Nevertheless, it is frequently desirable to discover unpriced social benefits—or at least the marginal benefits (MVs). One method of discovering their likely order of magnitude is to derive the implicit values placed at the margin by decision makers, to make them explicit and then to ask them—the responsible deciders—whether what they are actually doing is what they thought they were doing or what they wanted to do (see Lavers, 1972).

A technique that has recently been applied to maternity serivices (see Morley, 1972) and to library policy (in universities) is that of inverse linear programming. Ordinary linear programming (as we saw in chapter 2) usually begins by asking, 'What do you want to achieve?' (what is the 'objective function'?) and proceeds to find the technically most efficient way of doing it. Inverse programming begins by assuming that what is being achieved is being achieved with technical efficiency and then asks 'This is how you seem to value your different activities—do you think these really are the right values?' Thus, at the very least, the technique can derive a range of relative shadow prices that are implicit in current and past decisions and compare them with what one may suppose to be true social priorities as established, for example, by policy statements made from on high.

In the example we used in chapter 2, the slope of the objective function EE (Figure 2.5 on p. 21) was -1, indicating that each output had a unitary weight. One way of interpreting these weights is to call them marginal values. For example, if X_2 were regarded as three times as important as X_1, it could receive a weight ($= MV$) of 3 with the weight of X_1 remaining unity. This means that instead of one X_1 being regarded as equivalent to one X_2, three X_1s are now needed to be equivalent to one X_2. The objective function correspondingly has a slope of -3 as in line $E'E'$, and the new most efficient point C is located.

Libraries—especially university libraries—illustrate the problems of benefit measurement well, for not only do they not charge for any of their services but it is not altogether clear even what their services are (Hawgood and Morley, 1969). The first thing required therefore is to itemise as comprehensively as possible a mutually exclusive list of the most important outputs or services. Next the resources used in providing these services are itemised. For a university these two lists of outputs and inputs are presented in Table 11.6. Given these categories the fixed coefficients showing how much of each input is used up in producing a unit of each output is derived. The 'technology matrix' for Durham University library was as shown in Table 11.7.

TABLE 11.6 *Outputs and Inputs of a University Library*

Outputs		Inputs	
(A)	new books per term (accessions)	(S)	senior librarians (man-minutes)
(OILL)	obtaining inter-library loans	(J)	junior librarians (man-minutes)
(LML)	user-hours of library material in library	(C)	clerical (man-minutes)
(LL)	lending books on long loans (in book-fortnights)	(P)	porters (man-minutes)
		(£)	uncommitted money
(SL)	lending books on short loans (in half-day periods)	(St)	seats in seat-hours
		(Sh)	empty shelves (in feet)
(US)	user-services by senior librarian (man-hours)		
(UJ)	user-services by junior librarian (man-hours)		

TABLE 11.7 *Durham University Library Technology Matrix*

Inputs \ Outputs	A	OILL	LML	LL	SL	US	UJ	Resources available (£)
S	72	4	0	0.6	0	60	0	132,480
J	18	72	0.4	5	3	0	60	141,840
C	18	0	0	0	0	0	0	27,600
P	2	12	0.1	0.1	0	0	0	13,980
£	2.78	0.25	0	0	0	0	0	4,315
St	0	0	1	0	1	0	0	83,600
Sh	0.1	0	0	0	0	0	0	14,000

Source: Hawgood and Morley (1969), chapter 3.

In addition to the resource constraints in the technology matrix (only the last two of which were, in actual fact, inequalities), three demand constraints were set such that in the following term user-hours (LML), long loans (LL) and short loans (SL) must be at least equal to the existing rates of these outputs to allow for certain externality effects.

With these data, two further steps can be made. First, assume that library policy is rationally conducted. This implies that the MV of each service to library decision makers is equal to its MC and that, in turn, the ratio of the MVs of any two services will be equal to the ratio of their MCs. Now the ratios of the MVs define the slope of the objective function implicitly used by library decision makers and hence the position they select on the production frontier. Since rational behaviour implies an equality between the ratios of MVs and MCs, by calculating the ratios of the latter the ratios of the former can be obtained and hence the optimal levels and blend of outputs.

TABLE 11.8 *Marginal Costs, Predicted and Realised Outputs of Library in Next Time Period (term)*

	A	OILL	LML	LL	SL	US	UJ
Marginal cost	4.47	.89	.003	.045	.02	1.2	.44
Predicted output	1533	209	57,567	15,000	1,000	203	57
Realised output	1533	244	53,700	15,000	1,000	205	40

Source: Hawgood and Morley (1969), Chapter 3.

Table 11.8 shows the calculated average variable costs (assumed equal to marginal costs in linear programming) and the output levels predicted given the implicit ratios of MVs. Realised outputs are also shown for comparison with the predictions.

Assuming that the fixed coefficient, $MC = AC$, assumptions are reasonable approximations to reality, the rationality postulate is reasonably supported by these results—the principal discrepancies being OILL and UJ.

The second step is to ask what ratios of MVs would produce exactly the pattern of outputs observed. The library decision makers could then be confronted with these implicit rates and asked 'Are these really your priorities?' Because of the kinks in the production frontier, a variety of MV ratios may frequently produce the same output mix. The procedure here was to use the MC as the weight if it fell within the permissible range of weights and if not to choose the limit of the permissible weights nearest to the MC. Table 11.9 shows the results of these calculations. The reason for using one of the weights (US) in the first row as 'numéraire' for the second is, of course, so that we need not specify the units in which MVs are measured. The interpretation of the MV ratios is as follows. If the university were presented with a choice between one addition to stock and four inter-library loans it would on average, according to current policy, add to stock. If presented with a choice between one addition to stock and four hours of user-services, it would choose the latter. If presented with a choice between an addition to stock and 1,000 user-hours or 90 long loans it would add to stock. The library is run as if these were the relative priorities it set itself at the margin. Having got these relative priorities out in the open it is perfectly obvious that they need not correspond to what are generally felt (for example, by library users) to be the correct priorities.

TABLE 11.9   *Implicit Weights and MV Ratios*

	A	OILL	LML	LL	SL	US	UJ
Weight	4.05	.89	.003	.045	.02	1.2	.44
MV ratio using US as numéraire	3.4	0.74	.003	.037	.017	1.0	.37

Source: Hawgood and Morley (1969), Chapter 3.

The scope for applying this technique is obvious—it will almost certainly prove a useful source of dissertation fodder for graduate students of social policy. What implicit values are placed in your local library on fiction, travel, religion and art? What implicit values do local authorities place on the provision of different kinds of local authority housing? What currently hidden values exist in the present allocation of hospital beds—are they consistent with policy? Do maternity cases receive the kind of treatment regarded as most suitable for their varying needs by the experts? What set of relative priorities is implicit in current income subsidy schemes? To which types of clients do social workers give highest priority?

In addition, linear programming can trace out the consequences of changes in the resource constraints as input supplies alter and of changes in the technical coefficients as technical progress alters. And there are, of course, more sophisticated versions of the technique than that illustrated here.

Benefits from Reducing Health Insurance Cover in the USA

In the absence of moral hazard, complete health insurance is efficient in a risk-averse population if it can be provided at actuarially fair premiums. But the existence of moral hazard in practice, and the workings of the (private) health service industry in the USA, raise the possibility that too much insurance may exist (ignoring all externalities).

M. S. Feldstein (1973) derived a measure of the losses owing to excessive health insurance. If we imagine the MV curve in Figure 11.3 to represent the demand for hospital care (in, say, patient-days) then at the going price, P, Q days will be taken by a representative patient demanding hospital

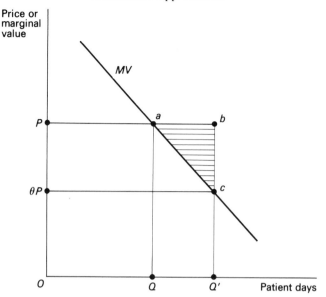

FIG. 11.3   Welfare loss of health insurance.

care. That is in the absence of insurance. If there is insurance together with coinsurance such that the patient bears some fraction, θ, of the daily hospital cost, price falls to θP, quantity rises to Q' and the welfare loss—the excess of cost over value—is the triangle *abc*. For convenience we assume the demand curve to be linear in the range *ac*. In equation form, the welfare loss (L) is

$$L = \tfrac{1}{2}(P - \theta P)(Q' - Q).$$

It is useful to define this loss in terms of the elasticity of demand:

$$\eta = \frac{dQ}{dP} \cdot \frac{P}{Q},$$

where $dQ = Q' - Q$ and $dP = P(1 - \theta)$. The equation thus becomes:

$$L = \tfrac{1}{2}\eta(1 - \theta)^2 PQ.$$

This expression enables one to calculate the reduction in loss (L) from increasing the coinsurance term θ from its existing value (taken as 0.33 in 1969 in the USA) to a higher one, say 0.5 ot 0.67, given data on total expenditure at the existing level of θ (viz. PQ) and elasticity estimates (varying from -0.4 to -0.8). In fact, Feldstein also allowed for the fact that increased insurance also raises the price of hospital care in the USA and raises its 'quality' in terms of the amount of staff, equipment, etc. used in hospital, by making estimates of the responsiveness of hospital charges to changes in insurance coverage and of the value to patients of the better quality of care. These adjustments would *reduce* the size of any change from increasing coinsurance. Table 11.10 reports the results without making these adjustments.

TABLE 11.10 *Welfare Gains from Raising Coinsurance Term θ*

η	Gain in \$m from raising θ to	
	0.5	0.67
-0.4	5,012	8,568
-0.8	10,024	17,136

Source: Feldstein (1973).
Note: Results based on 1969 private hospital expenditure (PQ) of \$12.6 billion.

Table 11.11 reports the results for the extreme values (minimum and maximum) predicted when price and quality increases are included, based upon a model of behavioral responses. Against these potential gains must be set the losses attributable to the increased bearing of risk by individuals whose insurance cover falls due to the postulated rises in θ from 0.33 to 0.5 or 0.67.

TABLE 11.11 *Adjusted Welfare Gains from Raising Coinsurance Term θ*

η		Gain in \$m from raising θ to	
		0.5	0.67
-0.4	highest estimate	4,284	6,394
	lowest estimate	1,205	1,856
-0.8	highest estimate	4,284	6,394
	lowest estimate	1,484	2,261

Source: Feldstein (1973), Table 2.

The measure used by Feldstein to represent the value to households of a change in the risk of having to make financial payments for health care was the maximum premium the household would pay to insure the risk. As we have assumed in earlier chapters, Feldstein assumed that the utility of income is independent of the state of health itself and is affected only by changes in income.

The expected utility of an uninsured household will be:

$$pU(I_0 - H) + (1 - p)U(I_0).$$

With insurance and coinsurance, expected utility becomes:

$$U(I_0 - q) - pU(\theta H)$$

where q is the (certain) premium paid.

The maximum premium q^* that the household would pay to avoid the uncertain expenditure would leave the household indifferent between accepting the additional risk from coinsurance and paying the additional premium (q^*) to avoid it, viz.

$$U(q^*) = pU(\theta H).$$

With risk aversion, or diminishing marginal utility of income, this q^* must exceed $p\theta H$, the actuarially expected expenditure, and the 'net cost of risk bearing' is the difference between them, viz.

$$q^* - p\theta H.$$

If we now consider a rise in θ from θ_0 to θ_1 together with an associated rise in q^* from q_0^* to q_1^*, the net cost of the *increase* in risk bearing will evidently be

$$(q_1^* - p\theta_1 H) - (q_0^* - p\theta_0 H) = q_1^* - q_0^* - (\theta_1 - \theta_0)pH.$$

Feldstein used a particular form of the utility function, together with data on annual hospital expenditures and length of stay in hospital, to compute the increases in the cost of risk bearing by raising θ from 0.33 to 0.5 and to 0.67, on three alternative assumptions about the degree of risk aversion. Results, adjusted for the price and quality effects mentioned before, are reported in Table 11.12.

As can be seen, the rise in θ could actually create gains (negative losses). This is because reduced insurance coverage can have the effect of reducing hospital charges, which will create savings if the elasticity of demand is less than unity (which the empirical work suggests it is) and greater savings the lower the (absolute value of the) elasticity.

TABLE 11.12   *Adjusted Welfare Losses from Increased Risk Bearing*

| η | | Loss $(+)$ or gain $(-)$ in \$m from raising θ to | |
		0.5	0.67
-0.4	highest	1,106	1,697
	lowest	$-1,346$	$-2,552$
-0.8	highest	2,780	4,086
	lowest	0	0

Source: Feldstein (1973), Table 3.

TABLE 11.13   *Net Welfare Gains from Reducing Insurance*

η		Gain in $m from raising θ to	
		0.5	0.67
-0.4	highest	5,630	8,946
	lowest	99	159
-0.8	highest	4,284	6,394
	lowest	$-1,296$	$-1,825$

Source: Feldstein (1973), Table 4.

Note: Results not obtainable directly from Tables 11.11 and 11.12 owing to the highest and lowest in these tables not corresponding to the same assumptions about the effects of insurance on hospital prices and quality of care.

The two sets of estimates are combined in Table 11.13. These results indicate a wide range of possible outcomes (in 1969 prices), depending on the assumptions. Taking a conservatively low assumption of $\eta = -0.4$ and supposing, plausibly, that the response of inputs to changes in θ is low but the response of hospital prices fairly high, the most plausible conservative estimate of the net gain from reducing insurance by raising θ to 0.5 is about $3,000m per annum (compared with total spending on private premiums of $17,000m in 1970). As Feldstein says (p. 277) 'It seems reasonable to conclude that an increase in the average coinsurance rate would increase welfare and that the net gain would be quite substantial.'

Should Tenants in Arrears Be Evicted?

Cost–benefit analysis can, as we have seen, be a useful exercise even though it is not possible fully to quantify every cost or benefit. A good example of a case where many effects cannot be quantified but where the technique gives quite positive guidance to social policy makers at the local level is in the treatment of council house tenants in arrears.

Arrears are frequently symptomatic of a far deeper social problem than irregularity of payment and this alone is sufficient for local authorities to exercise caution, before bringing in the bailiffs, by involving local social services departments at an early stage. An entirely different type of concern is also embodied in the Home Office and Department of Health circulars on this matter among which the potential burden of homelessness on local taxes is one. The standard cost–benefit framework with its unitary weights system regards these, however, as purely interpersonal transfers—the tenant's benefit or the rate-payer's cost—which cancel out. The most plausible alternative assumptions about weights would normally place a higher value on the tenant's than the rate-payer's pound, which makes one feel even less inclined to think that social welfare is much impaired by a shift of burden from tenant to rate-payer.

A study in Reading (County Borough of Reading, 1969), however, of the costs and benefits of eviction for rent arrears should make the problems raised by transfers clearer. The number of evictions in Reading for rent arrears was small—six in 1966/7 with outstanding arrears of £670 from former tenants—and the total collectors' arrears owed by current tenants varied quite substantially around £2,000. The choice facing the authorities is simply between eviction, once tenants become persistently and seriously in arrears, and non-eviction.

The pattern of pure transfer payments created as a result of eviction is broadly as follows:

Rent of temporary accommodation for evicted tenants
Rent of vacated dwelling from new tenants
Supplementary Benefits
Rent of husband's lodging

Real resource costs and benefits are shown in Table 11.14 together with an item by item comparison of the net benefit (+ or −) of eviction compared with non-eviction.

TABLE 11.14   *Costs of Eviction and Non-Eviction* (£)

Category	Policies Eviction	Non-Eviction	Net social benefit of eviction
1. Direct costs of eviction	25	0	−25
2. Preparation for new tenants (redecoration)	5	0	−5
3. Allocation of new tenants	5	0	−5
4. Lost consumers' surpluses of temporarily vacant property	+	0	−
5. Removal and storage of furniture	5	0	−5
6. Provision of temporary accommodation for one month	10	0	−10
7. Social services	10	0	−10
8. Tenant's loss of earnings while searching for new accommodation	10	0	−10
9. Effect on evictees	+	0	−
10. Risk of permanent split in family	+	0	−
11. Damage to tenant's property	+	0	−
12. Care of family	−(?)	0	+(?)

Source: County Borough of Reading (1969).

Even though it was not possible to measure all the items, it is quite clear that, with the single possible exception of the care of the family (especially the children), eviction imposed net costs upon family and authority. Possible benefits not so far included are chiefly (a) the replacement of an irregularly paying tenant by a regularly paying tenant and (b) the incentive effect that eviction may have on neighbouring tenants. If eviction is to be justified at all, it will needs have to be justified on either or both of these two counts.

Previous analysis has established a fundamental point about the provision of social services: that the socially optimal quantity is where the sum of all MVs is equal to marginal social cost. This condition implies that the sum of MVs should be set equal to the open market potential rent of local authority housing, this representing its social opportunity cost, not equal either to per unit historical cost or to per unit replacement cost.[5] If we assume an optimal stock of local authority housing in any area, the differential between open market rent and the rent paid by the tenants is the MV of the rest of society. If every tenant paid the same rent for the same type of dwelling, any tenant falling in long-term arrears would signal a permanent fall in *his* MV and, if there were no excess demand for the optimal stock of subsidised housing, would imply a case both for eviction, if it were costless, and a reduction in the subsidised housing stock. If the social costs of eviction are positive, as they are, the greater the short-fall of the tenant's MV (as indicated by arrears) and the difference between open market rent and the rest of society's MV, the greater the likelihood that eviction is a socially optimal policy. However, only if the social costs of eviction are zero does it follow that any permanent arrears require eviction.

Identical rents for all tenants implies, however, that all tenants have identical MVs—supposing subsidising policy to be efficient. The fact that MVs differ implies modifying the conclusion of the previous paragraph, for an accumulation of arrears may now be evidence for the need for a larger subsidy to the family in question—especially if it is owing to a change in the family's financial circumstances. Essentially, this amounts to an assessment of the comparative urgency of 'need' of the family in arrears and the family with the highest priority on the waiting list. Since in practice priorities on the waiting list are usually based on arbitrary criteria such as length of wait it seems unlikely that the new tenants would, on average, necessarily represent more urgent cases in the sense of imposing an externality on the rest of the concerned community than those who have got themselves into chronic difficulties with arrears. In such circumstances, the adjustment of rent would be a natural and consistent corollary, the case for non-eviction being strengthened by the positive social costs of eviction.

The incentive effect of eviction is mainly an empirical matter that we do not propose to explore in detail. The Reading study indicated that the effect of eviction on other tenants in arrears was small, was confined to tenants in the immediate neighbourhood and was, anyway, temporary. Viewed purely as an incentive effect, eviction is almost certainly an inefficient policy. Given both the small number of evictions in Reading and the relatively small size of outstanding arrears it does not seem likely that even the existence of the eviction right supplies much in the way of an incentive to pay, especially by comparison with the many ordinary social pressures on tenants not to default on payments.

But implicit in the foregoing is a criticism of the standard treatment of transfer payments as merely cancelling items, for transfers, like prices, provide a measure (though frequently a very poor one) of individual and social valuations. If, for example, neither an individual tenant nor the rest of society is prepared to pay (possibly only implicitly in the case of the rest of society) enough to keep the tenant in a council dwelling in the public sector of the housing market, that is evidence for the potential optimality of either reletting the dwelling in the public sector at a suitable rent or selling it. In this way transfers can be used as the basis for shadow pricing to achieve both a socially optimal stock of local authority housing and a socially optimal mix of tenants occupying it.

NOTES

1. But why use conventions at all? The answer in economics is implied by the answers to two additional questions—at what point should one stop 'considering' and act and how much information about two options is worth obtaining before one is selected?
2. The reader is left to devise a scheme that might increase the supply of organs while safeguarding the interests of donors, their relatives and recipients. Note that one way of increasing the availability of suitable cadavers for transplants may be to increase communications between doctors and between hospitals. This need not be cheaper, however, than increasing the supply of suitable organs, even if many were not used.
3. Why does this list not include rents? The answer has something to do with conventional assumptions about the treatment of redistribution in cost–benefit studies.
4. Why does the length of life of a new dwelling not feature in this equation? Why does not the initial value of the property being improved or demolished also figure?
5. Which is likely to be higher: open market rent, historical or replacement cost? Why?

QUESTIONS ON CHAPTER 11

1. What is the difference between cost–benefit and cost-effectiveness analysis?
2. In what respects is GNP maximisation alone an unsatisfactory criterion by which to evaluate the efficiency of social services?
3. Having read the summary account of Feldstein's study of British acute hospitals, and the details in his book, (a) explain how he reaches the conclusions quoted on pp. 282–3 of the present text and (b) discuss the reliability of these results.

4. Having read the summary account of Reinhardt's study in the text, and the original, explain how his results were derived and discuss their reliability.
5. What other evidence can you adduce to support or counter the proposition that medical inputs are substitutable one for another?
6. Discuss the strength and weakness of the various output measures used in the empirical examples in this chapter.
7. Having read the summary of the Layard–Verry study, and the original, explain how their conclusions are reached and discuss their reliability.
8. Are teaching and research complementary activities in universities? How would you test for complementarity?
9. Having read the summary account of the Klarman *et al.* study, and the original, explain how their results were reached and discuss their reliability.
10. If quality of life varies between renal dialysis and transplantation (as it does), how might one use the standard gamble method of chapter 8 to quantify the difference?
11. What rate of discount should be used in cost–benefit or cost–effectiveness studies of social services?
12. Contact your local housing authority and using data they provide advise them as to whether it would be cheaper to demolish and rebuild or to renovate their old properties for rent.
13. Having read the summary account of the Jones-Lee study, and the original, explain how his results were derived and evaluate their reliability.
14. What is the present value of your post-tax earnings over your expected lifetime (given your present age)? Do you feel that this over- or under-values the value of your life, (a) to you and yours, (b) to society in general (including you and yours)?
15. Having read the summary of the Hawgood–Morley study, try a similar exercise for your own library.
16. Contact your local social services department and calculate, using their data, the relative values placed upon the various activities of social workers in their employ.
17. Having read the summary of Feldstein's insurance study, and the original, explain how his results were obtained and discuss their reliability.
18. Are the *British* overinsured against health care costs?
19. How might you set about quantifying more of the categories in Table 11.14?
20. Choose any one area of social policy (e.g. hospital care), conduct a literature search using your local library facilities and bibliographies, references, etc., known to you, and assess the current state of the cost–benefit or cost–effectiveness art in that area.

FURTHER READING

The potential number of references is, of course, immense. Many have generated controversy that can be followed up in the journals. Others are tucked away in obscure places. Studies referred to in the text were:

Bottomley, J. A. *et al.* (1972) *Costs and Potential Economies.* Paris: Organisation for Economic Cooperation and Development, Centre for Educational Research and Innovation.

County Borough of Reading (1969) Eviction from council houses for rent arrears. In P. B. Kershaw (ed.) *Cost–Benefit Analysis*. London: Institute of Municipal Accountants and Treasurers.

Feldstein, M. S. (1967) *Economic Analysis for Health Service Efficiency*. Amsterdam: North-Holland, chapter 4.

Feldstein, M. S. (1973) The welfare loss of excess health insurance. *Journal of Political Economy, 81*, pp. 251–80.

Fox, K. A. *et al.* (1972) *Economic Analysis for Educational Planning*. Baltimore: Johns Hopkins University Press.

Hawgood, J. and Morley, R. (1969) *Project for Evaluating the Benefits from University Libraries*. Durham: Department of Economics.

Jones-Lee, M. (1976) *The Value of Life: an Economic Analysis*. London: Martin Robertson.

Klarman, H. E., Francis, J. O'S. and Rosenthal, G. D. (1968) Cost-Effectiveness applied to the treatment of chronic renal disease. *Medical Care, 6*, pp. 48–54. Reprinted in M. H. Cooper and A. J. Culyer (eds) *Health Economics*. London: Penguin.

Lavers, R. J. (1972) The implicit valuation of forms of hospital treatment. In Hauser, M. M. (ed.) *The Economics of Medical Care*. London: Allen and Unwin.

Layard, P. R. G. and Verry, D. W. (1975) Cost functions for university teaching and research. *Economic Journal, 85*, pp. 55–74.

Mooney, G. (1977) *The Valuation of Human Life*. London: Macmillan.

Morley, R. (1972) 'Comment' on Lavers (1972). In Hauser, *op. cit.*

Needleman, L. (1969) The comparative economics of improvement and new building. *Urban Studies, 6*, pp. 196–209.

Reinhardt, U. (1972) A product function for physician services. *Review of Economics and Statistics, 54*, pp. 55–67.

CHAPTER 12

Output Budgeting and PPBS in Social Policy

A. CASE FOR OUTPUT BUDGETING

In the introductory chapters we noted the importance of rational decision making in the formation of social policy and also that there is no automatic tendency for public authorities to pursue the genuine objectives of social policy or to pursue them as efficiency as possible. Much of our political machinery is simply incapable of doing any more than ensuring a usually thorough financial audit of public activities and, as a consequence, bureaucracies—and politicians—are left with varying degrees of discretion in what they do and how they do it. The planning techniques of chapter 11 not only have as a purpose the provision of methods by which policy aims may more effectively be accomplished but also impose upon those who formulate and carry through various social policies the necessity for explicitness and openness. Explicitness is also a main characteristic of the techniques to be described in this chapter. Less formal methods of policy appraisal—based on 'experience' or 'flair'—are basically uncommunicable and the 'truth' about social policy gets 'revealed' to but a few. Different programmes are not related to one another. Responsibility gets divided up in an arbitrary way. Democratic participation is minimised. The scope for the riding of personal hobbyhorses by administrators and policy makers is maximised. Explicit analysis has the signal virtue of forcing the decision maker to concentrate (a) upon the objectives of policy and (b) upon the trade-offs between and within policies that necessarily have to be made. As a result, relevant questions about policy are more likely to be asked (e.g. what additional information is needed to make a sensible decision?) and policy making becomes more open since the reasons for doing things (whether right things or wrong things) are more explicitly stated and hence discussable.

As we have illustrated, the scope for these techniques in social policy making is much wider than may be thought. Cost–benefit and cost-effectiveness can yield useful results even in the presence of substantial unquantifiables and without ignoring the unquantified factors or treating them as unimportant.

However, both the presence of important unquantifiables (at least, currently) and also the behaviour-constraining environment of decision makers and administrators means that frequently the information that is relevant to many decisions is simply never collected (e.g. earnings by educational attainment) while much that is collected is either almost entirely irrelevant (e.g. rental value of Crown properties) or, from the point of view of rational planning rather than financial control, rather unsuitable if not downright misleading (e.g. conventional depreciation accounting, wages of otherwise unemployed labour). These factors limit the extent to which cost–benefit techniques can currently be employed. Because people have not been forced before to ask the relevant questions the relevant data are not available. But, in any case, the high cost of such exercises means that it is pie in the sky to imagine their being systematically employed *every* time one of the innumerable policy decisions is taken, at whatever level, somewhere in the administrative and top policy formulating ranks of the public authorities. Output budgeting is a technique that is designed to overcome some of these difficulties.

B. What Is Output Budgeting?

The basic difference between output budgeting and traditional budgeting is that the former classifies costs (social opportunity costs so far as possible) according to the objectives for which they are incurred (outputs) while the latter classifies costs (financial costs) according to the type of resource purchased (inputs). It is for this reason that the term 'output budgeting' is preferred in this book rather than 'programme budgeting' (PPBS stands for Planning-Programming-Budgeting-System) for the former term really captures the essential distinguishing feature of the process, and programmes, or activities, can be defined independently of outputs (e.g. in terms of client groups). The reason for the input orientation of traditional practice is not hard to find in social policy. It is that markets do not usually exist for the outputs of social policy—frequently they have been deliberately withdrawn from the market. Consequently, the only 'hard' basis for assigning costs is on an input basis: budgets are divided up into capital versus current accounts, into wages and salaries versus equipment and materials, into administrative sectors such as hospital expenditure versus local authority health and welfare expenditure. The reason for this is clear: administrative units demand cash for spending on specific resources and traditional accounting is designed to ensure that money is spent on those things for which it was given and on nothing else. Moreover the costs considered— given the necessity for financial audit and control—are only those 'costs' that appear as money flows within and out of the public sector. The earnings forgone by children staying on at school for an additional year are not fiscal costs so they do not appear in the accounts, although they may be very substantial social costs and possibly larger than the fiscal costs (the fiscal costs may, of course, themselves be good approximations to some of the social costs of providing an additional year's education).

Major problems in output budgeting are likely to arise around four principal conceptual problems:

(a) policy objectives need to be defined clearly.
(b) output measures need to be divised to enable performance to be monitored and appropriate total, unit and marginal costs to be calculated.
(c) genuine social costs only ought ideally to be defined and measured.
(d) the social costs need to be attributed as nearly as possible to the outputs that give rise to them.

In addition, since output budgeting is to be seen as a routine exercise—as routine as traditional budgeting—the decisions taken on each of these heads must be such that too great a detail is avoided to keep the cost of the exercise as low as possible. Output budgeting consequently indicates only the overall deployment of resources and provides a framework for rational choice. Cost–benefit techniques provide a vital back-up to output budgeting for more detailed examination of specific social programmes.

Policy Objectives in Education and Health

Identifying policy objectives is equivalent to fixing the titles of social policy programmes and sub-programmes and they should be sufficiently broad to be manageable but not so broad as to be meaningless. Thus, for example, broad programme heads for the British education output budget together with some sub-programmes:

A. Compulsory Education
Objectives: provide highest possible standard of education according to child's age, aptitude and ability during present period of compulsory schooling; increase equality of opportunity; improve staff/pupil ratio; improve standards of provision in Educational Priority Areas. (Note that not all of these are genuine outputs.)
1. Maintenance of existing pattern and scale of provision
2. Improving teaching methods and curriculum
3. Changing availability of teachers

B. Nursery Education
Objectives: assist educational development and social adjustment of children below compulsory school age; release mothers for work; raise proportion of children attending in Educational Priority Areas. (Again the latter is a means to an end, hardly an end in itself.)
1. Maintenance of existing pattern and scale of provision

2. Change proportion of children attending and length of stay
3. Change availability of teachers

C. Education of the 16–19 year old
Objectives: provide education and vocational training for all in these age groups who wish it and who can profit from it: meet projected qualified manpower requirements; increase proportion of children in full-time, part-time and day-release education.

The identification of such objectives is itself an extremely valuable exercise. It highlights conflicts and potential conflicts between objectives (forcing explicit choices); it identifies logical interrelationships between objectives (some may be prior to others, others complementary); it compels the administration to think carefully about the most useful way of classifying objectives. There is usually a variety of ways of classifying objectives and the 'best' method is usually the one that is some compromise with existing classifications—which have the short-term advantage of familiarity and for which data are often collected as a routine matter—but that will also reflect the major strategic policy choices that will be made in the foreseeable future.

In the health and personal social services, for example, classification could be based upon client groups (e.g. maternity cases, children, the old) or in administrative terms (e.g. hospitals services, primary (GP) care, local authority services), or some combination of these two. Within the hospital service, for example, a programme structure might be based upon either diseases, diagnostic groups, medical specialties, client age groups or client dependency. The last of these is not currently feasible and the first, though probably the most attractive from the resource allocation point of view, unfortunately contains several thousand elements. The compromise structure with which the British Department of Health and Social Security is currently experimenting includes the following main programmes: general health; primary care; maternity; children and families; the elderly; the younger disabled, mentally handicapped; mentally ill; hospital surgical specialties excluding dental surgery; hospital medical specialties including paediatrics; dental services; ophthalmic services.

Output Measures

The sub-programme structure of the health and personal social services output budget would ideally carry through the basic client-orientation theme with each sub-programme representing a package of care. Unlike the educational system, however, where clients receive fairly homogeneous services according to their age and the type of institution at which they are studying, the package of care received by a client of the National Health

Service is almost infinitely variable depending on his condition, the judgement of the doctor or social worker and the locally available facilities. Thus, the elderly may receive a very wide variety of domiciliary and day care. As in the main programme structure again some compromise has to be made in order to make the budget manageable. One obvious method of doing this is to associate particular types of input with the basic programme structure and client groups. Thus, most main programmes in the NHS have the sub-programme structure shown in Figure 12.1.

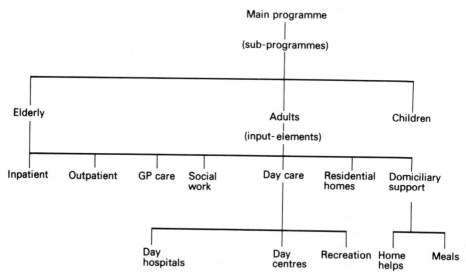

FIG. 12.1   Sub-programme structure of programme budgets in the National Health Service.

In addition, this procedure assists reconciliation with traditional budgeting conventions. Each input-element, for example, can be further subdivided into traditional expenditure categories such as recurrent gross expenditure, charges, capital expenditure, training and research. The demographic (client-group) basis of the programme budget in the Department of Health and Social Security illustrates a further use of PPBS—in forecasting public expenditure.

At the top level, medium-term public expenditure planning operates mainly through the Public Expenditure Survey (PES). This is roughly how it works: each November, the Treasury asks the spending departments of central government to estimate the cost of carrying on with present policies over the next five years (at the prices of that year). During March and April, the Treasury and the departments bargain over the projections on a bilateral basis, so the estimated 'demand' for public money on a no-change-in-policy basis is determined. Meanwhile, the Treasury does an econometric exercise for the next five years to forecast gross domestic product (GDP), imports, exports, private consumption, etc., and, in the light of the survey, of the forecasts of what resources in general will be available and of whatever medium-term macroeconomic objectives there may be, the Prime Minister and the Chancellor decide the total public expenditure that is actually planned to be available. In June the stage is set for the final round, where the differences between the PES aspirations and the totals for public expenditure are to be resolved. This takes place largely by ministerial bargaining in Cabinet sub-committees.

Now an important part of this process is political, but economic methods are also used, the Treasury's econometric model being one. In the DHSS, an important role in its PES exercise is played by the department's programme budget. Table 12.1 gives a numerical version of the DHSS's programme budget, and a brief description of it can be found in the 1976 Consultative Document on the NHS:

The programme budget is not a complex technical tool but a crude method of costing policies based on past expenditure. Its central purpose is to enable the Department to cost policies for service development across the board, so that priorities can be considered within realistic financial constraints. The programme budget is neither a forecast nor a plan: it is a way of exploring possible future strategies for development . . . . The programme budget covers all health and personal social services for England, as defined for the Public Expenditure Survey, at a national aggregate level. Some closely related expenditure is excluded because it does not fall within this definition, for instance sheltered housing, sheltered employment and blind home workers' schemes.

The programme budget also attempts to group expenditure into programmes which are more meaningful in considering options and priorities than the Public Expenditure Survey breakdown or the traditional estimates and accounts. In health and personal social services a complete breakdown of expenditure by objectives (e.g. treatment of specific medical conditions) would be extremely detailed and complex, and far too cumbersome for an across-the-board review; the necessary data is not in any case available. The programme budget does not therefore contain the kind of information needed for evaluating options in detail. However, there are certain major groups of services cutting across administrative boundaries, which provide complementary and alternative forms of care for certain important groups of users, in particular the elderly, physically and mentally handicapped, mentally ill and children. These 'client groups' are also the subject of special policies and priorities, and their numbers are changing in very different ways with the changing age structure of the population. It is also useful to distinguish maternity services for these reasons.

It is possible to carry out a fairly detailed allocation of expenditure to these 'client groups'. However, to facilitate comparison with planning by the NHS and local authorities, the programmes . . . are simply a grouping of services by major user. Thus, for instance, all home nursing and geriatric medicine are included in the 'elderly' programme, and health visiting (but not paediatrics, which cannot be costed separately) under 'children'; primary care and hospital

TABLE 12.1 *DHSS Summary Programme Budget (£m, November 1974 prices)*

	Average current growth p.a. 1970–71 1973–74 (%)	1973–74 Outturn Capital (£m)	1973–74 Outturn Current (£m)	1975–76 Provisional estimate Capital (£m)	1975–76 Provisional estimate Current (£m)	1979–80 Illustrative projection Capital (£m)	1979–80 Illustrative projection Current (£m)	Illustrative average current growth p.a. 1975–76 to 1979–80 (%)
Grand total	4.3	528	3,630	424	3,992	304	4,332	2.1
Primary care Sub-total	1.7	23	648	24	718	18	833	3.8
General medical services	1.9		209		223		249	2.8
General dental services	−1.9		120		129		139	1.9
General ophthalmic services	−8.5		19		24		27	3
Pharmaceutical services	3.3		276		312		382	5.2
Health centres[a]	25.2	23	2	24	3	18	5	11
Prevention	5.5		15		15		17	3
Family planning	66.6		7		12		14	4
General and acute hospital and maternity services Sub-total	3.7	300	1,572	233	1,670	155	1,733	0.9
Acute IP and OP	3.0		1,161		1,225			
Ambulances	4.0	300	75	233	79	155	1,574	1.2
Miscellaneous hospital[b]	9.2		174		197			
Obstetric IP and OP	3.9		136		143		133	−1.8
Midwives	−1.1		26		26		26	0

Services mainly for elderly and physically handicapped

Sub-total	9.0	96	512	76	593	44	673	3.2
Geriatric IP and OP[c]	5.2	34	195	31	212	28	243	3.5
Non-psychiatric DP	15.4		6		7		9	5
Home nursing	5.6		52		59		75	6
Chiropody	9.9		8		9		10	3
Residential care	9.1	54	117	35	142	15	154	2
Home help	14.8		80		91		98	2
Meals	18.9		8		14		15	2
Day care	—	8	12	9	17	1	20	4
Aids, adaptions, phones, etc.	—		9		12		17	9
Services for the disabled	8.9		25	1	30		32	1.5

Services for the mentally handicapped

Sub-total	8.0	32	167	29	189	25	211	2.8
Mental handicap IP and OP	6.6	14	136	12	146	9	156	1.6
Residential care	17.0	9	10	9	15	10	20	7
Day care	—	9	21	8	28	6	36	6.5

Services for the mentally ill

Sub-total	3.6	28	303	23	320	36	344	1.8
Mental illness IP and OP	3.0	23	280	17	291	25	306	1.3
Psychiatric DP	14.5		10		13		16	5
Residential care	12.6	2	3	2	4	3	5	7
Day care	—	1	3	2	4	4	7	15
Special hospitals	5.6	2	7	2	8	4	10	6

(continued)

TABLE 12.1 (continued)

	Average current growth p.a. 1970-71 1973-74 (%)	1973-74 Outturn		1975-76 Provisional estimate		1979-80 Illustrative projection		Illustrative average current growth p.a. 1975-76 to 1979-80 (%)
		Capital (£m)	Current (£m)	Capital (£m)	Current (£m)	Capital (£m)	Current (£m)	
Services mainly for children Sub-total	0.5	16	232	22	266	13	290	2.2
Clinics	2.9		25		26		26	0
Health visiting	2.5		33		34		43	6
School health	7.3		48		51		51	0
Welfare food	-44.6		8		8		8	0
Residential care	16.7	12	84	18	110	10	121	2.5
Boarding out	8.4		12		14		15	2
Day nurseries	7.2	3	17	3	20	1	22	2.5
Central grants and YTCs	-18.2	1	5	1	3	1	4	6

Other services Sub-total	11.0	33	196	17	236	13	248	1.2
Social work	11.0		88		105		114	2
Additional social services training			—		—		6	—
Other local authority services[d]		24	18	14	23	9	23	0
Miscellaneous centrally financed services[e]	17.3	9	90	3	108	4	105	−0.8

Rounding: illustrative growth rates 1975–76 to 1979–80 are generally rounded to the nearest 1 per cent p.a., except where expenditure exceeds £100 m. *All figures are approximate*. Discrepancies are due to rounding.

Abbreviations: IP = inpatients; OP = outpatients; DP = day patients; YTC = youth treatment centres.

Notes:

[a] Capital figures include expenditure on clinics and other community health.

[b] Includes extra costs of teaching hospitals, Regional Hospital Board and Family Practitioner administration (pre-reorganisation), mass radiography, blood transfusion services, income and accounting adjustments.

[c] Includes units for the younger disabled.

[d] Includes capital expenditure on land, vehicles, etc.

[e] Includes other health expenditure, departmental administration and research.

Source: Department of Health and Social Security (1976) Annex 2, Table 1.

services used by the whole population (including the elderly and children) are shown as two separate 'whole population' programmes, and maternity services are identified separately within the hospital services programme. There is so much overlap between services for the elderly and physically handicapped that these have been grouped together. [DHSS, 1976, p. 78]

The programme budget thus enables broad judgements of priority to be made. It may also suggest areas where more detailed cost–benefit type evaluation may be appropriate. It provides a useful general factual framework in which high-level policy can be developed as well as a basis, given underlying demographic developments, for forecasting future demands on resources.

The relative crudity of the 'output' measures will strike the reader—especially when contrasted with the discussion of outputs in earlier chapters. At aggregate levels, such crudity seems inescapable. On the one hand output measures are invaluable in monitoring the success of social policies and in helping decision makers to see and anticipate the consequences of increasing resource inputs or shuffling them around. On the other, it is only at the lowest level that one can normally economically justify output measures of any genuine sort, where a low-level objective is naturally defined. Thus, for example, the number of pupils staying on at school after the compulsory school leaving age is a fairly 'hard' output measure for that part of the educational output budget to which it refers. Equally, however, it is on its own inadequate. A short-list of other relevant output measures that would be useful might include: examination results; performance in non-examined subjects; pupils qualified for higher education; quality of social and sporting life of the educational establishment; quality of cultural life; employers' assessments of school leavers; output of school leavers with specialised qualifications; level of 'citizenship' attained by school leavers. In health, it is hard at the aggregrate level to do more than relate the figures in Table 12.1 to client populations, cases treated, etc.—in short: throughputs, not outputs. The role for finer measurement of time output in these fields lies, of course, not at this aggregate level but in further investigation of questions prompted by such analysis: health centres are expanding relatively fast—are we getting 'value for this money'? The cost of hospital maternity services rose by 3.7 per cent per year in 1970–73 yet the total number of births and of inpatient and outpatient maternity cases all fell. The consequential rising cost per case suggests itself therefore as an example of a sub-programme worth investigating in greater detail. Questions prompted by a programme budget may thus lead to the more refined methods of cost–benefit and cost-effectiveness analysis.

Treatment of Costs

The costs in an output budget ought to be the true social costs of each programme. This implies incorporating costs that the organisation itself may not bear (e.g. forgone earnings; value of time waiting) and excluding genuine transfers.[1] In the initial stages, however, of setting up an output budget, rather traditional 'cost' or expenditure concepts may perforce have to be used until the budgeting system has developed sufficiently for the bases to be altered upon which routine data are collected. Nevertheless, even within the traditional cost concept in public accounting, the problem of allocating costs looms large. Because most programmes have a number of outputs and several programmes may share inputs there is no uniquely correct way of allocating total expenditure/costs. On the one hand, the *marginal* cost of expanding any one programme is the additional cost necessarily incurred, no matter where or by whom. On the other hand, *total* costs must necessarily be treated with some degree of arbitrariness. If one output dominates several others then it is sensible to allocate all costs to that output, treating the others, perhaps, as costless bonuses. Otherwise the usual practice is either 'cost-slicing'—dividing total costs *pro rata* according to some measure of throughput or utilisation—or identifying a separate category of unallocated costs. While the former tends to overestimate the true costs, the latter tends to understate them. A final possibility that might reduce the unallocable costs is to compromise the programme headings somewhat by, for example, shifting away from final *outputs* to *activities*.

Perhaps the most difficult problem in cost allocation concerns the proper allocation of costs through time. For an output budgeting period of one year the problem is how to allocate (a) those costs whose benefits flow over a longer period of time than that over which the costs are incurred and (b) those costs that are inescapably incurred in future budgeting periods as a result of a decision now. In short, the problem concerns the proper allocation through time of what are conventionally known as 'capital' costs.

The purpose of an output budget is to show either the present distribution of incurred costs among outputs or, if future budgets are being forecast, what future distributions are expected, *ex post*, to look like. Given the purpose, the question is how to allocate the cost of, say, a £1 m building planned to last fifty years, whose building costs are to be incurred over the next three years. If the object were to cost a *programme*, it should be calculated in the way implied by cost–benefit analysis. For example, if the actual expenditure flows corresponding to the social value of resources used up were £500,000, £300,000 and £200,000, then the cost at time t_0 is

$$C_0 = £500,000 + \frac{£300,000}{(1 + i)} + \frac{£200,000}{(1 + i)^2} - \frac{£x}{(1 + i)^{50}}$$

where £x represents the net 'scrap value' of the building after fifty years. But this, it should be noted, is the cost of part of the *programme* not a cost of the *decision to build*. Building could always be stopped in the second year, and thus costs insescapably incurred by a planned programme are not the same as those inescapably incurred by the decision to begin the programme, or subsequently to continue it for another accounting period. Output budgeting is concerned primarily with the costs of decisions, whereas cost–benefit analysis is concerned with the costs of programmes over their planned lifetime. Thus, for output budgeting purposes there is no need to include the present value of costs nor to calculate the annual annuity whose present value over fifty years has the same present value. At time t_0 the appropriate building costs are, in fact, £500,000. At time t_1 the appropriate costs will be £300,000. At time t_4 they will be zero and at time t_{50} they will be $-£x$ (if the programme is carried out as originally planned).[2]

This important distinction between output budgeting and cost–benefit analysis has led to considerable confusion by being not fully understood. Some output budgeting practitioners have even felt guilty about entering capital costs as they are incurred instead of, say, annuitising them over the life of the programme and have defended their decisions on grounds of practicability whereas they were, conceptually, perfectly justified in doing just that!

There are, then, a great number of problems to be encountered in setting up an output budget. They are, however, not really the problems of output budgeting but the problems of policy decision making itself. Output budgeting raises the problems in a highly explicit way—indeed it is designed to do just this, on the grounds that it is better to identify the elements in social policy choices as clearly as possible for only then can there be any chance that they will be systematically considered. Only then will the basis for social policy making be sufficiently exposed for greater public participation in policy formation. Only then are the key problem areas systematically identified for research teams to get to work on them. Only then, moreover, have we a system whose avowed intention is to enable tomorrow's decisions to be better informed and more widely discussable than today's.

With these general considerations behind us we turn to an illustration of how output budgets may be worked out in a specific area of social policy: output budgeting in the police force.

Output Budgeting and the Police

The allocation of expenditures in a police force according to conventional accounting is illustrated in Figure 12.2. It is readily apparent how unhelp-

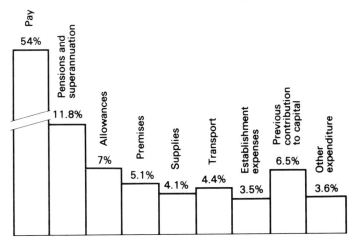

FIG. 12.2   Gross expenditure on police force distributed by conventional budget categories.

ful such a classification is in presenting police authorities, chief constables or the Home Secretary with relevant information about policy options. The budgeting categories bear no relation at all to the activities of the police force, to their function or to the outputs they produce. What are these functions? A reasonable list might include the following:

1. Maintenance of law and order and protection of persons and property.
2. Prevention of crime.
3. Detection of criminals and interrogation.
4. In England and Wales (not Scotland) prosecution, or not, as the case may be, of persons suspected of criminal activities.
5. Conduct (in England and Wales) of prosecutions themselves for less serious offences.
6. Road traffic control and advice to local authorities.
7. Duties on behalf of government departments, e.g. in respect of nationality questions.
8. A long-standing duty to befriend anyone needing help and to cope at any time with major or minor emergencies.

On the basis of such objectives for the police an entirely different budgeting system has been suggested. One such set of budget categories in a simple output budget identifying only major police programmes might be:

(a) Protection of persons and property from:
    (i) criminal activities
    (ii) traffic hazards
    (iii) miscellaneous hazards

(b) Treatment of offenders:
    (i) detection and apprehension
    (ii) process and trial
    (iii) training

Such an output budget is illustrated (in percentage terms)[3] in Figure 12.3.

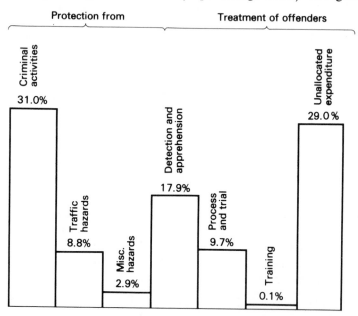

FIG. 12.3 Output budget for police force.

Each of the output categories in Figure 12.3 is drawn very broadly and within each programme head there would be, of course, a wide range of more specific outputs—classified, for example, by the severity of the criminal activity in the first programme. The advantages, however, of functional costing as against the more traditional budgeting are self-evident. What is perhaps less self-evident is the ease with which it becomes possible to link up the police output budget with other related activities both within and outside the Home Office. For example, in a comprehensive output budgeting system a non-police input into the protection of persons and property from criminal activity is the activity of the Criminal Injuries Compensation Board. In protection from traffic hazards, the Department of the Environment and the Welsh Office provide inputs, as do local authorities.

A difficulty that frequently arises with an output budget cast in strict output categories is that it is impossible to allocate all the costs meaningfully to a category, even using the rules of thumb outlined above. For example, in Figure 12.3, which was based on the work in the Home Office of one of the most resourceful and imaginative practitioners of output budgeting, 29 per cent of expenditure (assumed equal to cost) was left unallocated. Moreover, the strict output based budget poses the problem of output measures in its most challenging (intractable?) form. In the intermediate stages before output budgeting has become widely used and its problems and their solutions fully understood and worked out, it is therefore sometimes desirable to effect a compromise based more upon activities than upon the ends those activities are supposed to attain. Such a programme structure is usually more immediately practicable, involves less intensive collection and processing of new data and conforms, as a rule, more closely to the managerial form of the organisation. Such a structure for the police may be:

(a) *Operational*
    (i) Ground cover
        1. Supervision and administration
        2. Patrol
        3. Station duty
        4. Extraordinary events
        5. Vice squad
    (ii) Criminal investigation and control
        6. Supervision and administration
        7. Extraordinary events
        8. General investigation
        9. Specialised investigation
        10. Investigation support services
        11. Crime prevention
        12. Regional crime squad
    (iii) Traffic control
        13. Supervision and administration
        14. Patrol
        15. Road survey
        16. Traffic and accident information
        17. Traffic wardens
        18. Road safety
    (iv) Additional services
(b) *Support*
    (i) Management
    (ii) Training
    (iii) Support services
(c) *Overhead*
    (i) Pensions
    (ii) Accommodation

Of these, the first four programmes are 'front line' activities corresponding quite closely with broad output categories and capable of intelligent

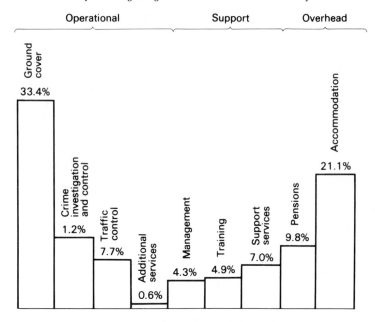

FIG. 12.4   Programme budget for police force.

division into sub-programmes. The output budget for major programme needs (more appropriately, the programme budget) resulting from this classification is illustrated in Figure 12.4.

Although this approach has some merit as an interim method it has the severe handicap that it is restricted to the police force's existing range of activities, while a genuine output approach identifies competing or complementary activities by other organisations and thus highlights the alternatives facing policy concerned with, e.g. road safety, punishment and care of prisoners, prevention of accidents. It has, moreover, been designed explicitly to avoid cutting across existing police organisational lines. Thus 'Ground cover', for example, refers to most of the work of the Criminal Investigation Department (CID). The strength of this method is that it avoids complicated cost allocations and is broadly familiar. Its weakness is that it may be too familiar to force radical thinking about efficient police activity and that it does not indicate what various police functions are costing, since the various inputs relating to a given function are not brought together as a routine matter. It is as well, though, not to criticise these kinds of attempts too harshly so long as the properties of a good output budget are never lost sight of, for the necessity for the kind of compromise illustrated here is the result of our extensive ignorance of the workings of society in general and of not having the results of appropriate criminological researches in particular. It is, of course, in areas such as this that interdisciplinary research comes into its own—economics posing the research questions but other disciplines contributing to, if not entirely providing, methods of answering them.

Enough has been said to show both the importance and the problems of introducing output budgeting systematically into social policy. The principal practical difficulty is to allocate (genuine social) costs to current decisions regarding programmes having clear and articulated outputs. The more detailed the output the more the 'overhead' problem looms and the more unsatisfactory one usually finds the existing organisation of the institutions whose budgets are being prepared. Not least of the many advantages of output budgeting is the clarity with which even an elementary exercise will indicate overlap between organisations (e.g. government departments) and many PPBS experts elevate the 'system' part of their brief into a full-blown systems analysis whereby an attempt is made to identify objectives and to relate the organisational forms themselves to these objectives. These latterday Florence Nightingales, equipped with all the techniques of modern management science, are engaged upon essentially complementary acitvities to the cost–benefit and output budgeting experts.

NOTES

1. Transfers are, of course, important from the point of view of income redistribution.
2. Corresponding to these are present values of cost of

   at t_0: £500,000 + £300,000/(1 + i) + £200,000/(1 + i)² − £x/(1 + i)⁵⁰

   at t_1: £300,000 + £200,000/(1 + i) − £x(1 + i)⁴⁹

   at t_4: −£x/(1 + i)⁴⁶

   at t_{50}: −£x,

   which are the building costs of completing the programme at t_0, t_1, etc.
3. Note that these expenditure categories ignore substantial social costs such as forgone earnings of prisoners (if they are members of the society whose welfare is to be maximised), value of the time of witnesses, jurymen, etc.

QUESTIONS ON CHAPTER 12

1. What is output budgeting?
2. What is programme budgeting?
3. What costs should be included in an output budget?
4. How does output/programme budgeting differ from normal budgeting?
5. What disadvantages, for resource allocation purposes and monitoring efficiency, do normal budgeting procedures have?

6. Identify programme heads as exhaustively as possible for either your college, work-place, church or club.
7. For any one of the institutions in question (6), how would you distribute (a) a 5 per cent *reduction* in the total budget across heads, (b) a 20 per cent *reduction*, (c) a 5 per cent *increase* and (d) a 20 per cent *increase*?
8. What does your answer to question (7) tell you about the marginal values you attach to the programmes and sub-programmes of your chosen institution?
9. How would you describe the outputs of the programmes and sub-programmes of your programme budget? What objective indicators of the outputs you have described would you develop to evaluate your success in meeting your objectives?
10. How would you allocate joint costs in a programme budget?
11. Evaluate the application of output/programme budgeting in any specific area known to you in which it has been applied.
12. How does output/programme budgeting link up with cost–benefit analysis?
13. How would you decide whether a cost–benefit analysis was worth undertaking?
14. Read the book by Martin and Wilson (1969) and assess the value of output budgeting in the police force.
15. What areas indicated in Table 12.1 would you select for more detailed study?
16. How would you set about eliciting the value of the activities listed in Table 12.1?
17. Whose valuations would you seek to elicit in question (16)?
18. Are output budgeting and cost–benefit analysis a substitute for or a complement to allocation by markets?
19. What is the link between output budgeting and production function analysis?
20. What incentives would you devise to encourage public decision makers to adopt output budgeting and economic evaluation *and to act upon their implications?*

FURTHER READING

Collins, E. A. (1966) The functional approach to public expenditure. *Public Administration, 44*, pp. 295–313.

Department of Education and Science (1970) *Output Budgeting for The Department of Education and Science.* London: HMSO.

Department of Health and Social Security (1976) *Priorities for Health and Personal Social Services in England: A Consultative Document.* London: HMSO.

Gray, A. and Steele, R. (1979) Programme budgeting in the health sector. *Omega, 7,* pp. 451–8.

Heclo, H. and Wildavsky, A. (1974) *The Private Government of Public Money.* London: Macmillan.

Hovey, H. A. (1968) *The Planning-Programming-Budgeting Approach to Government Decision-Making.* New York and London: Praeger.

Institute of Municipal Treasurers and Accountants (1969) *Programme Budgeting— the Concept and the Application.* London: IMTA.

Lyden, F. J. and Miller E. G. (1968) *Planning, Programming, Budgeting: A Systems Approach to Management.* Chicago: Markham.

Martin, J. P. and Wilson, G. (1969) *The Police: A Study in Manpower.* London: Heinemann.

Mooney, G. H. (1977) Programme budgeting in an area health board. *Hospital and Health Services Review*, 73, pp. 379–84.

Novick, D (ed.) (1965) *Program Budgeting*. Cambridge, Mass.: Harvard University Press.

Pole, D. (1974) Programmes, priorities and budgets. *British Journal of Preventive and Social Medicine*, 28, pp. 191–5.

Wasserman, G. J. (1970) Planning programming budgeting in the police service in England and Wales. *O & M Bulletin*, 25, pp. 197–210.

Williams, Alan (1967) *Output Budgeting and the Contribution of Microeconomics to Efficiency in Government*. CAS Occasional Paper No. 4, London: HMSO.

Williams, Alan (1978) The budget as a (mis-) information system. In A. J. Culyer and K. G. Wright (eds) *Economic Aspects of Health Services*. London: Martin Robertson.

Author Index

Subject Index

public sector
and profit motive, 51ff

quantification, dangers in, 181, 194

range of incomes, 118ff
rationing, non-price, 191
Rawlsian maximin, 62, 90, 146, 243
redistribution of income
cash *vs* kind, 71ff
through education, 127ff
efficiency of, 96ff
between landlords and tenants, 262
measurement of dispersion, 114ff
and the public sector, 133ff
specific *vs* general, 65, 188
theories of, 83ff
vertical and horizontal, 84, 139
regressivity, *see* progressivity
renal failure, 211, 224–5, 289–91
rent (housing), 115, 136, 140
arrears, 304–7
controls, 261ff, 269
imputed, 115, 136, 140, 266–8
and price of housing, 260, 266–8
replacement ratio, 163, 170
residual income progression, 115
returns
average and marginal, 240
constant, increasing and decreasing, 16
to an input, 15
to investment in education, 128, 238ff
to investment in health, 214ff
to scale, 15, 282, 287
social and private, 217–18, 239ff
rheumatic disease, 124, 209
risk aversion, 40, 303
and private property, 52
Royal College of General Practitioners, 197

sacrifice method, 188ff
Sainsbury Committee report, 211–12, 232
sanitation, 208
scaling in index construction, 151, 197, 219ff
scarlet fever, 207–8
school meals
and public expenditure, 66, 138
screening hypothesis, 237–8
secondary education, 244, 246, 313

self-interest, 50, 58ff, 99, 101ff, *see also* caring
Sen's maximin, 90ff
shortage (housing), 255, 259, 261
sickness
costs of and insurance, 40ff
iceberg of, 212–13
and poverty, 157
prevalence of by social class, 124
see also health
skills
and human investment, 37ff, 158–9
and poverty, 157
and universities, 287
slavery, 159
slums, 268–70, 291
smallpox, 205
social benefit, 25ff
social class
and education, 126ff, 236, 249
and poverty, 157ff
and prevalence of sickness, 124ff, 213
and redistribution, 136ff
social contract, 49ff
Rawlsian, 63
social cost, 27ff, 311–12,
see also external effects
social dividend, 168ff
social indicators
of deprivation, 150ff
in education, 199, 243ff
in health, 197–8, 219ff
as supplements to GDP, 193ff
value judgements in, 150ff
social security
benefits of, 142, 164–5
contributions, 136, 141, 164–5
and public expenditure, 66
social welfare expenditure, 66–7, 139ff
standard gamble, 222ff
streptomycin, 205
student loans, 249ff
subsidies
agricultural, 142
and education, 239, 243, 250–1
employment, 166
and external benefits, 27, 186–7
and health services, 218, 225
and housing, 264, 266–9
indifference curve analysis of, 71ff
and redistribution, 133ff
and skill-acquisition, 166
and specific consumption, 64–5, 185ff